LAMAR
HUNT

A LIFE IN SPORTS

Other Books by Michael MacCambridge

America's Game: The Epic Story of How Pro Football Captured a Nation
The Franchise: A History of Sports Illustrated Magazine
More Than a Game (with Brian Billick)

As Editor

SportsCentury
The ESPN College Football Encyclopedia

As Contributor

A New Literary History of America
Under the Arch: St. Louis Stories

LAMAR
HUNT
A LIFE IN SPORTS

MICHAEL
MacCAMBRIDGE

**Andrews McMeel
Publishing, LLC**
Kansas City • Sydney • London

Andrews McMeel Publishing, LLC
an Andrews McMeel Universal company
1130 Walnut Street, Kansas City, Missouri 64106

www.andrewsmcmeel.com

12 13 14 15 16 MLY 10 9 8 7 6 5 4 3 2 1

ISBN: 978-1-4494-2339-1

Library of Congress Control Number: 2012936730

For Robert Minter,
faithful friend,
fellow true believer

CONTENTS

"Play cannot be denied. You can deny, if you like, nearly all abstractions: justice, beauty, truth, goodness, mind, God. You can deny seriousness, but not play."

—Johan Huizinga, *Homo Ludens*

"Sports constitute a code, a language of the emotions, and a tourist who skips the stadiums will not recoup his losses at Lincoln Center and Grant's Tomb."

—Wilfrid Sheed

"I've always loved sports. Basically, I just consider myself a fan."

—Lamar Hunt

PROLOGUE

The day was crisp and the mood festive as the family of H. L. Hunt left home late in the morning of Monday, January 2, 1939.

H. L. was dressed, as usual, in a simple suit and tie, with a white linen shirt, his wife, Lyda, beside him in a Sunday coat, with a corsage she'd worn for the occasion. Their youngest daughter, the fifteen-year-old Caroline, had climbed in the other car, along with Hassie and Margaret. H. L. got in behind the wheel of his Oldsmobile sedan, Lyda at his side, and Herbert and Bunker happily chattering in the back seat. Sitting next to his brothers, the six-year-old Lamar Hunt gazed out the window, his deep-set eyes wide open.

As H. L. wheeled the car down Abrams Road toward Fair Park, Lamar watched the Christmas decorations still on the shops throughout Dallas, and the wreaths on the front doors of the homes. Then, as the traffic thickened, he could spot in the distance the initial glimpses of Fair Park—the congregating pedestrians, the flags fluttering in the New Year's breeze, the signs for parking in and around the Fair Park grounds. He had been to the park once before, for his first visit to the Texas State Fair three months earlier, but now he wasn't thinking about ice cream or rides or arcade games, but instead was eagerly awaiting a clear look at the giant concrete edifice where the family was headed.

They parked on the other side of Parry Avenue, and saw the distinctive cream-brick façade of the Fair Park Auditorium, near the front entrance. Taking his mother's hand for the walk, Lamar looked around at other families decked out in their holiday best, young couples walking and holding hands, an assortment of marching bands from all over the state, some walking into the stadium while playing rousing fight songs. Throughout the crowd were the red-and-black bedecked alumni of Texas Tech University, many wearing cowboy hats, with the spirit ribbons on their coats anchored with tiny gold footballs. Fewer in number, but still visible, were the supporters of St. Mary's College of California, wearing red, white, and blue, waving pennants and sporting shiny buttons that proclaimed "GALLOPING GAELS." It was a magnificent, good-natured bustle, and everywhere he looked, Lamar saw people who appeared just as happy to be there as he was.

As the Hunts reached the turnstiles, H. L. distributed tickets to each of the children—the brightly lettered stub announced that this was the "Cotton Bowl Classic"—and Lamar handed his to the man at the gate, before moving quickly inside to the stadium concourse, then tugging Lyda's arm to ask for a quarter so he could buy a game program. She fetched it out of her purse, waited while he gave the coin to the concessionaire, then took Lamar's hand and brought him with the rest of the family through the tunnel and into the giant cement bowl. A full half-hour before kickoff, they reached their row under a bright, cloudless Texas sky.

For a time, Lamar grew very quiet, and just stared down at the field. There was Texas Tech's star Elmer Tarbox, No. 21, in the all-red uniform, with black shoulders and piping on the arms, the white inset panels on the rib cage and the inside of the sleeves. Meanwhile, the St. Mary's Gaels, the young Cinderellas from the West Coast, were decked out in equally nifty uniforms, their blue jerseys capped with white-paneled shoulders.

As the teams headed to the sidelines for final pre-game preparations, out came the marching bands from Southern Methodist University and Woodrow Wilson High and Highland Park High, playing "The Eyes of Texas" and "The Bells of St. Mary's" and then, with the crowd standing at rapt attention, hands and hats over hearts, the National Anthem.

On what the Cotton Bowl's press-box statistician described as an "ideal" day for football, Lamar watched St. Mary's take a 20–0 lead, then thrilled to the sight of Tarbox and the Red Raiders rallying for 13 points in the fourth quarter, before St. Mary's ran out the clock to seal an exhilarating win.

Afterward, on the long walk back to the car, and the stop-and-start drive through the congested traffic toward their home on White Rock Lake, the boys in the backseat spoke excitedly about all they'd seen—the bright uniforms, Tarbox's remarkable touchdown reception, the public address announcer's updates of TCU's game against Carnegie Tech in the Sugar Bowl, the beautiful Cotton Bowl queen who spoke at halftime, the marching band that spelled out the letters "HELLO TECH" before the game, and the sharp roadsters parked in a line just outside the park.

Back home, while the ladies got changed, and the family maid, Pandora Waters, prepared dinner, Lamar thanked his mother, whom he still called by the pet name of "Papoose Mooze." He then rushed into the library to ask his father to turn on the radio. Dashing back to the closet under the front stairs to fetch his football, he returned to his favorite spot in the library, planted himself in front of the large console, and listened to all the talk about TCU's big Sugar Bowl win in New Orleans, and accounts of the Cotton Bowl game he'd just returned from, and then heard Graham McNamee's call from Pasadena, as USC scored a late touchdown to edge previously unbeaten, un-scored-upon Duke in the Rose Bowl.

Sitting there, pigskin at his side, paging once again through the Cotton Bowl program, Lamar Hunt was a picture of contentment. He'd seen his first football game that day.

•

When the end came, nearly seventy years and countless thousands of games later, the news broke too late to make the next morning's papers in the Midwest and East. By sunrise, December 14, 2006, word of Lamar Hunt's death the previous night was working its way through Dallas and Kansas City and Columbus, Ohio; the National Football League offices in New York; Soccer House in Chicago; and around the globe, from Wimbledon to Roland Garros; the Football Association headquarters in London to the Bra-zilian national team's training pitches in Rio de Janeiro. On that day, people throughout the world of sports shared in the loss of the kindly gentleman who had shaped so many of their lives. The news prompted sad smiles, and many raised a private toast to the man who never drank.

The obits wrote themselves. ESPN called him a "soft-spoken man who changed the face of pro football," and the New York Times referred to him as "the man who gave the Super Bowl its name." USA Today was one of many publications that described him as a "visionary."

The sports world in which Lamar Hunt's death was reported was not pre-cisely one of his own making, but it would have looked far different without his involvement. He did not build the networks that covered sports every minute of every day of every year, nor was he the architect of the omnipres-ent web of sports news, discussion, and tribalism that made up the messy realm of the Internet.

Instead Hunt instigated a series of audacious ventures—in pro football, tennis, soccer, basketball, and other sports—that implicitly recognized and celebrated the notion that many Americans would happily spend much of their discretionary time and income absorbed in the world of spectator sports, that even in a land of freedom and prosperity, there was still refuge and solace and camaraderie that could be found only in the world of games.

When it came time to catalog his contributions, it was inevitable that he would be remembered first for his work in pro football. As a quiet, shy twenty-six-year-old in Dallas in 1959, better known at the time as simply the youngest son of legendary oilman H. L. Hunt, he had politely but resolutely pressed his case to bring pro football to Dallas. After repeated rejections from the men who ran the National Football League, he decided to start his own league, founding the American Football League, which began play in eight cities in 1960. The AFL and its eventual success ushered in an era of widespread expansion in all American team sports. The universe of pro football nearly doubled overnight, growing from twelve teams in 1959 to twenty-one in 1960, then adding five more teams in the next eight seasons. In the same decade of the '60s, partly in response to football's rapid and successful growth, baseball grew from sixteen to twenty-four teams, hockey from six to fourteen, and pro basketball from eight to twenty-five.

In 1966, with the war between the NFL and AFL at a furious pitch, Hunt coolly negotiated the agreement that led to the merger between the two leagues, in which all eight of the original AFL franchises were welcomed into the NFL (making the AFL the first upstart American sports league to survive intact since the American League successfully challenged the National League in baseball in 1901).

The existence and viability of the AFL made necessary both the merger and the game that would first be played after the 1966 season, which the NFL originally called "the AFL–NFL World Championship Game." In this, Hunt took a special role, first suggesting that the game be called the "Super Bowl," then later proposing the arch but distinctive manner of identifying its component games with roman numerals, befitting something grand and majestic like, as one writer put it, "Popes or World Wars." After the 1970 death of Vince Lombardi, it was the AFL loyalist Hunt who suggested to NFL commissioner Pete Rozelle that the league rename the Super Bowl trophy after the Packers' patriarch. It was in this small gesture and a hundred others like it for which Hunt gained his reputation in football as a man who thought about the good of the game and the league first, and only then about what might benefit his own team's interests. The transformation of pro football in the '60s landed Hunt in Canton, Ohio, where he was inducted into the Pro Football Hall of Fame in 1972. Two weeks after induction, he presided over the opening of Arrowhead Stadium, an innovative, vastly influential structure that would become the first modern, classic, football-only stadium. By then, he was well on his way to transforming other worlds as well.

In 1967, with the sport of tennis still clinging to its Old World conventions of ostensibly all-amateur competition, Hunt signed on as a minority partner to a radical plan hatched by New Orleans entrepreneur David Dixon to push the game decisively into the professional era. With the advent of World Championship Tennis, he helped sign "The Handsome Eight," an octet of world-class players from around the globe; the circuit would eventually take pro tennis out of the station wagons and one-night stands of the Jack Kramer tours of the '50s and '60s. The very existence of WCT was a factor in bringing about the revolutionary change in tennis, when Wimbledon announced late in 1967 that its tournament would allow professionals to compete for the first time in 1968.

But even before that first open Wimbledon, Dixon had abandoned WCT, unable to keep up with the early losses. So Hunt agreed to bankroll the enterprise and, over the next five years, constructed the template of the modern tournament and tennis tour, which culminated with the weeklong WCT Finals in Dallas, the marquee new event in professional tennis. In 1972, in front of 40 million viewers on NBC, the WCT Finals played host to the legendary five-set final between Ken Rosewall and Rod Laver that many experts considered the finest match ever played. Though WCT would perish in 1990, Hunt was inducted into the International Tennis Hall of Fame in 1993. "He simply *made* pro tennis," said one observer. "We owe it all to Lamar."

If ever a sport were in Hunt's debt, it would be soccer in America. Transformed by watching the TV broadcast of the epic spectacle that was the 1966 World Cup Final in London, Hunt soon invested in the venture that would eventually be known as the North American Soccer League. In the face of massive public indifference, and nearly equal amounts of hostility, he worked quietly and tirelessly, over two leagues and the next four decades, to create the right environment for the sport to flourish in America. Even after the NASL died, crushed by the weight of the maniacal ambition of other owners—and the imbalance created by the New York Cosmos juggernaut built around Pelé and other superstars—Hunt continued to quietly support the cause of soccer in the United States. He was the co-chair of the Dallas host committee in 1994 when the World Cup came to the United States, and invested again, even more heavily this time, in Major League Soccer, which launched in 1996.

Along the way, he bought a stake in the NBA expansion franchise the Chicago Bulls in 1966, and stuck with the team through nearly a quarter-century of losses before reveling in the Bulls' six world titles of the 1990s. In the '60s, he invested in a minor league baseball team in the Dallas–Fort Worth area, with an eye to bringing Major League Baseball to the area. Around the same time, he was a part-owner of a seventy-two-lane bowling complex that included a bowling amphitheater, which hosted a short-lived venture in the early '60s called the National Bowling League. While running that complex, he came up with a precursor of the "Superstars" competition, a multi-event contest featuring stars from a wide array of different sports. By the time of his death, he had been chasing these sporting pursuits for more than fifty years. His very first business venture, in which he invested and operated during his college years at Southern Methodist University in the early '50s, was a baseball batting cage and miniature golf course.

"I would say certainly I had a penchant for what I call show business or entertainment or the sports business," he said. "They're all interchangeable in my mind."

When Hunt began the American Football League in 1959, the universe of sports in America was still operating at the margins, sitting over at the kid's table of American popular culture. Five years earlier, when Time, Inc., considered launching a weekly magazine devoted to sports, one executive surmised that the only people who would want to read such a magazine were "juveniles and n'er-do-wells." When the company subsequently launched *Sports Illustrated*, it found a surprisingly large and affluent audience, a vast swath of the American mainstream—Lamar Hunt among them—that built much of their social lives around playing and watching sports.

Those who were routinely dismissive of sports were missing the makings of a social revolution, of the ways that in a time of heightened social stress and splintering cultural divisions, the animating influence of games could cut across divisions of race, class, religion, and economics, serving as a safe common ground for social discourse and a vital social glue in a polyglot society.

Lamar Hunt didn't miss it. He not only saw it coming, he helped make it happen.

All through American history there had been well-heeled businessmen, tycoons, and heirs who indulged their love of sport; these so-called sportsmen were the moguls who helped develop the infrastructure of modern American sports.

But Hunt was different. Never before and not since has anyone with so many resources spent so much time watching, participating in, and being captivated by the absorbing ritual of sports and the suspended state of play. His accomplishments would put him in the company of the other giants of American sports—Charles C. "Cash and Carry" Pyle, Abe Saperstein, Rube

Foster, George Halas, Branch Rickey, Red Auerbach, Pete Rozelle. Each was present at a revolution. But Hunt, significantly, was present at a number of revolutions. And he was a catalyst for each one.

•

He was as well-mannered as he was rich, which is to say absurdly so. Writers could not resist pointing out the incongruity between his vast wealth and the decidedly unelaborate way in which he carried himself. Just under six feet tall, with a smallish head, chestnut brown hair carefully combed, blue eyes set close above an easy smile and a pronounced chin, Lamar Hunt looked exceedingly normal. At various times over the years, he would be described in print as resembling "a level G-18 federal bureaucrat," "a technical trouble-shooter for Monsanto," "a healthful, earnest accountant," "a junior executive or a minister," "a Methodist parson on his way to visit the sick," "a Baptist deacon at a sales meeting," "Mr. Peepers," and the "the guy who lives next door." Don Garber, the commissioner of Major League Soccer, described him as "a larger-than-life figure without being a larger-than-life personality."

To those who knew him best, the sum of the contradictions all made a kind of vivid, poetic sense. A shy, retiring figure by nature, he remembered being "horrified" the first time he saw his name in the newspaper. Yet he would give thousands of public speeches and interviews over the decades, in an attempt to further his various enterprises. The man who had a listed phone number in the Dallas phone book and answered virtually every letter ever sent to him until he died was also notoriously secretive and guarded. As his friend and onetime business partner David Dixon put it, "Lamar is the best super-rich guy I've ever known. But by his family practices, he's very secretive, a lot of times unnecessarily so." This was true throughout his life. Edward "Buzz" Kemble, his teammate at SMU and one of his closest friends in life, didn't find out Hunt had cancer until months after the diagnosis came in 1998, and then only because Lamar's wife Norma confided in Buzz's wife Dorothy. "He just wasn't one to volunteer personal things," said one friend.

If he was misunderstood by many, it was perhaps because they made as many assumptions about his wealth as the observers in 1959 who, upon hearing that the son of a wealthy Texas oilman was starting a new football league, expected a blustering man-child in a 10-gallon hat and cowboy boots, and found instead a soft-spoken young gentleman who would invariably greet his elders with courtesy titles, then frequently adjust his glasses and stare off in the middle distance before dutifully attempting to answer each and every difficult question.

The contradictions played themselves out across the decades: He would invest tens of millions of dollars in sports franchises, would shop extensively for art and rare antiques, travel the world and eat at its finest restaurants. And yet, as a wealthy man who usually flew commercial, and then invariably coach ("the back of the plane gets there at the same time," he happily pointed out), he became as well known for his parsimony as any American celebrity since Jack Benny. "I do detest ostentation," he once explained, and in so doing explained a lot. A charity roast for Hunt in the summer of 2000 consisted of more than a dozen friends and associates telling anecdotes about Lamar running out of money and/or gas, asking to borrow everything from 55 cents for a taxi to $20 to get his rental car out of the parking lot. Everyone had a variation on the "Lamar needed money" story. Hank Stram's son Dale once saw Hunt write a check in the sum of 10 cents to pay a toll on the Dallas Tollway.

"Lamar knew the value of two things," said Clive Toye, who traveled and worked with Hunt in the North American Soccer League. "He knew the value of a dollar, and he knew the value of his word."

He was careless and forgetful about so many things in his hectic life. The daily details of getting gas, getting his state inspection sticker renewed, having cash on hand, and replacing worn-out shoes, were all matters that eluded him. A notorious technophobe who left his cell phone turned off in the glove compartment, and whose VCR blinked "12:00" for years, he died without ever having turned on a computer. He was perpetually late in his meetings and correspondence, and he never seemed to have enough paper on hand for his thousands of memos and communiqués.

Yet the same man who could at times seem so disorganized in his personal and business affairs also had a draftsman's eye for balance and symmetry, and casually created one of the most enduring emblems in American sports—the Kansas City Chiefs logo, with its interlocking, block-shadowed K and C inside an arrowhead—while sitting in his kitchen one day in 1963. This was no one-off. For all his adult life, he'd sketch marvelously detailed renderings of logos, museum walls, stadium elevations, all the different elements of the world of sports that captivated his imagination (and most of his waking thoughts) since he was a boy.

In a sports world dominated by salty language and offhand profanity, he was an exemplar of probity. It wasn't simply that Hunt didn't swear. It was that people who *did* swear made it a point to swear less when they were around him.

He spoke in clichés and platitudes, and yet thought in terms of innovations, and was willing and able to discuss details down to a granular level. "One of the things that made him special," said NFL commissioner Roger Goodell, "was that the small stuff mattered. Incredible attention to detail. He saw the big picture, but he also saw how the little pieces built up to that."

A lifelong Republican who voted for the GOP candidate in every presidential election, he was at the same time a trail-blazer in race relations in pro sports, helping to integrate both private and public institutions, hiring the first full-time African-American scout in pro football and tapping into the rich vein of historically black colleges in the South. In 1960, he signed to his new pro team the first black to play football at a predominantly white four-year college in the state of Texas (Abner Haynes from North Texas State), and in 1967, his team featured the first starting black middle linebacker in pro football (Willie Lanier). In 1969, his Kansas City Chiefs were the first championship team in pro football history to have a majority of black players in their starting lineup. Lloyd Wells, the black scout who helped the Chiefs sign many of their stars of the '60s, summed it up in a sentence: "Finest white man I ever met."

Others would second the motion, without the qualifier. "He is the finest human being it has ever been my privilege to know," said Marty Schottenheimer. "I've never met a better human being in all my life," said Dick Vermeil. His friend Bill McNutt once said, "He's warm and genuine and straight as a string. If everybody were like him, the world wouldn't have any problems." His longtime lieutenant, Jack Steadman, said at Hunt's memorial service, "When God created man, he had Lamar Hunt in mind."

But to those outside his remarkably compact inner circle, the sum of all these heartfelt encomiums was to reduce Lamar Hunt to a bland, saintly figure. He was the kindly, reserved but enthusiastic uncle walking the perimeter of Arrowhead Stadium on game-day mornings in Kansas City, unfailingly cheerful and polite while meeting the public. Even those who admired him struggled with his seemingly boundless capacity for pleasantness.

"What a wonderful man," said Steve Sabol, the longtime head of NFL Films, before pausing a second. "And *boring*! What a boring man!" Sabol had wrestled with a film on Hunt's life that, in the end, became a long, uninterrupted flow of his acknowledged goodness and, in Sabol's opinion, less interesting because of this.

Those who worked for him, almost to a person, were fond and protective of him. They appreciated his approachability so much that they took pains not to take advantage of it. "He was busy, so he wouldn't just sit down and start talking to you, and you'd have this long, deep conversation for a half-hour," said his longtime assistant Thom Meredith. "That would happen maybe once a year, if that."

His innate shyness became one of his defining characteristics. There were people whose lives he dramatically shaped—Hall of Fame quarterback Len Dawson and tennis great John Newcombe among them—who could not recall a single conversation they had with Lamar that lasted more than a few minutes.

"He didn't *do* small talk," said one friend.

Many people in his sphere revered him at a distance, speaking to him briefly once or twice a year, grateful that he always answered their letters and returned their calls, wishing only that they could have known him better. "I wish I would have said to him, 'Lamar, let me come down to Dallas for a day and just follow you around,'" said Pat Williams, the longtime basketball executive who first met Hunt in 1969. "I'm sure he would have let me."

They loved his decency, his whimsy, his generosity of spirit, and his bottomless reservoir of ideas—always the ideas. Many of those closest to him put it precisely the same way: "He was a man of many ideas," each would say, before pausing and adding, at once affectionate and protective, "Not all of them good ones." And then: "Don't quote me on that."

He contained multitudes. He was described by his wife as being "both calm and constantly active." There was no doubt, both inside and beyond his family, that he loved his kin, loved being a father, loved being a husband, drew strength from the times he was surrounded by his children. And yet, there he was, out the door and off to the airport, flying for a meeting in Los Angeles, or a game in Cincinnati, or a dinner in New York, or a World Cup tournament overseas. Alone, if necessary.

He was his mother's son, unfailingly polite, and—with vast wealth at his disposal—he set out on a journey that would forever alter the landscape of American sports. He is not remembered, like his father, for being a mythic figure of oil and politics and manifest destiny. Instead, Lamar Hunt was renowned because he was perhaps the most unusual combination ever of decency, innovation, secretiveness, optimism, persistence, naïvete, politesse, shyness, loyalty, and an irrepressible love of the moment.

"If you just met Lamar, you'd never guess he was born rich," said the legendary sportswriter Dan Jenkins, who counted Lamar as a friend, a neighbor, and a subject at different times over the years. "You'd just think he was a football fan. He was a kid for life. You know, people in sports, they never get over being a kid . . . if they've got any sense."

There was something deep and abiding about his love of competition—something that went beyond the surface diversions that many people find in games. So the obituaries only got it half right. Lamar Hunt wasn't a traditional sportsman. He was a sports *fan*. And though publications and networks all across the sports world reported his many ventures and triumphs and innovations, none took the measure of the long road he'd taken to make his own dreams come true. Nor did anyone mention that of all of his many signal accomplishments, the greatest of these had yet to be fully grasped.

The score wasn't final just yet.

CHAPTER ONE

LATE ARRIVAL

H. L. Hunt sat at the kitchen table, fidgeting with the straw boater in his hands, trying his best to avoid a look of boredom. Seated at the end of the table, his oldest son, Hassie, wore the slightest trace of a smile.

Lyda Hunt had felt her husband's restlessness for days, almost as soon as H. L. and Hassie had returned from the oil fields to sit with them for what was surely going to be the family's last baby. But that had been two weeks ago, in mid-July. And now, as Lyda sat in the path of the electric fan, her breathing forced, she felt the weight of her husband's barely concealed exasperation, and reached a decision.

"June, you and Hassie need to get back to the field."

"No, Mom, everything can wait," H. L. protested, though not too strongly.

"No, it cannot," she said, firmly. "Our business needs attention, so do go back. I have done this six times. You two get on with the drilling, and Margaret will take care of me and the baby."

With that, H. L. Hunt exhaled, and stood up, and everyone relaxed. Very soon, he would be on his way, doing what he did best: Moving, acting, striving further in his journey to make his mark on the world. And Lyda, once again, would be the head of the household.

She had returned a month earlier, in the summer of 1932, from their new home in Tyler to El Dorado, Arkansas, where the family had lived for most of the 1920s. She wanted to be close to her physician, Dr. Murphy, and have her last baby in the comfort of the three-story brick English-revival house known as "The Pines."

Within the hour, H. L. and the fifteen-year-old Hassie were on their way, the car moving past Lyda's beloved tulip beds, its taillights disappearing behind the row of pine trees in front of the house. They would be back to work by the morning.

Lyda Hunt, pious, steady, and learned, stood barely five feet tall, and weighed 150 pounds when she wasn't pregnant. Now, two weeks overdue and bloated closer to 200 pounds, her face seemed wan, and even getting up to her bedroom on the second floor was an effort. Her oldest daughter, Margaret, just sixteen but already a second mother to the youngest three Hunt children—the nine-year-old Caroline, the six-year-old Bunker, and the three-year-old Herbert—looked concerned as she followed her mother from room to room.

Later that night, after the children were put to bed and the kitchen lights were out, Margaret came into her mother's room to check on her. Formally and unsentimentally, Lyda spoke directly to her daughter.

"I feel fine, Margaret, and I am sorry to put this burden on you, but people of forty-three do not customarily have children. So just in case anything should happen to me, the clothes I want to wear are in a suit-box in the closet."

Margaret Hunt had never considered *losing* her mother before, but she was beginning to understand the gravity of the ordeal ahead. She returned to her room and slept fitfully until, early the next morning, Lyda summoned her in the dark, and urged her daughter to drive them to the hospital.

Through the quiet streets of El Dorado, a nervous Margaret negotiated the family car to the hospital, stealing frightened sideways peeks at her mother seated beside her, face contorted with pain.

Several hours later, on the morning of August 2, 1932, "Baby Hunt"—the name Lamar would come weeks later, with no middle name, as H. L. and Lyda had already worked their way through homages on both sides of the family tree—was born at the El Dorado hospital. By the end of that week, Lyda was out of the hospital and back in the home in El Dorado, nursing her baby, with Margaret helping in any way she could. By mid-August, Lyda and Margaret and baby Lamar were back in Tyler, in the crowded, three-bedroom home on Wooldridge Street where the Hunt family had settled after their move from El Dorado.

So Lamar Hunt's story was just beginning, even as the legendary saga of Haroldson Lafayette Hunt and Lyda Bunker Hunt and their family was well underway. In a land convulsed and crippled by the seismic financial and social trauma of the Depression, men fought for their survival and fortunes in the same breath. The cities of America knew the breadlines, and the long procession of migrants, looking forlornly for regular work. But across the South, in the small towns and hollers, the transitory phenomenon was even more noticeable. Men picked up and embarked for new surroundings at the hint of money.

And when the real strike came, in October 1930, the southwest United States was transformed. They came on horses, trains, wagons, and cars (the latter often getting stuck in the quagmires of the unpaved streets in the oil boomtowns of Henderson and Kilgore, Texas). There was no sense of how long the boom would last or who might prevail. So the temper of the times was bruised, breathless, and distrustful. It was in this world that H. L. Hunt thrived.

He had forever altered his own future and that of his family with his shrewd play on Columbus Marion "Dad" Joiner's seminal Daisy Bradford No. 3 well in Rusk County, Texas, in the dwindling fall days of 1930, cannily capitalizing on the largest oilfield discovery in the world at that time.

H. L. Hunt had gained and lost and regained his fortune by the time of Lamar's birth, but he was by no means secure. Earlier in 1932, just a week after Charles Lindbergh's baby was kidnapped, a ransom note—written on wax paper, inside a burlap bag—was deposited among the azaleas on the Hunt property in Tyler. The note contained a threat to kidnap and kill one of the two oldest children, Hassie or Margaret, if H. L. Hunt didn't bring a ransom to the Blue Note Club in Tyler. The threat was viewed as serious enough, and H. L. Hunt's standing substantial enough, to call in the Texas Rangers, with Manuel "Lone Wolf" Gonzaullas personally handling the case, and apprehending the would-be kidnappers.

The outsized adventure was entirely in keeping with the tone and tenor of the life of Haroldson Lafayette Hunt, Jr. Born in 1889 in Carson Township, Fayette County, Illinois, to a Confederate War soldier father and a college-educated mother, Ella Rose Hunt, who'd served as a nurse on the Union side. Home-schooled and precocious, H. L. Hunt, Jr., quickly became known as June or Junie to his family. A restless soul, he left home at age sixteen, returning only after his father's death six years later. He'd learned a lot in those years, using his mathematical mind to its best advantage in both games of chance and in business. He'd also learned, on what was left of the frontier in the West, to fend and think for himself.

One of the stories he told his sons was about the night he won big at poker at a labor camp in California. After lying awake much of the night, H. L. concluded that in all likelihood he would be rousted while taking the only road into town the next morning. So he left then, in the middle of that night, avoiding the main road, and instead following the train tracks by the moon's dim light, walking 15 miles due west to the next town, still holding his winnings.

When he returned to Illinois, to bury his father in 1911, he was becoming a striking, if not handsome, young man, with soft skin, a cherubic face, and crystal blue eyes. With his $5,000 inheritance, June decided to go to Arkansas, where H. L. Hunt, Sr., had fought during the Civil War. His father had told June that during the fighting in the Battle of Ditch Bayou, he saw "the richest, best-looking farmland you ever saw."

H. L. wound up in Lake Village, Arkansas, a bucolic town built on cotton, and a refuge from the bustling Mississippi. The C-shaped lake seemed to jump out of the Mississippi River, just west of Greenville, Mississippi, and when H. L. Hunt arrived, taking up residence at the Lake Shore Hotel, he found a town and a tone to his liking. The town was dignified, cultured, and full of, in his own memory, "the comely ladies of Lake Village with their soft drawls."

He bought a 960-acre plantation due south of Lake Village, and commenced with the life of a gentleman farmer, overseeing his property. Two years in a row, the rising tides of the Mississippi washed out his crop. But he persevered by other means, keeping his hand in the town dealings and winning a good deal of poker games at the Lake Shore Hotel, as well as high-stakes affairs across the Mississippi River in Greenville.

Soon, H. L. Hunt made the acquaintance of the prominent Lake Villager Nelson Waldo Bunker, proprietor of the town's general store, postmaster for the village, and all-round lodestar of other community relations. The men hit it off, and soon enough, Hunt—always "girl-minded" in his own words—was courting Bunker's seventeen-year-old daughter Mattie. That summer, Mattie's older sister Lyda came home from her teaching job in Jonesboro. June and Lyda shared a few conversations in the Bunker parlor, and he quickly became convinced that he was courting the wrong woman.

Lyda was the third of Pap and Sarah Bunker's six children. Recognizing her thirst for education, her parents had sent her to a boarding school in Little Rock and then Potter College for Women in Bowling Green, Kentucky. She returned to Arkansas and found work as a teacher in Jonesboro, 200 miles north of Lake Village.

H. L.'s courtship of Lyda, held in the dining rooms, ballrooms, and front porches of Lake Village, was an exercise in willfulness. He respected her intelligence, grace, and self-possession, and the sense that so many had of enjoying the grounded warmth of Lyda's company. There was an earnest goodness to her that he found comforting, even civilizing.

Conversely, H. L. must have made a distinctive and convincing suitor. He was a distillation of the American virtues of honest craftiness, a keen sense of ingenuity, exacting thrift, and a disregard for pretensions borne of book learning and the trappings of high society. Possessed of a formidable mind, a certifiably photographic memory, and a strong sense of personal manifest destiny, he was a man serenely confident in his own abilities and specialness. His genes, he allowed to Lyda, were special and must be passed on to further generations.

They were married on November 26, 1914, and Mattie was the maid of honor. For a few years, H. L. and Lyda lived a life that was unremarkable, save for the traumatic shifts in fortune that H. L. experienced in the cotton business. Even as they were building a family—Margaret born in 1915, and Haroldson Lafayette Hunt III, or "Hassie," born in 1917—June's business acumen kept them solvent.

It was in 1921, while about to make yet another plantation deal, when June had a change of heart. He caught wind of the oil rush in El Dorado, 90 miles to the west, and decided after a mere few minutes of reflection to turn his attention to the burgeoning new business.

In the slapped-together oil towns, filled with card sharps and prostitutes, men and women possessed of empty bluster and a desperate need to make a score, H. L. Hunt confirmed something about himself. In matters of business, he was not merely smarter than most other men, he was more principled as well. Others might not have been able to cope with the convulsive uncertainty, but H. L.'s nerve was staunch. He could unabashedly ask for help when he needed it, confident in the rectitude of his mission. In his business dealings, he was content in operating at a profit in that space of chance where other prospectors and speculators might grow wary, wait for further signs of promise, and, in that moment, lose their opportunity. H. L. Hunt did not waver; he surged headlong into the fray, with an unshakeable will, and faith in his own powers of perception and instincts.

Over the next decade, June mastered the arcane art of oil drilling and the buying and selling of oil leases. Buying low, selling high, often keeping a share in leases that he would turn around and sell at profit, he became a premier wildcatter, with a reputation as an indefatigable worker and an honest debtor.

So by the fall of 1930, when H. L. caught wind of a test well being drilled near Kilgore, Texas, he had spent nearly a decade in the oil business. Driving over from El Dorado, he met Columbus Marion "Dad" Joiner, and wound up with a crucial stake in the East Texas Oilfield. While the immediate effect of the immense strike was a dilution in the market, with oil prices falling from a dollar to 15 cents a barrel, June knew the long view was good: In a country where cars were being produced in record numbers, and where interstate transportation was booming, the business to be in was oil.

In 1931, he moved his family to Tyler, Texas. By now the Hunts had five children—Margaret, Hassie, Caroline (born in 1923), Bunker (born in 1926), and Herbert (born in 1929). Lyda Hunt was ready to settle down, and quite ready to stop having children. Lamar would be her last.

Margaret later joked that baby Lamar had exhibited the family's trademark frugality even before he was born, delaying his arrival until August, when many of the (non–air-conditioned) hospitals in Arkansas offered a discount on their surgical procedures. Back in Tyler, Caroline followed the day nurse around the house, rushing to the kitchen when the woman asked for a napkin, only to realize that she'd meant for the girl to fetch a diaper. Fussed over by his sisters, doted on by his mother, Lamar Hunt had arrived in the world with an almost angelic disposition.

Two things happened in 1933 that would shape his early life. Having outgrown their first Tyler home, the Hunts moved into a regal white antebellum mansion on the end of Charnwood Street near downtown Tyler. With its white-columned front porch looking out at the massive magnolia tree abutting the front sidewalk, the home sat on the brick-lined "T" that marked Fanning Street meeting Charnwood. There was a wide yard on the side of the house, bordered by a rectangular walk and azaleas, room on the other side for Lyda to plant her rose garden, and servants' quarters in the back, where the chef Gertrude and the young maid Pandora Waters were housed.

By then seventeen, Margaret had taken some of the parenting responsibilities from her mother, often tending to Lamar and the toddler Herbert, but when she left for college at Mary Baldwin in Staunton, Virginia, in the fall of 1933, H. L. Hunt recognized a need for more help. That fall, he wrote Margaret a letter in college:

> While in New York I hired a Swiss governess, Eugenia de Tuggenier, for Lamar as I would like Mom to be less tied down to family obligations. Raising the first five of you has not left her adequate time for the traveling she enjoys and needs to do with you all to expose you to more of the world. I hired her on the basis of her impressive references, how-

ever, Miss Tuggenier's previous experience had not prepared her for living in Texas. Upon arrival she expected to be threatened by Indians. Also, she has never before experienced devoted colored servants. Bunker calls her "Toogie" to her face which he manages to get away with although she is quite strict otherwise. "Toogie" is teaching Bunker and Herbert to speak French which I do not suppose will damage them. Toogie has some *Flying Elephant* books which the boys read out loud with her in French . . . Hassie wants to play football in school but Mom and I are not giving our permission. I never knew of a football player who didn't end up with some permanent injury . . .

Taking residence at Charnwood, the governess shared a room with the infant Lamar, feeding him a bottle and singing him to sleep in French. That Thanksgiving, Lyda left to spend Thanksgiving with H. L., Hassie, and Margaret on the East Coast, while Toogie stayed in Tyler with the three youngest boys.

From an early age, Lamar proved to be keen and sweet; he loved chasing after his brothers and following after his sisters, and was a preternaturally patient and observant traveler. While she by all reports adored Lamar, the new surroundings strained Miss Tuggenier's Continental sensibilities. One summer day in 1934, supervising Lamar and his siblings out in the yard at Charnwood, the stout Toogie fanned herself and proclaimed, "I would not trade one acre of Switzerland for all of Texas."

In 1935, with Texas in the midst of a polio epidemic, the Hunts summered in Newport, Rhode Island, taking up residence at a house right off the Atlantic. As the family spent one of their days sunning on the beach, Caroline looked on at her littlest brother, and paused to take a picture.

She caught him that splendid day in his element, contentedly amusing himself in the wet sand, holding his toy boat, setting it in the water and snatching it back, utterly absorbed in play.

•

The same year that Lamar Hunt was born, the United States Caramel Company issued a set of thirty-two sports heroes cards, celebrating the famous athletes of the day. The makeup of the set provided a good index of the sporting popularity of the era: There were twenty-seven baseball players, three boxers, and two golfers. Zero football players. Had there been any, they surely would have been college stars. The National Football League, barely a decade old, consisted of eight franchises, including teams in Portsmouth, Ohio, and Staten Island, New York. The league did not have a championship game, divisions, or a uniform schedule. It was a pale echo of the college game. In 1925, when the Chicago Bears signed Illinois's Red Grange following his last college game, the Bears drew more fans for Grange's barnstorming off-season tour than the entire league drew for its 1925 season.

There is a conventional, and largely credible, history of American leisure that argues that, up until the middle of the twentieth century, spectator sports existed on the periphery of American society, as a diversion that knew and accepted its position. There was a time and a place for sports: weekends, mostly, and holidays; the quadrennial modern Olympics had developed a following, the World Series focused the nation's attention for a week in October, as did the New Year's Day bowl games, the Memorial Day running of the Indianapolis 500, Fourth of July doubleheaders, and Thanksgiving Day football games.

There were, as yet, no regular periodicals solely devoted to all sports. *The Sporting News*, the bible of baseball, would remain a baseball-only publication until the 1940s. Radio became more pervasive, giving the games a broader base, reaching beyond the shift workers and gamblers who were at the heart of sports fandom in the '10s and '20s. As movie theater attendance increased, even through the Depression, the opening short reels of sports coverage, often hosted by radio personality Bill Stern, helped create a new era of modern, mythic athletic heroes.

Outside of the large cities of the industrial Northeast, sports were still a decidedly parochial exercise, something to be done rather than seen. In Texas, baseball still ruled but college football was a passion of nearly equivalent widespread interest. The violent sport had swept the state, nourished by the widespread competition among the high schools and focused each fall on the seven major colleges comprising the Southwest Conference, all save the University of Arkansas within the state's borders. H. L. Hunt had grown up playing baseball in Illinois, but he grew to love football and he observed, more than once, that he was perfectly happy to gamble on either.

At Charnwood, there were daily lunches and nightly dinners served in the spacious dining room, with large bowls of meat, potatoes, and vegetables for the family and H. L. Hunt's numerous, unannounced guests ("he never called ahead," recalled Herbert, "he would just show up with one or two people"). The older children sat at dinner, attentively listening while June weighed in on the business of the day, politics, and foreign policy. Lamar, because of his youth, still took meals in a high chair in the kitchen, developing a rapport with and a trust of the domestic staff.

H. L. Hunt was prone to definitive statements, a product of a time when the exemplars of American manhood were known to have little patience for ambiguity of any kind. At dinner, he would take a break from his daylong smoking of La Corona Belvederes but not his running commentary on the events of the day. "Dad didn't do idle chitchat," said Herbert. "If you were talking about something and it was nothing, you'd be interrupted. Dad took over."

In the evenings when H. L. was at home, the family would often sit by the baby grand piano and listen to their father singing along with Lyda's playing. While she loved the church hymns, he was fond of the popular songs of the day, often crooning to Fats Waller's "I Can't Give You Anything But Love."

Lyda doted on all her boys, and both Lamar and Herbert used the same term of endearment, "Papoose Mooze" (or simply "Mooze"), in addressing their mother. There were crucial differences, though, between Lamar and his brothers. Both Bunker and Herbert had trouble reading, exhibiting traits that would generations later likely be diagnosed as dyslexia. And they were initially far more headstrong. After Herbert came down with pneumonia in the fall of '34, H. L. wrote to Margaret, "We have to bribe him to take his medicine. It has gotten to where he is charging five dollars to take castor oil." Around the same time, the confident Bunker took to walking by himself around Tyler and, during a vacation in England in 1936, he caught a bus to a movie theater by himself. By the time he got out of the show, the buses had stopped running, so he walked across London at night, the ten-year-old American boy searching for the familiar façade of a hotel.

By contrast, Lamar was more malleable in personal relations, in all ways the baby of the family. He was also precocious, with both words and numbers. He didn't have the photographic memory of his father or Hassie, but he was adept at math and showed a gift for names and numbers. He also developed an early love of sports and games. Caroline remembered, even before his fifth birthday, that Lamar was rattling off the names of his football and baseball heroes.

While all of H. L. and Lyda's children grew up feeling loved, there was a distinct sense of reserve in the family. Husband and wife slept in separate rooms; no one in the family was overly demonstrative. Margaret once relayed that her father had referred to her as "beautiful" on the day she was born, and "never gave me another compliment." H. L.'s pride was the young Hassie, who bore a haunting resemblance to his father (they won a father-and-son lookalike contest at a fair in the early '30s) and who, from the age of thirteen on, accompanied his father in the oil fields. But even Hassie was reproached when he once kissed his mother. "Stop that!" ordered H. L. "Don't be kissing people."

The Hunts did not talk a lot about their feelings. And, as it happened, there was a lot to not talk about. The gas leak in the house at El Dorado that led to the death of their fourth child, the month-old Lyda, in 1925. The growing spells of erratic behavior that Hassie suffered later in his teenage years. Then there was the chaotic fantasia that was H. L. Hunt's personal life.

Through the '20s and '30s, in Arkansas and Louisiana and Texas, he was known as an honest businessman. But in his personal life, H. L. Hunt—quite secretly at first, then later more or less unapologetically—was a bigamist. After baby Lyda's death in 1925, H. L. told his wife that he was setting out for an adventure in Florida, to capitalize on the Florida land boom. Down in Tampa, he met and courted a young woman named Frania Tye, to whom he identified himself as Major Franklin Hunt. They were married in a civil ceremony later that year. For the next decade H. L. Hunt traveled incessantly. He spent less than half his time at either home, and it wasn't until 1934, after H. L. had brought Frania Tye and their children to Dallas, that his two lives intersected.

One day, he brought Hassie with him to meet Frania Tye, providing a scant explanation as to her identity. When Frania Tye finally did what she'd long threatened—calling Lyda and divulging H. L.'s other life—there was little outward change. Ever stoic, Lyda reached out to Frania and offered to adopt her children. But even with this titanic breach, nothing was said. After the initial revelations, even more remarkably, Margaret Hunt never discussed the matter with her brother or anyone else in the family. "We never talked about it," she explained in 1989. "We still don't talk about it." Caroline would remember later, "I never heard my father and mother exchange an unpleasant word to one another." Instead, those that knew H. L.'s secret navigated around the wreckage and simply pretended it didn't exist. Lamar would grow up knowing about none of it, and he wouldn't find out until far later in his life.

But it would not be accurate to say he was unaffected. In 1935, Lamar Hunt's financial future was secured by the prudent insistence of Margaret. She had learned about Frania Tye and the second family on a train trip with Hassie to the Jumbo Gold Mine that H. L. had purchased in Winnemucca, Nevada. Later in the fall, dining with her father in New York on a weekend away from college, she did not confront him with the knowledge of a second family, but she did inform him, "Daddy, I think you need to set up trust funds for the kids. Hassie and I have a business but the kids don't have anything. Suppose something should happen to you . . ."

He agreed, and in December 1935, H. L. and Lyda Hunt set up trusts to benefit their six children. It insured that Lamar Hunt, upon reaching the age of eighteen, would be a multimillionaire.

Later, Lamar would have precious few memories of Tyler. He remembered playing in the yard outside the house, he remembered the pecan tree in the front yard, and he remembered the ice storm that threatened to kill the tree, and looking through the parlor window at his father, who was negotiating a wheelbarrow with a small fire in the tray, rolling it around under the tree to melt ice off the branches. And Lamar remembered the next morning, when the ground beneath the tree was black with dead birds.

In Tyler, Lamar was often along for the ride, joining the family for a drive out to the train station in Minneola, where the train would stop to bring Margaret to Dallas. The boys would flatten a penny on the rail and delight in picking up the hot copper wafer after the locomotive had passed. Children flattened pennies on rails all across the country; but in the Hunt family, H. L. hastened to point out to his children that it was *illegal* to destroy U.S. currency.

The standard dress for oilmen was khaki pants and khaki shirts. But H. L. invariably wore crisp white shirts, setting himself apart from his peers. When in town, he'd leave right after breakfast, head down to the People's National Bank Building, then return for lunch. At dinner, Lyda and the staff were always prepared for the unannounced guests, and the children were prepared to stand up during the meal and face a quiz about state capitals or American history or Texas heritage.

From the kitchen, where he was fed by the servants, Lamar could hear it all: the political and business talk from the dining room in front of him; the discreet knocks on the back door, as drifters and out-of-work locals asked Lyda Hunt for a small portion of food. The complex tapestry of human interaction was right there, including the ineluctable truth that the black domestic workers, to a great degree, made the household run smoothly.

Lamar could only have picked up shards of the big events of the time: the family's shock at the 1937 New London Gas Explosion, caused when a school tapped some of the gas from a Hunt Oil line; the continued concern over kidnapping threats; the endless discussion of the oil business and how it did and should work; and, always, in the background, H. L. Hunt speculating on his prospects.

One of the singular passions of H. L. Hunt was his love of numbers. "He loved to gamble because it was percentages," said his nephew Stuart Hunt. "He had one of the most active minds of anybody I've ever seen. Winning money was the way to keep score. The challenge was what he played for. He understood percentages. Everything he bet on, cards, dice, horses—his success was in his mathematical ability to calculate the odds. He never bet on hunches; he called himself a 'card locator' because he remembered the cards that had been played. He had the guts to bet them if he had them, and he always bet with the odds." (Which is not to say he didn't believe in intuition. Family lore was rife with stories of H. L., in transit to a new drilling site, stopping by the road en route to search for four-leaf clovers. When naming his companies, he was partial to six-letter names beginning with P, which led to Placid Oil and Penrod Drilling and Panola Gas.)

While Toogie was taking care of the young Lamar, Lyda was free to tend to her rose garden, and to oversee H. L.'s complicated mathematical system for betting the horses. In a 1935 letter to Margaret, Lyda mentioned:

> I have been his sole handicapper working hours on end to dope out the horses he would bet on. His system has been quite successful, but I have become exhausted by the endless lists of numbers. I told him that I would not go on doing this anymore and that he would have to hire somebody. I resigned. So when you return for vacation, do not be surprised to find the downstairs guest bedroom converted into an office for Messrs. C. O. Johnson and John Lee, who work full time on Daddy's horse racing venture which we should probably name Hunt Horses, which does not begin with a P and therefore will probably not be very lucky.

The French lessons continued for more than a year, then ended abruptly. H. L. grew weary of his youngest boys being more fluent in a foreign language than they were in English. In 1936, H. L. came home and summoned the family dog, Willie. The dog didn't come, until Lamar, not yet four, came into the parlor and called *"Ici, le chien,"* and watched as Willie bounded toward him.

"That's it," said H. L. "I can't even call my own dog." Toogie was let go, and more duties to take care of Lamar were passed off to Caroline, by now in her early teens, and the bright young kitchen servant, Pandora.

The family would remain in Tyler through the fall of 1937. At a picnic at Tyler Lake one day, the family lapsed into a discussion about whether the dog

Willie knew how to swim. H. L., quite sure of the dog's innate aquatic ability, picked him up, strode to the lakeside, and threw Willie into the water, watching him paddle back to the shore as five-year-old Lamar looked on in fraught concern. The shock and initial fear would linger in his memory for years.

Later that same fall, Lamar and Herbert joined Lyda, Margaret, and Caroline for an Alaskan cruise. After putting the boys down for a nap one afternoon, and locking them in their stateroom, Lyda, Margaret, and Caroline went ashore at one of the stops. When they returned to the room, the boys had disappeared and a porthole door was open. Lyda was aghast with fear, until she heard the boys giggling just down the hall, in the adjoining room. Lamar was sincerely contrite when he realized he'd given his mother a serious scare. "I'm sorry we scared you, Papoose Mooze," he said. "We would never scare you about kidnappers."

By now, H. L. Hunt's oil holdings were immense, and his travels were taking him more frequently to Dallas. It was where he did most of his banking—Nathan Adams at the First National Bank having granted him the crucial $50,000 loan that allowed him to maximize his play at the Daisy Bradford No. 3. Tyler, off the train line and increasingly out of step with the rapidly changing realities of Texas business, had a population of 28,000 people. Dallas, always striving to improve and grow larger and more modern, had become the hub of southwest business. It had gleaming skyscrapers and a population nearing 300,000.

It was H. L. Hunt's considered opinion that Margaret, now twenty-three and having graduated from college, would find a more suitable mate in Dallas than in Tyler. So on December 22, 1937, the family bought a property in Dallas. By Christmas Day, they were in the process of moving.

They would spend the beginning of 1938 in a new city, in a house that for the next eighteen years Lamar Hunt would know as home.

This, too, came at a crucial time. As one family member put it, "The rest of the family grew up in the oil patch. But he really ended up growing up in a metropolitan city."

CHAPTER TWO

MANSION ON THE HILL

Lamar burst through the front door and didn't stop to take in the view. He headed straight through the vestibule and up the staircase, at a six-year-old boy's sprint, trailing closely after Herbert and Bunker.

His brothers had seen the house back in December, and returned to Tyler with breathless stories of the "secret" chute that led all the way to the basement. On moving day, that was all Lamar wanted to see.

"The first time there we rushed to the laundry chute," he'd say later. "There were the older brothers showing me this neat thing. We didn't care how many rooms it had or how many square feet or how good the kitchen was, the ten acres, the lake. No. The laundry chute." The boys spent much of that first day experimenting to see what could safely be dropped down the chute from the second floor to the basement laundry basket.

When he stopped long enough to take in the view, he discovered a house of outsized dreams. The home into which the Hunts moved at the beginning of 1938 was called Mount Vernon, and it was modeled after George Washington's Mount Vernon (but at roughly twice the scale), with six grand white columns lining the front porch and a graceful, glass-lined cupola at its apex.

The house stood on Lawther Drive, just to the west of White Rock Lake, a reservoir built by the city of Dallas that at one time had been the city's main source for water. Development in the area had begun shortly after 1917, when fishing became legal on the lake. By the time the Hunts arrived in 1938, Franklin D. Roosevelt's Civilian Conservation Corps had begun building docks and other improvements around the lake, and it had become a popular picnic and recreation spot for Dallasites.

H. L. had paid $69,000 in cash to purchase the home from Thomas Y. Pickett, a tax appraiser who by 1938 had run out of money and into trouble with the Internal Revenue Service. The house had been commissioned by Pickett and built by John F. Staub, the residential architect renowned for his work in the stately homes in the River Oaks neighborhood of Houston in the '20s.

The deed of sale, signed December 22, 1937, included the house and the ten acres overlooking the still unpaved Lawther Drive, as well as "two peacocks and all chickens . . . one cow, and a calf." Lyda noted that she'd never had a cow in her life, but now, upon moving to the big city, she would finally have one.

By mid-January, they had mostly unpacked, and H. L. had set up his office in downtown Dallas, resuming his frequent travels. The changes to the house began almost immediately, with the paving of the long semi-circular drive that came up to the front of the house. Soon, Lyda had a pair of live oak trees planted on either side of the driveway. On one side of the house, she installed a rose garden, having imported the ideal sandy loam from Tyler.

It had been six years since the Lindbergh kidnapping, but the wealthy still lived in fear. After hearing the details of a nearby robbery, H. L. insisted that the house's five safes be locked in the open position, so any potential intruders wouldn't think he was hiding something of value in them. Lyda used the basement safe for her canned preserves. Lamar used the safe under the front stairs to store his football, baseball, bat, and glove.

Very soon, H. L. built a fenced-in area in the back for the six deer he brought onto the land. The enterprising young Herbert took over the chicken coop and began selling eggs to his parents. H. L. would sometimes walk through the backyard, visiting his deer, pulling pecans off the trees, and cracking the shells to eat them. H. L. was neither an athlete nor a fan of extended socializing—a four-hour round of golf would have been torture to him—but he did occasionally take a pitching wedge out in the front yard and hit a few golf balls.

Lamar was not yet seven in the summer of 1939, when the men from the Paddock Pool Company came from California to build the second private swimming pool in all of Dallas. Playing outside, he would watch the workers, who camped outside during the duration of the project, using their mule team to excavate the tract for the pool. On the day the men poured the cement, they took a break just long enough for Bunker, Herbert, and Lamar to slide through the fresh mix. Lyda was apologetic to the workers and, as always, discreet. "She never told on the kids to daddy," said Caroline. "My parents never did tell on us."

Perhaps it was the recollection of his father throwing Willie the dog into the lake back in Tyler, but Lamar was initially frightened of the pool. When H. L. came home from work in the afternoons, Lamar would hide in the upstairs bathroom, trying to avoid his daily swimming lesson. But he would be located, June would don his swimming trunks, and the two would head out to the pool. By the summer of 1940, Lamar was a serviceable swimmer.

Mount Vernon was a wealthy house in Texas in the first half of the twentieth century, which is to say that the Hunts employed several black domestic workers, and that both parties observed the racial customs of the day. H. L. Hunt was hardly a progressive, but he had stayed clear of racist organizations like the Ku Klux Klan, and he had developed a reputation as an honest, even kind, employer. There was a sense of familiarity and affection among the house staff. One April Fool's Day, Pandora Waters made a beautiful chocolate pie for the family, with a crisp flaky crust and meringue top, all of which perfectly concealed a center consisting entirely of mud. After the boys tried the fateful first bites, Pandora was laughing along with the rest of the family when she produced the real pie, with a chocolate filling.

Another of the family's servants, Armstead B. Smith, was a part-time cook who had played football in college, and whose mother was the beloved cook at Camp Waldemar for girls (where Margaret and Caroline had spent parts of their summers). Smith would arrive in the afternoons from his day job, about the time the boys would come home from school, and often agreed to play football with Lamar and Herbert, provided Herbert helped him later in the kitchen. Armstead taught Lamar the finer points of tackling and helped him master his grip around the laces of a football. The half-hour games would end in time for Smith to go to the servants' quarters and take a quick bath, then return to make dinner, served in the dining room at 6 p.m. sharp.

Smith also cooked at the family's parties and outdoor barbecues, making enormous hot sweet rolls that the brothers adored. "We called them 'stomach-breakers,'" Lamar said. "Bunker, Herbert, and I would eat until we couldn't manage another bite, and then we'd lie down on the floor gasping."

Because of the lingering kidnapping fears, H. L. declared that the children needed to ride to school, usually with one of the house staff driving them. Caroline was soon enough driving herself, while Lamar was driven to the Dallas Country Day school and, later, Lipscomb Elementary. After quickly thanking Armstead for the ride, he would get out of the car, flushed with embarrassment, and hurry up the schoolhouse steps. Though he could not articulate the feeling for decades, the experience—to have Armstead, a man he liked and admired, chauffeuring him to school—made Lamar sheepish. "It wasn't a limousine or anything, it was just a normal car," he remembered, "but it still felt odd."

There were few houses in the neighborhood, and even fewer children. But right next door to the Hunts was a stockbroker named Dallas Gordon Rupe II. His son, Dallas III, was known to everyone as Buddy. Lamar and Buddy became best friends almost instantly. When they met, Lamar was six years old, Buddy was four, both were the youngest children in their families, and both had already fallen in love with sports. It would be the first of many relationships in which Lamar's natural reticence would be complemented by a friend who was more outgoing. "Lamar was a very quiet boy at the time," said Rupe. "It was very tough to get a smile out of him. I think the problem and reason for it was that Lamar was simply very shy."

Before long, Lamar started calling Buddy "Root," and Buddy called Lamar "Sap." They would take turns sleeping over at each other's house every other weekend, join each other's families for dinner, even go away to summer camp together. The Rupes, like the Hunts, sent their children to summer camp in Hunt, Texas (Camp Stewart for the boys was not far from Camp Waldemar), about 100 miles west of Austin.

"I can remember, I'd get a letter from home and I was tremendously homesick," said Rupe. "And Lamar would read it to me, as I would cry and he would cry."

Lamar and Buddy loved football most of all. There's a photograph from early in the Dallas years, of a scene in the Rupes' backyard. Herbert, with a football, is running to daylight, while little Buddy, dressed in a full football uniform save the helmet, is in pursuit. Moving in for the tackle is Buddy's older sister, Paula ("she was a hard tackler," remembered Herbert). Chasing the runner, in a striped shirt and sporting Buddy's snug-fitting leather helmet was Lamar, intent, smiling, closing in to make the play.

In their enduring friendship, Lamar and Buddy learned to turn everything into a game or contest of some sort. They held all manner of competitions: races through the house at Mount Vernon on inclement days, football games and contests out in the yard when it was nice. They would race to see who could pick the most pecans off the trees in 15 minutes (with Buddy getting the benefit of a longer fishing pole). In the middle of summer, beset with chigger bites, they'd even count who had the most.

But best of all, they were their own football heroes. In the Hunts' backyard, the grove of pecan trees would yield piles of leaves each fall. Lamar and Buddy would rake up the leaves, and then use the pile as the defenders in their games. When they were playing on the same team, pretending to be the Southern Methodist University Mustangs, the leaves were the defenders. Lining up in a virtual single wing, they would call intricate plays, Lamar spinning the ball to himself to simulate the snap before sprinting into action and then pitching to Buddy. When they played one-on-one games against each other, the leaves were where they would make their tackles.

By 1939, when he ventured to his first Cotton Bowl, Lamar had fallen in love with the *idea* of spectator sports, and the visions of crowded stadium scenes—Yankee Stadium, Madison Square Garden, Soldier Field—were the grand datelines of his early imagination. "I was always interested in the attendance at sporting events," he said. "I would open the newspaper and go to the box scores, and one of the first things I would look at would be attendance. The Phillies drew 7,211. Or 30,228 saw the Indians sweep a doubleheader."

On Sundays came the double helping of newspapers, the fat *Dallas Morning News* and the *Sunday Times Herald,* with acres of coverage in the usually tight sports sections. And since both H. L. and Lyda received a copy of each, there was always a sports section for Lamar to examine, save, and clip out. He would look at the quarter-by-quarter score and the scoring summaries at college football games around the country, and see what the writers had to say about the games he'd listened to on the radio the day before.

From his earliest days, Lamar was a planet orbiting the sun of his mother. From Buddy Rupe's perspective, there was only one head of the household at Mount Vernon. "Lamar's mother was the leader of the Hunt clan, and I just adored her," he said. "Mr. Hunt was very interesting, but he wasn't around that much."

While H. L. traveled extensively, Lamar gravitated to another male figure. An auditor named Al G. Hill had begun courting Margaret early in 1938, and the young Lamar found in Hill a warm, affable presence. Hill was a calmly assured man with a cherubic face and a level head. By the second week of his visits to Margaret at Mount Vernon, Lamar would end his nights by curling up in Al's lap and falling asleep. During much of Al and Margaret's courtship, Lamar tagged along, joining them while boating on White Rock Lake, or going to the movies at the Lakewood Theater.

Al and Margaret were married at Mount Vernon in October 1938, with Lamar sitting on the piano bench in the front room, swinging his legs and smiling happily. As they were waiting for their own house to be built, Al and

Margaret moved into the poolhouse next to the house at Mount Vernon, and Lamar visited them frequently—partly because he revered Al, but also because he could go into their small refrigerator and pinch bottles of Coke, which weren't available in the main house.

In his youth, he dressed as most children around him did. Dungarees, slacks on Sunday, short-sleeved collared shirts, and the same tightly cropped crew cut that was standard issue for most boys in Texas in the middle of the twentieth century. The severity of the haircut accentuated his smallish, close-set eyes, and his prominent chin. But what most struck those who knew him was the degree to which he stood apart—in demeanor and attitude—from the men in his family. The rest of the Hunts, from H. L. down to Bunker and Herbert, strode headlong into life. Lamar, however, did not. He was not exactly meek but somewhat withdrawn. He smiled easily, daydreamed often. And his disposition was more restrained. It was not just politesse—a lot of his peers were well-mannered. There was something more . . . he was at once playful and modest, and he lacked the air of malevolence and entitlement that sometimes infected rich boys of privilege. He was, in the nomenclature of a different time, a gentle soul.

•

Summer Saturday mornings. Sun coming through the gauze curtains. Chickens pecking in the backyard. Lamar would wake up and get dressed, then head downstairs to breakfast, with Pandora preparing pancakes and eggs. He would thank her, then ask Lyda for a dollar to go to the Lakewood shopping center.

Out the side door and down the back driveway, he would head out of Mount Vernon and walk across Fisher Drive, the sun coming up high on the lake, and the distinctive sound of the green parrots in the trees. There was little development in the area, so Lamar could move almost as the crow flew. He'd skirt the edge of the Sanford property, home to Cotton Bowl director Curtis Sanford, across a creek and over a set of railroad tracks, then cross the bridge above the creek into which Caroline had once driven her car. From there he'd wind his way down to Lakewood Drive, and the end of the Lakewood Bus line, where he'd catch the bus into Lakewood, getting off at the intersection of Lakewood and Abrams Road. Back on foot, he could see the art deco tower of the Lakewood Theater, which opened the year the Hunts moved to Dallas, the hub of a bustling new shopping district.

Lamar often went early, so he could stop up the street at Harrell's Pharmacy and buy a comic book or a sports magazine—*Bill Stern's Sports Stories* was his favorite—and have a strawberry milkshake at the counter, quietly reading while sipping from the white paper straw with the red swirls.

If time permitted, he would head around the corner to the Abrams Road Pharmacy and its pinball machine. "He always had a competitive fever," said his friend Bob Chilton, who knew Lamar around the neighborhood and would wind up attending college with him a decade later. "There was this pinball machine at the drugstore, and he used to play it all the time. One time, I was watching him, and I left to go out and get on my bike. As I was leaving, I brushed the machine. He followed me outside and threatened to beat me up if I ever messed with the pinball machine again."

One morning, Buddy accompanied Lamar to the Abrams Road Pharmacy, and the two were playing the pinball machine. Buddy was just recovering from a particularly strong case of poison ivy, and much of his face was covered in calamine lotion. When another boy, standing by the pinball machine, made a remark about Buddy's appearance, Buddy turned away, ignoring the slight, then turned back when he heard the commotion—Lamar stepping up and threatening to pummel the boy for teasing his friend.

The Lakewood Theater double feature would begin at noon and on summer Saturdays Lamar would arrive in time for the serials and both movies. Then it was a late afternoon bus to the edge of White Rock Lake and the walk back home. "Nothing better than on a Saturday morning getting up and seeing *The Lone Ranger* serials," he said. "They would have fifteen, so you'd have to come back every week and see what happened."

Back home in the evenings, Lamar gravitated to the library, where he'd sit by the large radio, pet the new dog, Whiskers, and listen for his favorite shows: On Friday nights, it was *Bill Stern's Colgate Sports Reel*, the 15-minute assemblage of legend and lore. On Saturday nights, Lamar would bring a Big Chief tablet into the library and mark down the top ten songs in *Your Hit Parade*, comparing it to his own predictions. On Sunday nights, it was NBC's powerhouse lineup of Fred Allen, Jack Benny, Fibber McGee and Molly, Edgar Bergen and Charlie McCarthy. With Pandora off for the day, H. L. sometimes did the cooking, often frying up scrambled eggs for dinner, along with fried chicken leftovers that remained from the week.

Autumn weekends were different. Sometimes Lamar and Buddy would journey over to a vacant lot near the lake with friends and play touch football in the morning. But before noon, Lamar would be back in the library, lying on his stomach in front of the radio, listening to five solid hours of football. On a good week, Bill Stern would be calling a game from South Bend or Ann Arbor or Minneapolis, with an 11:30 a.m. kickoff. Then, at 2 p.m., it was the Humble Oil Southwest Conference Game of the Week ("Go to the Games with Humble"), and the inimitable call of announcer Kern Tips.

From Austin or College Station, or sometimes nearby in Dallas or Fort Worth, Tips would spice his play-by-play with a tangy blend of gridiron colloquialisms ("We've got a good, old-fashioned family squabble ahead of us today . . ."), a direct cousin to the purple prose of sportswriting that Lamar had already grown to love. When a running back fumbled a handoff from a quarterback, Tips announced there had been "a malfunction at the junction." A kicker converting an extra point was "making sevens out of sixes." A quarterback tackled behind the line of scrimmage "had to peel it and eat it this time."

As he grew older, Lamar was allowed to borrow the family's tape recorder, and he and Buddy would sit up on the third floor of Mount Vernon, beneath the cupola, playing games and imitating their favorite announcers: Lamar managed a passable imitation of loquacious boxing announcer Harry Balogh ("and now ladies and gentlemen, may the better man emerge victorious"), as well as the flat intonations of Graham McNamee, and, inevitably, the arch yet folksy Tips. "He's a rolling bundle of butcher knives down there on the field," Lamar would mimic, "that's TCU's Bounding Jimmy Lawrence." The sound of these voices, the hushed gravity in a pre-game introduction—these things connoted big events for Lamar, and entry into the world to which he'd witnessed only a few firsthand glimpses.

Lamar soon surmised that his father's interest in football wasn't solely a sporting one. While Lamar pored over his *Street & Smith's Football Pictorial Yearbook*, H. L. was often heard in his study on gameday mornings, talking to his personal bookie, querying contacts around the country for inside dope, and talking to his nephew, Tom Hunt, who was charged with monitoring the latest weather reports at the venues where H. L. was considering placing bets.

Though H. L. would, in later years, become infamous for the vast sums he bet on football games, Lamar developed a slightly different perspective on his father's fandom. "He was more of a baseball fan than a football fan," he said. "He was a fan of football, certainly. But he didn't go to school—he didn't go to high school and college, so he didn't have the connection, and he never played football."

But H. L. loved to move, and he loved to gamble, so football trips became common. On the Saturday morning after Thanksgiving in 1939, Lamar and

Herbert traveled with their parents on a special train out of Dallas's Union Station bound for College Station, Texas. It was the annual Texas A&M–Texas game, and it carried a special significance as the Aggies were unbeaten and in contention for a mythical national championship. There would be higher-toned "specials" on the rails for TCU or SMU road games, but what the seven-year-old Lamar remembered best was following his brother to the dining car, which was a converted boxcar with men selling snacks and beverages on crates. One car back was the men's toilet car, which was a series of holes cut in the bottom of the boxcar, into which a boy could urinate while watching the trestles rushing along below.

For a seven-year-old sports fan, College Station could appear altogether exotic. In the midst of a Kyle Field crowd of rapturous Aggie Cadets, Lamar looked on in wonder to see if star fullback Jarrin' John Kimbrough could keep A&M undefeated for its Sugar Bowl date with Tulane. Earlier in the fall in Austin, UT's Jack Crain had transformed the Longhorns with his open-field running in a 14–13 upset of Arkansas. But on this day, Crain and Texas were no match for the bigger, deeper Aggies. Lamar returned to Dallas having determined his first true football hero.

Though relatives had given him the starter-sets for stamp and coin collections, he had instead gravitated to scrapbooking, and by the summer of 1940, as he was turning eight, it had become his favorite hobby. Sitting on his bed in the evenings, he would borrow his mother's scissors and paste pot and construct highly detailed, elaborate scrapbooks. He'd gotten a black embossed leather cover, with "Scrap Book" in a jazz-age gold print on the front. Inside, on the first page, he pasted a picture of the 1939 All-America football teams as selected by Grantland Rice, United Press, and the Associated Press, along with a picture of Kimbrough, "the pigskin pulverizer of the Plains," in the words of UPI sportswriter Henry McLemore.

The Aggies' agronomy major was the star of the first book, as Lamar carefully clipped out the photo of a letter-jacketed Kimbrough standing next to a steer in a *Life* magazine publicity photo, and following Kimbrough's signing of a pro contract with the New York Yanks of the ill-fated American Football League.

By the summer of his ninth birthday, Lamar began a new section, which he titled "Texas A+M in 1941," carefully lettering the headline with red pencil and outlining it in blue, over a publicity photo showing A&M's two returning starters lining up in formation with nine empty pairs of shoes, to dramatize, as the headline put it, "Nine Men Who Weren't There," Kimbrough and his eight Aggie teammates whose eligibility had run out.

When his brothers were gone, or Buddy was away, Lamar always found solace in his books and games. "I played a lot alone," he said. "My older brothers were like three and six years older than I was, so it wasn't that big a difference, but there were times when they were away at school, or whatever, and I do remember playing a lot in the yard by myself. I'd go out in the front yard, and I'd throw the ball up and play like I was in Yankee Stadium, and be hitting the ball in the imaginary field there, and then I'd run, chase the ball, and hit it back the other way. Or football, you know, the same type of thing: throw myself passes and catch them." Siblings would remember him playing football in the backyard, lining up Whiskers' litter—three black puppies, three spotted—into opposing teams, then running plays while the puppies happily chased after him.

He also loved to invent new games. "I'd take a ball and bounce it off a wall and then scratch out a little court with my foot, and there'd be scoring," he said. One of the nicknames given to him around this time was "Games." His family never called him that—"I never knew he ever *had* that nickname until much later," said Herbert, and Caroline said she'd never heard him called that—but Lamar enjoyed the moniker, and as an adult would mention it frequently when discussing his childhood.

Lamar was a keen student, a good reader, and strong in his studies. In January of 1940, he wrote a letter to Caroline, off at college. In an unusually neat hand for a seven-year-old boy, he wrote, "Pan[dora] is with us while Mother has gone over to Margaret's to fit some clothes. We like the stamps you sent. We saw Gulliver's Travels and the Hunchback of Notre Dame. Sind[sic], Lamar."

In his memory and in fact, he felt sheltered and nurtured, safe and secure inside his family. But the family's preoccupations, to a great extent, were not his own. Lamar was by now allowed to sit at the adults' table, but he often daydreamed while the adults spoke of business and politics. "There was lots of discussion at the dinner table, and lots of important political people," Lamar remembered. "But I never had much interest in politics." Sundays were often a time when H. L. would drive his family out in the country, surveying the varied elements of his kingdom. "We'd go look at the cows and steers in the field and Dad thought it was the most marvelous thing in the world," said Lamar. "To me it was the most boring."

On Sunday, December 7, 1941, the Hunt family was out in Denton, Texas, testing a well, when the news broke of the attack on Pearl Harbor. Margaret, who had traveled to Pearl Harbor with Al on their honeymoon two years earlier, was perhaps the most shocked. "When the news came over the radio," said Lamar, "just hearing it—a Japanese attack! On Pearl Harbor!—of course to me it all sounded very exciting, war and airplanes. But I can remember Margaret's reaction to it best. She just bolted up. She was aghast."

H. L. knew well the implications. Within days, Hassie had enlisted in the military, and the fifteen-year-old Bunker was angling for an early entry. H. L.'s oil reserves would be crucial to the war effort, and he knew it. Before Christmas, he had a large flagpole erected in front of Mount Vernon, with the Stars-and-Stripes flying throughout the day.

The details of the days changed—even the Hunts were affected by gas rationing and the other sacrifices of wartime—but the tenor did not. Armstead and Pandora still served dinner at 6 p.m. sharp, but now a small radio was brought into the dining room, so that the family could hear the news of the day—Paul Harvey, Gabriel Heatter, William L. Shirer reporting on the war effort.

"We thought the war was romantic," remembered the writer Dan Jenkins, "because we didn't have to fight in it." So it was with Lamar. His primary focus remained on sports, but he also became more cognizant of the massive war effort. He became a plane-spotter, learning to identify the distinctive characteristics of the Japanese Zeros. The prospect of the war's conclusion was enough, by 1944, to prompt him to begin a scrapbook devoted to the D-Day Invasion.

By then a student at J. L. Long Middle School, Lamar had grown more serious about sports. He didn't simply play games on vacant lots but had started actively training for a time when he would get his first experience of organized team sports.

Remembering her childhood, Caroline Hunt said, "I never saw my mother lose her temper." H. L., absorbed in his own world, also was slow to anger. Both Caroline and Lamar would remember receiving but a single spanking in their childhood, each of them from their father for what Lamar would describe as "being impertinent at the dinner table."

Some of his siblings suspected Lamar received the benefit of being the baby of the family. "I think she was probably very lenient," Lamar said of his mother. "I was the last child and my mother and dad used to kiddingly say that the only reason I didn't get spanked was 'cause they were all spanked out. My mother was a real soft touch, I'm sure."

But there was more to it than birth order. H. L. and Lyda—without consulting any parenting tracts—offered absolute authority over major areas ("when he said something, that was it," recalled Caroline) and gentle guidance, if not benign neglect, in others. "I don't ever remember being reprimanded about *anything*," Caroline said later.

It was in this environment that Lamar learned manners. Lyda remained chipper through her private torments, through the fear and anguish of having two sons in the military. At Mount Vernon, voices were rarely raised. It was a splendid way to raise a child to show kindness and equanimity and respect. But it left Lamar ill-equipped for instances that elicited genuine sorrow and grief.

One night during the war, the Hunts were awakened by screams of distress from the backyard, and awoke to see the servants' quarters above the garage ablaze. The people and cars were safely rescued, but the bedrooms burned to the ground. Standing out in the darkness, under the light of the dying flames, the clang of the fire department's belated arrival in the distance, Lamar watched one of the male servants weeping openly, as all of his possessions were lost. "It touched me considerably," he would recall decades later. "The memory is still sad to this day."

That wouldn't be the only calamity. One spring morning in 1945, Lyda woke Herbert and Lamar with a worried shout, and told them to get down to the lake fast.

Bounding down the stairs, still in their pajamas, the boys rushed out the door and ran down to the bottom of the hill, scurrying across Lawther Drive to the lakeside where a young man in his late twenties was in a state of hysterical despair.

"My father!" he shouted. "He's down there somewhere! And I can't swim!" It took a while for the boys to make sense of the man's rambling, but it became clear that out on the lake that morning, the man and his father had capsized while checking on a trout line. The man made it to shore, but his father had been wearing hip waders, and when the water filled his boots, he sank to the bottom.

Lamar and Herbert, by now both gifted swimmers, dove in and spent 20 minutes trawling under the surface to search for the body, to no avail. When they came ashore finally, breathless and exhausted, Herbert dejectedly walked up to the house to take a shower and change. But Lamar stayed on the shore with the man.

"When the fire department finally came and pulled the dead man out of the water," said Herbert, "that was something that had an effect on Lamar for months."

Or perhaps longer. It was nothing that the family talked about. Open sorrow, like affection, was frowned on.

Neither did they discuss the plight of Hassie. After returning from his military service, he became increasingly irrational and irritable; at one point, he threw a grapefruit at his mother. H. L., desperate to act, to make it better, declared Hassie should go in for a prefrontal lobotomy and electroshock therapy. The cure, in this event, was at least as bad as the disease—it muted Hassie's personality, and he became an often vacant, listless presence, losing all interest in his previous oil and gas pursuits. If anything, it changed H. L. Hunt even more, as he spent years haunted by doubts about whether he'd done the right thing.

But nothing was said. What Lamar observed, from watching his mother and father, was to soldier on.

•

In the summer of 1945, near the war's end, the family put the twelve-year-old Lamar on a train in Dallas, and he traveled alone to Brunswick, Maine, to visit Caroline and her new husband, Lloyd Sands, stationed by the Brunswick Naval Base. Lamar traveled with his name, address, and phone number on a sheet of paper safety-pinned inside a pants pocket. Meek and quiet, carrying a single small suitcase, he successfully managed to change trains in St. Louis, taking another Pullman sleeper all the way to New York and then a connection up into Maine. While Caroline was indifferent to sports, she knew her "favorite sibling" loved them, so during his three-week stay, Lloyd and Caroline brought him down to Boston, where he watched the Braves in action at Braves Field, and even went to a harness-racing meet, where they slipped him a few dollars to bet on the races. Lamar was back in time for V-J Day.

He was filling out a bit by now, drinking milkshakes every day at Harrell's to put on weight for his first organized football experience. He'd been playing the game for nearly a decade—with his brothers, with Buddy, with Armstead, and by himself in the backyard at Mount Vernon. But he had yet to prove himself in any organized competition (though there had been a gymnasium at J. L. Long Junior High School, for physical education and pick-up basketball games, Lamar had yet to experience being on formal sports teams, with uniforms, practices, and officiated games). That would change soon enough. Working harder than ever before at his pass-catching and ball-handling technique, he'd added a regimen of exercises, counting his daily jumping jacks, push-ups, and still-dips. He'd taken to doing sprints up either side of the semi-circle driveway at Mount Vernon, and was continually frustrated by his inability to match the time on the east side as he had on the west. Finally, after more than a week of consternation, he measured the distance of each and discovered that the west side was five yards longer than the east.

In early September 1946, he got on another train, with Herbert, traveling to Pottstown, Pennsylvania, to The Hill School, a preparatory boarding school for boys. He brought along a new wardrobe of clothes—The Hill had a dress code requiring coats and ties six days a week—and a scant handful of personal possessions: large kitchen shears, so he could continue his scrapbooking, a football, a baseball mitt and ball, and a copy of Ring Lardner's *You Know Me Al*. Lyda sent off her two youngest boys with a cheerful goodbye. They were used to this by now. "Mother and Dad never went with us," said Herbert. "It was strictly put you on the train at the Highland Park Train Station."

Prior to September of 1946, Lamar's journeys had consisted of a few carefully guided vacations with his mother, heavy on museum visits, and some brief excursions to summer camps, at the Culver Military Academy one summer in Indiana and at least two summers at the Stewart School for Boys in Texas. Each time, Lamar was constantly accompanied by his older brother Herbert or his close friend Buddy Rupe, to ward off homesickness.

This time would be different. After they changed trains in St. Louis, Herbert and Lamar took a Pullman car to Philadelphia, then boarded the Reading Railroad out to Pottstown, Pennsylvania, about 35 miles to the northwest.

Lamar was going into a new and thoroughly different environment, one about which he was pensive and anxious. But as he would throughout the rest of his life, he would find his solace, sense of confidence, and friendships in the world of sports.

CHAPTER THREE

"HERBIE"

At The Hill School, where families of wealth had been sending their bright, earnest young boys to boarding school for nearly a hundred years, the lush campus on the hill above Pottstown, Pennsylvania, made for an august approximation of English boarding schools of another century.

Each morning, the boys gathered for chapel. While some of the Hill experience could be called carefree, chapel was decidedly not. Sitting in alphabetical order on the phalanxes of dark mahogany pews, with light shining through the tall stained glass casting a muted glow beneath the vaulted ceilings, the gangly schoolboys, in tight ties and blue blazers, looked up at an almost gothic scene of written exhortations in Old English typeface painted around the church: The mood was as arch as the language ("Watch ye," "Quit yourselves like men").

The students were restless some mornings, not quite daring to look bored, trying not to fidget through the procession of prayers and scripture and hymns. Yet even here, in this stentorian setting, Lamar soon figured out a way to play a game.

The challenge was specific and isolated. On the wall in the front of the cathedral was the day's list of hymns, and when the boys stood up to sing the first hymn of the day, Lamar and Graham Humes, sitting next to him, would have a contest, in which each cracked opened his hymnal at once and then checked to see who had opened his book to a page number closest to the hymn to be sung.

The winner usually sang with a touch more conviction. The loser bought a milkshake that afternoon at Doc's diner, just across High Street, and the only spot off the Hill campus where the boys could go without being considered to be "off campus." This was the insular world where Lamar lived for five school years, and where he would thrive.

The Hill, fittingly, stood at the top of a sharply sloping hill right on High Street, the main thoroughfare through Pottstown. The school prepared youth for the real world by, to a great extent, shutting them off from it, and inculcating them in the eternal verities and the exacting requirement of both academic and personal standards. Rigorous cleaning inspections. Strict adherence to courtesy titles and deference. A well-rounded education stressing the humanities. Even an English nomenclature: There weren't freshmen through senior classes at The Hill; there was the Third Form through the Sixth Form.

Under the stern, enterprising leadership of headmaster James I. Wendell, The Hill had grown in stature and fact since the late '20s, commencing with a major building effort at the height of the Depression. Wendell signed his memos "Jas. I," and thus earned the nickname "Jazzeye" from some of his students, though nothing about his manner particularly evoked that American art form.

The Hunt family had already made an impression on Mr. Wendell before Lamar's arrival. Bunker had been the first to attend, on the recommendation of some of Margaret's friends in Dallas, and had found the strait-laced ritual at The Hill less oppressive and marginally more pleasant than his time at Culver Military Academy. Headstrong and confident, he'd bent the rules to suit his personality; he quickly started making book for football games and also ran a craps game out of his dorm room.

But what got him into trouble with the staff was when he left campus to drive with some classmates to Philadelphia for the Cornell–Penn game in 1942 (they had permission to leave; he didn't). When Bunker didn't show up to work off his demerits that day, Wendell discovered the deceit and summarily expelled him. Though Bunker's classmates, in a sign of protest, refused to sing at chapel the next morning, Wendell would not be swayed. When H. L. received the news by telephone, he was typically pragmatic. "Fine. I understand," he told the Hill headmaster. "Just find another school for him up there and let him transfer. No point in him coming home and missing schoolwork." As it transpired, Bunker attended another prep school in New Jersey for several weeks, then was permitted to return to The Hill after Christmas break. Herbert traveled a smoother path, playing sports and largely staying out of trouble.

It was a time and place in American life that was rife with nicknames. Some were furtive, a few were profane, but almost everyone had at least one. When Herbert began attending The Hill, the year after Bunker left, virtually all of the upperclassmen started calling him "Bunker" or "Bunk."

So traveling to The Hill in '46, Lamar wouldn't have known that his nick-name was more or less inevitable. "We'd heard that there were a group of Texans coming," remembered Tom Richey, an eager, gifted youth of Lamar's age who had come down from Riverside, Connecticut, a year earlier, and earned a spot on the baseball varsity team, where Herbert was a teammate. On the quadrangle, at a new-student mixer in September, Lamar hit it off with Richey, who was first to bestow on him the nickname of "Herb." It was only a few days into the new term before most of his other classmates were calling Lamar "Herb" and, not long after, "Herbie."

Whatever the Hill School boys had heard about Texans, they hadn't ex-pected one quite so reticent as Lamar Hunt. Head ducked, smiling nervously, he made it through the opening weekend of social mixers, then quickly and naturally gravitated to the other athletes, playing on the "Far Fields" teams in his first year—junior varsity football in the fall, midget basketball over the winter, then junior baseball in the spring.

The self-consciousness that Lamar had occasionally felt earlier in his schooling vanished here. There was no awkwardness about Armstead drop-ping him off to school, no notice initially of his father's standing or his magnificent home. Virtually all the Hill boys hailed from wealth. All were dressed the same, in a blazer and tie each and every day of the week, and on Sunday morning for chapel. Very quickly, Lamar Hunt found his way and blended in.

Alarms went off at 5:30 a.m. in the middle school dorm. It was up and to the showers, and then report to the high-ceilinged dining hall, which could feed 400 at a time, the boys grouped by their age, always sitting only with boys of the same form (the sole exception being the "training table," to the side of the hall, for the athletes in season).

After a brief break, when some students worked off demerits by raking leaves or pushing brooms, classes would begin by 8:30 a.m. Lamar quickly proved to be strong with numbers and facts, but less assured in other class-es, with Spanish proving a particular challenge.

Popular with his classmates for his spirited play on the field and his unaffected, somewhat bashful friendliness off it, he soon gravitated to Richey, who shared his nearly insatiable love for sports. A fondness for sports was a given at The Hill, but even in this athletic-minded group, Lamar stood out. He bought the newspaper each Sunday, to keep track of college games. And in class, and sometimes in his dorm, he would draw elaborate stadium scenes, including a full-page rendering of the minor-league baseball stadium Rebels Field, home of the Double-A Dallas Rebels.

He returned from his first semester at The Hill full of talk about the sports teams, the guys in the dorm, and the rigor of the daily life. That Christmas Day, 1946, Lamar and Buddy Rupe went along with Bunker and Herbert to the first annual Yam Bowl game, played at Dal-Hi Stadium, between the historically black colleges Southern University and Tuskegee Institute. Bunker, back from the war, had developed a sense of belonging anywhere, but the quieter Lamar registered the irony: He and a small portion of the whites sitting in a segregated area, while the majority of the black crowd enjoyed the game. Lamar and Buddy were enchanted by the stylistic flourishes of Southern University's players. The Jaguars broke the huddle and fairly danced to the line of scrimmage, bodies swaying, hands above their heads, splayed toward the opposing goalposts.

A week later, Lamar joined his family for the annual trip to Fair Park and the Cotton Bowl. Then it was back to The Hill for the spring semester. Though Herbert had promised his parents that he'd keep an eye on his little brother at The Hill, he soon found he didn't have to. Rushing to classes, extending himself during afternoon practices on the far fields, Lamar quickly came into his own. "We'd hardly see each other that year," said Herbert.

•

By the fall of 1947, Herbert had matriculated to Washington & Lee (with the implicit assumption being that Lamar would follow). That fall, Lamar made the junior varsity team but broke his leg early in the season, and was confined to a wheelchair for much of the fall term. His roommate, a golfer named Johnny Fisher, from Dayton, Ohio, spent part of the semester wheeling him around campus and helping him up and down stairs. But Lamar's life would be altered not by what happened in Pottstown but what was going on back in Texas.

The SMU Mustangs were coming off a subpar 4-5-1 season in 1946 and were predicted to finish in the middle of the pack in 1947. They opened with an early-season road win over Santa Clara, in a game marked by the exploits of a 5-foot-10, 173-pound sophomore from Dallas named Doak Walker.

Ewell Doak Walker, Jr., was just about everything that a young, sports-loving, God-fearing, football-silly Texas boy could ever hope to grow up to be. Over the coming years, Lamar would study his manner and his expressions, the way he walked, and the way he ran on the field. He stared at the pictures of Doak with his fiancée, Norma Peterson, the Cotton Bowl beauty queen. He committed to memory Doak's manner and the way he wore his hip pads. Remembering it later, Lamar was very matter-of-fact: "He was my idol."

Lamar had seen Walker—and then-teammate Bobby Layne—playing high school football for the Highland Park Scots, and he'd attended the last three games of SMU's 1945 season, when the Mustangs had shut out Arkansas, Baylor, and TCU, earning the freshman Walker All-SWC honors. But Doak had been away for military service in 1946, and he was returning to what was considered to be a diminished team in '47. Just days before taking the train to Pottstown, Lamar listened from Mount Vernon as Walker broke touchdown runs of 97 and 44 yards against Santa Clara. After three bye weeks, the Mustangs returned to action with a taut 35–19 win over Missouri on October 4, in a game that featured two more mazy Walker touchdown runs—for 76 and 57 yards.

That fall, the sense of being physically inert weighed on Lamar, but he compensated. In their dorm room, he and Fisher used to set a fedora upside down in the corner and have a contest to see who could flip the most cards into it from a seated position across the room. Unable to actively play for the first time in his memory, he began devoting even more energy to following SMU and the "Mustang Miracle Man." Lamar had known heroes before he got to The Hill: He'd grown up a Yankees fan and could recall hearing Lou Gehrig's "Luckiest Man Alive" speech from Yankee Stadium on the radio on July 4, 1939; a year later, he'd become enamored of A&M's Kimbrough. But in the fall of 1947, he was transformed.

SMU had started generating national headlines when they knocked off No. 15 Rice on October 18. A week later, they traveled to UCLA and edged the 16th-ranked Bruins, 7–0, with Walker scoring the game's lone touchdown. That led to a showdown in Dallas, between the ascendant Mustangs, who had moved from outside the Associated Press Top 20 to No. 8 in the nation in the space of three weeks, and unbeaten Texas, which had been sitting at No. 3 all season long. Interest in the game was so intense that SMU had to move it off the campus, from Ownby Stadium to the Cotton Bowl.

From his dorm room in Pottstown, Lamar was able to listen to the national radio broadcast, and heard those old Highland Park high school classmates, Walker and Bobby Layne, battling it out for the Southwest Conference crown. Late in the Texas–SMU game, Walker made a breathtaking catch on the sideline from a Gil Johnson pass, then ran to the one-yard line to set up the go-ahead score. SMU prevailed, 14–13. Lyda sent Lamar clippings each week from the Dallas papers, and he would scour the Sunday editions of the Philadelphia Inquirer for more news of Doak's heroics.

The next two years would find Lamar absorbed in the mythology of Walker. He and Richey would spend long hours at The Hill's library, looking through issues of *Life* and *Look* and *Collier's*, along with the big-city newspapers of the day, for pictures of Walker's exploits. Richey was an Army fan, still smitten with Glenn Davis and Doc Blanchard, while Lamar longed for the Texas greats. "We'd call to each other when we found a picture," Richey said. "Lamar especially loved the color pictures. I can remember that we'd be looking at one, and I might suggest, 'Come on, let's just tear it out—nobody will know.' But he would always just smile and say, 'Naw, we can't do that.'" But with the clippings his mother sent from home, along with the magazines he bought during his trips into town, Lamar constructed a scrapbook of Doak's exploits.

It was almost baseball season when the April 5, 1948, issue of *Life* hit mailboxes and newsstands. The cover featured a gatefold photograph of 150 Dodger rookies, at the team's camp in Vero Beach, Florida. But it was a different story, inside, that would be the talk of the dorms at The Hill.

There, on most of a full page, was a grainy black-and-white photograph of H. L. Hunt, walking to his office on Elm Street one weekday morning, along with the headline that read, "Is This The Richest Man in the U.S.?"

As this conjecture was a surprise to the rest of the family, it was a jolt to Lamar as well. "That was the first time I had ever had any inkling or thought," he said, "although I knew we lived in a nice house, and it just wasn't all that important. It wasn't that big of a deal."

Even amid the routine wealth at The Hill, the news was a big deal. Lamar's roommate, Johnny Fisher, was the first one to ask the question: "Is this your father?" Lamar granted that it was, and suddenly found himself cast back to the days at Lipscomb and J. L. Long when his family's wealth made him the focus of attention.

"He made it a non-event," remembered Tom Richey. "We asked him about it and it was clear he didn't want to talk about it."

What Lamar would perfect around this time was a figure of speech that he would use throughout his life. When asked if that was his father under the headline, he would reply with the single-word affirmation "Yeah," but with the word clipped off at the end, and rounded in the middle so as to hint at two syllables. The word, uttered by Lamar, sounded more like "yowt," and it had an air of dismissive finality to it, connoting that he wished for the subject under conversation not to continue.

"Hey, Lamar, was that your dad in *Life*?"

"Yowt," he said, nodding his head curtly. And that was that.

In the fall of 1948, Lamar returned to Pottstown and won a spot on the varsity team. That season, he began wearing Doak Walker's number, 37. The Hill School football team of '48 was a young one, with only five lettermen returning, and the team fell short in several close games, before building confidence ahead of its traditional season-ending game against arch-rival Lawrenceville, the prep school from nearby New Jersey. The oldest interstate rivalry in prep football, the game had been played since 1887. Very early on, the sporting enmity between the two schools was consecrated by "the Dirty Red Shirt," worn each year by the Lawrenceville captain the week before the Hill game. The tradition evolved into a bet, in which a Lawrenceville victory over Hill meant a celebration of the supposed power of the unwashed shirt, while a Hill win over Lawrenceville meant the Larries had to wash the shirt. In '48, the Hill upset previously unbeaten Lawrenceville on Dell Field, holding onto a 13–7 lead throughout the second half, before marching off the field toward the Hill grandstands, where students were waving a large bedsheet reading "WASH THAT SHIRT!" Lamar, celebrating with his teammates that night, was already talking about the next season, and how good The Hill could be if the upperclassmen dedicated themselves to the task ahead.

All of the players on that Hill School team were encouraged by the big win to end the season. But with Lamar there was something else pushing him forward. It was Doak. Early in that '48 season Lamar and Richey came to the library and found what Lamar had been hoping for. There, on the cover of the September 27, 1948, issue of *Life* magazine, was his hero. The terse cover line read, simply, "Doak Walker of Southern Methodist," but the image was an undeniable triumph of iconography. The pensive star had posed in full uniform, left arm in front of him, as if to ward off a defender, and right arm cocked, holding the ball back by his helmet, poised to pass. Walker looked serene, surveying an imaginary field of defenders to pick out the right man.

Lamar took to heart his idol's humble airs, easy rapport with fans, and earnest patience with questioners. When the news came, that December, that Walker had become the first junior to win the Heisman Trophy, some of Lamar's classmates congratulated him. He was home for Christmas (and another Yam Bowl) and got to spend his New Year's Day again watching his hero in action against Oregon, as Walker—celebrating his twenty-second birthday—led SMU to a 21–13 win in the 13th Annual Cotton Bowl (and, as Lamar was proud to report, his eleventh straight).

In the spring of 1949, as the school year wound down, the boys would take more breaks at Doc's. Lamar's standard order was a malted—as he continued trying to put on weight—while he and his teammates discussed the season ahead. On campus, after baseball practice, they would often linger and talk with Epps Maugher, proprietor at the athletic store in the gymnasium. Maugher kept close tabs on the boys' athletic exploits. In the small talk in the late afternoon, as the boys would discuss an upcoming dance, Maugher would counsel, "If you're serious about athletics, there's not enough time for that kind of business."

In chapel, he and Graham Humes continued to vie to see who could come closest to the page number of the evening hymn. Humes brought two quarters for the collection plate each Sunday, and Lamar would routinely ask him to borrow a quarter, so he'd have something to put in the plate as well. And when the chaplain would close with the prayer, "God bless the old boys of The Hill wherever they may be this night," Lamar latched on to the phrase.

"Someday," he told his classmates, "we'll be 'an old boy from The Hill.'"

•

In the summer of 1949, Lamar made his way out to his father's new property, the Palette Ranch, a picturesque getaway in Wyoming, hard by the Shoshone National Forest. His sister Caroline invited him to join her and some of her friends. One night, Lamar showed them his favorite dorm room pastime. He put a cowboy hat in the middle of the living room floor and invited all the guests to take turns trying to pitch playing cards into the hat.

He spent plenty of time riding horses and fishing, but even at the ranch, Lamar was preparing for football, consumed with getting into top physical condition. He'd run laps around the house and practice his punting on the sloping yard outside the main cabin. That summer he corresponded with Tom Richey, back home in Connecticut, and made plans to head out to the East Coast nearly a month early; they'd spend two weeks training at Richey's parents' Riverside, Connecticut, home, then drive to Pokety Farms, Maryland, and spend another ten days on the estate owned by the family of teammate Ed Garbisch.

When Lamar arrived in Connecticut that July, Richey recalled his friend's single-minded demeanor:

> Lamar was the author and task master. If you let up one bit, he was the judge ... jury ... and executioner.
>
> It consisted of a wake up call at 6 a.m. . . . . a light breakfast ... A heavy workout with a weight set and chin up bar in my back yard ... off to the Riverside school grounds for wind sprints, passing drills, punting and kicking, and open field tackling drills. To finish off the program, an hour's pitching and hitting in an improvised baseball batting cage I had constructed on the school grounds ...
>
> Lunch was a light affair of turkey or chicken with no bread, of course, all the while talking football. The afternoon session started promptly at 3 p.m. and lasted for two hours. It was a repeat of the morning session with more heavy weight lifting and a two-mile run.

Sitting in the Richeys' Riverside home one night, Lamar was unusually adamant. "There is nothing more important in our lives right now," he said. "All that matters is that we have the best football team we can possibly have. Mark my words, if we believe, it will happen."

Another conversation that the pair had that week always remained with Richey. Talking one night before going to sleep, the boys discussed their future. At one point, Richey recalled his friend saying, in an unusually resigned tone, "You see, Tom, no matter what I do, I'll always be H. L. Hunt's son." He recognized then that he wanted to make a name for himself, but he had no idea how to go about doing so.

On Thursday, July 21, the boys went into New York City to watch the Giants finish a homestand against the Reds at the Polo Grounds. They were among the sparse crowd of 4,155 in attendance that afternoon. Richey had been scheming for weeks to snatch a hat from a major-league ballplayer, one of the badges of honor among teenage boys at The Hill. According to Richey's plan, he and Lamar would both race out onto the field after the game and each grab a player's cap, then sprint for the opening in centerfield that allowed fans to exit onto the street. As the Giants' 9–5 win over the Reds was winding down that day, Richey and Lamar moved down to the front rows in front of third base and first base, respectively. After the final out, Tom ran out to centerfield and swiped his hero Bobby Thomson's cap. Thomson himself chased Richey out of the centerfield exit and caught up after three police officers wrestled Richey to the ground, snatching the cap back. When Richey rendezvoused with Lamar later—they had arranged to meet at a nearby sub-way stop—Lamar was abashed and apologetic. "I just couldn't do it," he said. It was not the only time that Richey would serve as the instigator of hijinks from which Lamar would beg off.

"He was not really a rule-breaker," said Richey. "In my defense, a lot of kids were doing that at the time. Even the cops, after they got Thomson's cap back, said, 'Nice try, kid.' But Lamar rejected that as not the right thing to do."

The next week, near the end of their time in Riverside, the boys drove up to Storrs, Connecticut, to spend a day watching the New York Football Giants training camp. Late that afternoon, as they were returning to the Richey's home, a light drizzle started. On a winding road on the way back to River-side, a truck directly in front of them stopped suddenly. Richey, driving his mother's cream-colored Oldsmobile convertible, slammed on his brakes but wound up rear-ending the truck.

The scene that followed might have been much worse: Richey emerged from his car furious, and was confronted with a formidable Italian-American truck driver who was just as upset. As their language intensified, Tom grow-ing more shrill, Lamar came out of the passenger side and stepped between the truck driver and Richey.

Looking at his friend, Lamar said, "This is not the right thing to do, Tom. Let's do what we need to do and then get on down the road." With Lamar act-ing as diplomat, the two drivers exchanged contact and insurance informa-tion, and soon went on their way, with the self-described "hot-head" Richey having been placated. "Lamar was the great mediator," he said.

At the end of July, they drove to the Cambridge, Maryland, home of Richey's roommate, Ed Garbisch, Jr. His father had been an All-American at Army who'd kicked four field goals to beat Navy in his final game in 1924. Ed Garbisch was more than happy to run his son and his friends through the paces of two-a-day workouts, beginning with a 5:30 wake-up call, fol-lowed by a two-mile run by the banks of the Choptank River before break-fast. Through this week, Lamar kept a faithful record of all of his placekicking performances, his accuracy from various distances, and how he performed wearing high-top or low-cut shoes. In the evenings, the boys would bowl at the estate's bowling alley, then sit around the fireplace in the Garbisch living room and hear tales of the Army teams of the '20s.

With all the traveling, it was later than usual in the summer before Lamar spied the new issue of *Street & Smith's Football Yearbook*. He turned to the

Southwest Preview and read intently: "Parade that Red & Blue band up and down the field, Mr. Drum Major, and tell the trumpeter to blow his hat off, for here they come again—Doak Walker and Gil Johnson! Theirs has been a two-ring circus of pigskin razzle-dazzle which has never been equaled in the Southwest, where there is no razzle more dazzling."

The distinctive prose of that era's sportswriting insinuated itself into Lamar and Tom's banter. They would archly intone their favorite phrases from the annual previews—"built like a spark plug and dripping with power" or "It's the arms that hit you, sir"—as they went about their day, on the field or off.

And when they arrived at The Hill, they were primed for the season ahead. Under the tough but largely calm coaching of Wilbur "Jack" Riley, the Blue-and-Gray installed a new offense that season, with the single-wing of past years morphing into the "Michigan Spin," in which the team would line up in the single wing, with Lamar as a blocking back, then often shift into a T formation, where he was the quarterback.

The team voted Jim Yonge, the left end from Florida, as its captain during training camp. He was a large, shambling, well-liked presence, often joining (in fact, often leading) a group of players who would duck out of campus after chapel and grab a beer or two at a local Pottstown bar. "Lamar was not prone to breaking the rules," Yonge remembered. "I was prone to breaking the rules. There was a group that thought I was doing a bad job as a captain, and they would give several lectures about me being a bad influence. But Lamar was never in that group. That wasn't his style. He was a quiet, quiet guy. He exuded confidence. You knew you could depend on him."

Lamar was by now quite comfortable at The Hill. He roomed with Phil Woods, a champion diver from Tampa (who had roomed with Lamar's friend and fellow Texan John Torbett the year before). Their third roommate was Dick "Digger" Davis, a brash and sometimes grating Texan whose calling card was the catchphrase "Fab-o-lous." Lamar and the likable Woods hit it off, at times growing exasperated enough with Davis to set "bear traps"—a small bucket of water nestled just above a slightly open dorm door—that would splash on the unsuspecting Davis when he walked into the room.

The 1949 football season would serve as a touchstone for Lamar and his teammates for the rest of their lives. Lamar was reliable and sure-handed as the T quarterback, and played a solid defensive back. His friend Richey, one of the halfbacks, was intense and difficult to tackle. The Louisiana fullback, Stan Dossett, was deceptively fleet, and made some of the season's biggest plays.

The Hill opened the '49 season with a 32–0 trouncing of Williamson Trade School, with Lamar intercepting a pass and scoring two touchdowns. After a win over the Franklin & Marshall freshman team, The Hill earned a key road win over Mercersburg Academy, breaking Mercersburg's eleven-game win streak. By now, the team's exploits were earning extra space in the pages of the *Pottstown Mercury*, where sportswriter Joe Much was chronicling the local heroes.

Lamar, wearing a modified facemask to protect a broken nose sustained in training camp, helped the team to wins over Woodberry Forest and Peddie School. As the win streak grew, the campus was transformed on a weekly basis. Bunker Hunt, encouraging his young brother's exploits, had taken to sending a large shipment of steaks from Texas, so the football team could have a special training-table meal on the eve of every game. (Bunker also financed the filming of games, providing the coaching staff another teaching tool during the season.)

On the mornings of games, the upper-school dorm would ring out with the college fight songs, Tom Richey's playing 78s of college anthems and team marches on his turntable, the sounds blaring from the window of the dorm he shared with Garbisch, out into the quadrangle, where it could be heard by all.

In the whirl of excitement over the season, Lamar's studies actually improved. Some mornings before school, or in the evenings, after practice, dinner, and homework, he found himself drawn to the team's gridiron, Dell Field, which was within 100 paces of the upper school dorm. Looking around at the stadium—its humble, hand-operated scoreboard and the wooden bleachers—he found a kind of grandeur and respite, and even more motivation to complete the team's quest.

In early November, the week before the final game of the season with arch-rival Lawrenceville, students erected large banners reading "Wash That Shirt!" Buses of parents and schoolmates followed the team bus for the trip over to New Jersey. As the Hill squad sat in the visitors' dressing room at Lawrenceville, Riley walked through the room, his cleats clicking on the cement floor, and made a rare inspirational speech. "Gentlemen, you're going to play a football game today," he said gravely, "that you will remember for the rest of your life."

In this, he proved prophetic. Lamar barged out of the locker room, Richey remembered, "like he was going to kill somebody." Both sides were motivated for the traditional rivalry, but the months of preparation and dedication by the Hill squad proved decisive. Lamar intercepted a pass and scored a touchdown, as Hill won going away, 40–7. With the large contingent of parents, faculty, and classmates in the stands, the postgame celebration was effusive.

Even as the game was ending, many players went their separate ways. Richey, planning to attend Yale the following year, went with his parents to Princeton, where the Tigers would host the Eli the next day. Lamar and Ed Garbisch, Jr., traveled with Ed's father to see Army square off against Pennsylvania, earning a steak dinner in Philadelphia, and then choice seats to watch the Cadets nip Penn, 14–13, the next day. That day's copy of the *New York Times* featured a write-up on the game (including a picture of Lamar and an erroneous reference in the game story identifying him as "a New York City product").

When they all returned Saturday night, there was as delirious a celebration on the quadrangle as a strait-laced Pennsylvania boarding school would allow. The team gathered for the first "victory bonfire" since The Hill's undefeated team in 1922; Lamar's friend Torbett played the school fight song on his trumpet. The boys sang into the night, and later the players and their friends snake-walked around the quadrangle and, in the midst of the revelry, Torbett led the school band in a rendition of "The Eyes of Texas" that everyone understood was for Lamar.

By the end of the '49 regular season, Lamar and Ed Garbisch both had decided to stay over for an extra year at The Hill. The school offered the option of extending the studies, usually for students who needed more seasoning, but also for young men who wanted to spend another year in the idyllic setting, delaying the transition to college life for one more year. Though Lamar and Garbisch urged Richey to join them, he'd already been accepted at Yale and was reluctantly on his way.

Though he knew he was going to spend another year at The Hill, Lamar was firming up his college plans in the spring of 1950. With Herbert successfully working his way through Washington & Lee, less than an hour from where Margaret had studied at Mary Baldwin College, it was understood that Lamar would go there as well. But each night, Lamar would look at the wall above his small dorm-room desk, where the *Life* cover of Walker was displayed.

Late that school year, he called Margaret at the Garden of the Gods club in Colorado Springs.

"I really don't want to go to W&L," he told his sister. "I want to come home. Would you talk to mother and see if I can't come back and go to SMU?"

"Why don't you just speak to her yourself?" asked Margaret.

"Well, I feel like I need representation, some influence in high places."

Margaret agreed to argue the case to their mother. When presented with the message, Lyda said, "It will be lively to have those college boys around" again, and Margaret called back to share the good news.

His last year at The Hill felt more like a coda than a culmination. He was captain of the football team, vice-president of the Sixth Form, president of the Hill Christian Association, and president of the Athletic Association committee.

Richey and Yonge were gone, but Lamar roomed with his training camp partner Ed Garbisch and, again, Phil Woods. For all his football pedigree, Garbisch was becoming a talented golfer, who routinely would practice hitting eight-iron shots out of the dorm room window, across the quadrangle, and, with alarming frequency, into the headmaster's yard.

Lamar, Ed, and Phil shared a mutual love for games, so there were almost constant contests in their dorm, Room 30 on the third floor of the upper school residence. When they weren't tending to divot marks on the carpet, or the pockmarks on the wall from Garbisch's errant golf shots, they would clear out the floor and develop their own miniature golf course, placing books under the pulled-up carpet in strategic locations for breaks in the green, using glasses on their sides to serve as the cups.

It was Lamar's idea to run a heavy cord across the top of the room, just a few feet from the wall, then hang a bedspread over that, for modified skeet-shooting exercises. With one classmate holding the cord taut, another would sit nearby and occasionally toss paper plates up against bedspread while the third roommate, aiming carefully from the other end of the long room, would shoot the portable skeet with a BB gun. "I don't know how in the hell we ever graduated from that place," said Woods.

Dorm life was charmed in the fall of 1950, but it was a difficult season on the football field. Injuries plagued the team, as it fell to a 2–5 record, its final loss to Lawrenceville exacerbated by a small plane that flew overhead and dropped fliers declaring "We Won't Wash That Shirt" on bleachers and Dell Field.

In the spring came baseball and more hijinks, and what by then felt to Lamar like a victory lap. At the Hill spring dance program, Lamar played against the Haverford School in the afternoon, showered, and arrived for dinner at 6:15, watched "The Silver Whistle," presented by the Hill School Dramatic Club, then spent three hours dancing in the Common Room. He was comfortable with his friends but still somewhat sheepish around girls. "I never liked dancing," he would say later. "I wasn't good at it and I didn't enjoy it."

As with any group of teenage boys, there was plenty of discussion about girls and sex and the future, though most of it was from a gently sheltered remove. The "Purity Test" was popular among teens in this era of postwar America, featuring a questionnaire that docked points for kissing and petting, from a Fifty (pure) to several levels below (corrupt). One classmate of Lamar's signed his yearbook, "Good luck next year at college, and keep your P.T. score at 50. That way you always have something to look forward to."

But that was never the focus at The Hill, nor was the idea of a career. Many students had already begun considering their paths, but Lamar was more sanguine. "The only thing I was worried about," he said, "was coming to SMU and being the next Doak Walker."

Yet he stood out among his classmates for his decency, kindness, and resolve. Lamar was voted the Student Most Likely to Succeed. His classmate Tommy Taylor wrote, "Herb, I thought for a while we might be seeing each other at W&L, but I'm sure SMU is the place for you after all. . . . I'm sure Walker's and Rote's shoes can be filled with your spirit and determination." Other students wrote that they expected to see Lamar on the All-American lists.

On June 3, 1951, two months short of his nineteenth birthday, Lamar graduated with the Centennial Class of The Hill School. There were Cold War tensions reflected in the valedictorian's speech. That morning, he received a telegram from the Rupes: "Congratulations we are proud and happy that you have so successfully reached this important mile post in your life our prayers and best wishes are with you now and will attend you throughout the difficult years which seem to lie ahead for all of us Mr. and Mrs. D. Gordon Rupe Jr and Buddy."

And so Lamar headed back to Texas. During his five years in Pennsylvania, he'd gained a sense of his own potential, as well as a significant measure of self-confidence. Less painfully shy than he was when he left home at fourteen, he'd grown into a strapping young man, even with the eyeglasses he began wearing in his final year. Nineteen years old, wealthy, confident, and exquisitely well-mannered, he was beginning to realize that his dreams were more bound up in the world of football and sports than with oil and business. And now, as he enrolled at SMU, he prepared to play the same position as his idol, on a team playing all of its home games at the stadium that had been synonymous for him, since the age of six, with the glory and grandeur of sports. The world was opening up, and Lamar Hunt was following that dream, running to daylight.

CHAPTER FOUR

"POOR BOY"

In June 1951, Lamar returned to live at a far different Mount Vernon than the one he'd left in 1946. Hassie, after his lobotomy, required constant attention, and his diminished state was a source of pain for H. L. that the old man couldn't begin to articulate. The very month of Lamar's return, both Herbert and Bunker were married. Once the weddings were done, Lyda grew even more absorbed with her church and gardening activities, staying closer to home, traveling less frequently to shop for her beloved antiques.

Then there was his father's heightened profile. When Lamar was at Mount Vernon in the early '40s, H. L. was a private figure of some stature, but by Lamar's return in 1951, his father had become a decidedly public figure with both the intent and, by his reckoning, the means to influence the course of U.S. politics. Disappointed in Truman and galvanized by the Cold War, H. L. spent much of 1951 angling for General Douglas MacArthur to seek the Republican presidential nomination.

H. L. had long professed to see things that others could not. In the '50s, what he saw—and perceived much of the rest of the country was blind to— was the threat of communism in America. It was this threat, rather than the prospect of nuclear war, that was his primary concern, and would remain so for the rest of his life. Hair cottony white, long fingernails tapping on a tabletop when wanting to emphasize a point, he became a man motivated by what scared him most. With his wealth secure, he devoted more time and energy to sharing his views, launching the educational foundation Facts Forum, which became a hub for anticommunist literature and broadcasting. So there was more than just business for H. L. to contend with in the new decade: more weighty pronouncements, more letters to the editor, and often now he would dictate them at home, frequently asking his secretary, a compact, energetic woman named Ruth Ray Wright, to come to Mount Vernon to help with his correspondence.

On Sunday, August 5, 1951, Lamar was returning from El Paso, where he'd attended the wedding of his brother Herbert and Nancy Broaddus. His fellow Hill School alum Dick "Digger" Davis had been calling Lamar regularly since they returned from school, and on this day insisted on picking Lamar up at the airport. Davis was interested in a Hockaday student named Sharon Ramsey, and wanted Lamar to meet Sharon's friend, a comely high school junior named Rose Mary Whittle.

"This guy Dick said, 'You've gotta meet this friend of mine—he's funny and he's great,'" Rose Mary recalled later. "So we go to the airport and meet Lamar, and he had on glasses, and I really didn't think much of it. I just met him; I had another boyfriend at the time."

Rose Mary was young and luminously beautiful, possessed of a small, inquisitive face, delicate features, and graceful arms gently tapering to slender wrists. Lamar wasn't merely smitten, he was stricken. Growing in confidence after his limited early dating experiences, he invited Rose Mary and her friend to come to Mount Vernon to go swimming the following week.

When they visited Mount Vernon, Lamar was comfortable in his domain and unusually bold. Standing in the pool at one point, he reached out from the water to grab Rose Mary's ankle as she was walking poolside, then playfully refused to let her go.

"What are you doing?" she asked.

"I won't let go," he said, squinting up at her, "until you agree to go out with me."

She consented, and their first date was Lamar's favorite place in town, Fair Park, for the annual summer operetta. The musical had moved indoors to the State Fair Theater in '51, and they saw *I Married an Angel*.

Lamar won her affection over the coming weeks because he was cheerful and made her laugh. The quality that his friend John Torbett had written about in Lamar's yearbook two years earlier—"I've never known a more modest guy for one with so many achievements"—was notably present beyond The Hill. Lamar's easy self-effacement was disarming; unfailingly courteous, able to poke fun at himself, he was a young man who embodied the distinctly middle-class notion of good, clean fun.

"After a few weeks of going out with him, I really started liking him," Rose Mary said. "And I was really surprised, but he was the funniest person in the world, and everyone said so." They'd go out with friends, to a soda shop or a movie or an ice-cream parlor, or simply spend hours necking in the pool at Mount Vernon.

Driving in the car one night with another couple in the backseat, they were rushing to reach an ice-cream stand before it closed when they pulled up to a red light. They sat there for an elongated moment, and then another, before Lamar deadpanned, "Feel free, light." It was a throwaway, but Lamar's friends in the backseat started laughing so hard that soon Lamar and Rose Mary were laughing as well. "He had a real sharp sense of humor," said Rose Mary, "but it was always nice, it was never mean or arrogant."

When Lamar met her, Rose Mary was sixteen years old and attending the Hockaday School, the same tony private Dallas girls school that Margaret and Caroline had attended. Rose Mary flourished in what she would later describe as her "very protected little bubble" of north Dallas life. "We did nothing," she would say of her teenage years, hanging out with her friends at the Dallas Country Club or Northwoods Country Club. "We were so good-for-nothing. But it felt like something at the time. Everything had to be right; we'd take forever to pick out the right bathing suit for the summer. We were all so vain and shallow."

Whittle Construction was a significant presence in 1950s Dallas. The Tennessee-born Ralph Whittle was a pioneer in both public construction (his company had dug the trenches that later became the North Central Expressway) and in private recovery, where he was a member of the city's first Alcoholics Anonymous chapter and, later, a benefactor of a halfway home for men in recovery.

From August 1951 onward, Rose Mary's life began revolving around Lamar. She would spend her weeks as a conscientious Hockaday schoolgirl, wearing the forest-green pleated skirt, bloomers-and-blouse "combination" beneath, with white socks and saddle oxfords. Then on weekends, she'd go out with Lamar. His courtship of Rose Mary was conducted at stadiums and gymnasiums, movie theaters and ice-cream shops and, more than anywhere else, at Fair Park. "He just loved it," Rose Mary said. "We would go out there twice a week in the summer. I was very scared. I had been raised in a situation where the Cotton Bowl was in a dangerous part of town, but he enjoyed it, didn't think anything of it. He was comfortable." At Fair Park, Lamar was drawn to the carnival games, where he'd endeavor to win Rose Mary a stuffed animal at the arcade. They would ride the rides, play the games, eat some ice cream, and take the long way back to her home. "We were sort of just us," she said. "We had our own little world, and we were so madly in love with each other."

•

On September 1, 1951, Lamar began training camp with a class of dozens of other freshmen trying out for the Southern Methodist football team—most were prized scholarship recruits, while he was among a handful of freshman who had chosen to walk on to try to earn a spot on the roster. Even in the midst of his early dating with Rose Mary, he'd maintained his intense training efforts, visiting Ed Garbisch at his parents' house in Maryland for two weeks of preseason training.

He was undaunted by the first day of camp, when freshman coach Herman Morgan passed around a sheet for the incoming players to sign their names and list their high school football honors. In the midst of the numerous "All-State" and "All-District" accolades of his classmates, Lamar wrote down that he was the captain of his Hill School team.

In the dressing room at Ownby Stadium, Lamar's locker was next to a glib California single-wing tailback named Phil Jones, who had been all-Orange County in 1950 and whose grandmother lived not far from the Hunt house on White Rock Lake.

Jones was an extrovert who developed an easy rapport with Lamar. After seeing Lamar changing from glasses to a pair of contact lens before one practice, Jones began calling him "Six Eyes," rather than "Four Eyes," and soon shortened that greeting to simply "Six." Lamar liked the way Jones could take as well as he gave, fielding the incessant teasing from SMU equipment manager Wayne Rudy and the starting freshman tailback, a heralded, granite-hard runner from Port Arthur named Frank Eidom. "There were mostly Texans," said Jones, who got more than his share of teasing as a Californian. "Eidom would always call me 'The Laguna Flash' and Wayne Rudy would ask me if I knew any 'queers.' But Lamar was much more sophisticated and discreet. He didn't go in for that kind of stuff."

On a Friday in mid-October, Lamar took the field with the rest of the SMU Colts freshman team, wearing jersey No. 35 and playing halfback, in front of an Ownby Stadium crowd estimated at 1,600. He caught a touchdown pass in the 26–6 win over the Rice Owlet freshman squad. After the game, he continued doing just what he'd done at the Hill—composing a scrapbook with every newspaper story on his team, culled from the pages of the school and area newspapers. At SMU, he added an array of black-and-white glossies, purchased from Laughead Photographers, the Dallas business that shot all of SMU's games, and many of the dances and graduation pictures as well. To the glossies, Lamar added his own captions. "Lamar Hunt snags a Malcolm Bowers pass and goes up the sideline for 17 yards," he wrote in his neat, precise hand, "before he is knocked out of bounds by Gordon Kellog (41), Rice Owlet defensive back."

Lamar and Phil Jones had three classes together that first year at SMU. One was Air Force ROTC, and another was Speech 1-A, where they practiced presenting and receiving awards, and giving brief introductory and acceptance speeches. A more difficult class, at the new Fondren Science Building, was Introduction to Zoology, with Professor E. D. Cheatum, who had developed a reputation for his laborious, detailed chalkboard diagrams, which invariably turned up on exams.

Lamar and Phil often took their homework to Phil's grandmother's house, as Lamar was partial to Mrs. Jones's easy hospitality and fried peach pies. After one session, Jones discovered that Lamar had left his zoology notebook behind. The oversight demanded a prank, so he carefully mimicked Lamar's handwriting (which he described as "a very fine teeny little style of micro-writing") on Lamar's transcription of one of Dr. Cheatum's diagrams, of the malaria-carrying mosquito that had caused an epidemic during the building of the Panama Canal. Drawing in Lamar's notebook, Jones drew a bump on the back end of the mosquito, then added an ersatz label by spelling his name backward, writing: "SENOJ GLAND (FUNCTION AS YET UNKNOWN)."

The next day, Jones returned the notebook to Lamar without comment, just a week or so before the test. A few days after the test, they went to the door of Dr. Cheatum's office to collect their papers and see their grades (Lamar got an A). They made their way over to the gymnasium to shoot some baskets, as Lamar carefully examined his graded paper, and began looking quizzically at one of his diagrams. Dr. Cheatum had circled Lamar's notation of the "Senoj Gland" and written in red ink, "What is this?!" Lamar stopped short of the gym and, looking perplexed, said, "Let me see your mosquito diagram." Jones bit his tongue and handed over his paper, to which Lamar said, "You left off the Senoj Gland!" At that point, Jones collapsed to the ground in gales of laughter and, only after composing himself, looked up at Lamar and mustered the line, "Spell 'Senoj' backwards."

As Lamar looked at his friend, a smile slowly creased his lips.

"Lamar could always laugh at himself," said one of his college teammates. "Not a lot of guys were able to do that. It made a difference."

The '51 season ended with the SMU frosh shutting out the TCU frosh to complete an undefeated season. Lamar took Rose Mary to the Mustang Club banquet at the Grand Ballroom of the Hotel Adolphus, honoring the team on Friday, December 7, the ten-year anniversary of the Pearl Harbor Invasion.

When not losing himself in the by-now familiar protective camaraderie of the team with the other freshmen on the football squad, or toiling through his early class load, Lamar spent much of the fall of 1951 at fraternity mixers and rush parties, trying to decide which fraternity he should pledge. Among the major Greek organizations at SMU, the SAEs were known as the party frat, and were never likely to be a good fit for Lamar's more reserved sensibilities. That left two major contenders: Phi Delta Gamma, the fraternity where Doak Walker and most of SMU's most prominent athletes pledged; and Kappa Sigma, a mainstream fraternity with fewer athletes.

While the Phi Delts were prestigious, they also, by the early '50s, had gained a reputation on campus for rigorous hazing rituals that were, to some minds, humiliating. Neither side of this equation held any fascination for Lamar. He understood and respected authority, but found the screaming of drill sergeants disquieting. The prospect of a twenty-two-year-old spending a semester paddling eighteen-year-olds seemed ludicrous to him (as it did to his teammate Don McIlhenny, who originally pledged Phi Delt before switching to Kappa Sigma).

The Kappa Sigmas were earnest, idealistic, and decidedly mainstream, and there was a collegial egalitarianism in the group that pleased Lamar; it was as close as anything to what he'd experienced at The Hill. They also had the advantage of fellow Dallasite and Hill alum John Torbett, who through his musicianship and the force of his personality had a spellbinding effect on many of his fellow students. "I chose Kappa Sig probably because of John Torbett," Lamar said. "I'd gone to school with him and he recruited me." It wasn't merely musicianship with Torbett—he also possessed a near-photographic memory, reminiscent of H. L., and an ineffable social magnetism; Lamar loved hanging around him.

"The Phi Delts nearly slit their throat when Lamar went Kappa Sig," said fraternity brother Roger Blackmar.

By the spring of 1952, Lamar was helping the cause, hosting Kappa Sigma rush parties at Mount Vernon, where H. L.'s cook Jeff would make chicken spaghetti for the guests, who had dubbed the swimming pool "The Huntry Club."

But when frat brothers would arrive at Mount Vernon, they needed to be ready to compete. "First we'd jump in the pool just to cool off," said Bob Chilton, who pledged Kappa Sigma the same year Lamar arrived. "But then Lamar would go to a locker, and pull out a stopwatch and a clipboard. He had established a set of printed records: Best time under water from side to side, best time on backstroke from the diving board to the ladder. And he'd have a list of personal records and pool records."

"Lamar was a great rusher," said Blackmar, "but he was low-key."

He was also consistently kind. At the Kappa Sigma House, the stone building on fraternity row, there was a cook and cleaner—'50s mores in Texas dictated that he was known as a "house boy"—named Frank Stanton. Cheerful but unpolished, Stanton's Southern drawl reduced "Kappa Sigma" to "Kappa-Zima," and when he went to the Texas State Fair in the fall of 1951, he bought a customized cap that read "Zima." Lamar loved it, but he took pains to not belittle Stanton over the error, telling him "Zima's actually a better name than Sigma."

Though Lamar was now back home, his daily experience was radically enlarged. Rather than walking from the dorm to his classes in the hermetically sealed world of The Hill, he was now living at Mount Vernon and driving to school each day. In place of the required blazer and tie, he sported a more casual look: jeans and khakis, collared sport shirts and team T-shirts. From the carefully regimented schedule at The Hill, Lamar came to an environment in which he was in charge of his own hours. And he went out of his way to play down his assets. The phrase of the era was "big-timing it." Lamar was allergic to it.

In fact, at times he seemed to take pains to go in the opposite direction. One day he stopped at the home of LeVon Massengale, who was dating Rose Mary's sister Joanne. They were going to double-date later that evening but had some time to kill. As LeVon was heading upstairs to change clothes, Lamar asked, "You got anything that needs done here?"

LeVon, a little puzzled, told him he could watch television.

"You got anything else?"

"Well, Lamar . . . the lawn needs mowing."

And so Lamar did it.

Those eccentricities would endear him to Massengale and Rose Mary and Joanne's brother, Dick Whittle. For his birthday one year, they got him a card that read, "For the man who has everything . . ." on the front, then opened to reveal a tiny piece of plastic, with a sign reading "navel comb." Lamar laughed heartily and vowed that he'd save it.

"Everything he did, he dressed down," said Phil Jones. "He was probably the worst-dressed guy on campus: Levis, no socks, leather moccasins, probably trying to overcompensate from looking like the rich boy. And I probably would have done the same thing. He looked more like he maybe belonged at a state school, not a private university."

His friend Bill Adams concurred: "Nearly every day a cashmere sweater over a T-shirt, blue jeans, and penny-loafers. He didn't even have a checking account until he was twenty-one."

Even then, Lamar found it a nuisance to manage and keep track of his money. He didn't want to have to *think* about how much to bring for a particular occasion. By his sophomore year, he had asked his frat brother Sam Hunt, no relation, to manage his spending money for him, keeping track not only of where he spent it and on what, but often actually physically holding Lamar's money for him.

"With Lamar his shyness made him sort of back away from the fact that he did come from tremendous wealth," said Buddy Rupe, who followed him to The Hill, SMU, and Kappa Sigma. "He had a tremendous amount of money in his trust, and he didn't want anyone to be aware of it, and he certainly didn't want to flaunt it in any way. In no way was he flamboyant."

Though busy with school and sports and the fraternity, he always found time to spend with Rose Mary. Phil Jones went on several double-dates with Lamar and Rose Mary, and found Lamar's girlfriend "beautiful and vivacious and kind of rapid-fire. Maybe a little high-strung, a little nervous."

Rose Mary as a teenager was a beauty with a trove of insecurities. She was taking voice lessons but too embarrassed about that to even tell Lamar; she was embarrassed by being a high school student accompanying Lamar to college functions, where she felt intimidated by the talk. She would come out to Mount Vernon for dinner, be quietly polite throughout the meal (though she did pass on the oyster stew, despite H. L.'s admonition that it would be marvelously healthy for her digestive tract), but felt self-conscious whenever she was around Lamar's parents.

When she was with Lamar and his friends, she found him endearingly odd in his habits, and she learned to accept his foibles.

"He didn't have any money to carry," remembered Rose Mary. "His parents, they gave him everything, but not cash, I guess. And he never asked, he was too embarrassed to ask, he said. He felt funny asking, because he was older and he should have a job, and he should be doing something to earn his own money. Going to the operetta, he'd have just enough gas to get us out there and back. And he never thought ahead, he just winged it. He even borrowed money from the house boy at his fraternity, 50 cents to get three or four gallons. He would even use a nickel sometimes. He was awful, but he was funny, the way he did it, because he always laughed at himself."

During this period, Lamar drove an old Pontiac with a broken-out headlight. After Lamar dropped Phil Jones off at his grandmother's house, she asked her grandson, "His daddy's real rich. But why does Lamar look so tacky?"

"Oh, Granny," Jones replied. "That's just Lamar."

•

In the summer of 1952, after Buddy Rupe graduated from The Hill, he and Lamar decided to take a driving trip, and were joined by Lamar's Hill School roommate Phil Woods. The trio drove from Dallas all the way out to San Francisco, then returned through Colorado Springs, taking a jaunt up to the Palette Ranch before returning to Dallas.

Woods flew in from Tampa and joined the Hunts for dinner one night. The phone rang during the meal and the butler Jeff answered the phone, but not before H. L. Hunt called out, "If that's the president again, tell him I'll call him back—I'm having dinner." Later that night, Lamar and Phil joined Rose Mary and a friend for *Kiss Me, Kate* at Fair Park.

The next night, as Lamar and Phil were getting ready to retire, Lyda summoned them into her room, where she was sitting at her dressing table.

"Now, Lamar, you're going to be gone five or six weeks," she said. "Do you have enough money?"

Lamar flushed, smiled faintly and said, "Oh, yeah, I'm sure I'll be fine."

She looked at him levelly. "How much money do you have?"

"I've got some cash and a $100 U.S. War Bond."

Lyda shook her head and exclaimed, "Lamar! You're going to need money for food, and gas, and staying in hotels."

"Oh, it'll be fine—we're going to stay in a lot of college towns, and we'll just sleep in the fraternity house."

She shook her head, and reached into her purse and gave him about $300. He assured her he would spend it carefully, but she already knew that. She whisked them away.

They set out from Dallas at midnight on July 18, driving Lamar's brand new Oldsmobile 88 (it was a company car, leased from Penrod Drilling), the "Rocket 88" of rhythm and blues lore, heading straight for Carlsbad Caverns, three teenage boys rapidly becoming men, still young and energetic and daring enough to start a 3,000-mile, three-week road trip with a 500-mile drive starting through the middle of the night.

"The first time we stopped for gas, we all got a Coca-Cola," said Phil Woods. "We took off from there, and we're *flying*. There's either no speed limit, or the speed limit's 80. Buddy Rupe finishes his Coca-Cola, and chucks it out the window. Well Hunt about had a conniption fit. And it wasn't because he was littering. It was because Lamar knew a place in Wyoming, where he could turn in the bottles and get a five-cent rebate. And so from then on, every time we'd stop in a gas station and get a Coke, we'd have to put 'em on the floor of the back seat. And after a while, the floor in the back seat was just covered with Coke bottles, every time you turned a corner you could hear them clinking and clanking."

They checked out the Carlsbad Caverns the next day, then moved on to El Paso, walking across the bridge into Juarez (where Lamar tossed some spare change at a group of begging Mexican children, pausing to record this in a small spiral notebook he kept in his back pocket, where he cataloged every single cent he spent on the trip). The next day, they went from Texas up into New Mexico, through the Petrified Forest National Park, and into the Grand Canyon. From there it was up to Bryce Canyon and Zion Canyon in Utah, and across the Painted Desert and into Las Vegas.

The Nevada trip included the predictable gambling stops. Lamar had been preparing for it, walking around with a small roulette wheel in his pocket for weeks, trying to devise a new mathematical system to beat the casino. Years later, he would grasp the ineluctable truth that every toss of the coin was a fifty-fifty proposition, regardless what had happened in previous flips, and that either red or black was less than a fifty-fifty proposition in roulette, with the green "0" and "00" spaces tilting the odds in favor of the house. But on this trip, he was convinced he'd found the key to fortunes. "I remember our system well," said Phil Woods. "If one color or the other came up two or three times in a row, we would bet the other color."

They got to Vegas, drove out to see Boulder Dam, then went to the Horse-shoe Club on the Strip. At a $5 table, Lamar and Phil were both employing the system, with Rupe looking on bemusedly. "We were ahead probably $150 or $200," said Woods. "We were sitting and hooping and hollering."

From behind them, a graying man in a nicely tailored suit approached and tapped one of the boys on the shoulder. When they tuned back to look at him, he said, "You guys are doing that wrong."

"What do you mean?"

"You can get a run of seven or eight or more all the same color in a row. You keep doing what you're doing, it's going to cost you." He then turned and walked away. The boys were slightly fazed, but shrugged it off.

"You know who that guy was?" asked the croupier. The boys shook their heads. "Nick the Greek."

Lamar and his friends were impressed; they knew the legend of Nick "The Greek" Dandolos. But they stuck with their system. And later in the night, they discovered that "The Greek" was right. Lamar bet on red ten consecutive times and watched the roulette wheel turn up black on just as many occasions. His winnings turned into $70 in losses.

After two days in southern California, and taking the boat out to Catalina Island off the coast of San Diego, they headed north, into Los Angeles and to the La Brea Tar Pits, then arrived in the Sequoia National Forest at 8 p.m. There was no vacancy in any of the lodges, so they had to sleep in the car.

Rupe had done most of the driving, so it was decided that he would sleep in the front seat. Jones and Lamar flipped a coin to see who would get the backseat and who would be left sleeping in the trunk. Lamar won the toss, but since he was by now short on money, he offered to sell Jones the rights to sleep in the backseat for $1. After Jones agreed, Lamar headed to the trunk. Temperatures dipped into the 40s overnight, and when Lamar emerged from the trunk the next morning, he had donned all of the dirty clothes that the boys had been throwing into the trunk during the previous week and now, as the sun was coming up over the Rockies, he came out in layers of soiled clothes, greeted with cascades of laughter from Rupe and Woods.

The rest of the trip was somewhat less eventful. They headed up to San Francisco, where they ate dinner at the famous Omar Khayyam's ("I had something I couldn't pronounce if I had to," wrote Woods in his trip journal. "It was very good"). From there, it was on to Reno for more gambling ("'The System' didn't work too well! In fact, we dropped $105.20"), then up to the Palette Ranch. After a day at the ranch, the boys got up at 4:30 in the morning and drove to Denver, and then on to Colorado Springs, arriving at the Garden of the Gods club just before noon on Lamar's twentieth birthday, August 2, 1952. After three days of rest, a trip to the dog races and up Pike's Peak, the boys headed back to Dallas in time for Lamar to make SMU's preseason football training camp.

That fall, as he began his sophomore year at SMU, Lamar kept in his binder a page titled "Games I Have Seen This Year," and in his exacting hand wrote the date, opponents, score, and location of each game he'd watched that season, along with a "Television" notation if he'd watched the game on TV. The weekend of September 26–28 was a typical one in Lamar's life. He spent that Friday evening at the Cotton Bowl, working as a spotter for the radio broadcast of SMU's season-opening loss to Duke (Lamar still hadn't qualified for the varsity squad). The next afternoon, he returned as a fan to watch Texas A&M play Oklahoma A&M. On Sunday afternoon, he and Buddy Rupe were in the stands yet again, for the regular-season home opener of Dallas's new professional football team, the Dallas Texans. Owners Giles and

Connell Miller had purchased the team from the league after the New York Yanks washed out in 1951. The Miller Brothers had high hopes. But when the Texans took the field—in royal-blue jerseys and helmets, with an outline of the state of Texas on the jersey sleeves—only 17,500 fans were in attendance for the Giants 24–6 win over Dallas. It may not have been that many.

"I remember going to the first game," said Lamar. "They were playing the New York Giants, and they were playing against Kyle Rote. There were maybe 10,000 people at the game, so even though it was big-time pro football, with Kyle Rote, who'd been playing for SMU just a couple of years before, the public didn't perceive it as that big a deal. To my recollection, that may have been the only game I saw, the opening game."

The prospect of pro football coming to Texas had intrigued Lamar. He had spoken at least once with Bunker about someday owning a team, and now the NFL was coming to Dallas.

"I was excited, but it wasn't as big a deal as college football," said Lamar. "Frankly, SMU was drawing 55,000 and 60,000 average crowds at that point, and at some games in the 70,000s, so it wasn't that big a deal. The biggest deal as far as I was concerned was that Doak Walker was playing in the NFL, and that he would come back."

It wasn't only Lamar, of course; Walker's profile in Texas during the period was akin to Babe Ruth in New York or even Jackie Robinson among black Americans. Walker would return to Dallas each August, when the Lions played in the Salesmanship Club game at the Cotton Bowl, an exhibition put on by a group of Dallas businessmen.

The only pro football games that regularly appeared in Dallas during the period were Lions games, on week-old kinescopes, so that the Lions–Bears game of October 28, 1951, aired in Dallas on November 4, the same afternoon the Lions were playing the Green Bay Packers. College football's dominance could be seen in obvious ways and more subtle ones as well. Even as he was playing at SMU, Lamar still eagerly awaited the *Street & Smith's Football Yearbook*. The magazine's focus was typical of the national mood: The 1952 book included 113 pages on college football and just seven, in the very back of the magazine, on the pros.

After the Texans' disappointing opener, there were even fewer fans in the stadium the following week when Hugh McElhenny and the San Francisco 49ers thumped the Texans, 37–14. By November 9, when the Rams overwhelmed the Texans, 27–6, there were precious few fans in the stadium—the announced attendance of 10,000 was pure fiction. Within a week, the franchise was gone. By November 12, they'd had their last practice in Dallas, and on that day, Giles Miller sent a telegram to Bert Bell that read, "I regret that it is necessary to inform you the Dallas Texans Football Club, Inc., is as of today unable to complete the current season because of a lack of finances." The team's operations were taken over by the National Football League (the team would find a home a year later, as the second incarnation of the Baltimore Colts and, with Gino Marchetti and Art Donovan anchoring the defensive line, would grow into the dominant team in the league by the end of the '50s). But for Dallas, pro football had been tried and proven a failure.

At the same time, Lamar was captivated by the *idea* of crowds. "I can only say that I do remember so clearly that in the small agate type in the box scores, always looking at those attendance numbers and going, 'Isn't that great?' The Boston Braves moved to Milwaukee [in 1953], and it was a big story every day what they drew at Milwaukee, and they broke every kind of record, I think, for attendance. That was just a monster story, just day after day, you know, the headline would be 'Braves Win In Front of Crowd of 36,000' or 'Braves Draw 41,000' That was more important than if they won or lost, it was just a great story. And I think I first thought of owning a football team back then."

•

Lamar's first business venture was decidedly more modest. On a trip to Fort Worth in '52, he'd seen a baseball pitching machine concession and noticed "it was just minting money: 25 cents for ten balls." Lamar had also been intrigued with the mechanized pitching machine that the Hill baseball team used his final year there. It was a useful tool for practices, but what struck him was the allure of the challenge . . . even boys not on the baseball team, just walking past on their way to soccer or track, often asked for a chance to step in and take a few cuts. There was also the appeal of the metronomic efficiency of the machine, allowing Lamar to track how many line drives he hit for every ten swings. By 1953, he decided that a pair of batting cages could succeed close to the SMU campus. That spring, he signed a lease for a parcel of land at the southeast corner of Yale Boulevard and the North Central Expressway. In a nod to Frank Stanton at the Kappa Sigma House, Lamar called it "Zima-Bat."

Tom Richey had also invested in the project, and, soon enough, Lamar hired frat brother John Torbett to work as the night manager, and Bill Adams to help as well. Joe James, Caroline's friend who'd met Lamar at a stay at the Palette Ranch in the '40s, was driving from his job at the bakery one evening, and remembered "as I entered the Expressway service road, northbound, an outdoor batting cage suddenly sprouted. I stopped. Lamar was sitting on a folding chair, ready to take thirty-five cents from anyone who wanted to try hitting pitches that whizzed by the plate."

Lamar's best customer was Bunker, who stopped by every morning on his way into work, and spent $10 hitting baseballs. "He'd be there in his dress shirt, and he'd be soaking wet," said Lamar. "He wasn't doing it to help me, but it was good exercise for him."

Paying a rent of just $500 a month for the land, Lamar made a profit his first summer and poured the profits back into the site, debuting Zima-ture Golf in the spring of 1954 and a watermelon stand called Zima Melon later that summer.

"We would go there every Friday," remembered Rose Mary. "I'd be picking up balls in the outfield and other strange things. A carload of friends drove by once while I was picking up balls and someone said, 'Hey, Rose Mary, have a wonderful date!' They all thought I was crazy."

Lamar visited the site every day and worked hard to find ways to increase business. He had a regular promotion in the spring in which the fraternity with the highest percentage of players on the miniature golf course during the evening won a free keg of beer. He also issued a series of cards offering a free game to the low score in a foursome. Zima-Bat was making money, and in 1954, Lamar opened another location—in a lot adjacent to Burnett Field, where the Dallas Eagles, the American Association minor league baseball team, played its games.

The main location was ripe for expansion, and Lamar moved aggressively. "We made a very unwise decision to expand too fast," Lamar said. "We put in a watermelon garden, so you could get slices of watermelon, and the real downfall was that we put in a miniature golf course, and man that thing ate us alive from a maintenance standpoint. It was very difficult and very expensive. So we made profits on the batting range, but we blew it on the miniature golf and the watermelon garden." (In 1956, by the time losses reached $12,000, Lamar decided to shut it down.)

With the business venture, the football team, his first serious girlfriend, and fraternity activities, Lamar was hard-pressed to find time to study, but he remained dedicated, though somewhat distracted. He had a three-ring binder in which he kept his class notes, but he spent as much time doodling on the pale yellow section dividers that separated his subjects. He would list his teammates and bestow nicknames to each one (Little Gorilla, Watermel-on Walt, Hossy Head, Pin Chin, Banana Nose, Native Dancer, and Grand Old Man, about whom he wrote, "only man in history to have a son on the frosh team before he graduated"). He'd sketch out team awards for "Biggest Lover," "Biggest Loafer," and "Biggest Griper." He would enumerate the highlights and lowlights of his freshman season: "Carl Johnson digestive trouble on the opening day of practice," "J.V. cold cuts, pregame hash and French toast after game." On the divider before his chemistry class was his neat listing of the SMU backs for the 1953 season, cataloging the class, number of letters won, name, jersey number, position, and weight of more than thirty different play-ers, including a list of "graduated" players and "fade aways."

Back home at Mount Vernon, he'd turned the alcove on the second floor into his private study area, the walls plastered with pictures from magazines, and a full-page tear-out from a newspaper of Doak, the shelves lined with textbooks and his own early library. There was Ring Lardner's *You Know Me Al: A Busher's Letters*, which had accompanied him to The Hill and back, along with such less-celebrated titles as the golf instructional book *If I Were in Your Golf Shoes* by Johnny Farrell (with an introduction by Bobby Jones), *Do You Know Your Baseball?* by Bill Brandt, with baseball trivia like "Q: What pitcher played right-field in the longest game of his career and won it with a home run in the 18th inning?"

Nearly all of his books were textbooks or sports books, but there were a few exceptions. He'd acquired a book on stamp collecting, though few of his classmates in high school or college saw him spend any time on it, as well as a well-thumbed title called *Youth's Courtship Problems* by Alfred L. Murray, which posited itself as a frank (for its era) discussion of the politics of dating, with chapter titles like "How to Get A Date" and "The Meaning of a Kiss."

Among Murray's chapters was one on smoking and drinking, which in-cluded the question, "Why Do People Smoke and Drink?" along with the answer, "They are ignorant of the ill effects these narcotics have upon their bodies. Too often their actions are determined by popular opinion or inner desires. They do not know the true facts." It seems unlikely that Lamar would have lapsed into a life of alcohol and nicotine under any circumstance, but it's true that he got through his college years remarkably unscathed, and never developed a taste for nicotine. "He was never much of a drinker," said Rose Mary. Elsewhere, Murray spent a chapter on the subject "How to Be Popular," in which he noted that "The Popular Fellow" would have these traits: 1) Un-derstanding, 2) Thoughtful, 3) A Gentleman, 4) Charitable, 5) Kind Words, and 6) Command Respect.

Whether he gleaned any useful tips from a book or not, there was, even at this young age, a kind of relaxed rectitude to Lamar. He never touched cigarettes, and rarely if ever drank, explaining when asked that he simply didn't like the taste. While others drank a beer after a golf outing, he always asked for a Dr Pepper.

In the classroom, he mastered the gentlemen's B. He was a conscientious student with an aptitude for mathematics and architecture. His handwriting had matured into a symphony of precision. In printing, his headlines were crisp and light, with delicate winged serifs extending from his capitals. His cursive was a marvel of delicate acuity, distinguished most by its compact dimensions. Perhaps it was because he was nearsighted, or perhaps it was because he was by nature secretive, but his handwriting grew quite small during his college years (and would shrink toward microscopic later in life). The pages of his architecture notebooks were pristine.

By contrast, his geology notebooks were clouded with smudges from erasures, scratched-out definitions, and accompanying notes on dihexagonal bipyramids and the fluvial cycle in domes and folds. He dutifully copied down all the minutiae, noting that "Novaculite—looks like limestone but isn't," and committed to memory the myriad charts and tables of the science, including ones with headings like "Crustal Layering in Km. to Mohorovic Discontinuity."

He was a geology major and not a semester went by when he wasn't reminded of that fact. This was the field of study that had made his family spectacularly wealthy. Lamar studied it, copied it, and memorized it. But he never fell in love with it. "It was just the sort of the thing to do," he said, "because my older brothers had done that, too, and we were in the oil business, and I didn't have a focus in other directions."

•

Athletic dreams aren't dashed in an instant. They are defeated incrementally over time, as hope comes up against humbling experience, and confidence crumbles under the weight of scrimmage setbacks and time spent on the bench. Lamar faced this evidence on a daily basis, and persevered, even as those around him were deciding to give up their dream or, like Phil Jones, pursue it elsewhere. Though Jones beat Lamar out for the second-string halfback spot behind Frank Eidom on the freshman team, he transferred to San Diego State, realizing he was "never going to play" at SMU. And that was before the arrival of heralded halfback Don McIlhenny in 1952.

And yet Lamar persevered, after any real hope of athletic glory failed him. When he wasn't talented enough to make the traveling squad as a sophomore in 1952, he traveled with the team anyway, volunteering to act as a spotter in the press box for radio broadcasts. And he remained an avid fan; even while not playing, he still kept a meticulously detailed scrapbook of the 1952 season, carefully pasting in ticket stubs, press passes, newspaper headlines, magazine articles, and, at the end of the book, a photograph showing head coach Rusty Russell in front of a framed news clipping of SMU's 27–20 upset of Notre Dame a year earlier. The photo was taken minutes before Russell announced his resignation at SMU, saying it was "too big a job to coach football and have to answer criticism at the same time."

After the little-known, and less regarded, Woody Woodard took over prior to the 1953 season (the rumor around campus was that he had applied for the job by postcard and was hired because he came cheap), SMU remained a team in search of past greatness. There was plenty of talent, though not all of it balanced. Phil Jones remembered "SMU signed about fifteen all-every-thing backs, and maybe two linemen weighing 220 pounds, or at least that's how it seemed."

Buried in the depth chart at halfback, Lamar moved in his sophomore year to end (where he'd soon begin wearing jersey No. 80) and continued to work diligently. "Lamar had good hands," said teammate Don McIlhenny. "He just wasn't very big and he wasn't very fast. Which isn't to say that he was small and slow." In the football coaches' timeless jargon, Lamar Hunt, at a shade under 6 feet and weighing 180 pounds, was not a "difference-maker."

If anything, the competition proved more brutal at end than it had been in the backfield. He now found himself at a position that was studded with Mustangs who would go on to future pro football careers. There was Ed Bernet, who joined Lamar for training sessions out at Mount Vernon, running wind-sprints up the hills in the off-season. There was the graceful Doyle Nix, who was a bit taller, a bit heavier, and a bit faster than Lamar. And then, emerging in 1953 and 1954, was the dedicated junior-college transfer Raymond Berry, the quiet, purposeful son of a coach from Paris, Texas, who by his college years was developing a reputation as an exacting athlete, willing to spend hours in obsessive pursuit of a small edge. Berry was drawn to Lamar, for both his lack of pretension—"he was just a good, low-key guy," said Berry—and his dedication to the sport.

Lamar responded by training harder himself. "Bunker used to train Lamar," Margaret Hunt Hill recalled. "He would drive the car at ten miles per hour and

Lamar would run alongside." Later, Lamar would say he had no specific recollection of those sessions, but Herbert vouched for the truth of the story. "That
sounds like Lamar," he said. "And that sounds like Bunker."

Though Lamar recognized he would likely never be a star, he continued to
show up each day to take part in the long afternoons spent sweating on the
Ownby Stadium field, the pungent smell of the freshly baked bread from the
Mrs. Baird's bakery wafting through the air. As the drills and scrimmages accumulated, and the afternoon shadows lengthened, some of the players would
sneak a peek at the large clock on the tall cream-brick tower of the Dr Pepper
plant, visible from a block away, calculating how many more minutes they had
to sweat. Then came the long walk to the dressing room, for showers and re-
freshments after which, weary and bruised, they'd head back to their lives as
students. Some of the players would gravitate to Gordo's, the pizza and beer
joint, or further down Mockingbird, to Mac's College Inn, with its joke-diplo-
mas for beer-guzzling and its high content of local women who were not SMU
students. But Lamar got in his Oldsmobile and headed to the library or back
to Mount Vernon.

On the field, Lamar was out to practice every day, taking snaps with the scout
team, faithfully executing drills, and being a good teammate, even if at times
that meant taking his punishment from friends. Forrest Gregg, the All-Southwest
Conference lineman who would go on to a Hall of Fame career as a Green Bay
Packer, faced off against Lamar daily in practice. But for more than a year, until
another teammate told Gregg about visiting Mount Vernon and swimming in
the Hunts' pool, Gregg had no idea that his teammate came from wealth. "That's
how smart I was, and how unassuming Lamar was," Gregg said. "You'd never
know. He wore the same thing I did, which was penny loafers, and socks we stole
from the athletic department, SMU T-shirts, and blue jeans. That was him, and
he was one of the guys. I always appreciated that about Lamar."

Some of his teammates took to labeling him with the ironic "Poor Boy,"
but Lamar took it well and remained an avid team player, although one who
came in for a highly specialized form of ribbing. One of his friends was John
"Bubba" Kelly, a raw-boned back with a pompadour, who came up to Lamar
after one practice in which Woody Woodward was particularly critical and
said, "Lamar, why don't you buy this place, fire all these guys, and let us just
play football." Lamar ducked his head and smiled through the laughter, content to be one of the guys.

He wasn't even listed in the program for the 1953 spring game, but he
played his way onto the junior varsity team. On Monday, November 9, 1953,

he intercepted a fourth-quarter pass and returned it 54 yards for a touchdown, the only points in the SMU junior varsity's 6–0 win over previously unbeaten Fort Sill.

In the 1954 SMU team prospectus, Lamar was listed as a second-string player, behind Raymond Berry at left end. "Lamar was one of the outstanding players on the Junior Varsity last year and showed up well in the spring intra-squad game," said the brochure. In 1954, his fourth season of college football, he got into four varsity games, playing a total of 20 minutes. He never lettered. But he remained steadfast in his enjoyment of the team experience. At the end of that season, in the annual game against TCU, Lamar came in at end and blocked the Horned Frog safety (and quarterback) Chuck Curtis so persistently on one play that a frustrated Curtis incurred a 15-yard unnecessary roughness penalty. Lamar joked that it was the only positive yardage he was ever responsible for in his SMU career.

"Lamar had his fraternity," said McIlhenny, who was both a teammate and a fraternity brother, "and he had the football team. But you have to understand, football is a fraternity, too. And I think, if anything, he liked that fraternity even more than the Kappa Sigs."

•

There was a girl Lamar had dated during his early days back in Dallas. He later confided to Rose Mary that he was so sure he would marry this other woman that he'd bet a friend $50 that she would be his wife one day. Instead, he later discovered that the girl he'd pined for—who'd gone to Woodrow Wilson High and worked as a model for Neiman-Marcus—was not only going out with someone else, but pregnant to boot.

So by the time Lamar and Rose Mary began dating seriously in the fall of 1951, he was affectionate but somewhat reserved. "He was very cautious with his words," said Rose Mary. "By the time he finally told me he loved me, which was a year or so after we started seeing each other, I was almost over him."

As a suitor, Lamar Hunt was neither crude nor pushy, but he was prone to jealousy. Like most young couples, Lamar and Rose Mary had traumatic near-breakups over things that would, in retrospect, strike both of them as comically insignificant. When they had been dating about a year, Lamar invited Rose Mary and her best friend, Dorothy Chandler, over to Mount Vernon. The pool hadn't been cleaned recently, leaving some twigs and leaves on the surface of the water. Accustomed to the pristine pool at the Northwood Country Club,

Chandler proclaimed upon seeing the Hunts' pool, "Oh, I'm not going to put my foot into that!" When he felt slighted, Lamar could grow very quiet, and on the rest of that day he was almost still, though courteous and cordial when the girls left. But he didn't call Rose Mary for several days after. She, still in high school and already a self-described "humongous worrier," locked herself in her room and refused to eat. Days later, when Lamar finally called the Whittle House, Orene Whittle told her daughter to pick up the extension in her room, and then she brought Rose Mary a plate of fried chicken while Rose Mary was on the phone. Orene knew that now, finally, she would eat.

"He would get mad at me," Rose Mary said, "and disappear for three days, and not say a word to me. Kind of punish me. But he wouldn't even tell me what he was mad about."

The pattern was set: Lamar avoided direct conflict whenever he could, often withdrawing. He was loyal and honest but unequipped for the vulnerability and intimacy that relationship problem-solving required. So they struggled—Lamar with his jealousy, Rose Mary with her anxiety—but they were in love and they soldiered through. In the fall of 1953, she matriculated to SMU as well.

A year later, in the fall of 1954, Lamar and Rose Mary were pinned. The ceremony was done with mock solemnity at Rose Mary's sorority, the Kappa Alpha Theta house, with Lamar and Rose Mary standing on a second-floor balcony. After he affixed his Kappa Sigma pin next to Rose Mary's Theta pin on her jacket, Lamar's fraternity brothers in the front yard serenaded the couple with the Kappa Sigma anthem, "Mister, He Kissed Her":

> *One day while out walking a coed came in view*
> *And they started talking, now what should he do?*
> *He couldn't resist her, this little campus queen*
> *For she seemed to fit his romantic scheme.*
> *He promised to meet her that evening at ten*
> *He rushed up to greet her, and what happened then?*
> *Why, Mister, He Kissed Her, the finest ever seen*
> *And now she is wearing the scarlet, white and green*

That fall, Rose Mary came to his games, sat for long hours out in the parking lot afterward, kissing and consoling him through the numerous disappointing days when he didn't get to play.

Though he was completing his fourth year at SMU in the spring, Lamar was not ready to graduate yet, still needing to take a few more classes. In the summer of '55, he had a summer school assignment, an on-site geology camp at the University of Colorado at Boulder. Talking with Tom Richey one day, Lamar shared that he had no enthusiasm for it.

It was May of 1955 when he was pulled from one of his classes with urgent orders to head home: Lyda, who had been suffering severe back pain for days, was rushed to Baylor Hospital, reportedly from a stroke. The local specialist recommended immediate surgery, but H. L., as he had in 1946 when Hassie was spiraling out of control, leaped into action, seeking the nation's finest physicians and an immediate remedy. He decided to fly her to the Mayo Clinic in Rochester, and the family chartered an American Airlines DC-6, not wanting to risk the flight in the unpressurized cabin of the Hunt Oil private plane.

Once at Mayo, H. L. approved the suggested treatment of surgery to reduce the pressure from what was believed to be a brain tumor. But in a matter of hours, it was discovered that Lyda Hunt was not suffering from a tumor at all but rather a brain hemorrhage, which the surgery only exacerbated. She suffered a massive stroke and died on Friday, May 6, with Lamar and Caroline standing vigil in her hospital room. Just that suddenly, the Hunt family matriarch was gone.

On receiving the news in the hospital, Lamar sought out Caroline, the sibling with whom he was closest. Tears in his eyes, he spoke of his beloved Mooze, and then walked alone down the hall at Mayo. He was twenty-two years old and could hardly conceive what his life would be like without his mother, the pious, benevolent anchor.

There was not merely shock, but, for a family that did not show emotion easily, a kind of muted anguish, a pain that couldn't articulate itself. Herbert remembered a "very quiet" plane ride back. The plane pulled into Love Field on a hushed Friday night.

On Sunday, Mother's Day, in the library at Mount Vernon, the stricken family gathered to hear Paul Harvey's broadcast. Harvey, by then among the best-known voices in the country, for his crisp, dulcet diction and his melodramatic stop-start pauses, came into the Hunt living room as he had so many times before. And this time, he was speaking directly to the family: "Tomorrow at 4—Dallas, Texas, will say goodbye to a remarkable woman ..."

The day after the funeral, still bereft, Lamar called on Rose Mary, driving to her home and accepting condolences from the Whittles. After thanking them, he asked to speak to Rose Mary alone, and they moved out to the front porch. He was still despairing, still stunned. But the next step was quite clear to him.

"We have to get married," he said to Rose Mary, *"right now."*

CHAPTER FIVE

A MAN ALONE

The death of his mother was the single most traumatic event of Lamar Hunt's life. As the youngest child in a far-flung family, he had relied on his relationship with her from his earliest years. Now, without her, he seemed to temporarily lose his bearings, as well as the comforting illusion that everything would always turn out okay.

About his father, he could be respectfully matter-of-fact and descriptive. But thoughts of his mother brought him up short. He could never begin to articulate what she meant to him. "She was a neat, neat person," he once managed. "I guess one of the things that I most got from her was a love for nature and gardening and things like that, 'cause she did love that, and that's one of my favorite things to do."

He went through the week of the funeral in something of a daze, and then he did what the Hunt family did when faced with major traumas: He tried to move forward. In her book *H. L. and Lyda*, Margaret would remember the weeks following the death of her baby sister Lyda in 1925, and a visitor coming over to the house afterward to console her mother, remarking that if such a thing had happened to him, he would've collapsed. Lyda Hunt remained gracious but after the man left, she sat down with Margaret and Hassie and said, "Ignore what you just heard. We do not collapse."

So Lamar Hunt didn't collapse. But by all indications, he felt his mother's loss acutely then and for the rest of his life. He was not one to regale friends and family over his favorite memories, or enumerate her most endearing qualities. But one family member, decades later, remarked that nearly every time Lyda was mentioned in Lamar's presence, "he grew very quiet, and he looked away, almost as if he still couldn't bear the thought of her being gone."

His most obvious response, in the immediate aftermath of Lyda's death, was to hasten the marriage to Rose Mary. She was unusually steadfast about needing to wait until early 1956, at least, since she had agreed to be the rush chairman for her sorority that fall, and it was an obligation she took seriously. In this he relented, agreeing to a date in January 1956. Decades later, it all seemed clear in retrospect to Rose Mary, who said: "He wanted a mother. He wanted someone to take care of him."

In her will, Lyda left Lamar, among other things, her half-share of Mount Vernon. His father asked him to sell it back to him, but Lamar offered to give it to H. L., pointing out that it was his parents' house in the first place. But H. L. wouldn't hear of it, insisting, for tax purposes, to pay his son half the book value of the home. Lyda also left Lamar her 1910 Victrola that he had been fascinated with since childhood, and her blue Cadillac, which Lamar appreciated but was embarrassed to drive. Friends would see Rose Mary driving the car, dropping Lamar off two blocks from the SMU campus. (One reason she was driving was because, in June of '55, the Texas Department of Public Safety revoked his driving privileges. Even at this age, Lamar had earned a reputation among his friends as not so much a bad driver as an absent-minded and occasionally reckless one, routinely ringing up speeding tickets and taking his eyes off the road. He had other things on his mind.)

Lamar found Mount Vernon, without Mooze there, to be unbearable. H. L. was disoriented at first but soldiered on quickly, and was unable to say much at the breakfast table beyond "I miss mom." It was a sad truth, and neither of them knew what to add. Within weeks, H. L. began more frequently summoning his personal secretary, Ruth Ray Wright, to the house for work. By the end of the summer, she was often staying for dinner.

Lamar did not protest or make a scene, but quietly informed his father that he was going to rent an apartment closer to the SMU campus. Within a month of his mother's death, he had asked his Kappa Sigma friend Bob Wilkes if he wanted to share an apartment. Even among the more business-like Kappa Sigs, Lamar found in Bob a kindred spirit ("I was as square as he was," said Wilkes), someone who loved sports and largely avoided bars and drinking. They found a split-level apartment in University Park, and Lamar moved a few of his things over there. That same spring, he brought home a new dog, a long-haired Chihuahua he named "Herschel."

They were not roommates for long before Lamar left to spend part of the summer in Colorado, taking part in a pair of field-study geology courses on research methodology and field geology. When one of the students on the project expressed disgust at the thought that a private individual could actually own the Seven Falls landmark in nearby Colorado Springs, Lamar certainly didn't volunteer that the person in question was his sister Margaret, along with his brother-in-law Al. He did share these details with his friend and former SMU teammate Edward "Buzz" Kemble, a jovial, carefree character who had always been especially nice to Lamar on the football team, and who was in Boulder with a teammate taking summer school classes.

Neither Hunt nor Kemble had matched their high-school promise on the football field, but they'd both toiled cheerfully on the SMU third string in 1954. Now they shared a dose of homesickness and desire for escape. They would make the 40-minute drive on Tuesdays and Thursday nights to the Mile High Kennel Club in Commerce City, where they'd watch the dog races, soaking in the scene of a live band playing between races, and the bugler whose clarion call brought the greyhounds onto the track. "Lamar's system was you don't bet favorites and you don't bet longshots," said Kemble. "He wanted the 9-to-1-ers and the 10-to-1-ers. We didn't do too well with that system." One night that summer, Lamar met Buzz and his girlfriend Dorothy, visiting from Dallas, for dinner in Denver. As the couple was leaving for the airport, Lamar asked Dorothy if he could borrow 75 cents to pay for gas and tolls on the way back to Boulder. "Lamar didn't have much money," said Kemble. "And after we lost at the dog races, he had even less."

By the mid-'50s, the pattern was set: Lamar rarely carried much cash, and when he ran out, he would ask to borrow the smallest possible amount to see him through to his return, then promptly repay the debt at his earliest convenience. For those who knew only his family's reputation, it was bewildering that the son of one of the world's richest men would go through his days nearly penniless. But for those who understood Lamar's worldview, it was plain; he was going to be a young man who would appreciate the value of a dollar, and the work required to earn it. Nothing could be worse, in his mind, than the stereotypical rich Texan flashing around a wad of bills. So he limped along and spent judiciously, with the one obvious exception being his penchant for gambling.

Over the summer, Lamar kept up a steady correspondence with Tom Richey, stationed in Germany, who kept him apprised of military life ("Most of these German gals look like female Chris Cringles but occasionally you meet the Marlene Dietrich type") and inquired about Zima-Bat ("I've been worried about the range lately . . . I know you haven't felt much like writing, so I haven't been sweating too much.")

In one letter, dated July 8, 1955, Tom asked Lamar about his sports plans. "Are you going out for football this fall? I hope so 'cause I certainly don't want the same thing to happen to you that happened to myself. You never can tell who will get hurt, and after all that big play in the final game of your senior year is worth all the work the other years. Give it a lot of thought."

Lamar had. But he was still grieving his mother. He'd already devoted four years to college football, and though he had one more year of eligibility left, he chose not to come back to the team for his final year.

He returned to the apartment he was sharing with Wilkes and the Chihuahua Herschel. He and Wilkes would often dine at the frat, and he and Rose Mary went out more often—he even smuggled in Herschel with them to the movies. That fall, Lamar spent much of his time at the frat house and the Fondren Library, and took to loaning his Oldsmobile out to his friend John Marshall. "You can't take these pretty SMU girls out in that car of yours," said Lamar. "Just borrow mine when you need it."

He continued dropping by the Kappa Sigma house between classes, testing his frat brothers each weekday morning by reading out loud from Dr. George W. Crane's "Test Your Horse Sense" column in the *Times-Herald*, or heading up to the top floor of the frat house for ping-pong games. "He was absolutely the world's worst sport at ping-pong," said Bill Adams. "He must have broken five or six paddles. He could not beat me, and I wasn't very good."

Christmas 1955 was somewhat muted. Margaret took over the role of the Hunt family matriarch, though her relations with H. L. were strained—she already sensed that his secretary Ruth meant more to him, and she didn't like her near-constant presence in the house so soon after Lyda's death. Lamar and Rose Mary attended their last Cotton Bowl as SMU students, watching Ole Miss rally to beat TCU, 14–13. It was, Lamar was proud to attest, his eighteenth straight Cotton Bowl game.

With January, Lamar was greeted with a light class load in his last semester, as well as the rush of last-minute wedding plans, and the inevitable bachelor party. Lamar's future brother-in-law, LeVon Massengale (by then married to Rose Mary's sister Joanne), had been reluctant to attend Lamar's bachelor party, held in a conference room at the Stoneleigh Hotel. "I'd met his brothers at a New Year's Eve party and wasn't impressed," he said. "Bunker and Herbert were just loud, obnoxious boys—I suppose most of us were back then. But Lamar was different. Terrifically well-mannered." Massengale and Rose Mary's brother Dick had both been invited but reasoned that anyone who didn't smoke, drink, swear, or enjoy dirty jokes probably wasn't going to be much fun at a bachelor party. Out of loyalty to their future in-law, though, they decided to attend, and upon arrival found out the featured entertainment was going to be the stripper Candy Barr. The buxom blonde dancer, already a Dallas legend, showed up that night without music, having assumed it would be provided. Thinking fast, Roger Blackmar rushed down to the parking lot and paid $5 to borrow the parking lot attendant's radio. Ms. Barr disrobed to a Top 40 station, before a blushing Lamar, and enthusiastic yet gentlemanly applause. "I think he was adequately embarrassed," said Bob Chilton. "Candy Barr was one of the all-time great strippers. I think Lamar turned a color red that I never saw before. And everybody else was enjoying themselves."

The wedding, a week later, was a quiet, tasteful affair. Lamar's grooms-men consisted largely of fraternity brothers or football teammates, or both: Rupe, Bob Wilkes, Carl Shannon, Sam Hunt, and John Torbett. H. L. Hunt and Ralph Whittle met for the first time and seemed to enjoy one another's company. Buddy Rupe was slated to be the best man, though Lamar deferred at the ceremony and let H. L. serve in that role.

The next day, Lamar and Rose Mary left for their honeymoon, skiing at Sun Valley, Idaho. On the third day, Lamar decided to go from the beginners' slope to the intermediate hill, and wound up wrenching his knee in a fall. The newlyweds retired to their room for much of the rest of the stay, then left early, stopping in Reno for some gambling before their return to Dallas.

They were greeted, back home, by Rose Mary's mother Orene, looking stricken and apologetic, explaining that she had accidentally let their beloved Herschel out in the front lawn, where he'd been attacked by a neighboring dog. The little Chihuahua, always carefree and affectionate, had received stitches but was even more mentally than physically scarred. "Lamar loved that dog so much, and he just pulled it on to the bed with us, and wrapped it up," said Rose Mary. "But the poor thing was never the same again."

They stayed at Mount Vernon for a while, before taking up residence at a small apartment at 4508 Abbott in north Dallas, then moving into their first home, a small three-bedroom home with a den, done in the early American style, at 6831 Orchid Lane in Dallas.

And though the future looked promising, the contours of Lamar's life were closing in on him. He was married. Rose Mary quickly got pregnant, and they were expecting their first child in October. There was a degree in geology in May. And then there would be an office waiting for Lamar at Hunt Oil. He did not talk a great deal about the future, and his friends didn't often inquire.

"Honestly, as a nineteen-year-old kid and your father's the wealthiest man in the world, nobody even asked what Lamar was going to do," said Don McIlhenny. "We all knew: He was just going to be another millionaire, and how lucky he was. Rose Mary was going to be pretty, and that was going to be that."

•

It was the heart of the 1950s and Cold War tension was high. But change was, unequivocally, in the air. On Wednesday, February 22, 1956, Rosa Parks was arrested in Montgomery, Alabama, for refusing to relinquish her city bus seat to a white passenger, and Elvis Presley entered the Billboard single charts for the first time, with his new song "Heartbreak Hotel." Lamar didn't have any classes in the afternoon, so he drove downtown to the Hunt Oil office and a meeting with Al Hill. Al was not merely his brother-in-law and trustee of the Lamar Hunt Trust, he was a man whom Lamar had always looked up to, from the early days at Mount Vernon. The visit was Lamar's surrender to the inevitable—seeking out advice for the next stage of his life. It also was an indicator of his regard for the rock-solid Al, whom he described as "always a very conservative, sound business man. He was not a risk-taking person."

It was a relaxed, if somewhat formal, meeting, with Lamar sitting attentively while Al talked about the future, Lamar's obligations, and his options.

After the meeting, Hill took the time to write a follow-up letter, in which he restated his general advice and outlined to Lamar the most prudent course of action. Hill extolled the virtues and tax advantages of oil exploration and advised Lamar to "secure the services of an experienced and high-class geologist" and to "employ a landman who could scout drilling wells, buy leases, and help in making deals."

"Debts should not be incurred to go into side ventures," Hill counseled, all but singling out the Zima-Bat franchise as a foolish endeavor. "These side ventures can be made down the line when capital has been accumulated through the depletion allowances and capital gains transactions."

In closing, Hill advised that Lamar move calmly and prudently with his fortune. "I would say that if you take your taxable income each year, use good advice and counsel in expending it in an oil exploration program and do not try to become a boy wonder over-night, you will surely end up a happy, wise, and healthy man."

There was little to argue with this sound approach. Lamar, receiving the letter later in the week, saved it and studied it. But for whatever reason, he chose not to follow Al Hill's recommendation. He didn't start hiring men for his own oil company—perhaps because he sensed that doing so might cast him irrevocably down his father's path. Neither did he openly rebel against the advice; instead he kept working on his geology degree at SMU and dutifully dropping into the Hunt Oil office when he was asked.

Later in the spring, Lamar traveled to Europe with a forty-man delegation from Hunt Oil, staying in Madrid for two nights and then heading on to Pakistan, where he sent Rose Mary a postcard with a picture of a grizzled snake charmer ("that's a friend of mine around my neck"), and outlined his itinerary: "Oh well, Harumph, lunch with the president, dinner with the Iranian ambassador, tomorrow night the American ambassador." Later, he went to Karachi with the group, for a ceremony accompanying the arrival of $3 million of drilling equipment for exploration of oil reserves on the Makran Coast. On April 22 and 23, he and Herbert spent two nights at the Imperial Hotel in Tokyo, before stopping off in Hawaii on his return.

He was back for his final exams, and, on Monday evening, May 28, 1956, at a ceremony beginning at 5:30 in the evening at Ownby Stadium, he received his Bachelor of Science in geology. The family was there, and all agreed that Lyda would have been so proud.

The following Monday, Lamar reported for duty at Hunt Oil, taking a humble office on the same floor but far removed from his father and brothers. His own memories of his early professional career were decidedly humble. "After I graduated from SMU, I had a very small office," he said. "And I trailed around after my next two oldest brothers, and they tried to look after me and teach me."

He embarked on a summer of glum oil work, joining company executives as they christened two new drilling barges in Orange, Texas, on June 15, and two months later, the christening of a drilling barge called the "Jim Garrison," during which Lamar, wearing a bow tie, looked on rather meekly for company pictures.

After shutting down Zima-Bat that summer, he vowed to be more prudent before undertaking his next independent endeavor. He and Tom Richey talked at one point of investing in a television pilot. A would-be Dallas producer named Herb Friend had contacted them, but both Lamar and Tom thought him worryingly glib, and wondered if Friend had the substance to succeed in the business. They considered investing in an all-purpose wrench being developed by a man in Ohio, but ultimately passed because they doubted whether it could be a truly profitable venture.

One night, after Tom had begun working as a marketing rep for *Life* magazine, stationed in Dallas, Lamar pointed out how hard it was to find parking spaces in downtown Dallas. This led them to bandying about the idea of a more practical car, perhaps modeled on a smaller European design. For a number of months they considered the idea of building the LATOmobile (combining the first two letters of their first names), but the start-up costs were prohibitive. Lamar wanted to be his own man, but he was also not ready to risk his entire fortune on a start-up venture he knew little or nothing about.

The respite from his new life came where it always had, from sports. At their new house on Orchid Lane, Lamar installed a backboard and a basket for basketball. "He would always want to play H-O-R-S-E," said his friend Bob Wilkes. "But Lamar wasn't a very good basketball player—he'd take off on the wrong foot on lay-ups." At the same time, he grew passionate about golf, taking a standing tee time at 9 a.m. Saturday mornings at the Dallas Country Club. Lamar's enthusiasm outstripped his talent, and his friend Tom Richey saw him flash a combustible temper on the course. "He would never cuss, though," said Richey. "He would just say 'Gee-yah!' It wasn't 'God,' it was 'Gee-yah,' through clenched teeth. I must have heard that 100 times." Golf clubs were never safe when Lamar duck-hooked into an adjoining fairway, and more than one pitching wedge found its way into water. But he craved the camaraderie and the competition, often bringing along Richey and his classmate and groomsman Johnnie Harris after which everyone would adjourn to the 19th hole for drinks, with Lamar ordering his inevitable Dr Pepper.

In the fall and winter, he continued traveling to football and basketball games. Earlier in the '50s, Bunker and Herbert had hired a private pilot, a salty, omnicompetent Army vet named Jake Cobb, and bought a company plane, a small Cessna. Though they were frequently using it during the week, Lamar began checking it out on weekends, to follow the SMU basketball team around on its quest for another Southwest Conference championship.

Jake Cobb would, in the coming years, play an increasingly important role in Lamar's life. The pilot was another in a long line of self-reliant Texas adventurers. He'd earned his pilot's license before World War II and spent much of the war ferrying fighters fresh off American assembly lines across the Atlantic and into the European theater. Throughout the 1950s and beyond, Cobb made himself indispensible by flying the Hunt brothers wherever they wanted to go whenever they wanted to go there, but also by displaying a sixth sense for the kind gesture, and for understanding the truism that, in his words, "rich people, because they have money, are the worst planners in the world." Jake was a pilot, mechanic, babysitter, secretary, valet, consigliere, aide-de-camp, and friend. And when H. L. Hunt suffered a rare loss in Vegas, he would send Jake out to the Sands to drop off a satchel with Jake Freedman at the Sands Hotel.

On trips with H. L., it was Cobb who made sure that H. L.'s "readings," his voluminous brochures from Facts Forum on the dangers of Communism, would get distributed on each floor of whatever hotel Hunt was staying. (Just as importantly, it was Cobb who tipped the bellboys, instructing them to remove some copies from the table every hour or so, so that H. L. could at least have the illusion that his message was getting through.)

"He was the frontman," said Bob Chilton. "Jake was the all-time colorful guy. He would sacrifice his body, just to do whatever had to be done. He was forced to have dates with some of the worst-looking ladies in Las Vegas."

For years, Lamar would call, bring a few friends, and they'd all pile in the Cessna, where Jake would take them where they wanted to go—which was, as often as not, to an SMU football or basketball game. In the spring of '56, the newlywed Lamar followed SMU to its regional final in Wichita, and then to the Final Four in Evanston, bringing along Bill Adams, Bob Wilkes, and Buzz Kemble.

It was an era in American sports when one could go to the box office on the day of even the biggest games and still hope to buy tickets. Even when games were sold out, tickets could often be purchased at face value or slightly above it outside the stadium or arena. Things usually fell into place beautifully, a result which some of Lamar's friends chalked up to his sunny disposition and eternal optimism. And when all else failed, they improvised.

If tickets couldn't be purchased, they'd track down a writer from one of the Dallas or Fort Worth papers, and see if one or two of them could get in as a "photographer's assistant."

When no tickets or friendly writers could be found, they would resort to the matchbook-cover trick. Lamar and each of his friends would find a young, friendly looking ticket taker and walk up to him, presenting a matchbook cover as a ticket stub, with a folded $5 or $10 bill clearly visible beneath it. "He'd look down at that damn thing and give you a smile, and sometimes tear that match cover in two, but he'd always peel that money off and keep it," said Jake Cobb.

Once inside the arena, Lamar and his friends grew adept at cherry-picking better seats. They might start in the back row, or standing in the concourse, but throughout the game, they'd carefully work their way down toward the action. There was an art to it: Seem agreeable, look respectful—Lamar and Buzz and the rest were almost always in coats and ties—and slip into some empty seats when something exciting happened and everyone was looking at the field or the court.

It was just such a dodge that Lamar and Buzz used in the spring of 1958, winding up on the court, under the scorers' table on press row, watching Kentucky and its Fiddlin' Five beat Elgin Baylor and Seattle for the NCAA title in front of a packed, partisan crowd at Freedom Hall in Louisville.

In the fall, Lamar fell into his normal routine, following the SMU football team around on its schedule. He also continued to search for a system that would consistently win betting on college football games. He corresponded with Richey, who was doing service duty overseas in 1956, sending him a few preseason annuals and asking for his help in evaluating the relative merits of the teams. Back in the states, he shared some of his betting philosophy with Kemble. One of his trusted gambits was one he called "The Slaughtered Favorite." The rule was to always bet against a team coming off a loss of 15 points or more, yet still favored to win its next game. "It got to be where that was all he'd bet," said Kemble.

Married life was pretty much like SMU life, though with a smaller circle of friends and fewer nights spent eating out. Shortly after their marriage, Rose Mary realized she'd need to come to grips with her limited cooking skills. After one occasion, when it took her nearly an hour to conjure up scrambled eggs for a friend of Lamar's who was staying over, she made a vow to become proficient, and did. But in a year, she had gone from a life of sorority parties and pre-nursing studies to an entirely domestic existence, as a young wife who was being coaxed by Margaret to join the Junior League. Lamar's quirks that had charmed her in college—his beat-up car, his penchant for running out of gas, his near-obsessive attention to college football—began to wear thin. Lamar's Oldsmobile had a splitting seat cushion in the front seat, with the tan foam clearly visible. When he took her out, he'd simply throw a towel over it, but when Rose Mary began participating in society functions, she occasionally had to pick up other women, and found herself mortified by the condition of the car.

On Saturday mornings in the fall, Buzz and Dorothy Kemble would come by, as would Lamar's Kappa Sig friend Bob Chilton and his wife Linda. Mid-mornings, Lamar would duck into the bedroom and call his bookie, quietly laying out his bets for the day. "He would say, 'Let me put 11 on such-and-such, and 12 on this team,'" said Rose Mary, "and I thought that meant 11 or 12 dollars. But he was betting 11 or 12 *thousand* dollars. I almost had a heart attack. I just got so furious with him. And I was so pitifully ignorant at the time, I didn't know what anything cost, didn't know anything about money. I just thought it was so trashy."

He bet far less on the pros, but he still watched. Doak Walker had gone on to great things with the Detroit Lions, and each Sunday he would watch the Lions game on TV (the local CBS affiliate had taken to showing mostly Detroit games, as the constituency in Texas for Walker and Bobby Layne was vast), and marveling at the sophisticated ball-handline, the wide-open passing, the growing crowds.

In the final month of Rose Mary's pregnancy, Lamar worked to make her more comfortable. Margaret had arranged a nurse to come in for six weeks, pointing out to Rose Mary more than once that, "When I had my first child, my feet didn't touch the floor for four months." But Rose Mary still planned to travel with their friends to the SMU–Rice game on October 20, the day before her due date. That Friday, as she was frosting the cupcakes she'd made for the flight, and wondering if she'd be able to make the trip, she felt a sharp pain, and her water broke. Lamar brought her towels and helped her with her bag to the car. Racing to Baylor Hospital, he gamely tried to calm her, remarking about the interesting architecture of a new building going up on the expressway. On October 20, 1956, the twenty-four-year-old Lamar and the twenty-one-year-old Rose Mary became parents, with the birth of Lamar, Jr. The arrival of the baby was a lifeline for Rose Mary, who was almost bewitched by their child. "I just thought he was the most beautiful baby ever," she said. "I know everyone says that, but I thought Lamar, Jr., really was." She came home six days later, to a shower of small gifts that Lamar had wrapped for her and placed around the house.

At work, Lamar remained lost, on the margins of the Hunt Oil universe. Across the hall from Lamar's office were the two full-time Hunt Oil landmen, a pair of deal-closers named Mack Rankin and Jim Beavers. They noticed early on that Lamar was different, quieter, less involved—and also clearly less headstrong—than his brothers. Tax laws encouraged Lamar to engage in a certain amount of drilling each year. Rankin noticed that when either he or Beavers would present Lamar with a prospective deal, Lamar was always unfailingly polite. He would ask a few questions, and be sure he understood the financial aspects. And then he would, invariably, say yes.

"Lamar had no interest in the oil business whatsoever," said Mack Rankin. Elsewhere at Hunt Oil, there was a young, SMU-educated accountant named

Jack Steadman, who would occasionally stop by Lamar's office. It became apparent to Steadman, as well, that the youngest of the Hunt sons felt detached from the family business. "He would just sign whatever he needed to sign, and that was that," said Steadman. "But you could tell it didn't really capture his imagination."

Lamar would come home in the evening, eat dinner, play with the baby for a while, and then he would lay down on the sofa in their living room, and, for a brief time, he would stop moving. By that point in the evening, it would be too dark to shoot baskets out in the driveway, or to trim the hedges. With no games to watch, there was nothing on their small black-and-white television to hold his attention. With the baby asleep, Rose Mary would sit on the couch, and Lamar would lay his head on her lap.

"I just don't know," he would mutter. "I don't know what I can do to be worthy of all that I've been given."

In these years adrift, he'd thought often of leaving it all behind. He mentioned more than once to Rose Mary that perhaps what he wanted to do was get into coaching, move to Pottstown, back to The Hill. "Whatever you want to do," she'd told him when he floated the idea. But even as he suggested it, he knew it wouldn't work. Rose Mary was finding keeping house and having one child a challenge, even with a housekeeper. Lamar realized that though she was beautiful and devoted, she was not flexible, and she would not have enjoyed the humble life at The Hill, serving as den mother for a floor full of teenage boys.

There were small crevices of discontent that others could see, though most were noticed only in retrospect. Rose Mary spent much of her time fretting over her mother, Orene, who had taken to wearing a hat at all times, out of concern that her head might fall off. By the time Ralph Whittle got his wife to see a psychiatrist, she was wearing two hats at most times during the day. Lamar continued to press for a busy social schedule, but Rose Mary was content to be at home with Lamar, Jr.

Then in November 1957, the other shoe dropped. H. L. married his secretary, Ruth Ray. Back home on Orchid Lane that fall, as Rose Mary was feeding Lamar, Jr., his bottle, she was visited by Herbert and Bunker's wives, Nancy and Caroline. Talk soon turned to H. L., before Nancy confided, matter-of-factly, "Don't you know all those children are his?"

Rose Mary didn't know it, and initially couldn't believe it. But then her in-laws spoke further and she could.

"Just look at them," explained Nancy. "Ruth's kids look just like H. L." It was true—H. L. had begun his romance with Ruth more than a decade before the death of Lyda, and shortly after the marriage, their children moved in with her to Mount Vernon.

Rose Mary passed the news on to Lamar that night, with less sensitivity than she might. "It took a long time," she recalled, "but finally he did believe it. And he just *hated* it. He was very upset with his father, but he didn't tell him. He just—he always acted the same. Everything was secretive."

Later that winter, Don McIlhenny and his wife Jan joined Lamar and Rose Mary to visit a private club, a modern-day speakeasy, located just on the outskirts of west Dallas. It was a dinner club with gambling in the back, and a password required at the door. McIlhenny had visited once before, and Lamar was eager to go with him, so they took their wives. On the way out there, the wives in dresses, the husbands in coats and ties, Rose Mary remarked to the whole car, "Lamar, how come Don dresses so sharply and you wear such drab old clothes?" And Lamar, not flustered but quick, responded, "Because he's a high-paid professional football player, and I'm not." Everyone laughed, including Rose Mary.

Rose Mary had begun to master the kitchen, but by the end of 1957 was pregnant again, and the couple welcomed their second child, Sharron, born February 28, 1958. But later that year, Orene passed away and Rose Mary went into a deep funk. Hoping to rouse her from her torpor, Lamar presented her with an Atlantic crossing for her birthday.

On July 12, 1958, Lamar and Rose Mary left Dallas at 7 in the morning, embarking on a three-week European vacation. Arriving in New York that afternoon, they were in Brussels the following day, and spent three days in Belgium, visiting the World's Fair, Lamar snapping pictures of Rose Mary under the giant Atomium, before flying to Zurich. Later, they traveled by train to Geneva, then flew to France for four days. Lamar was an avid tourist, wanting to see the Louvre and the Cathedral at Notre Dame, visiting the Moulin Rouge and walking to the top of the Eiffel Tower (Rose Mary, scared of heights and confined spaces, chose to stay below). On July 23, they set sail from Le Havre aboard the *Ile-de-France*, arriving in New York on July 31, before flying back home to Dallas.

The trip had been a tonic for Rose Mary, who had been somewhat overwhelmed by the arrival of her second child. It had also proved to be a clarifying experience for Lamar. He was twenty-five years old. He had two children and a high-strung but loving wife still rocked by the sudden loss of her mother. He had a fortune in the neighborhood of $100 million at his disposal, and a building full of oil executives to help him succeed even more in the oil business. But as he sat in his small office each day at Hunt Oil, he felt rest-less and extraneous. Around this time, something began to coalesce in La-mar's mind. He could not get passionate about oil or real estate or the stock market (although he did enjoy the statistical give-and-take of monitoring his stocks). What he loved most were sports. The places he most wanted to visit were stadiums and arenas. His free time was spent largely watching or playing sports. He did most of his reading in sports. What he and his friends talked about most, even after marriages and kids, was sports.

It was also becoming clear to him that there would be little joy in follow-ing in his father's footsteps, little pleasure in—as he had described it to Tom Richey back in the Hill School days—being "just another son of H. L. Hunt."

"Different people have different interests," he'd say later. "And I just had, I had more of a bent toward the entertainment business. I was thinking about the appeal of attracting people to a spectator event, that was more appealing to me than finding stratigraphic traps underground. Well, that was interest-ing, too, but I just, you know—some things are more interesting than others."

•

The Hunts didn't waste money, and they certainly took business seriously. So if Lamar was going to enter into the world of sports, he would have to convince at least himself—and ideally his father and siblings as well—that it made sense as a business proposition. Following his return from Europe, he began to look for signs pointing to sports as a prudent business investment. They weren't hard to find: Eisenhower's Interstate Highway Act of 1956 was drastically changing the nation's housing and travel patterns, as was the ad-vent of jet travel. By 1958, the GNP had grown more than 50 percent from where it stood in 1950. The sale of televisions had exploded, from 7,000 in the country in 1946 to a total of nearly 50 million near the end of the 1950s. Consumer spending was up—the handful of shopping centers that existed after the war had grown to 4,000 by the end of the '50s.

If people were going shopping more often, it meant they had more mon-ey—and consumer spending had grown dramatically in constant dollars during the decade. What did sports teams need to thrive? They needed de-voted fans with the means to buy tickets, and they needed advertisers who would spend money to reach those customers. Companies had spent $5.7 billion on advertising their products in 1950; by the end of the decade, that number had nearly doubled.

The universe of spectator sports was growing, but Lamar couldn't decide, initially, which sport was the most desirable. With the move of the Dodgers and Giants to the West Coast, there had been plenty of discussion about expansion in Major League Baseball. At the same time, attendance had grown in the NFL every year during the '50s, and Lamar and his friends were spending more time in front of the TV sets on Sunday afternoons.

In 1957, he had traveled to Kansas City for a three-game series between the Yankees and Athletics, with his brother-in-law Lloyd Sands (his sister Caroline's husband at the time) and cousin Tom Hunt. The group stayed for all three games, and Lamar was struck by the support in the small city for a team that had been a consistent doormat. By the end of the '58 season, expansion talk in baseball was heating up. With Ebbets Field and Polo Grounds sitting empty, and the fans of the Dodgers and Giants still bitter, the New York lawyer Bill Shea had been agitating for another team in New York. In this pursuit, he recruited the legendary baseball man Branch Rickey, in exile since leaving the Pirates in 1955.

Early in 1958, Lamar began considering the possibility of investing in a minor-league baseball team in Dallas, in hopes of bringing a major-league franchise to the city one day. That spring, he visited one of the best-known minor-league organizations in the country, the Denver Bears, owned by Bob Howsam, who in passing mentioned to Lamar his other passion—his as-yet fruitless attempts to bring pro football to Denver.

Football, of course, appealed to Lamar as well. By this time, the NFL was insinuating itself more thoroughly into the Dallas market. There were two games televised most weeks, both of them live. The more he watched pro football—and it had become a preoccupation, an all-day Sunday commitment of time—the more he became convinced that the NFL should bring a team back to his hometown. "It just seemed clear to me that a pro football team could really succeed in Dallas," he said, "because you had a 75,000-seat stadium and, well, it was just incomprehensible to me that a college team could draw well, and why wouldn't it translate to a pro team?"

In the summer of 1958, Lamar invited Don and Jan McIlhenny for a picnic, on the north side of White Rock Lake. McIlhenny had just finished his second pro season, and first in Green Bay, after a promising rookie campaign with the Detroit Lions. It wasn't unusual for the Hunts and McIlhennys to get together, but the venue was somewhat odd.

"Lamar went up there to the picnic," said McIlhenny, "and I don't want to say he subjected me to a grilling but he wanted to know everything there

was to know about professional football. I was one of the few guys that Lamar knew that was playing at the time. He sat there and asked me about the
coaches, the locker rooms, the pre-game schedule, the money that you got, if
you got any to play the exhibition games. Lamar wanted to know everything
like that; I mean he wanted to know about the trainers, how you travel, when
you went to California, what did you do—did you fly out there, did you stay
out there?—he wanted to know about that. And training camp, what you did
in training camp, how the rookies were treated, what did I think about the
hazing, who had hazing. He just wanted to know everything. He was really
interested, because he'd never gone to training camp. How do guys get cut?
Did you hit a lot? Did you scrimmage? All of it. And I said to Jan, driving
back in the car that night, 'What in the world was that all about?'"

Lamar was still undecided about whether he would want to buy a baseball
team or a football team when he called NFL Commissioner Bert Bell's office
in the summer of 1958 to inquire about an expansion franchise in the NFL.
Bell told him pretty much the same thing he'd told people in Seattle, Orange
County, Houston, Atlanta, New Orleans, and Minneapolis for years: "The NFL
won't be expanding any time soon. If you want a team, call the Wolfners."

The downtrodden Chicago Cardinals, once owned by the late Charley
Bidwill, by now belonged to his widow Violet and her new husband, St. Louis
businessman Walter Wolfner. For the Cardinals, whose business was on the
south side, in the shadow of George Halas and the more-celebrated Bears,
second-best was a way of life. While Bidwill had been among George Halas's
best friends, the relationship between Halas and the Wolfners was poisonous.
The irreparable split came in 1957, when the Cardinals had negotiated for
the rights to play at Northwestern's handsome Dyche Stadium, just north of
Chicago in Evanston. Halas nixed the deal, producing a twenty-eight-year-
old agreement—subsequently honored by Bell—which forbade the Bears to
play home games south of Madison Street, or the Cardinals to play home
games north of there. Walter Wolfner had vacillated for years among the
choices of selling his club, moving it elsewhere, or remaining in Chicago to
fight Halas and the Bears to the death.

That fall, Lamar called Wolfner and arranged a visit.

"My modus operandi would have been, 'I'll be in Chicago next week, and
I wondered if I could spend some time with you—I'd appreciate it—and I
had something I wanted to talk with you about football.' And he said, 'Fine,
I'd be happy to talk with you, what day would you get here?' And I said I
could make it any day, I could adjust."

Lamar could adjust, of course, because he had no reason to be in Chicago beyond wanting to speak with Wolfner. When Lamar visited the team offices in the fall of 1958, he was astonished at the dilapidated nature of a pro football team's headquarters. Located at 511 Plymouth Court, just off Printers Row, there was no sign on the front. "I remember it being fairly archaic," he said. "I don't mean that critically, obviously, but it wasn't a very affluent business then." Visitors walked into an old warehouse, and took an old elevator—with the movable wooden slats on the door—up to the threadbare Cardinals offices.

While young Lamar eventually got around to politely inquiring about the details of the franchise and the possibility of buying a stake in the Cardinals, Walter Wolfner focused on the actuarial tables. It seemed nearly an obsession for Wolfner. "Halas is way up there in years," he said. "He's liable to pass away any time soon." (As it transpired, Wolfner died in 1963; Halas died in 1985.) Over that meeting, and two more in the fall, Lamar proposed buying the team outright and moving it to Dallas and, after that was rebuffed, put forth a series of proposals that would give him a minority interest, with some prospect of buying a controlling interest later, provided he had the option to bring the team to Dallas.

"And they just said, 'No, we're not going to do that,'" Lamar remembered. "'Halas is going to die, and we just hired a new coach,' and, you know, there was always—they always had this glimmer of hope that they were going to win the battle of Chicago."

That battle was costing the NFL money. Since telecasts of NFL games were blacked out when either team was at home, and since the Cardinals or Bears were at home nearly every week, the lucrative Chicago TV market was nearly bereft of pro football on television. For that reason, Bell had been hoping for years that the Wolfners would sell their franchise or simply move themselves, to give the Cardinals a chance to succeed elsewhere and the Bears a chance to flourish. But efforts to get Wolfner to budge had been unsuccessful.

Lamar's early talks with the Wolfners were unproductive, and his reticence and frugality did not impress Violet Wolfner. "Lamar had more money than God," remembered Charley Bidwill's son, Stormy, who'd taken an active interest in the franchise from an early age and who along with his brother Bill would eventually inherit the franchise from his mother. "Well, the only thing that he ever spent that we could figure out was that he *might* have spent some money for his clothes. Otherwise, he never spent a nickel. My mother turned to me at one point and says, 'I don't understand—I've never seen a man so cheap.'"

Shortly after his first meeting with the Wolfners, Lamar began discussions in baseball with Amon Carter and J. W. Bateson, owners of the minor-league Dallas Rangers, and their general manager, Warner Lewis. The Rangers administrators were interested in the prospects of placing a Dallas team in the new Continental Baseball League, and spoke with Lamar about whether he would be interested. When news of the meeting leaked to the press, Lamar was, in his words, "horrified when I saw my name in the paper."

Branch Rickey had described a new baseball league as "inevitable" in May 1958, and joined forces with New York lawyer Bill Shea some months later for the Continental League, meant to be a third major league. Lamar and the other investors traveled to New York to hear Rickey speak late in 1958, and he would later recall Rickey being a "very convincing person, a very reasonable person—he wasn't a flamboyant salesman or anything like that." At the time, what stuck with Lamar was the elegance of Rickey's proposal for the teams in the league to divide television revenue equally, as a way to minimize income disparities between big-market and small-market clubs. "I remember clearly," Lamar said, "that Mr. Rickey preached the idea of equal sharing with television."

All of this was on his mind as he traveled to Houston with his friend Bob Wilkes right after Christmas of 1958, to watch SMU play in the Southwest Conference Holiday Basketball Tournament. There were no games on Sunday, so Lamar sat on the edge of the bed at the Shamrock Hilton, watching transfixed as the 1958 NFL Championship Game between the New York Giants and Baltimore Colts went into overtime. There was his old teammate, Raymond Berry, making a series of dazzling catches to help rally the Colts in regulation, and again as they marched down the field in overtime.

After seeing Alan Ameche plunge over for the game-winner to lift the Colts past the Giants in overtime, he sat on the hotel bed and realized that his mind, finally, had been made up.

"My interest emotionally was always more in football," he said. "But clearly the '58 Colts–Giants game, sort of in my mind, made me say, 'Well, that's it. This sport really has everything. And it televises well.' And who knew what that meant?"

Lamar went back to the Wolfners early in the new year and pursued negotiations further, though with no better success. In February 1959, he traveled one final time to discuss a deal, this time in Miami, where Wolfner spent his winters and owned a dog track. Lamar had offered the Wolfners a variety of options, each offering the prospect of the team moving to Dallas or Lamar eventually gaining a controlling interest. But by the time of his last visit,

Walter Wolfner seemed newly intent on staying in Chicago, and offering nothing more than a minority share.

"Do you know Bud Adams?" Wolfner asked Lamar at one point. He said he didn't, and Wolfner explained that Adams, an oil millionaire from Houston, had also been interested in acquiring the team. Others had approached him as well, he boasted, mentioning the potential ownership group in Minneapolis and Denver. But he wasn't selling; the team would stay in Chicago and would be controlled by the Wolfners.

Lamar shook Wolfner's hand and wished him the best of luck. Then he took a cab to the Miami airport for his American Airlines flight back to Dallas. Coming out of the meeting, and in the taxi on his way to the Miami airport, Lamar felt an unusual emotion—discouragement. "I realized that I wouldn't accomplish what I had in mind, of getting a team to Dallas," he said. "If I made the deal with the Wolfners, I'd be a minority stockholder of a team in Chicago that was not particularly well-run, and not doing well, and did not have much prospect it was going to do well—stuck on the south side, playing in Comiskey Park—and had a negative image."

On the American Airlines flight back to Dallas, he wound up in the very front seat on the right-hand side. The two-engine propeller plane took more than four hours to get from Miami to Dallas, and en route on that winter evening, Lamar glumly considered the fact that he was no closer to owning a football franchise than he'd been a year ago, when he'd first placed a call to Bert Bell.

"I thought to myself, I've had all these conversations with these people, and they're not going to do what I want them to do, they're not going to move to Dallas," he said. "But in the course of conversations, they had asked if I knew Bud Adams in Houston. They had asked if I knew Bob Howsam in Denver. 'Do you know Max Winter in Minneapolis?' And I did not, and anyway, over the course of these friendly conversations with them, they mentioned every one of these people and told me that each of them had gone the same path that I had, that they all wanted the Cardinals to move to their city. And so there it was—the light bulb came on—and I said, 'Why not go see *those* people and put together a new league?'"

Lamar had long had a habit of taking copious notes on whatever paper was available, and many of his brainstorms had been sketched out on the backs of envelopes or in the margins of magazines. But with this thundercrack of inspiration, he knew he needed more. He asked a stewardess for some stationery, and he hurriedly sketched out the plans on three sheets of onionskin writing paper with an American Airlines letterhead.

Under the heading "ORIGINAL 6; FIRST YEAR'S OPERATIONS," he began outlining the particulars of a prospective new league:

(1) 15-game schedule (3 have 8 at home, 3 have only 7)—play each team 3 times with clubs splitting net gate after visitors are paid for travel expenses.
(2) 3 exhibition games.
(3) Split net gate 60% to home–40% to visitor with visitors having a choice of 40% or $35,000, whichever is larger.

He next penned a college draft plan, granting each team territorial rights for one player, then conducting a thirty-round draft. Knowing that owners in Houston and Denver were already interested, and remembering how well Buffalo had supported its All-America Conference team, he included these cities while adding teams in the vital media markets of New York and Los Angeles along with, of course, Dallas.

Clubs shall draw for positions of draft and first 10 rounds shall be thus, i.e. (1) Los Angeles, (2) Denver, (3) Dallas, (4) Houston, (5) Buffalo, (6) New York, (7) New York, (8) Buffalo, (9) Houston, (10) Dallas, (11) Denver, (12) Los Angeles—each club getting two players. At the end of the 10th and 20th rounds, a fresh draw will redetermine the order of draw. At end of draft, each club shall have drafted 60 players.

He had looked at the Cardinals financial statements (the club had lost nearly $220,000 during the 1956 and 1957 seasons alone), and so he knew enough about the economics of football to come up with a prospective profit-and-loss statement for a hypothetical pro team.

Writing in short, neat printing strokes, he had finished his outline by the time the plane landed, drawing up provisions for owners, even making rough estimates on the costs of equipment and the revenue for ticket sales. He had even drawn up a rough schedule for the first season, going so far as to sketch out the likely weekends the regular season would begin and end.

He got into his car at the Love Field parking lot and drove home to Orchid Lane. And by the time he reached the driveway, this protracted bout of floundering helplessness had dissipated. For nearly three years, Lamar had cast about in the halls of Hunt Oil, taken trips in which he had no compelling interest, and gone through the motions of pursuing an oil career. Now, suddenly, he was energized. For the first time since he'd given up the dream of being the next Doak Walker, he had a sense of purpose.

And the landscape of American sports was about to change forever.

CHAPTER SIX

SURVEYING THE FIELD

When H. L. Hunt was considering a new financial venture, he would send a couple of assistants out in the field to do extensive research on the industry and its accompanying peculiarities, with orders that they weren't to return and report to H. L. until they felt they understood the business perfectly. Only then would he decide whether to pursue it.

But Lamar didn't have any assistants, so he would have to do the field research himself. He showed up at the Hunt Oil offices on Monday, February 16, 1959, and began collecting information systematically—and, consistent with his personality, as unobtrusively as possible. In the coming weeks, he began to look at the entire sports universe with fresh eyes. From his office, he accumulated background information on the prospects of virtually every large city in the United States. On a single sheet of legal paper, he spent weeks meticulously compiling a chart of the strengths and weaknesses of prospective cities, calling the Chamber of Commerce in dozens of big cities. His data on the forty-four potential markets, which ranged in size from New York, Los Angeles, and Chicago to Akron, South Bend, and Lubbock, included: a list of the stadium capacity of the stadium in each city, with a notation of whether it was owned by the public or a local college; the city's proximity to an existing pro team; a classification of whether the market was "virgin territory" (like Dallas and Houston), "semi-virgin territory" (San Diego), had an "existing pro team" (like Los Angeles and New York), or was in a "highly competitive" environment, usually with a college team (South Bend and Columbus); the expected effect of NFL television broadcasts on home games in the new market; population within a 50- and 100-mile radius; and Lamar's personal rating, ranging from E for excellent (Dallas, Houston, and several other cities) to P for poor, and any remarks on the rating. The first eight cities on Lamar's ledger were rated excellent, with one exception. By the entry on New Orleans, he noted the city's persistence of Jim Crow laws, and racial segregation in stadiums and arenas, describing the problem as "major." Other cities—including Memphis, Atlanta, and Little Rock—carried the same concern.

At the same time he was surveying possible cities for the new league, Lamar was also querying local business leaders to gauge their interest in supporting a new football team in Dallas. The week of March 11, the secretarial pool at Hunt Oil was particularly pressed, typing up 200 letters that Lamar sent out to presidents and CEOs in the community, with a three-page questionnaire. The correspondence to each business began with the note, "I have recently seen a copy of the Dallas–Fort Worth Bi-County Sports Committee Survey, pertaining to bringing Major League Baseball to the Dallas–Fort Worth area. While studying this report, I noted that you were one of the 200 business opinion leaders surveyed. As an aid to help me put together some loose-end ideas I have, I would like to impose on you for a personal survey, the questions of which follow."

The survey questions began with the caveat, "These questions refer to a professional football team, which would be a Dallas team and play its home games in the Cotton Bowl."

He opened with a loaded question: "Are you aware that plans are underway to form a new major professional football league with Dallas having a chance to be a member city?" There was no mention, there or elsewhere in the survey, that Lamar was the one planning to launch the new league, and that he would be the owner of the Dallas franchise.

With that decision came the corollary realizations. Lamar knew his days of gambling on football were over. He also needed to improve his public speaking skills. He realized that it would be a costly, improbable venture, but within weeks, he was imbued with an unshakeable belief that his idea was perfectly timed. If Major League Baseball, with sixteen franchises and slumping attendance, was in need of expansion—as Branch Rickey had so persuasively argued—then there was an even greater necessity for expansion in pro football, with just twelve franchises and rising attendance throughout the '50s.

At some point early on, he shared his plans with his friend Tom Richey. "We would spend long days, with maps on the floor of his home on Orchid Lane," Richey said. "Lamar would have all this information on different cities, and we would look at what would be the best cities. It felt like we did that for weeks."

The next step in Lamar's field research would be another call to NFL commissioner Bert Bell. Lamar phoned Bell on March 15, ostensibly to inquire again about the possibility of an expansion team for the NFL. The two men had spoken by phone the previous year, but it took some time for Bell to recall Hunt. When he did, Bell asked after Davey O'Brien, the TCU star of the '30s who had played for the Eagles when Bell coached the team, and for a time after his football career worked for H. L. Hunt. When Lamar brought up expansion, Bell reiterated that the league couldn't consider it until resolving the Cardinals situation, but added that the owners were not at all impressed with Dallas, because of the poor performance of the Texans in 1952, and that their first commitment was to the city of Buffalo. After Lamar pressed further for an appointment with the expansion committee, Bell suggested he call George Halas, then vacationing at the Arizona Biltmore in Phoenix. Lamar called Halas on March 18, but "Papa Bear" was no more accommodating. When Lamar suggested he wanted to visit Halas to "throw my hat in the ring," Halas dissuaded him and called it a waste of time, adding that "expansion is probably a long way off."

With that clear indication that the NFL was staying put, Lamar decided to move forward with his idea, and he began to seek out his potential partners for the new league.

His first prospect was Kenneth S. "Bud" Adams, also the son of a Texas oilman and much more in keeping with the traditional stereotype of Texas millionaires. Adams progressed from a burly youth who played football at Kansas to a heavyset adult best known for his distinctive flair in office decoration. In his subterranean office in downtown Houston, next to the tasteful displays of Native American art, Adams had a cage full of rare doves, a lily pond, and an indoor barbecue pit. He had been known as "Jabber" at his college prep school, and his Texas patois was at once cocksure and elusive, wholly unintelligible to some from the North. One of Adams's peers would later say, "To be honest it took me about two or three years to understand a single word of whatever the hell it was Bud was saying. He always seemed to be talking out the side of his mouth, not so much figuratively as literally."

Lamar and Adams had never met, but Bunker Hunt knew Adams from their time at Culver Military Academy. Lamar asked his older brother to call to see if Adams would have dinner with Lamar in Houston. Bunker called, relayed the invitation, and Adams said he would be glad to do so, then asked if Bunker knew what was on Lamar's mind. "I don't tell Lamar my business," Bunker explained. "And he doesn't tell me his business."

Lamar called the next day, polite but brief on the phone, asking Adams if he could meet his flight later that week at Houston Hobby Airport. On a balmy Texas evening in March 1959, Adams picked up Lamar in his Cadillac, and took him to the Charcoal Inn, a steakhouse he owned in Houston.

After some discussion about Bud's relationship with Bunker, Lamar and Bud spoke about their respective high school careers, the brilliance of Rice's Tommy Lewis, the best college games they'd seen, even their favorite uniforms. Lamar was cordial, but seemed slightly nervous to Adams, who wondered to himself about the younger man's agenda. After dinner, Adams drove Lamar back to Houston's Hobby Airport to catch his return flight to Dallas. As Adams pulled up to the airport terminal, Lamar finally confided the reason for his visit.

"You tried to buy the Chicago Cardinals, right?"

Adams, eyebrows raised—they hadn't discussed either man's pro football aspirations during the entire visit—allowed that he had.

"So did I," said Lamar. "I didn't have much luck—and you didn't either from what I understand." They shared a laugh about Walter Wolfner and his stubbornness. Then, grabbing the handle of his attaché case on the passenger floorboard, Lamar said, "Bud, I'm thinking of starting a new football league. If I do, would you be interested in owning a team?"

Adams' face brightened, and he replied, "Hell, yeah!"

Lamar explained he'd be in touch in the weeks ahead, the two men shook hands, and then he got out of his car and headed to his gate.

With that brief exchange, Lamar had set his course. Throughout the spring and into the summer, he continued collecting information, exchanging correspondence and building a dossier on the most attractive cities for a new league. Though the brothers shared equally in Penrod Drilling, they each spent the great majority of their time on their own deals—and Lamar was by far the least active brother in the daily running of the organization. When he disappeared for a game, or to explore a new city, no one asked. "No one noticed," said Hunt Oil landman Mack Rankin. "And if they had noticed, they wouldn't have cared."

•

In 1959, the headquarters of the National Football League were not in New York City. They were not even in Philadelphia, where they'd been located since 1946. Instead they were located across the street from the Philadelphia city limits, in the bucolic neighborhood of Bala-Cynwyd (pronounced ba-luh kin-wid). Reporters covering pro football in the 1950s often had exchanges like this when they phoned the NFL offices:

"Hello," a voice would say, "National Football League."

"Yes, I'd like to speak with Commissioner Bell, please."

"Speaking."

In the five-man office, with no secretary and no receptionist, Commissioner Bert Bell often answered the phones. Bell still bore vestiges of his old self, the playboy raconteur of the 1920s with slicked-back hair, by now silver, and an estimable paunch, neatly draped in blue serge suits during the fall and winter, and tan gabardine in the summer months. His voice was a thing of wonder, a deep, growling baritone that projected through office walls and over static-filled phone lines. Bell was a voluble man of motion, generally heard before seen. And since 1946, he'd been the one-man soul of pro football, championing the game to the public and to Congress, riding herd on the cantankerous and often divided owners, running the game with a concussive voice and near absolute authority.

On June 2, Lamar flew to Philadelphia for a lunch with Bell, and they went to one of Bell's favorite restaurants, the Tavern in Narberth, along with one of Bell's sons, Bert, Jr., and the Eagles' president Joe Donoghue. After plenty of small talk, Lamar finally mentioned that he was still interested in bringing an expansion franchise to Dallas. Again, Bell told him that the NFL wouldn't consider expansion until the league solved its "Chicago problem" and achieved a greater measure of competitive balance. "My dad told him they weren't ready for expansion," said Bert Bell, Jr. "He wanted the bottom teams to win three or four games, same amount of games, before they were ready for expansion."

After the meal, Bell called Lamar over to the corner of the restaurant and said, less vexed than perplexed, "What in the world did you come up here for? What in the world do you want?" Lamar steadfastly repeated his interest in expansion and Bell reiterated, "The owners are not interested in any kind of expansion, they have no expansion plans, and it's just a lost cause as far as Dallas is concerned." Then Bell added, "As far as I am concerned, I don't believe they will ever vote to expand."

Lamar by now had asked the NFL on three separate occasions about expansion and been told in no uncertain terms on three separate occasions that such a thing was impossible, at least in the foreseeable future. With that, he quickened his own pace and started touring the country to visit prospective owners he'd only corresponded with in the past. On June 20 and 21, he saw Bob Howsam in Denver and an ownership group in Minneapolis, headed by former Minneapolis Lakers owner Max Winter. Howsam's Denver Bears had increased the capacity of Mile High Stadium from 17,500 to 25,600, in hopes of attracting an NFL team. In Minneapolis–St. Paul, Winter and his partnership proved eager to join the venture. "We Folks here in Minnesota have been trying to get a franchise for some time," wrote Ole Haugsrud later, "but it seems as though the National League does not care to move or expand." As he went from city to city, meeting with investors, Lamar did not have a formal prospectus. "The only thing I had on paper was my football map of America," he said. "The NFL was concentrated in the north and east, with only two teams out of that area, in Los Angeles and San Francisco. To the NFL, having a team in Washington was having a team in the South."

Feeling he needed a franchise in Los Angeles and New York, Lamar began casting about for prospects in those cities. Through friend and former tennis star Gene Mako, he was introduced to Barron Hilton, son of hotel magnate Conrad Hilton, who agreed to consider a Los Angeles franchise.

But New York still beckoned. It seemed clear that any new league that was to be taken seriously needed a franchise in New York. In his meetings with Branch Rickey to discuss the Continental League the previous fall, Lamar had also been introduced to Bill Shea, the lawyer (and onetime owner, in the '40s, of the NFL's Boston Yanks) who had teamed up with Rickey to launch the league. In late June, Lamar invited Shea to dinner.

Lamar's friend Tom Richey had just been transferred from Dallas to the home office of *Life* magazine, in the Rockefeller Center in New York. La-mar called him that morning, and invited him to come along. "I recall the real purpose of the meeting was twofold," said Richey. "To see what obstacles Shea was having starting the new baseball league and to see if it was feasible to start a football franchise in New York. Another purpose was to see if Bill Shea would like to be a principal owner or could he recommend ownership."

They met at the fabled 21, on West 52nd Street, and Shea arrived in a blue suit, with a white shirt and a silver tie. Lamar spent much of the dinner in his usual mode of polite, persistent inquiry, asking Shea about his own difficul-ties, budgets, venues, and the challenges that might be faced in promoting a team in a city as large as New York.

The dinner started cordially, with Shea bringing Lamar and Tom up to date on his own efforts with the Continental League. But then Lamar shared that he was contemplating starting a football league of his own, and inquired if Shea would have any interest in owning the New York franchise. Shea most certainly did not. At that point, in Richey's memory, the tone of the eve-ning soured. "Shea was adamant that a new football league was too tough a venture with too many factions involved," said Richey, who viewed Shea's tone the rest of the meal as being one of "guarded condescension." When

Lamar asked if he could think of any possible New York owners, Shea half-heartedly mentioned the ebullient national broadcaster Harry Wismer, a small minority partner in the Detroit Lions, as someone who might enjoy the attention and challenge of a new franchise in a new league. But Shea emphasized that the venture was fraught, and implied strongly that if Shea himself—with all his experience and connections—was struggling to start a new baseball league, the callow novice Lamar would never get a new football league launched. At the end of dinner, after Lamar thanked Shea for his time and they parted, Lamar and Tom walked together up Fifth Avenue toward the southeast corner of Central Park.

Lamar was in an unusually reflective and talkative mood, and close to midnight, he and Tom sat down on a park bench just inside Central Park and began discussing the situation. They rambled around topics old and new, touching on the challenge that Lamar faced, their days at The Hill, the times when they would visit each other before football seasons. Hours later, they were still there on the bench, reflecting on the challenges of going forward. At that point, Tom reminded Lamar of his words in the night during their preseason training in 1949: that no matter what he did with his life, he would always be H. L. Hunt's son.

Richey was emboldened—he knew his friend well enough to press him in the way many others didn't, and at one point he proclaimed "Lamar, if you don't follow through with this decision and make a name for yourself— 'cause this is your big chance to be your own man—I'm not sure I *want* to be your friend!"

It was a dare more than an ultimatum, and Lamar understood it as such. He also understood, at least in theory, if he went ahead and launched the league, his life would change in ways that he couldn't begin to grasp. At the meal, Shea had alluded to his hectic schedule drumming up support for the Continental League. Lamar already sensed the strain in his marriage to Rose Mary, as his travel had increased to drum up support for the football venture, and she'd grown more anxious and homebound.

By the time they got up from the park bench, it was past the middle of the night in New York City. The first hint of dawn was appearing over the Hudson to the East. Lamar stood up and said, quietly but firmly, "I'm going to do it. I'm going to give it everything I've got." He said goodbye to Richey, who caught a bus to his apartment on Second Avenue, and he walked alone to his midtown Manhattan hotel. For nearly six months, he'd been flirting with the idea. He was now, despite Shea's stern warning, ready to go through with it.

Lamar's next step would be characteristic of the reticence that would later be seen, by his detractors, as a sign of deviousness, and by his friends as proof of his modest demeanor and methodical business style. Lamar himself would later admit, "I possibly have an indirect way of finding things out." Intent on moving forward, but still not ready to make any announcements, Lamar instead went back to Bert Bell, this time through an emissary. He called up Davey O'Brien; the former TCU star was a staunch businessman, longtime FBI agent, friend of H. L.'s, and a Dallas legend. Lamar asked O'Brien if he could hire him to travel to Philadelphia and make a request on his behalf. He wanted O'Brien to tell Bell that a group of investors was going to launch a new football league, and to ask Bell if he would agree to be the commissioner of the new league. "I was at least intelligent enough to know that I did not want to start a war," Lamar would say later.

O'Brien was instructed not to name anyone involved, not even Lamar. Before he left for Philadelphia, Lamar gave him a typewritten summary of talking points, including the directive, "Give position as a representative of a group which has formed to make a 2nd league. From the start indicate that your position is one of a non-associated party who is acting whatever way you wish to describe." Lamar also noted, "Point out that they are a group which is not going into this thing out of any vision of financial gain, but rather out of a love of football; however, they are not going into it on a charity basis." In outlining the broad contours of the new league's proposed structure, he added "Two divisions—with the winners meeting in a championship game. After several years of building their player strength, they feel it would be a natural for their champion to meet the NFL champion for an overall championship."

The outcome of the mission was predictable. O'Brien visited and was greeted warmly by his old coach, but Bell declined the offer to be the commissioner of the new league, though he wished them luck and, as O'Brien was leaving, added, "Incidentally, tell that young friend of yours in Dallas that he can come to me for advice any time."

Lamar was at Love Field, waiting for O'Brien when his flight returned. "He told me about the meeting he had with Bert Bell, and that he was representing a group of people in Texas," Lamar said. "And, in fact, Davey O'Brien wouldn't have known who the other people were because I was very close-mouthed. I didn't tell him I'd gone to see Bud Adams, but I told him there was a group. I guess that in my own mind, you know, this will be good to at least see what kind of reaction we'll get, and I was naïve enough to think that in baseball there were two leagues and one commissioner, so why shouldn't there be in football? And he told Davey, who was a dear friend, that it just wasn't practical for him to do."

It seemed as though the visit accomplished little, but its immense importance became clear a few weeks later, on July 26, when Bell himself phoned O'Brien and explained that he was due to testify before Congress, part of the NFL's long and as-yet fruitless efforts to gain legislation that would provide the sport with the same antitrust exemptions as baseball. The Subcommittee on Anti-Trust Monopoly, part of the Judiciary Committee in the U.S. Senate, was sure to ask him about expansion, Bell explained. He wanted O'Brien to ask Lamar if it might be okay to mention the proposed new league.

"And I thought about it," said Lamar, "and never dreamed how positive it would be, but it seemed like it could be a very positive thing. So I told Davey, 'Yes, he can mention this.' And I wasn't going to ask anybody—Bud Adams didn't know Bob Howsam existed, Howsam didn't know any of the others existed. So I said, 'Yep, okay, you have my permission.'" Even then, Lamar had O'Brien instruct Bell not to mention any names at all.

So on July 28, while Bell amused a subcommittee with his free-flowing dissertation on the state of pro football, Lamar sat silently in the back of Room 318 of the Senate office building, listening. As Lamar would later put it, "I sat in the back and got to hear the actual birth of the American Football League, as told by Bert Bell."

He couldn't have asked for a better salesman.

"The more football there is and the more advertisement of pro football, the better off we are," Bell told the committee. "We are in favor of the new league." He added that he considered the years of the NFL's rancorous war with the All-American Football Conference in the late '40s as "a great thing for pro football. Every newspaper was arguing who was the best and they would keep it in the papers." Michigan Senator Philip Hart interrupted Bell to point out that many of the owners didn't consider the AAFC's challenge a great thing for the sport at the time. "I know," Bell replied. "But I can't help what the owners think. I know what it did. I will tell you this is great and I have talked it over with every owner and not one of them has an objection to it, not one of them." (In fact, Bell hadn't spoken to any of the other NFL owners about the new league before speaking to Congress, but he did call George Halas the day after the speech, telling him that he thought the league was nebulous and might never get off the ground.)

That same evening after Bell's testimony, Lamar and O'Brien visited the Commissioner at Bell's summer home in Margate, New Jersey, arriving after 10 o'clock and sitting for a wide-ranging discussion until almost 2 in the morning. Bell was jovial and helpful, repeated that he was too busy with other things to entertain the thought of running a new league, but peppered Lamar with helpful advice. He pointedly urged the new league to go with eight teams in the first season, rather than six, on the grounds that eight was necessary for scheduling purposes, and it also allowed a league to plausibly split into two divisions, bringing about a useful rationale for a championship game at the end of the season. "All of you will enjoy this," Bell told Hunt at one point, "and all of the owners will get to become good friends down through the years. However, there is one thing that will separate you: when you start to fight over players." Lamar thanked him for advice and promised to stay in touch.

"I really liked Bert Bell," he said. "I really thought we could all get along." He would later characterize this opinion as "one of the more naïve thoughts in the history of American sports."

After returning to Dallas, Lamar called Bud Adams, who was ebullient, praising the Bell announcement as "great publicity."

"Bud, I think it's probably time for us to announce this. Would you mind if I came down to Houston—would you step forward with me?"

Adams enthusiastically agreed, and Lamar suggested they make the announcement the following Monday morning, August 3. His reasons were clear in his own mind: "'Cause I didn't want to be the only guy, the only idiot in the world identified with this thing, so I flew down and Bud and I had the press conference."

On the day after his twenty-seventh birthday, Lamar joined Adams in Adams's Houston office to announce the start of the American Football League. He was unusually nervous at the announcement, prompting one writer covering the event to whisper to a colleague, "Wait 'til Papa Bear gets ahold of this guy—he's going to eat him alive."

But now Lamar was in it, and there was nothing to do but move forward.

•

The news hit suddenly around the country. Up until Bell's announcement, Lamar hadn't even mentioned the names of the other investors to any of his potential partners.

In addition to Lamar in Dallas, Adams in Houston, Howsam's group in Denver, the ownership group in Minneapolis–St. Paul, Lamar soon met with the announcer Harry Wismer in New York, who was enthusiastic about joining.

In Los Angeles, Barron Hilton had been receptive after Mako introduced him to Lamar. The younger Hilton had grown up around football (after his father and mother divorced, his mother had been remarried to Mack Saxon, the longtime coach at Texas School of Mines), and as a teenager sat on the bench for some of Saxon's games. Lamar first met with Hilton at the offices of the new Carte Blanche credit card company in the summer of '59, and they hit it off. "He immediately struck me a dignified and honorable man, with an affable manner," said Hilton. "During our meeting, I could sense Lamar's determination." Within weeks, Hilton signed on to own the new league's Los Angeles franchise.

Lamar's office, where previously months had gone by without the presence of any outside visitors, was suddenly a beehive of activity. There was plenty of talk about the venture around the building, but no word from H. L. Hunt. "My dad would never tell me *not* to do something," said Lamar. "But I knew he thought I was crazy, because he made a particular point of offering me the advice of others."

H. L. finally summoned Lamar to his office and asked him to sit down. The elder Hunt explained that he was going to place a call to Jim Breuil, a business associate who had, in the '40s, owned an interest in the Buffalo franchise in the All-America Football Conference. H. L. knew about the financial troubles of the AAFC and was undoubtedly hoping that Breuil could provide a dose of reality for his son.

When they got on the phone together, Breuil did confirm that he'd lost money in the venture, but he also was very enthusiastic. "You'll have a great time," he said to Lamar, as H. L. sat behind his desk, frowning.

"I don't think my father was expecting that," said Lamar later.

H. L. was not the only one with doubts about the pro game. Al Hill, as well, looked down on the professional game. "My dad did not like pro football," said Al Hill, Jr. "He loved college football; he thought it was honest, hearty, and healthy. But dad thought that players in the pros were a bunch of thugs."

H. L. drafted one of his assistants, George Cunyus, to "go out and help Lamar, and get him out of it if you can, but if not, keep him out of trouble." Cunyus would report back to H. L. that Lamar's dedication to the start-up was unswerving, but he did help Lamar by drafting the new league's constitution, bylaws, and player contracts.

If much of the family thought Lamar was wasting his time and money, at least Bunker Hunt was excited. The week after the announcement, he walked into Lamar's office and said, "Hey, Lamar, I'd like to invest in your team."

"Oh, thank you," said Lamar. "But I prefer to go this one alone."

Bunker looked quizzically at his brother for a moment, shrugged his shoulders, and said, "Okay." And then he left.

It was a rare moment when Lamar asserted himself with one of his older brothers. "If it was going to bust, I didn't want to be saddled by having led somebody down a path," Lamar said, "and I just felt like it was my baby, and if it was going to fail, I wanted it to fail. I'm not averse to having partners at all, but that was one I felt it was the thing to do, to just stay with the 100% ownership."

("Not that it mattered," said one friend. "Bunker would tell Lamar what to do all the time anyway. Bunker *acted* like he owned part of the team.")

Preoccupied with his vision of the new league as part of a tandem—"like the American League and National League in baseball"—Lamar wanted to call the new league the American Football League. There had been other, aborted AFLs in the past, but none made enough of a dent on the American sports fans' consciousness to pose a problem. Lamar tried out the idea on Harry Wismer, who was instantly effusive. "That's great!" he said. "Let's go with it! That's fantastic, kid. Congratulations!"

Wismer was equally enthusiastic about Lamar's idea to adopt Branch Rickey's revenue-sharing plan from the Continental League. In doing this, the new league established a bedrock principle that would, in time, change the way American sports leagues did business.

"Harry was the guy, theoretically, who had the most to lose," said Lamar. "Not that anybody had anything to lose at that point, 'cause we weren't—we really didn't have a league yet, they hadn't committed. But everybody else said, 'It's all right.' Minneapolis and Dallas and Houston, they all would have shared, but when it came to the bigger cities, I remember that Harry very clearly accepted that."

Little else was decided at that point. The first meeting of the new league was held August 14, 1959, in the Imperial South Suite on the twentieth floor of the Chicago Hilton. For most of the men, it was the first time they'd ever met. There were only six franchises—Dallas, Houston, Denver, Minneapolis–St. Paul, Los Angeles, and New York. They were all sportsmen in the classic sense of being wealthy fanatics, and they adjourned early so all in attendance could make it to Soldier's Field to watch the College All-Star Game. A week later, they met again in Los Angeles, at the Beverly Hilton, and there, the league officially voted to call itself the American Football League.

Though Lamar had originally thought he'd have to go through the first year with six teams, it quickly became apparent that there was enough interest to field eight. Willard Rhodes, a grocery executive from the Pacific Northwest, had contacted him about placing a franchise in Seattle. Ralph Wilson, an insurance salesman in Detroit, called Lamar after reading about the new league in the *New York Times*; he was interested in bringing a franchise to Miami.

Both men were stymied by stadium problems. Lamar had known that venues would be important, but he hadn't anticipated how much of an impediment colleges would be. In both cities, the universities that occupied the stadiums—the University of Washington in Seattle and the University of Miami—were determined not to let pro teams play.

"We didn't have places like New Orleans available to us," said Lamar. "Because that was Tulane Stadium, and it was a college stadium, and they didn't want a pro team there. We were told that you couldn't get into the Orange Bowl in Miami, even though it was a city-owned stadium. Atlanta had no stadium, but there was a group that came forward, and they were willing, but we couldn't get into Georgia Tech, and they were willing to try to put a tinker-toy stadium together, and we danced around them."

A minority partner in the Detroit Lions who'd built his Sundays around football games, whether watching the Lions at Tiger Stadium, or joining his friends and family in front of the TV when the team was out of town, Wilson visited Lamar in Dallas and came away impressed. "He wasn't a man that had to have gala things," said Wilson. "He had a very small office, and he showed us around. At that time, the Hunt family was probably the richest family in the world." Though all efforts to get a team in Miami were stymied, Lamar was impressed with Wilson. "There was a genuineness to Ralph," he once said. "You didn't have a feeling there was any con in him at all. You felt like this was a first-class guy."

Rhodes would eventually drop out, the Seattle stadium situation proving intractable. But Lamar was keen to keep Wilson in the league and, later in the fall, encouraged him to consider Buffalo. After a meeting with civic leaders, Wilson signed on. That made for seven solid franchises, and the future looked hopeful.

All that changed on Saturday afternoon, August 29. Lamar was cutting the hedges outside the house at Orchid Lane, when Rose Mary came to the front door and told them there was an Associated Press reporter calling for him. When Lamar got on the phone, he got the gist of the news of the day: At a press conference before the Steelers–Bears preseason game in Houston, George Halas and Art Rooney had announced that the NFL would be expanding, and the cities the NFL was targeting would be Dallas and Houston, with plans to award franchises the following January and begin competition in 1961 (the timetable was later moved up to 1960 for the Dallas franchise, so it could start at the same time and in direct competition with Lamar's AFL entry).

The man in line for the Dallas NFL franchise was Clint Murchison, Jr., like Lamar, a son of an oil millionaire. The diminutive, sharp-tongued Murchison had played football in high school, then went to college at Duke and later graduated from MIT with a master's in mechanical engineering.

When greeted with the news that afternoon, Lamar remained outwardly calm, asking the reporter if he could have a few minutes to compose a reply. After writing out a statement while sitting on his bed, he phoned back and read his response. "Everybody has been knocking on their door for years and they've turned everybody down. It is obvious what they are trying to do, and it can get them into trouble . . . They're trying to knock out Dallas and Houston, but this doesn't change our plans at all and we're moving ahead. We'll be adding our seventh and eighth teams this fall."

He then got off the phone and sat down on the couch, visibly shaken. "He was just stunned," said Rose Mary. "Crushed. But he came right back and it made him all the more determined. Every time he'd get a little bit down, he'd get more involved, and become a better speaker, and work harder."

Lamar called Bell the following Monday, but the Commissioner protested that the matter was largely out of his hands. "What can I do?" Bell said. "They want to expand. How can I stop them?" Bell remained reassuring both privately (he sent Bud Adams a copy of the NFL bylaws, to help the AFL construct its constitution) and in public. "There are plenty of players," he told a reporter in September. "There are 250 kids graduating from college every year with pro football ability. We keep about five per team, a total of sixty. That leaves 190 unemployed in football."

But with the prospect of the NFL coming into the AFL's two anchor cities, many more observers thought that Lamar's quest had gone from daring to foolhardy. To some, continuing with the new league seemed pointless if the NFL were coming to those cities anyway. "If Adams and Lamar Hunt insist on war, then they themselves and the cities they represent will be the losers," wrote the *Houston Post's* Jack Gallagher the week after the Halas and Rooney announcement. "From here it would appear that the wisest move the AFL can make at this time is to disband."

•

Even as the announcement by Rooney and Halas indicated that the NFL was hoping to smother the new league before it could start, the older league kept sending emissaries to informally negotiate a truce that would have instantly brought Lamar and Adams what they'd wanted in the first place: franchises in the NFL.

In September, the Rams' co-owner Ed Pauley, Jr., had invited Lamar and Barron Hilton to a private meeting at the Beverly Hilton. "Mr. Pauley's pitch seemed to be centered around telling us how sure the American Football League was to fail," said Lamar, "and how I would end up supporting all the teams, and that he and his dad felt it could be worked out so that Bud Adams and I could get an NFL franchise. In fact, they were convinced then that I was supporting all the teams. It was just an ad-lib. Everybody was being their own commissioner, everybody had their own idea. But he was primarily pointing out that Bud Adams and I could get a franchise in Dallas and Houston and they would take Barron into the Rams ownership and the American Football League would fold up its tent." But Lamar was steadfast, saying he'd already given his word to his fellow AFL owners and couldn't renege on them.

Then, on October 11, while attending an Eagles–Steelers game, Bert Bell died of a massive heart attack. His death left a vacuum at the center of the NFL. The prospect of the AFL had made conditions highly unstable within the universe of pro football. Now, it seemed, the back-channel offers only increased.

There were numerous informal gambits from NFL owners, secret offers to take in Lamar, or Lamar and Adams, or even those two and two other franchises. One phone call came from George Halas himself. Lamar asked the Hunt Oil landman Mack Rankin to come in and listen to the call on his speakerphone, so he'd have a witness. Politely explaining to Halas that he couldn't accept the offer of an expansion franchise now, Lamar then weathered a full-blown Halas harangue: "Do you know how much goddamn money this is going to cost us?!," the Bears' owner demanded, before cursing Lamar for his stubbornness.

The talks were revived again in late October, when the NFL's expansion plans in Houston were hurt by Rice University's announcement that it wouldn't allow its stadium to be used by any pro teams.

But Lamar was steadfast, and by mid-November, he had lined up the AFL's eighth franchise. The team would be placed in Boston, with an ownership group led by Billy Sullivan, a former Notre Dame football publicity director. Sullivan joined just in time to attend the league meeting in Minneapolis the weekend of November 21–22 for the first AFL draft. "I talked to Billy Sullivan maybe five times, maybe seven times over a several-week period," said Lamar. "And he was a charming, loquacious guy—this was all on the telephone. Bill was not a guy that had any money to speak of, although he was a president of a fuel oil supply company. But he was a great talker, and he convinced me that he could put together a ten-person group and they put up this $25,000 check, and they would be at our draft meeting, in late November."

It was to be a big event: The Chicago Cardinals had agreed to play two of their home games in 1959 in Minneapolis, and that Sunday was to be the second one. Since Minneapolis was one of the AFL's flagship cities, the new league's owners planned to upstage the NFL's presence with their own meeting and a series of announcements coming from their first college draft.

That Sunday evening, on the eve of the draft, as the owners sat in a banquet room at the Cedric Adams Hotel waiting to begin their regularly scheduled evening meeting, Harry Wismer burst in the door, visibly agitated, carrying a newspaper under his arm. Someone asked Wismer if he was ready for dinner.

"Yes!" he shouted, slamming the paper on the conference table. "And this is the last supper!" Pointing to Max Winter of the Minneapolis group, he added, "And he's Judas!"

In this instance, the flighty Wismer's outrage seemed justified. The headline of the next day's edition of the *Minneapolis Star-Tribune* read "MINNESOTA TO GET NFL FRANCHISE" and detailed the secret negotiations by Halas of convincing the Minneapolis group to bolt the AFL in favor of the NFL.

While Max Winter fumbled for a response to Wismer's rant, Lamar gathered his bearings and tried to survey the damage done. While the Minneapolis group had not been the very first to join the new league, they were considered a crucial franchise in the upper Midwest and had played a vital role in the league's early formation, and their apparent abdication to the NFL, expertly engineered behind the scenes by Halas, was a major blow to the AFL, and a victory for the older league, which seemed likely to approve expansion to Dallas and Minneapolis–St. Paul at its annual meetings in January.

The Minnesota franchise went ahead and participated in the first AFL draft the next day, though it was a draft more in name than in fact. Concerned that some franchises would have a heavy advantage over others if the draft were conducted by normal means, the league went instead to a thirty-three-round blind draw. "And the theory was," said Lamar, "we recognized it would be terribly unfair if some teams had a huge advantage in scouting. After all, Billy Sullivan and Boston had only been in the league for about three days. We didn't want to get off to a start where it was that unbalanced."

Each team was granted a "territorial selection," a chance to designate the one college player they most wanted to have a shot at signing (Dallas's was the SMU quarterback Don Meredith; Houston took LSU's Heisman winner Billy Cannon). Then, for the rest of the draft, the three of the league's personnel men (some teams hadn't even gotten around to hiring scouts yet) put together a list of the best seniors at each position in the country, and separated them into groups of eight. For each flight of eight quarterbacks and centers, the owner of each team would reach into an envelope and grab a name.

It would be more than a month before the Minneapolis franchise formally withdrew its membership, pledging its allegiance for the rest of the year, at least publicly, to the AFL.

A week later, Lamar traveled to Chicago to sign Joe Foss, the legendary World War II flying ace, to be the AFL's first commissioner. Foss, the former governor of South Dakota, had attended just two pro football games in his life, but he retained a high profile, boundless energy, and the willingness to talk enthusiastically and at length about the prospects of the new league.

Foss agreed to move down to Dallas, where the league offices were located, though he also maintained his residence in South Dakota. "He was kind of a transient person," said Lamar. "He just flew everywhere."

Lamar dispatched the Hunt Oil accountant Jack Steadman to set up the AFL office and books of accounting, in a small, three-room office in the Southland building in downtown Dallas. Foss brought his secretary, Maxine Eisenberg, from South Dakota. The league hired Milt Woodard, an executive of the Western Golf Association, as the league president; Foss's friend Thurlo McCrady, a former coach, as the director of officials; and Dallas sportswriter Al Ward as the league's publicity man.

As the new year dawned—with Lamar and Rose Mary joining the rest of the Hunts for Lamar's twenty-second straight Cotton Bowl game, watching Ernie Davis leading the national champion Syracuse team past Texas, 23–14, someone in the group pointed out to Lamar that some of these players might be playing for his team the following fall.

After that respite, the parade of seemingly endless details continued. The Minnesota group finally conceded the obvious—they had sided with the NFL—and they dropped out, leaving the AFL with an urgent problem, since the new league now needed an eighth team.

With Foss in tow, the AFL established its official football, choosing Wilson rival Spalding, to be the manufacturer. The company introduced the new

"JV-5," which was a quarter-inch longer and a quarter-inch narrower than the official NFL game ball, making it easier to pass, though that was not the main rationale. "Spalding was going to give us the balls for free, so we didn't care about if it was an eighth of an inch longer," said Lamar.

At one meeting, someone mentioned Bill Veeck's innovation of putting player's names on the backs of their jerseys, and that was approved as well. The most debate came over whether the AFL should adapt college football's new option of running or passing for two points rather than kicking one on the conversion following the touchdown. Lamar was originally opposed.

"I didn't think we should do anything different than what the NFL did," he said. "I didn't want us to have five downs, or have it be fifteen yards for a first down, not that anybody suggested that, but Canadian football had three downs and the one-point rouge. So I was opposed to it, and the vote was 4–3. And now you say, 'Why was it 4–3?' Well, we only had seven teams at the time. We had lost Minnesota, and were still looking for Oakland, but now we're in January 1960, and we were still making up rules and things like that."

It would be two more months before the AFL would find an eighth franchise, and the choice of Oakland was one of necessity, since Los Angeles owner Barron Hilton was threatening to drop out if he didn't have a natural geographic rival on the West Coast.

"He was out there all alone in Los Angeles," said Lamar. "And it suddenly dawned on him, 'Wow, we've got to have a rivalry.' The biggest rivalry in football, attendance-wise, was the Rams and 49ers; they drew huge crowds, of 100,000 or more to watch those games. So we focused on Oakland, which obviously had no stadium to play in, and an ownership group put together including Oakland and San Francisco people, over Atlanta. But Atlanta didn't really have a stadium either. It was kind of a hollow contest."

The Oakland ownership group was led by Chet Soda, an ebullient Oakland businessman fond of calling everyone he met "Señor." At the press conference announcing the new team, Soda showed up with a beatific smile and distributed sombreros to many in the press corps, before announcing that the winner of the name-the-team contest was "the Oakland Señors." This prompted perhaps the most animated public display shown toward the team all year, as the nickname was roundly panned. Within a few weeks, the club relented, opting for the nickname the Raiders instead.

In late January, the NFL held a torturously long annual meeting in Miami Beach, stuck in a seven-day deadlock in its quest to name a new commissioner. The league finally settled on an unlikely and little-known compromise choice, Pete Rozelle, the thirty-three-year-old general manager of the Los Angeles Rams. Lamar had met Rozelle in passing at his meeting with Ed Pauley the previous fall. Though Rozelle was more polished, the two men had developed an affinity, as both were by far the youngest men in their respective circles. At the end of that meeting, the inevitable occurred: An expansion franchise for Dallas was awarded to Clint Murchison, Jr.—which would begin play in 1960, rather than '61—and another was awarded to the Minneapolis–St. Paul group that had defected from the AFL.

It was difficult to know, even in retrospect, what convinced Lamar to persevere through that year from the summer of 1959 through the summer of 1960. His most trusted elders, his father and Al Hill, both doubted his judgment and the venture in its entirety. George Halas, a man whose exploits he'd grown up listening to and rooting for in his library in Mount Vernon, had rebuffed him, ignored him, then attempted to induce him into taking what he'd wanted all along, cursed him when refused to do so, and then questioned his motives after the fact. His upstart venture had seemed doomed on a number of occasions; yet after standing firm with his new partners throughout much of 1959, one of his closest allies—the Minneapolis group—betrayed him, throwing the entire venture into doubt. And through it all, Lamar Hunt stood there, undaunted, holding tenaciously onto his dream.

At one point that long fall, he was asked by a newspaper reporter if the business was more personal to him because he'd started the league.

"I can't separate what part of pro football is business and what part is personal with me," he said. "I just know that it is very important that I succeed."

CHAPTER SEVEN

"GO TEXAN!— GO AMERICAN!"

In early October 1959, Lamar received a postcard from Rome, with an aerial view of the crumbling grandeur of the Colosseum, and the note, "Have just contacted local authorities and it may be available for 1960 season. Let me know if you want to put a team here and I will make formal request. Bunker."

Lamar was spending less time at home and more time traveling, trying to manage the wide-ranging responsibilities involved in forming a new league. But by November he realized he needed to concentrate on his own team.

His first priority was a proper name. That month he called Giles Miller, the man who had been a co-owner of the doomed Dallas Texans who'd played in the Cotton Bowl for part of 1952 before being taken over by the NFL.

"I told him I was considering a team name," said Lamar. "And I really liked the word 'Texans' because it was descriptive of where the team played and there was some history to it. I asked him if he would have any objection to our using the name, in terms of copyright or anything like that. And he said, 'Heck no! I've been having nightmares about that name for seven years, and I'll be happy to get it off my back.'"

So the franchise had a name. At a league meeting later that fall, the issue of team colors came up. "I had my heart set on Columbia blue," said Lamar. "It was my favorite color. And in one of the earlier meetings, we didn't have much to do or think about, and someone said, 'Well, we've got 15 minutes before lunch; why don't we decide team colors?' And I said, 'Okay, good.' And Bud Adams said, 'Okay, I'll speak first—I'd like Columbia blue as my principal color.' And my jaw almost hit the floor." Lamar settled on red and gold, a combination he had always liked, and soon set out to find a head coach.

His first few stops were in Norman, Oklahoma, to woo the legendary Oklahoma coach Bud Wilkinson, who'd already won three national championships and was, at the time, the most respected college coach in the country. Wilkinson had been courted by the pros before, but he recognized Lamar's wealth and enjoyed the young man's respectful manners. Lamar had brought Rose Mary up to visit at one point in the fall, further ingratiating himself with Wilkinson.

Lamar offered Wilkinson more than he was making at Oklahoma, but after weeks of talk, the coach balked, sending a telegram to Lamar at the Desert Inn in Las Vegas: "TRIED TO PHONE. DEPTH OF OBLIGATION TOO GREAT TO BREAK AWAY. AM GRATEFUL FOR YOUR CONSIDERATION AND TRUST YOU UNDERSTAND LETTER FOLLOWS BUD."

On October 30, Lamar flew to New York to talk to Tom Landry, the cerebral assistant for the New York Giants, on a weekend the Giants were home, about to stifle the Green Bay Packers, 20–3. The interview didn't go well— Landry was even more reticent than Lamar, and was skeptical of the new league. Additionally, he had already been contacted by Clint Murchison, intent on hiring Landry for Dallas's pending NFL franchise.

A week later, Lamar visited Wilkinson one last time, before finally accepting the coach's definitive no. Flying back from Norman, in the private plane with his friend Bob Wilkes, Lamar admitted that he "didn't have a clue" now whom he could hire to be his coach. Wilkes brought up Hank Stram, the well-regarded college assistant who'd worked at Notre Dame, Purdue, and SMU in the '50s, before moving onto Miami.

Lamar had only met Stram once—in the locker room at SMU, after a Mustang win in 1956—but had heard from others at the school about Stram's reputation as a bright, innovative thinker. Stram was a plump, prideful, chattering man, a dandy bantam with a prematurely balding pate who had inherited from his father a haberdasher's attention to detail; he never left home without seeing that his shoes were shined, often sporting one of the hundred or so suits in his closet. Behind the style, the self-regard, and bluster, Stram had demonstrated an uncommon mastery of the technical details of football. The two hit it off almost immediately, a perfectly mismatched pair.

After the initial meeting in Miami in November, Lamar called Stram in December and flew him to Dallas to offer him the job. Stram took a cab downtown from Love Field to meet with Lamar in his offices at the Mercantile Bank Building. Late that afternoon, as Lamar was preparing to drive Stram back to the airport, he first needed to make two more calls before they left. He asked Stram if he would go over to a nearby parking lot and pick up his car, so they could head to Love Field as soon as possible. It was parked several blocks away (the parking lot was both less expensive than the lots closer to the building and offered the added benefit, as Lamar saw it, of exercise walking to and from). When Stram went to pick up the car, he was shocked to find, rather than a Rolls or a Cadillac, Lamar's eight-year old Oldsmobile 88, with a dent on the outside and the same hole in the seat cushion that for years had caused Rose Mary such embarrassment. On Stram's way out of the lot, the parking-lot attendant yelled to him, "Don't forget to tell Mr. Hunt that I still want to buy his car!"

By the fall of 1959, the city of Dallas was mobilizing for the war between the leagues, the teams, and, not incidentally, the two best-known oil families in the community. Among the press, both Hunt and Murchison were well liked, though they cut far different public figures. While Lamar was sincere and polite, Murchison evinced a sharp, wizened wit. A writer for *Sports Illustrated* asked what he thought of the perception that the NFL's heavy-handed tactics made Lamar and the AFL the underdog. "I'll be damned," Murchison said. "You're the first person I ever heard call a Hunt an underdog!"

"There was an immediate contrast between them," said Gary Cartwright, who covered the Texans for the *Dallas Times-Herald.* "They're the sons of the two richest guys in Texas, and one—Clint—is so outgoing and urbane, while Lamar looks and acts like the guy next door."

The Texans took out the lease on the corner of the North Central Expressway and Yale Boulevard, the same spot where Lamar had earlier operated Zima-Bat. They built a movable building for a locker room and auxiliary team facility, housing Stram and his coaching staff along with trainer Wayne Rudy, hired away from SMU. (The Cowboys, for their part, would wind up practicing across the Trinity River at Burnett Field, with its dilapidated locker room, home to a succession of minor-league baseball teams.)

During the fall of '59 and throughout the first half of 1960, Lamar was often flying to meetings or traveling in Texas for speaking engagements. Though he seemed timid and mortified in his first press conferences, he grew more comfortable in front of a microphone. He was not a natural speaker, but he eventually gained confidence, on the strength of his disarming ability to laugh at himself as well as his persona, which was very much that of a fan who just happened to have the means to buy his own team. He possessed a few lines that he would repeat at every speech, one of them playing off of the widespread belief that George Halas had engineered the NFL's belated move for a Dallas franchise. "I don't think it's appropriate," Lamar would say, "that there's a team called the Halas Cowboys." Lamar invariably closed by mentioning that he had a season-ticket order pad in his pocket.

"The great coup that I thought we had is that the Cowboys came out and announced that their ticket prices would mirror the college football ticket prices, which were $3.90, that was SMU," said Lamar. "We came in at 10 cents above them, at $4, which showed that we were more major league than they considered themselves to be—we were the established highest ticket price in town. There wasn't a thing in the world they could do about it, once we had said four dollars. They couldn't go back and say, 'Well, we're going to charge four dollars, too.'"

The Spur Club, consisting of businessmen who helped with the season-ticket drive, was formed late in 1959, and held its first function in January at the Memorial Auditorium in Dallas. Later in the year, the team inaugurated the Texan Hostesses, a group of thirty comely women, mostly teachers, hired to help with the summer season-ticket push. That summer, the Texan Hostesses could be seen driving around the city in the new French imports, Renaults, with the team's emblem on the doors. At a small conference room in the Texan offices, announcer Charlie Jones led the Hostesses, and other members of the sales staff, through the Dale Carnegie course.

"There was a lot of talk about it, but not much wild excitement" said the radio announcer Bill Mercer, who would call the Texans games on KRLD radio in 1960. "It was kind of funny around town. The view was sort of like, *These two rich guys.* And there was some question about who was going to win. You knew two teams couldn't make it."

While the teachers were an effective means to get the attention of the business community, Lamar's other hires were less assured. The team's first general manager, the robust sporting goods executive Don Rossi, had no previous experience in pro football, though he'd once been a high school coach and later a college official. "He worked for Spalding," said Lamar, by way of explanation, "and he was someone who applied for the job, and he was a good-lookin', athletic-lookin' guy and, I thought, *Why can't he be general manager?*"

"Don didn't have any experience," said Bob Halford, the team's publicity man. "He had been a coach at Jesuit High school in Dallas, and he'd been an on-field official in the Southwest Conference. But Don was like a lot of the rest of them. He just went to Lamar and applied for the job. All of a sudden, he was a general manager."

For scouting, the team hired Will Walls, a TCU alum and a former New York Giants end. The handsome, shambling Walls managed to look unkempt even in a suit and tie, but he had a good sense for what kind of man could succeed in pro football. With Lamar, Rossi, and Walls, the Texans managed to assemble a representative core of players, including Abner Haynes, a stand-out running back at North Texas State; Chris Burford, an All-America end from Stanford; and the versatile back from LSU, Johnny Robinson, who had signed contracts with both the NFL's Lions and, later, the AFL's Texans, before a judge's ruling allowed him the choice to come to Dallas.

Before they embarked on their training camp, the Texans held a public tryout. Stram spotted Lamar in running shorts and football cleats, just stretching his legs ahead of the opening of the tryout. He asked Lamar to run a 40-yard dash and timed him in 5.1 seconds. That prompted Stram to come up with a bar to measure the hundreds in attendance. "Now, you receivers and backs," he said to the throng of hopefuls. "We're cutting everybody that can't run faster than the owner."

•

One of the enduring mysteries of the birth of the Texans is how and why the club wound up holding its training camp 500 miles from Dallas, at the New Mexico Military Institute in Roswell, New Mexico. Decades later, even Lamar professed not to remember. "I'm sure there were economic reasons," he said, "But I can't remember. We didn't think about going to exotic places, but I don't know specifically why Roswell was chosen. It may be probably their rate was good."

Lamar and Stram had agreed that a spartan setting was appropriate, but no one was prepared for the humid, buggy desolation of Roswell. Chris Burford would recall the stifling summer heat and many on the team "spurning the 'training table' food of what must have been war surplus fare left in the commissary of the military school kitchen weeks before we arrived, necessitating an evening journey a couple hundred yards across the campus to the Dairy Queen, kitty corner from the dorms, so we could actually get something edible, all the while listening to Patsy Cline, Willie Nelson, and Eddie Arnold through the jukebox music of 'The Queen' and with the primary entertainment being the pinball machines to sustain and fire up our competitive senses."

The prized rookie Johnny Robinson recalled teammate Marvin Terrell, the guard from Ole Miss, having to adjust to his own biases. "Marvin came up there and they had all these colored guys there. They were all drinking out of this—well, we had oranges in a big tub of ice. Marvin came up there and he was watching all those colored guys, and he was dying. Finally he got down and reached in there and said, 'I don't give a God damn, I'm so thirsty I'll drink after anybody.' That's how you break the color line."

The players survived camp, but they nearly didn't survive leaving Roswell, aboard a chartered DC-6. With equipment manager Bobby Yarborough loading up the team's entire equipment inventory in the plane's cargo hold, the rest of the gear had to be stored in the first few rows of the plane. Smokey Stover, the rangy, well-liked linebacker, was sitting near the front when he heard the captain tell Rossi that the plane was carrying more weight than it should. Rossi told him not to worry, that he would be "personally responsible."

"I remember thinking, 'What good is you being 'personally responsible' going to be if we all die?'" said Stover. The plane lumbered down the runway and just cleared the trees to the East of the Roswell Army Air Field.

"When the flight landed, the pilot came out of the cockpit, just drenched in sweat," said Stover, "and said 'I'm never going to do that again.'"

On July 30, 1960, Lamar prepared to board a commercial plane in Dallas to San Francisco, where the Texans would play their first exhibition game, against the Oakland Raiders. He ran into a friend—the fellow sports fanatic Bill McNutt from Corsicana, whom he had seen at numerous SMU football and basketball games in the '50s.

"Why are you going to San Francisco?" Lamar asked.

"I'm going to see your football team!" proclaimed McNutt happily. McNutt's Collin Street Bakery was just then expanding its reach beyond north Texas, as an innovator in telemarketing and mail-order sales, turning the deluxe fruitcake into an annual holiday staple; but he and Lamar hit it off not over business but football—the chain-smoking McNutt had played in college at Vanderbilt, and he was like Lamar in that he thought nothing of traveling halfway across the country to see a game he wanted to watch.

Before this first game in franchise history, which the Texans won on a touchdown catch by Chris Burford, McNutt took a sequence of pictures scanning the interior of Kezar Stadium (the Raiders had yet to secure their own facility in Oakland), showing Lamar standing in front of an acre of empty seats. The crowd, announced at 13,000, might have been half that amount. But the adventure had started. There would be plenty of friends and acquaintances around Lamar, but McNutt—along with Kemble, Richey, Rupe, and a handful of others—remained in the inner circle. Lamar's life had changed drastically over the previous year, and the people with whom he felt the most comfortable were the same ones he knew best before he became a public figure.

After preseason games in Oakland, Boston, Tulsa, Abilene, and Little Rock, the Texans returned home to Dallas for their final preseason game, a charity benefit in the tradition of the Salesmanship Club exhibition games that were an annual staple at the Cotton Bowl in the 1950s. Over 50,000 fans showed up to greet the new team, which ran on the field wearing white pants, red jerseys with white numerals trimmed in gold, and red helmets, with the silhouette of the state of Texas on the sides in white and a gold star, approximating Dallas's location, inside the state. They won again, to go to 7–0 on the preseason.

Five days later, Lamar received a note from his stepmother, Ruth. "Because your dad may never tell you this," she wrote, "I just want you to know that he is very proud of you. Last Friday night it started raining before we reached Fair Park, but that didn't slow us down, and throughout the entire evening he literally beamed. He does realize that what you have accomplished is remarkable. He may be a man of very few words but he surely does recognize that you are wonderful. Everyone is so proud of you, Lamar, and let me just thank you again for always being so sweet to us. Affectionately, Ruth."

The Texans played their first regular-season game in Los Angeles against the Chargers, in front of just 17,724 fans in the cavernous Los Angeles Coliseum. Behind the runs of Abner Haynes, Dallas took a 20–7 halftime lead. As the teams were coming off the field at the half, Lamar fell into step with Stram and said, "Boy, I hope we don't beat them too bad. I don't want to make them look bad in their home opener." As soon as the words came out of his mouth, he felt a sense of unease. It was well founded: The Chargers rallied to win the opener, 21–20. "I learned at that first game that you do not ever let up in pro football," he said later. "You do not ever feel sorry for your opponent; you play 'til the game is over, and whatever the score is, it is."

The home opener against the Chargers two weeks later drew 42,000, though a large portion were the thousands of boys in the end zone general admission areas, brought in as part of the Optimists' Club 'Friend of the Boy' Day. In the two-team town, the Texans would never drew as many fans for a game again, but it wasn't for lack of trying. The promotion ideas, many of them from Lamar himself, were numerous. "He was always outwardly calm," said Bob Halford, the team's first publicity director. "But he could get excited about the smallest idea, and would be off and running."

For $1, children junior-high age and younger could get a Huddle Club membership, entitling them to free admission to all games, an official Texan T-shirt, and a "contract" with the team. Adult shoppers at Wrigleys Supermarkets in Dallas making a $10 purchase could buy one Texan ticket at face value and get another one free. On September 30, the Cowboys played a home game on Friday, and that week, for their home game two days later against the New York Titans, the Texans offered high school students free admission "if you present the torn ticket stub from any high school game you have attended this week."

It was also "Friend of the Barber Day," offering free admission "to all Dallas and Fort Worth barbers—wear your smock for free entry." This was Lamar's idea. "After all," he reasoned, "who talks to more people than a barber?" The crowd was announced at 37,500, though by some estimates at least half of those were high school students, and people granted entry wearing cook's aprons, lab coats, even women in their husbands' white dress shirts.

The initial novelty quickly wore off and soon the team was struggling to draw 20,000 fans. "One of the most discouraging moments for me was after the Texas–Oklahoma game, which is always a sellout in Dallas," said Lamar. "We played the next day, had eight All-Americans on our team, and obviously had superior personnel to either Oklahoma or Texas. We drew only nine thousand, and you had to start asking yourself where you were going."

As the crowds diminished for both the Texans and the Cowboys, the two teams moved even more aggressively to ingratiate themselves to the press.

"We'd sit around and talk about it: Who was going to give you the best Christmas present?" said Dan Jenkins, who was writing a column for the *Dallas Times-Herald* at the time. "The two PR guys were Larry Karl at the Cowboys and Bob Halford at the Texans, and all they wanted to do was take you to lunch and dinner every fucking day. They'd give you binoculars and typewriters and . . . they'd almost offer you a car. It got to be a joke among sportswriters. The teams would say, 'Okay, here's the deal: You're on the team plane, we're going to New York. We'll pay for everything we do, or we'll give $200 a day per diem.' And they'd ask Sam Blair or whoever, 'Which do you want?' And they'd always say, 'Both.' Bob was pretty much a march-to-the-sound-of-the-drummer type guy. Whereas Tex and Clint gave Larry Karl carte blanche. He'd buy you a fucking airplane."

Though much of Dallas was still segregated, the Texans' best player—and soon their most popular one—was Abner Haynes, the rookie who'd integrated the football team at North Texas State in the late 1950s, and whose surging runs became the team's surest selling point. The members of the Huddle Club made him a favorite, and, after one Texans game, even the PA announcer singled him out, saying over the Cotton Bowl loudspeakers, "Be careful on your drive out of Fair Park, ladies and gentlemen. The life you save may be Abner Haynes's."

But in the 1960 season, it wasn't the signing of Haynes, and it wasn't the pending lawsuit with the NFL that would shape the course of Lamar's career. Instead, it was the decision he made in late September to fire general manager Don Rossi.

Rossi had been assured and affable during the luncheons and radio interviews of the first half of 1960, helping to drum up awareness of and support for the Texans. But as the season began and decisions were being made, his lack of football experience showed.

"Don Rossi didn't know *come here* from *seven*," said Hunt Oil landman Mack Rankin. "He was a total incompetent."

There were more problems. There was grumbling over rumors that Rossi had brought a mistress with him to the team's training camp in New Mexico, and though Lamar never publicly disclosed it, there were also allegations of financial improprieties. "Rossi was an idiot," said the *Times-Herald's* Gary Cartwright. "I remember that there was a lady friend, but Rossi was just totally incompetent. I can't imagine why he was hired in the first place."

By the end of the season's first month, Lamar had grown alarmed about the team's expenses, which had spiraled far beyond his original estimates. Attendance was lower than expected, player expenses were far higher than he'd originally forecast, and the team's costs—from Will Walls's scouting budget to Wayne Rudy's training supplies to the numerous items requisitioned by Stram—continued to escalate. The question was less about financial wherewithal, which Lamar certainly had, than business soundness. Part of his decision to start a new league was his belief that it could be run prudently as a business. But the hemorrhaging losses in the first season were casting doubt on that notion.

Lamar needed someone he could trust. While he was pleased with Stram's handling of the team, and confident the Texans' talent was competitive with the rest of the league, the team as a business proposition was foundering. This wasn't the oil business, where Hunt Oil had thousands of employees steeped in a company tradition of frugality and fiscal soundness. And it wasn't Zima-Bat, run by Lamar with a few employees and partners, all of whom were personal friends. No, running a football team, if it was to be done properly, was going to require a true businessman. In his mind, Lamar didn't need a football man who could josh with cronies all day. He needed someone who could be tough on his behalf. This time, he knew exactly whom to hire.

•

The Hunt Oil accountant Jack Steadman was in Monroe, Louisiana, when he got a call from an unusually direct Lamar late one weeknight in the fall of 1960.

"Jack, I need your help here in Dallas," Lamar said. "I'm about to fire my general manager and I wonder if you can get here in the morning."

Jack Steadman, 6-foot-5, 250 pounds, with big feet and an erect bearing, was many things that Don Rossi had not been: He was a straight-arrow, tee-totaling family man who tithed at his Baptist church, studied his Bible, and sang in the church choir.

While Steadman was a product of the new school of accounting ("people think it's about numbers," he would say for the rest of his life, "but accounting is just a way to manage and analyze business information"), his corporate approach belonged to a much older tradition of the fiercely loyal company man. He would represent his bosses with bulldog tenacity to both the outside world and, whenever necessary, to others inside the company as well. He had developed a reputation as an uncompromising worker, as well as a worker with paper-thin skin, sensitive to any slights. Mostly, he was smart, loyal, and tough.

After driving all night to get to Dallas, Steadman displayed some of the maddeningly intractable resolve—the same quality would save Lamar millions of dollars in the decades ahead—when he negotiated his contract. Already receiving a raise from $12,000 to $15,000 to move from Penrod Drilling to the Texans, with an assurance from Lamar that if the team failed, he could have his old job back, Steadman argued for an additional $500 per year to offset the $500 he was giving up by leaving his post as choir director of the Ross Avenue Baptist Church in Dallas. Lamar made the announcement at a press conference in early November.

Inevitably, Steadman's attention to cost-control would run afoul of Stram's quest to build a first-class football team. Steadman had anticipated as much and brought it up to Lamar before taking the job. "I said to Lamar, 'I'm not the football guy,'" Steadman said. "'If Hank wants to deal with you, that's fine. But when it comes to cost control, he needs to report to me. And you need to tell him that.' And Lamar agreed to that. But Lamar never told him."

Stram soon was complaining about having to fill out extra paperwork and explain himself to Steadman, but Lamar reassured him that he would have everything he needed to field a winning football team.

With Steadman handling expenses as the general manager, the financial picture, though still grim, began to stabilize, and Lamar turned his attention to the myriad small details that captivated him. "He walked into my office one day, and told me that the AFL and NFL standings in our game program the previous week were an eighth of an inch off center," said Bob Halford, who examined the page and discovered Lamar was right. "He would never interfere with Hank Stram's coaching, but he worries about every tiny detail that might affect the image of the league."

After two tough late-November losses on the East Coast, the Texans returned home and closed their season with a three-game winning streak, finishing 8–6. But the last three home games were all sparsely attended, and even with Steadman's help, the team lost nearly $750,000 in its first season.

The problems were felt around the league. The Los Angeles Chargers were drawing so poorly at the L.A. Memorial Coliseum that their AFL title game match-up with Houston was moved to the high school stadium in Houston, Jeppesen Stadium, where the Oilers played their games. The Broncos first ownership group, led by Bob Howsam, lasted just the first year. "We weren't prepared to lose that kind of money, because we didn't have it," he said. The team was sold to a consortium including Cal Kunz and Alan and Gerry Phipps, and remained in Denver. Finances were dire throughout the league, particularly in Oakland and Boston, but the other owners remained, though in some cases just barely. It was around this time that the legendary quote from H. L. Hunt was first reported. Some thought Sid Ziff of the *Los Angeles Mirror* wrote about it first after cornering H. L. getting off a plane in Los Angeles and asking him if he was concerned about Lamar, who had reportedly lost a million dollars in his first year in pro football. "At that rate," H. L. replied, "he can only last another 150 years."

It was a great line. The only problem was the lack of concrete proof that H. L. Hunt ever actually said it. In the end it didn't matter—it was repeated often, like a mantra about the AFL's staying power—and if it provided some reassurance to those involved, all the better. But Lamar was convinced his father never uttered the words. "My dad would never say something like that," he said. "And the numbers were overly flattering anyway."

Back in Dallas, Will Walls was relieved of his duties after this first season with the Texans. Walls was a legendary figure in scouting circles, as much for his prodigious appetites and hard-headed nature as for his sharp eye for talent. "He was a great scout, when you could find him," said Mack Rankin. "He would go away and disappear for a week, and be drunk in a motel room. So I think it was about then that Lamar decided he needed some help."

With two leagues competing for players, the job now required more than the ability to discern players' talents. Early in 1961, Lamar replaced Walls by hiring Don Klosterman away from the Chargers, and made him the team's head talent scout (two decades later, the same job would be known in football circles as "director of player personnel"). Klosterman, the magnanimous former quarterback from Loyola Marymount (whose skiing accident in the '50s ended his playing career), was a movable feast, a witty, nattily dressed charmer who was also a sublime raconteur in the occasional dark art of player signing. Sitting with the announcer Howard Cosell in a Beverly Hills lounge once, Klosterman called to a friend, "Hey, come over here and help me listen to Cosell." But Klosterman was more than good company; he was a great scout and, in the parlance of sales, a consummate closer.

"He had a Rolodex that wouldn't stop, and he knew everybody in the country," said Gary Cartwright. "That was a turning point for the franchise."

In the cat-and-mouse game of player recruitment, the self-proclaimed "Duke of Bel-Air" was an expert at coercion. But not the only one. Lamar also called on the Hunt Oil landmen Mack Rankin and Jim Beavers. They had both grown up in the small east Texas town of Gladewater, gone into the military, and come out with a sense of confidence and what passed for worldliness. They could talk to people and were unquestionably loyal and skilled at earning trust quickly. Rankin possessed a homespun charm and an earthy sense of humor. They had one other key quality. They understood sports. They didn't need coaching—they knew they would need to ingratiate themselves to young athletes, and do whatever it took to sign young players to an AFL contract before they signed with the National Football League. It wasn't a twelve-month-a-year job, but it was fulltime when they were on it. Rankin once spent a night in a rental car, in December 1960, waiting outside of the apartment of Fred Arbanas, whom the Texans selected in the 1961 draft, to make sure an NFL scout didn't abscond with Arbanas in the middle of the night. Rankin helped sign Ohio State's huge All-American lineman Jim Tyrer, as well as SMU's Jerry Mays. Rankin lost a few too—TCU's Bob Lilly signed with the Cowboys, and the University of Texas standout Joe Don Looney wound up with the Giants—but most of the players he recruited signed with the Texans.

Rankin proved a good complement to Lamar's polite reserve. Sitting up in the hotel in San Francisco, the week leading up to the East–West Shrine game, Lamar was up much of the night talking to Texas Tech All-America E. J. Holub about the different elements of his contract, the oil business, the ranch on which E. J. grew up, and the state of college football in the Western

Athletic Conference. At one point, Rankin pulled Lamar aside and promised that if he would only leave, he and Beavers could close the deal. "Lamar kept bringin' up shit," said Rankin. "Lamar wanted to help, he wanted to work. But he was not a natural salesman." The moment when the talking stops and the deal gets made—that was not a turn Lamar was comfortable making.

As the team prepared its publicity campaign for 1961, Lamar sprung for a $75,000 four-color glossy brochure mailing. Though much of Dallas remained racially segregated in both attitude and fact, Abner Haynes's success proved that at least a portion of the city's fans would embrace a black star. On the Texans' foldout promotional poster, Haynes was front and center, larger than any other player, silhouetted with the red state of Texas in the background. His was the picture on the team's schedule card, and he was a co-captain, alongside running back Jack Spikes, in the Texans' Huddle Club.

Many of Lamar's college teammates and fraternity brothers belonged to the Spur Club—and Lamar himself sold 110 season tickets in 1960, to earn the right to wear the red blazer with the spur and Texans emblem on the breast pocket. Even as the Texans were struggling to find a broad following, the monthly luncheons—catering to the most fiercely loyal and involved fans—were well attended. At one luncheon, middle linebacker Sherrill "Psycho" Headrick bolted out to the dance floor to do The Twist, prompting eight supporters to get up and join in, with each winning a free ticket to the Texans' first home game of the fall.

Right before another luncheon, emcee Roger Blackmar called for the invocation and saw two different pastors rise from their seats. As Blackmar looked on helplessly, realizing that somehow the Texans had double-booked for the event, Lamar stood up at the dais and quickly announced, "Ladies and gentlemen, we're going to flip a coin, to see who will kick and who will receive." After the laughter subsided that's what happened: One minister gave the invocation, the other the benediction. "Lamar was always thinking football," said Blackmar.

In public, the 1961 season—which featured a bright 3–1 start, then a brutal six-game losing skid, was more of the same. Lamar remained the earnest, optimistic champion of football in Dallas and the American Football League. The mantra "Go Texan!—Go American!" was stamped on all Texans' merchandise and stationery. He continued attending SMU games whenever he could on Saturdays and joined the Texans' staff for their weekly bowling outings on Monday nights.

But behind the public cheer, his marriage was falling apart. Rose Mary blanched at the high-profile, high-pressure role of being the wife of a public figure, choosing more often to stay home with Lamar, Jr., who was just starting his first year in kindergarten, and the three-year-old Sharron.

Lamar and Rose Mary had both grown up sheltered, having things their way. Though their early married life hadn't been idyllic, they had managed, finding a rough equilibrium. But the strain of raising two children wore on Rose Mary, as did Lamar's hectic schedule. Chris Burford and his wife were invited to the Hunts for dinner one night in 1961, and Burford didn't notice Rose Mary's poise or beauty, only her frazzled state. "She just seemed very fragile," he said.

They groped for a way to rescue the relationship; Rose Mary was pregnant again in 1961, but miscarried that September. She was still carrying the dead fetus that October, when they were joined by two other couples for a flight to Buffalo. "We went out to Buffalo that fall, and she was just hounding him on the plane," said one friend. "Lamar was a gentleman, he wasn't going to make a scene, but you could tell that it tore him up."

In the hotel room near Niagara Falls, where the group stopped Friday night, a bereft Lamar, searching to find the words, said, "I don't think I love you anymore." It was all he could muster in the way of an explanation. Back home, the days and evenings were terse, largely mute. Lamar occupied himself with the children when he was home, and the two grew further apart.

"You did not talk about feelings in those days," said Rose Mary. "If you had them, you certainly didn't discuss them."

Finally, late in the fall of 1961, Lamar packed up a few things and moved out. He called his sister Caroline and asked if he could move into her house for a few weeks. It was one of the rare instances when he confided in a family member about a serious personal matter. "I'm a happy person," he told Caroline. "But I don't feel happy when I go home."

After a few weeks with Caroline and, later, with Al and Margaret, Lamar wound up in the apartment complex that he and his brothers owned on Bahama Drive. It had been a popular spot, with tenants including Dallas Times-Herald columnists Blackie Sherrod and Dan Jenkins, Don Klosterman and his wife, and several of the Texans players. Jenkins was impressed at once with his affability and his naïvete, best exemplified by the week Lamar got his first car with power windows.

"So he came over to the apartment one night," Jenkins said. "He wanted to show me his new car. Knocked on the door, came in, we talked a while, then he said, 'Come see my new car.' Went outside and, I forgot what kind of car it was, but he said, 'Watch this!' He pushed the button and the window came down. I said, 'Lamar, everybody on the sports staff at the *Herald* has one of those!'"

Slowly, the word got around that Lamar and Rose Mary had separated. One of their friends, Al Flannes, said the couple never recovered from the emotional toll of Rose Mary's miscarriage. But there were signs that the problems went deeper. "He had a hard time being intimate," Rose Mary said. "He needs a real relationship that is very going and coming and happy and loud and lots of people and all that. And I had two babies at home, and he just didn't want me to stay home with them."

On the field, the 1961 season turned irrevocably on November 3, 1961, a chilly Friday night in Boston, when the Texans, storming from behind, moved close to the Patriots' goal line with time running out. On the last play of the game, Cotton Davidson spotted Chris Burford on a look-in pattern in the end zone, but the ball was deflected by a Patriots fan who'd run onto the field during the play. Somehow, the referees hadn't seen the intruder and ignored Davidson's apoplectic protest. Stram grew incensed two days later when he saw the evidence on the coaches film, but Lamar asked him not to say anything to the press. Lamar was as furious as Stram, but he also knew that publicly pointing out the egregious nature of the error would only underscore the AFL's reputation as a second-class league. Instead, he wrote a note to Joe Foss's office:

> Our coaches are highly critical of the officials who did not see this spectator join the Patriot [defensive] backfield just before the ball was snapped. It is hard to visualize why they didn't see him but my position is, unfortunately, they just didn't. The whole point of this letter is that I feel you should demand that the Patriots construct a wire fence (as was done in Houston) to keep fans off the field. To say that our coaches, players, and staff feel we were cheated of a fair opportunity to win this game would be an understatement; however, the solution is not with officials or newspaper protests, but rather an edict from you that the Patriots correct this problem.

It was an early instance, the first of many, when Lamar put the interests and reputation of the league above his concerns for his own team. It mystified Stram, who knew just how competitive Lamar was, but couldn't fully appreciate how much Lamar felt responsible for the league as a whole.

The season ended at 6–8, as the Texans won three of their last four and Lamar ignored fans calling for Stram's firing. But Lamar was growing profoundly concerned over the fate of the league as a whole, as well as the long-term prospects for the Texans, who had lost $735,000 in 1960 and another half-million in 1961. Jack Steadman sat down with Lamar after the 1961 season and told him that the prospects were grim. The team was not making significant inroads into the Dallas market—season ticket sales had declined, despite the best efforts of the Spur Club and the Texan Hostesses—and the battle between the Texans and the AFL's Cowboys for the loyalty of Dallas football fans was being fought to an expensive stalemate. By the end of '61, there was a pall over much of the AFL. When the league convened for its annual meetings on January 8 at the El Cortez Hotel in San Diego, the mood was decidedly gloomy.

Lamar showed up at the El Cortez just in time to hear Harry Wismer being paged in the lobby. He'd seen the ruse before and knew that very shortly Wismer would emerge from near the banks of pay phones to accept the call (which he'd surreptitiously placed to himself), then talk loudly for a few minutes about some real or imagined deal. Lamar remembered when he was thrilled to have Wismer join the league, but he'd grown weary of the man's bluster and heavy drinking.

The first day's session was contentious. The Chargers' Sid Gillman continued to press Bud Adams and the Oilers to end the segregated seating at Jeppeson Field in Houston, while Adams assured the owners that when the team moved into a new stadium there would be no segregated seating.

Jay Michaels of MCA—the talent agency that was helping the AFL with its TV negotiations—gave the report on the ABC-TV deal, noting that the AFL's rating suffered in its second year, for which he cited a range of factors including "the poor press received by the Titans in New York City," thus prompting yet another testy exchange with Wismer.

At one point, the owners in executive session went around the room and revealed their operating losses from the previous season. "How can anyone be proud to have lost a million dollars?" exclaimed the Raiders' Wayne Valley. "I propose that we rename this league 'The Foolish Club,' because that's what we are." Everyone laughed, ruefully, at the time. But it was Lamar who seized on the phrase and began using it in the Christmas cards he sent out to the other AFL owners.

The best news of the meeting was Cal Kunz's announcement that the Broncos were changing their team colors to orange and white for the 1962 season and doing away with the vertically striped brown-and-yellow socks, which prompted unanimous, sustained applause.

After the league meetings, Steadman sent Lamar a memo in which he mentioned that he was being pressured by family members over the team's losses. The tax laws were such that if a new enterprise didn't show a profit by the fifth year, it would be considered a hobby, and all previous tax breaks would be reversed. "I know you do not want to leave Dallas, nor do I," he said, "but the Cowboys have the NFL behind them, and it doesn't matter to the League whether they are successful or not. But you are the Founder of the AFL and you need to have a successful franchise and continue as the leader for the League. Dallas is not big enough to support two pro football teams. We cannot continue to tell the other owners that the League will be successful unless we take action to make the Texans a successful franchise. We need to find a city that wants us and where we can build our operation without local competition." Lamar did not respond immediately, but from that point on, the question of the Texans long-term survival in Dallas became a question that preoccupied him.

The 1962 season dawned with some new hope. Stram, who had coached quarterback Len Dawson at Purdue as a collegian, saw him in 1961, and told him he still felt he could be a terrific quarterback. Dawson had played five years in the NFL, mostly on the bench, and watched his skills and confidence erode during that time. Stram told Dawson that if he could ever get out of his NFL contract, the Texans would sign him. After his second season on the bench in Cleveland, Dawson asked Paul Brown for his release and Brown agreed to do it. Right before the '62 training camp, Dawson signed with the Texans.

"After a while, I had serious doubts of my ability," said Dawson. "In five years in the NFL, I never played two games in a row. I never started and finished a game. I had to ask myself why. One conclusion was that I wasn't good enough." Shocked in the early weeks of training camp by Dawson's sloppy fundamentals, Stram overhauled his quarterback's footwork, throwing motion, and follow-through. He restored Dawson's confidence and by the time the Texans began the '62 season, Dawson had supplanted Cotton Davidson as the team's starter.

Days before the season began, Lamar—ever sensitive to the league as a whole—engaged in his single instance of owner meddling. To the Oakland Raiders, who were struggling to stay in business and bereft of a quality quarterback, Lamar traded two-year-starter Davidson (who had been the MVP of the league's 1961 All-Star Game) for the Raiders' first-round choice in the '63 draft. After making the trade, Lamar asked Steadman to give Stram the news.

Stram, "absolutely furious" at the time, even briefly considered quitting over the deal, and wouldn't speak to Lamar for days. Lamar fretted for the rest of the season, though he was convinced it was the right deal both for the league and for the team. Stram had been prepared to carry three quarterbacks on the team—Dawson, Davidson, and rookie Eddie Wilson—virtually unprecedented in the days of the thirty-six-man roster. Besides being a veteran backup, Davidson was one of the league's better punters and, in his absence, the punting job went to Wilson, who was one of the league's worst—finishing last in the league with an average of just 36.0 yards per punt. But the team, with Dawson at the controls and Abner Haynes radiant in the backfield, proved an offensive revelation, averaging nearly 28 points a game, and jumping out to a 6–1 start.

Yet even with the on-field success, the Texans' gate wasn't improving. The announced figures were largely fiction, and it would be years before Lamar realized how bad things were. "We averaged 10,100 paid per game, and the Cowboys averaged 9,900 paid per game. So, what a hollow victory that was. Both of us were going straight to the poorhouse with the attendance we drew, and we did it with a 3,000-season-ticket sale and every kind of promotion we could think of."

Quietly, Lamar and Steadman continued discussing the possibility of moving the franchise. As late as October 18, Steadman had grown more cautious, urging Lamar to stay in Dallas and possibly sell shares in the franchise to help offset his losses, reasoning that a new market would not solve the team's problems. "I feel our chances here are as good if not better," Steadman wrote. "Our biggest competitor is television rather than the Cowboys, although they are a factor, and we cannot get away from television. I would have to see a large season-ticket sale with a big stadium at a low rental plus concessions before I would be in favor of a move."

For much of the fall, the only candidate was the city of New Orleans. The city was starved for pro football, and Lamar already had a connection, with the glib, well-connected insurance salesman named David Dixon. Dixon had offered to serve as a broker, though in this he had already faltered. He had originally hoped to persuade the board of directors at Tulane University to grant the team the right to play in Tulane Stadium, the site of the Sugar Bowl, but he couldn't gain provisional approval for the use of the stadium. By the time he met with Lamar and Steadman, at Steadman's house in Dallas on the evening of Friday, November 9, Dixon was talking about having the team play in a high school stadium at New Orleans City Park until other arrangements could be made.

At the dinner meeting at Steadman's house, Dixon produced a typed agreement that night, which guaranteed that he'd find a place for the team to play in New Orleans in 1963, in exchange for a one-fourth interest in the team. Growing concerned that Lamar might actually sign the document, Steadman animatedly—and perhaps heavy-handedly—interceded, insisting, "Lamar, we *need* to discuss this first." Over Dixon's protestations, Lamar finally consented to think about it for a few days rather than agree to anything on the spot.

Later in the weekend, Lamar confided in Mack Rankin, whose area included Lafayette and New Orleans, and who probably knew more oilmen in Louisiana than in Texas.

"Lamar, you're gonna make the biggest mistake of your life," warned Rankin. "Everything down there is a payoff. You have not ever paid off one nickel in your life, to anybody for anything, other than it wasn't above-the-table business transaction. And you're gonna end up down there, and the first thing that's gonna happen to you is you're not going to pay off the police, you're gonna get out there and there's not gonna be any traffic control in the place. The next thing you know, the concession people, you haven't paid off them, and you're going to get to the game and you're not gonna have any concessions. It's gonna be one thing right after another one. Besides that, you're gonna be hounded by every politician down there to pay 'em off, but you're gonna want to get improvements to the stadium, or do this or that or whatever. You're gonna have to pay somebody off to get it done. You're making a terrible mistake."

Lamar looked pained. And then he gently admitted the rest of the deal. "I'd also be giving Dave Dixon a quarter-interest in the club."

Rankin, already forceful, turned apoplectic.

"*Jesus Christ!* This guy is nothing but a goddamn promoter!" said Rankin. "Doesn't have a nickel in the deal. All he did is he went out and made a deal with Tulane and got a five-year option for a lease on the stadium. Lamar, this is just exactly what I'm telling you about, what you'd have to deal with down there. You'd have to give him a 25 percent interest in the team, and he don't have to put up any money. Now you tell me if that's a good deal?"

Though he didn't commit to anything that week, Lamar was not optimistic about his choices, and was pretty sure he'd need to move the franchise somewhere prior to the next season. Meanwhile, with Dawson en route to AFL Player of the Year honors, Haynes about to set a pro single season record

for touchdowns, and Kansas fullback Curtis McClinton sweeping to the AFL
Rookie of the Year award, the youthful Texans were about to win their first
Western Division title. Though the Broncos began sharply, Dallas defeated
them on the road on November 18, with Dawson hitting Tommy Brooker on
a 92-yard pass play to break open a close game. A week later they clinched
their first division title and a chance to play their home-state rivals in Houston for the 1962 AFL title. But first there would be the final home game at
the Cotton Bowl, against the San Diego Chargers. With the Western Division
title wrapped up, the advance ticket sale was even lower. While having dinner in Dallas the night before the game, Lamar and Chargers' owner Barron
Hilton joked about locking the gates and just watching the game themselves,
from opposite sides of an empty stadium. The next day, though, Lamar
thought better of it, and the Texans faced the Chargers in front of another
small crowd, announced—inevitably—at 10,000.

A broad confluence of events worked in the favor of the 1962 AFL Championship Game, making it a watershed moment in AFL—and pro football—
history. The game was going to be played at the site of the Eastern Conference
champion, which meant that Houston's cozy Jeppeson Stadium would be
packed. The AFL had successfully gambled that the game wouldn't be challenged by a divisional playoff game in the NFL (the older league allowed for
a week in the schedule between the end of the season and the championship
game, to allow for any tiebreaking playoffs, like the one the Giants used to
beat the Browns in 1958). So there were no other pro football games being
played that weekend.

   For the writers covering the AFL title game, there was a bonus: The fourth
annual Bluebonnet Bowl, played in Houston's Rice Stadium the day before, featured Missouri against Georgia Tech, and brought in more writers from the Midwest and Southeast, who could piggyback the two games in a single weekend trip.

   As December 23, 1962, rose chilly and overcast in Houston, weather was
dreadful all up and down the East Coast. And the television competition
that Sunday was spectacularly bad: Among the scant offerings were several
holiday-themed shows, including the *NBC Opera* presentation of Menotti's
Amahi and the Night Visitors, Ted Mack's Amateur Hour, reruns of *Ozzie
and Harriet,* and game shows.

   Lamar, Lamar, Jr., Bunker, Herbert, and some friends were in the corner
of one end zone, about fifteen rows back. In truth, Lamar'd had the option of
a few seats in a covered area near the press box but chose to be able to sit with
a larger group among the fans. "You see the man in the Western suit who's

up there and warm?" he joked to Tom Richey. "He's the Oilers owner. The Texans owner is down here with everyone else."

He was delighted by it, and by the 37,981 that were hemmed into the permanent bleachers and temporary seating at Jeppeson Stadium. The Texans scored early, Haynes catching a pass from Dawson near the sideline and running untouched to the end zone. By halftime, it was 17–0, Dallas. Lamar was hopeful but still guarded, while the rest of the traveling party was beaming in anticipation of a championship. But a blue norther blew in during halftime, and by the time the second half began, it was much colder, with winds in excess of 25 miles per hour. George Blanda and the Oilers worked their way back, as Lamar's pocket of friends and family grew increasingly worried. Houston had a field-goal opportunity to win the game near the end of the fourth quarter, but the Texans' Sherrill Headrick blocked it to keep the game tied at 17. A late long pass fell incomplete and the fourth quarter ended in a tie.

Lamar, in the stands, realized the gravity of the moment—it would be only the second overtime game in the history of professional football, and the first since that seminal 1958 NFL title game that he'd watched, transfixed, from his hotel room in Houston. But there was a more urgent concern: Lamar, Jr., needed to go to the bathroom, so Lamar took him quickly as the two sides rested for a moment and prepared for the coin flip to begin sudden-death overtime.

He couldn't have known that he'd missed a piece of history. In the moments before the coin toss to begin sudden-death overtime, Stram had advised Haynes that if he won the coin toss, he should take the brisk wind. The Texans did win the toss, but when given the choice by the game referee, Haynes replied, "We'll kick to the clock." By declaring first that his team would kick, Haynes inadvertently surrendered the choice of which goal to defend to Houston. The Oilers, already receiving, chose to have the wind at their backs. On the sidelines, a frustrated Stram shook off the error and reassured Haynes.

But as Lamar and Lamar, Jr., returned to their seats just a few minutes later, everyone in his group was looking out at the field, in various stages of frustration and bewilderment, while an apoplectic Bunker was hurling epithets at Abner Haynes.

"Get him out of there!" said Bunker, fiery with anger. "What the hell is going on?!"

"I don't know," replied Lamar evenly, as he arrived at his seat and looked back out onto the field. "But 50 million people are watching."

With the wind at their backs, the Oilers threatened throughout the quarter. One drive was ended by Johnny Robinson's interception, the Texans' fifth of the day. But late in the quarter, with the Oilers moving into field-goal position, another crucial play swung the momentum. Reserve defensive end Bill Hull picked off George Blanda's short pass and returned it to midfield. As the sixth quarter began, the Texans finally had the wind at their backs, and began moving the ball. Dawson hit Jack Spikes for a first down on a key third-and-7 play. Then Spikes ran for 19 yards to move the Texans within the Houston 20. Four plays later, Tommy Brooker kicked a 32-yard field goal that ended what was then the longest pro football game ever played, at 77 minutes, 54 seconds.

Entering the locker room, Lamar was overcome with nervous energy. He reached up to an overhanging water pipe and did three quick, joyous chin-ups, then punctuated that with a war whoop. Later, he even took a brief sip of champagne.

"I've never seen a team fight for a win like this one did today," said a proud, champagne-drenched Stram in the locker room. "None of us will ever forget it." The game became an instant classic, watched by 56 million Americans on ABC. In the *Washington Post,* columnist Shirley Povich wrote, "The AFL was born at the age of three, so magnificent was this game."

Lamar had put a terrific team on the field in 1962, and the nucleus of his AFL champions—the youngest team in pro football—promised to be a perennial contender for years to come. But the team had lost money even in its championship season. Looking at the Texans' own financial numbers and the Cowboys' slow, but steady emergence, Lamar was convinced that the franchise would continue losing money and, in fact, might never succeed in Dallas. He would have to move.

He kept all this to himself, as he walked into the Hunt Oil offices on Christmas Eve morning, accepting congratulations for the previous day's big win from almost everyone he saw along the way.

It was a light day with a skeleton crew, and most of the messages on his desk were from friends and business associates offering their congratulations and Christmas wishes.

But there was another message, classified as confidential and extremely urgent: "Please call Mayor H. Roe Bartle in Kansas City."

CHAPTER EIGHT

THE HEART OF AMERICA

On December 26, 1962, Lamar drove to Love Field and boarded a Braniff jet bound for Kansas City. When he arrived at Kansas City Municipal Airport, he claimed his luggage and caught a cab across the Missouri River to the Muehlebach Hotel, where he had reservations under an assumed name. Upon arriving to his third-floor room, he placed a phone call, then took the elevator to the lobby, and exited onto 12th Street, the avenue of mythic nightlife, jazz, and much of Kansas City's vivid reputation as a town of outlaws and artists.

As Lamar walked to the curb, a blue limousine pulled up. He opened the back door and stepped in.

"Mr. Hunt, it is wonderful to have you visit," said the 320-pound man with the cigar, extending his hand.

"Thank you, Mayor Bartle," said Lamar. And with that, the next phase in the undercover courtship of the Dallas Texans by the city of Kansas City began.

Pro football was on the rise across the country. John F. Kennedy was in the White House, the First Family was playing touch football on the lawn in Martha's Vineyard, and the game had been featured on the cover of *Life*, *Time* ("The Sport of the '60s" read the tagline), and *The Saturday Evening Post* in the previous year. What H. Roe Bartle and the civic leaders of Kansas City recognized at the time was that pro football was conferring its own big-league status.

If Dallas was convinced it was something special—the business hub of the Southwest, a breed apart for being in Texas—Kansas City, Missouri, in the early 1960s sought respect as a growing, cosmopolitan city. Instead, it was still saddled with its reputation as something of a cow town, and a crooked, nickel-and-dime one at that. In fact, the city had for nearly forty years been on a track of careful urban planning, often with breathtaking results. The

Country Club Plaza, designed by J. C. Nichols and modeled after the city of
Seville, Spain, was the nation's oldest shopping district, and its Spanish architecture, the hundreds of fountains and small statues, gave the area a quaint,
civilized air. While Kansas City was still butcher for much of the Midwest and
had a Ford plant on the east side, it was also less beholden to heavy industry
than other Midwestern industrial cities and featured as its number one employer Hallmark Cards.

The city's predominant characteristic, shared by its mayor—the rotund
ball of mellifluous eloquence, H. Roe Bartle—was a mission for self-im-
provement. Kansas City was earnest about being a major league city. Bartle
had risen through the ranks of Kansas City politics with a mix of forceful-
ness, deal-making, shrewd calculation, and a magnanimous presence. The
man who spent many of his nights presiding over a local Boy Scout troop
had earned the nickname of "The Chief," for both his scout work and political accomplishments. Now, late in his political career, he was convinced
that bringing a football team to town would clinch Kansas City's status as a
bustling, modern, relevant city.

Bartle had been in Atlanta in the fall of '62 when he learned that Lamar
had visited that city earlier in the year, with an eye to moving the franchise.
Typical of his decisive nature, Bartle flew directly to Dallas and presented
himself at Lamar's office, counseling him to consider Kansas City. Lamar demurred at the time, saying he couldn't risk the public relations disaster of
being discovered shopping for a new city while the Texans were still trying
to draw fans for the '62 season. But he said he'd keep it in mind, and Bartle
promised him he'd stay in touch. Then the morning after the '62 championship game, Bartle reached out again.

There were times in his life when Lamar's penchant for secrecy seemed
excessive, even obsessive. But this was one occasion—others would follow in
the years ahead—when it was appropriate. From the Christmas Eve phone
call in which Bartle renewed his interest to bring the Texans to Kansas City,
to Lamar's visit later in the week, to negotiations in the first part of 1963, the
meetings were conducted quietly, urgently, and with a maximum of secrecy.
Lamar loved it.

"I was impressed with Mayor Bartle," Lamar said. "He spoke highly of
Kansas City, and I felt he believed what he said even though he said it in a
flashy way. We were looking for a home where we would be welcome and he
just made me feel that we could do well in Kansas City. I was also impressed
with the stadium facilities. I had seen so many bad ones in Boston, Buffalo,
and other places."

When Lamar visited again in January, this time with Steadman, Bartle brought them into his office. From his speakerphone, he called Bill Dauer, head of the Kansas City Chamber of Commerce, and explained that he had two men in his office whom he couldn't identify but who represented a pro football team that was considering a move to Kansas City. He wanted to know if Dauer thought the city could support a team. Dauer asked for a few minutes to speak to a friend, and then called back, joined on the line by Ray Evans, former Kansas All-American and head of Traders National Bank. Both were enthusiastic in their response that the city was ready for pro football, and that the community would support a team.

The same day, Bartle took his guests to the Kansas City Club, introducing them to acquaintances as "Mr. Lamar" and "Jack X." Those curious about the odd name were put off when Bartle confided that "Jack X" was an IRS agent in town exploring cases of income tax evasion. (The ruse was successful because the tall, closemouthed Steadman looked like someone on just such a mission.)

As the furtive negotiations proceeded, Kansas City offered generous terms: A seven-year lease at Municipal Stadium, with the rental for the first two seasons at $1 per year (the Texans had been paying $10,000 per game to rent the Cotton Bowl). In subsequent years, the city would get 5 percent of gross receipts after ticket sales topped $1,100,000, but if they didn't reach that mark, the $1 per year lease rate would remain in place. The team and the city would share equally in profits from concessions. The city also agreed to install 3,000 more permanent seats—and the option of 11,000 more temporary seats into the stadium—as well as constructing an office building and a practice field for the team. As Lamar and Jack left Kansas City, they had committed to nothing but had the framework for a deal in place.

The Cowboys knew nothing of the Texans' plans when Steadman called Tex Schramm later in January to set up a private meeting. Steadman told Schramm the team was considering leaving town, and inquired if the Cowboys would like to purchase the temporary locker facility that was built on the grounds of the team's practice field at North Central Expressway and Yale Boulevard. The Cowboys not only offered to buy the facility, they quietly agreed as well to pay for the Texans' moving expenses to leave town.

Lamar called a February 8 press conference in Kansas City, announcing that he had entered an agreement with the city of Kansas City to move the franchise there, provided the city could sell 25,000 season tickets by May 15. Taking great pains to thank the fans that had supported the Texans for three seasons, he explained that the time had come to move.

His points were clear, the reasons were self-evident, and he made them again a day later in Dallas, when he confronted the local media, most of whom sympathized with his reasons for making the move. Writing the following day in the *Dallas Morning News*, Gary Cartwright noted that with the free rental of the stadium and offices, the threshold for breaking even was far less in Kansas City than it would be in Dallas. "The Texans are on their way and so, possibly, is all the bitterness and frustration which has made Dallas a tragic comedy for three years," Cartwright wrote. "Someone had to go. It's sad, but it would have been a lot sadder if this insane war had continued."

The group most shocked by the news may have been the Texans' players. "Things looked great after we beat Houston," Chris Burford said. "It was so good we couldn't wait for the next season to start. We were going to drive those Cowboys out of town. They were getting clocked repeatedly, and we just really felt like we were going to take the town."

Many players were frankly angry—Jerry Mays threatened to retire—and some of the rest were bewildered about their new home. Len Dawson was with his wife Jackie in Pittsburgh when he heard the news. "I mentioned to some friends that the team was going to Kansas City and they said, 'Kansas City, Missouri, or Kansas City, Kansas?' I said, 'You mean there's two of them?' So I had no idea which one. The thought then, particularly back East, was, 'Man, you're going to a cow town. They have horses and cattle running in the middle of the main street in the city.'"

After the announcement, Lamar did something he'd never done before and would rarely do again. After a year that saw the dissolution of his most fervent professional dream (owning a pro football team in Dallas) and personal dream (finding a way to preserve his marriage to Rose Mary), he took a step back and left for an extended vacation. He knew that it wouldn't help to be hovering over the Kansas City proceedings regularly, and he didn't relish daily encounters with his fellow Dallasites who might try to convince him to keep the team in the city.

He sensed, at a level far deeper than intellectual, that he needed to get away for a time. And with only a vague notion about what he might discover—about himself or the world—he bought a plane ticket to Dublin.

•

For nearly four years straight, Lamar had been working ceaselessly, building a league and also a team, then finding a new home for the team that was, quite clearly, unloved in his hometown. Along the way, he'd lost the belief that he and Rose Mary could ever work out their problems. He'd done everything he could think of to save the relationship, quietly filed for divorce in the spring of 1962, and then grieved for its loss.

Now, as the new year dawned, and he faced the prospect of a fresh start on the football field, he also embarked on a new romance.

In Dublin, Ireland, taking a year of postgraduate study as part of the Rotary Club's overseas fellowship program, was the woman who had drawn Lamar's notice from her first days as part of the Texans Hostess Program.

She was the smart, pretty, self-possessed Richardson native Norma Knobel, whose magnetic presence had caused her to finish among the leaders in the ticket-selling contest (her first sale was to her father, who'd taught her to love football at an early age) and made her ideal company at Hart Bowl, for the Texans' staff Monday night bowling league. "You could see on those bowling nights that Lamar was impressed with her," said Jack Steadman. "And you could see why—she was impressive."

A graduate of North Texas State University with a degree in secondary education, she had taken classes with Abner Haynes, and seen the impact of his presence, integrating college football fields all around Texas. After spending her high school years as part of the Richardson High drill team, she had developed a love for sports and the way it served as a social glue for people of different ages and backgrounds. Women liked her, men were drawn to her, and she had become adept at putting people at ease, often while talking about sports.

As one of the Texan teachers driving around town in a Renault, she cut a fetching figure. Lamar had early on noticed her bubbly, infectious enthusiasm. Rose Mary even recalled an evening when the Hunts had a group of Texan employees over for dinner: "He said, 'I want you to meet this wonderful person, she has the most positive attitude —I want you to try to pick up some pointers from her. Look at her; just watch her.' So I did, and I thought, 'She is just so happy. Isn't that great?' Didn't help, though."

With the divorce set in motion, Lamar had begun casually dating again in 1962. He'd spent some time dating Joan Ryba, one half of the Ryba twins, formerly cheerleaders for Rice, then the Houston Oilers, before winding up in Vegas as part of Dean Martin's stage act, the "Thunderbird Twins." He'd briefly been linked with Don Meredith's first wife, Lynne, who herself was going through a divorce. But very quickly, Lamar began courting Norma. When she left for Dublin in the summer of 1962, he took her to Love Field to put her on the plane, bringing his nephew, Al Hill, Jr., along to meet her for the first time.

Lamar liked it that she wasn't self-conscious around him and others, the way Rose Mary had been. For Christmas in 1962, when she returned to Dallas for the holidays, he presented her with a gift, a gorgeous cashmere sweater he'd picked out at Neiman-Marcus, in a festive panorama of colors. When she unwrapped it, she was lavish in her gratitude but also forthright enough to gently explain to him that the sweater was at least two sizes too big, but that she'd love it if he could exchange it for one in her size. Then, as the weeks stretched into months with no sign of the smaller sweater, she also had the grace not to pester him about it. ("I said maybe once or so, 'How's the sweater coming?'" said Norma. "And Lamar would say, 'Oh, yeah. I'm gonna work on that.'")

Lamar arrived in Dublin that winter with no agenda beyond spending time with Norma. They traveled in and outside the city and watched Kilkenny face Croke in hurling, with the ash sticks swinging at Croke Park. They saw Dublin battling Galway in Gaelic Rules football, and were dazzled by the pandemonium of the fans. And they traveled to Milltown, the legendary stadium in Glenmalure Park where the Shamrock Rovers, the country's most successful soccer club, played its matches. The Hoops—playing in green and white horizontal stripes—were in their heyday, with a run of domestic championships and night games played in the European Cup competition. Lamar and Norma were in the standing-room-only terrace section, where the tightly packed crowd helped ward off the chill, and he looked on with avid interest at a game that looked so different from the one he'd seen played slowly and sloppily on the Far Fields at The Hill.

He took in the sports, he took in the weather, he took long walks, and he continued to fall irretrievably in love with Norma Knobel. He returned to the states in March (she would remain in Ireland until the summer), caught up on his correspondence ("forgive me, for I've been out of the country for much of the past two months"), and then began rebuilding his new life.

Besides the move to Kansas City in the offing, there was other good news from the AFL, though it was not universally recognized as such at the time. Writing in the *New York Times* after the possibility of the Texans move was announced, Arthur Daley cast a skeptical eye on the bankrupt Titans, Lamar's wayward champions, and the entire league: "Yet the hopelessness of the Titans and the uncertainties of the Texans make those on the sidelines wonder how much future the A.F.L. was left. The Chargers already have been driven to San Diego from Los Angeles by the Rams. The Oakland Raiders are dead in trying to combat their neighbors, the San Francisco Forty-Niners. Protests to the contrary, the situation has to be shaky."

But it was about to get much better. Harry Wismer's tragicomic run as owner of the New York Titans had ended in the fall of '62, when Wismer ran out of money and the franchise had to be taken over by the league. At that point, Lamar had been convinced that the league should just give up on the market. "I, personally, favored the league moving the team out of New York," he said. "We had a chance to sell to somebody in Miami, and I didn't think it was worth staying in New York, playing at the Polo Grounds in front of 5,000 people. I was very short-sighted; I didn't know how strong a guy Sonny could be."

Sonny was David A. "Sonny" Werblin, one of the heads of the Music Corporation of America, and the leader of the five-man ownership group that paid $1.3 million to take over the failed Titans franchise. Werblin had given the AFL a hand in securing its first TV deal, with ABC, in 1960, and now bought in as a full partner in the enterprise. He was smooth, understated, calmly self-assured, and wealthy—in short, everything Harry Wismer was not. In the polished persona of Werblin, the entertainment world saw a new breed of showman, less carnival huckster than professional dealmaker. Werblin's contacts within the industry were a matter of legend; he had negotiated Ed Sullivan's lengthy CBS deal, as well as represented the likes of Jackie Gleason, Alfred Hitchcock, Jack Benny, Andy Williams, Ozzie and Harriet Nelson, Ernie Kovacs, and scores of others.

As the Giants' Wellington Mara would put it, "We didn't know much about Sonny Werblin when he bought the Jets. And we didn't like what we eventually found out. He was a much more formidable man than Harry Wismer, and we pretty soon sort of knew it meant trouble."

On April 15, 1963, Werblin announced the launch of the "Gotham Football Club, Inc."—essentially the reconstituted Titans, now renamed, with plans for a new stadium (Shea Stadium, then under construction in Queens, right next to the site for the 1964 World's Fair), a new nickname (Jets, which neatly rhymed with Shea's co-tenant, baseball's Mets), new colors (green and white, in honor of Werblin's St. Patrick's Day birthday), and a new coach (recently deposed Colts leader Weeb Ewbank). Just over a month later, on May 22, Lamar announced that the Texans would move, and by the spring of '63, two of the AFL's major problems—the Texans and the Titans—were well on their way to being solvent, profitable franchises.

With the woeful Raiders finishing last in the league in 1962, Lamar's lone act on the football operations side—the trade of Cotton Davidson to the Raiders—had netted the first overall choice in the AFL draft. The team chose and quickly signed the mammoth Grambling defensive tackle Junious "Buck"

Buchanan, about whom Klosterman raved, "He can run a 220 in twenty seconds flat with a goat under each arm."

Besides Buchanan, the draft included Maxwell Award winner Bobby Bell
(whom Stram would call "the best athlete I've ever seen"); Michigan State's
bruising guard Ed Budde; the versatile Southern Miss punter Jerrel Wilson
(who could also play fullback, tight end, and on special teams); and solid
right tackle Dave Hill. It was a landmark draft for the team, one of the greatest in football history, and further established Klosterman as a key player in
the Chiefs hierarchy. One of the things Matt Rankin noticed was how comfortable Klosterman was around the black players, whom he seemed at ease
with and—even more importantly—was able to put at ease.

"Jim Beavers and I were born and raised in East Texas," said Rankin. "And
didn't have that California charisma of being able to talk those people's language. And it definitely was a different language."

Late in 1962, Klosterman spent a week in Minneapolis with Bobby Bell,
the All-American whom everyone assumed would sign with the NFL's Vikings. "The Vikings and [coach] Norm Van Brocklin just sort of had this
attitude like, 'Oh, don't worry about it, he'll come here,'" said Bell. "But Don
Klosterman was a *salesman*. He said, 'Bobby, we really want you with us;
what's it gonna take here?'" What it took in this case was Lamar flying up and
approving Klosterman's offer of a five-year, no-cut contract, a rarity even in
the days of sky-high bonuses.

Lamar didn't have all the paperwork with him the day he visited Minneapolis, but he sealed the deal with a handshake with Bell and his advisers, and
welcomed Bell to the team. The next day, both Lamar and Bell happened to be
on the same flight from Minneapolis to New York. After arriving at Idlewild
Airport, they shared a cab ride into the city. "We're coming out of [the air-
port], and as we cross the bridge, the cabbie reaches back and says, 'I need 15
cents for toll,'" said Bell. "Lamar reaches in his pockets and doesn't have any
change, so I hand the guy 15 cents. So we stop at Lamar's hotel first, and he
gets his stuff out of the trunk, and I'm sitting in the car. Then he knocks on
the window and says, 'Hey, Bobby, do you have any cash on you?' I say, 'Yeah.'
He said, 'I'm sorry, I don't have any cash on me; I'm gonna need you to pay for
the cab.' And I said, '*Oh*-kay.' So now I'm going to my hotel. I jump out of the
cab, I run into the hotel, I check in as fast as I can, rush up to my room, and I
call back to Minnesota, and I say, 'Hey! Hey! Hold on, what's the deal here? I
just signed with this guy Lamar Hunt to play there.' And he says, 'Yeah, what's
wrong with that?' And I said, 'Hey, man—Lamar Hunt's *broke!*'"

In Kansas City, despite the massive effort, season-ticket sales had fallen short of the goal of 25,000, but even at 15,182, they set a new record for an AFL team, and on May 22, Lamar made it official, announcing that the team would move to Kansas City.

Throughout that month, Lamar surveyed the hundreds of variations of entries he received in the "Name the Team" contest. There was everything from "Royals" to "American Royals" to "Monarchs" (the moniker of the city's old Negro Leagues team) to the "Mo-Kans" and "Meat Packers." The most popular of the 4,866 entries to the contest was to call the team the "Mules," followed by Royals, Pioneers, Steers, Stars, Mavericks, Plainsmen, Scouts, and Hunters. None immediately swayed Lamar, and for a time, both he and Stram wanted to retain the nickname Texans.

"Lamar, we can *not* call the team the Kansas City Texans!" Steadman insisted.

Lamar, still sanguine, argued that the Dodgers had kept their name after leaving Brooklyn, and the Lakers had kept their name after moving from Minneapolis.

"It's a completely illogical argument," he would admit later, "but I was so wrapped up in the name at the time that it didn't seem that way. Jack said it would have been a disaster and, of course, he was right."

Lamar finally succumbed to Steadman's logic and selected a new name. On May 26, he announced that the franchise would be called the Chiefs, owing to the area's Native American heritage and, as well, as a nod to Mayor Bartle. A week later, in the kitchen of his Dallas apartment, Lamar sketched out the team's new logo on a napkin, placing the elongated, interlocking "K" and "C" inside a white arrowhead. Soon enough, the silhouette of the state of Texas came off the red helmets, and the arrowheads went on.

Lamar announced that he would keep his residence in Dallas but spend much of his time during the football season in Kansas City. He persuaded Steadman to move his family to Kansas City, so the team would have an executive presence in the city. Steadman had already spent much of the spring in Kansas City, helping to scout out the location of the team's new office building and training site, on 63rd Street in Swope Park.

On Friday, June 21, 1963, the staff of the Dallas Texans and the moving vans accompanying the team set out north for Kansas City. "I was crying like a baby as I drove out of town," said Hank Stram, "just thinking about the fact that we were having to leave. I was the last guy to leave Dallas. Lamar had explained the economics to me. I understood. But I was just hoping against hope that he would change his mind. I felt like Dallas was our town."

Actually, Lamar would be the last to leave, driving up with Lamar, Jr., as well as Stu and Dale Stram on July 13. On the morning of July 14, the team reported to training camp at William Jewell College in Liberty, about 15 miles northeast of the city.

The team's initial reception in its new home was largely positive. Before the season, fifty-two different Kansas City companies purchased at least fifty season tickets. In three years in Dallas, only four companies had reached that threshold, and one of them was Hunt Oil. At the first team luncheon, in front of a crowd of 270, Lamar said, "It feels strange to be in a city that does not suffer from an overpopulation of football teams. But it feels good." Lamar, ever optimistic, was fairly beaming that summer. His football team, reigning champions, were getting a fresh start in a city that seemed glad to have them. Norma had returned from her fellowship in Ireland, and they had started to date regularly. She was along with him for a preseason game against the Oilers, played in Wichita, Kansas, on August 30.

The game was a chance for the team's impressive rookie class to get work. Few were working harder than Stone Johnson, the Grambling running back who—on a team with the deepest roster of running backs in the league—was also playing on the specialty units. Johnson had been an Olympic sprinter (at the 1960 U.S. Olympic trials, he equaled the world record in the 200-yard dash, running it in 20.5 seconds), but he was determined to prove he wasn't just a trackman in shoulder pads.

In the first half of the game in Wichita, Lamar was about twenty rows back in the crowd, with Norma, when Johnson made a block on an oncoming defender and, losing his footing in traffic, crumpled up against an Oiler defender, falling to the ground.

Lamar knew instantly that it was bad. He could tell not just from Johnson's prone form but also from the hasty way that the other players on the field stepped back, and then began motioning furiously for the medical staff to come to the field. But on this muggy summer night, in a small stadium in Wichita, there was no one on either sideline prepared to administer first aid for the convulsive trauma that Johnson had suffered. Lying on the ground, Johnson looked up in horrified fear, unable to move his legs, while his teammates grew more concerned. Stram's son Hank, Jr., who had befriended Johnson in camp, looked on from the sidelines, tears in his eyes. After a few minutes, Lamar went down to the field himself. "Sometimes, it seems like forever before help comes," said Abner Haynes. "But this *was* forever." There was no ambulance at the stadium, and it took about 20 minutes before one arrived on the scene.

"At that juncture," said Curtis McClinton, "everyone knew it was serious. And nobody wanted to play football." The injury, diagnosed as a compression fracture of the cervical vertebrae, left him in critical condition at Wichita General Hospital.

The teams played out the game in a distracted haze. Lamar didn't wait for the finish but instead followed Johnson to St. Francis hospital. He then made the call to Johnson's parents in Texas. Late that night, he got through to Stone's college coach, Grambling's Eddie Robinson, and delivered the bad news.

"Mr. Robinson," he said when he reached him at home. "I have some terrible news. Stone Johnson's been hurt in our game in Wichita. And it looks very serious."

Back at Wichita's Veterans Field, the team dressed and got aboard the charter bus heading back to Kansas City. But Stram and some of the players stopped by to visit Johnson at the hospital. Johnson would never leave. He died a week later from complications related to the surgery.

"Lamar stayed," said Curtis McClinton. "He stayed there with Stone, in the hospital room. He was there the next morning, and he was there a week later when he died."

In a way, the shock from the incident was felt throughout the season. Buck Buchanan packed up his roommate's belongings, to be mailed to Johnson's parents in Texas. At his new home in Kansas City, Stram was left mute by his son Henry's anguished and repeated question, "Dad, how could he die? It's only a game." At the funeral in Texas, as Mr. and Mrs. Johnson watched their son buried, Lamar and several of Johnson's teammates wept.

Lamar set up a trust fund for Johnson's parents, and at his behest, the team retired Johnson's number 33, though he never played a down in the regular season. From there, the team shored up its own safety procedures and tried to move on. Abner Haynes, especially, seemed deeply troubled. He still had his bravado, but there was something missing, some telling sense of abandon in his play that was gone. "Abner was never the same," said Chris Burford.

Despite the tragedy, the Chiefs began the season in convincing fashion, routing Denver 59-7. For Lamar, game days were distinctly different in 1963, since every game was a road trip. It meant even more travel, but by now that was second nature to Lamar. He'd still frequently fly to SMU or some other big Southwest Conference game on Saturday, then head to Kansas City the night before a Chiefs home game.

He was also, undeniably, transformed by his new relationship, out of his divorce languor and deeply in love with Norma. "He took dancing lessons at

Arthur Murray," said Bill Adams. The courtship of Norma continued through the fall. Jake Cobb, piloting the Hunts' private plane, quickly noticed that she brought a different air to the festivities. "She was more of a people person than Rose Mary was," said Cobb. "She made people feel at ease around her."

There was more to it than that. Norma went beyond an appreciation for the moment. Other women might point to the pageantry of a game, or the sound of a band, but she was an unabashed fan and a quick study, attuned to the technique of the athletes, able to follow some of its strategy. She also gravitated to the good-natured partisanship between the AFL and the older league (of NFL loyalist Tex Maule's withering dismissals of the AFL in *Sports Illustrated*, she would recall, "I would read his articles and just practically gag").

On the first weekend in October 1963, Lamar and Norma went to the Cotton Bowl on a Friday night to watch SMU play Navy, then returned the next morning for the annual rivalry game between Texas and Oklahoma. After the game, they drove to Love Field, where Cobb flew them down to Waco, for the Baylor–Arkansas game. They returned that night, then flew commercial to Kansas City Sunday morning, to watch the Chiefs' satisfying 28–7 win over the Oilers, in a rematch of the '62 title game. Back in Dallas on Monday, they went with Chiefs' talent scout Don Klosterman back to the Cotton Bowl, for the night game between Prairie View A&M and Wiley College. It was not uncommon to see multiple games in a weekend, but even Lamar was impressed that Norma had been game for all five. "We saw a *fipple-header!*" he declared.

On the trips to Kansas City, they'd often stay in town afterward and have dinner with Stram and his family. Outwardly, Hank and Lamar made an unlikely pair: Stram, raised in poverty, had a striver's sense of purpose; with his tailored suits and monogrammed shirts, he was exquisitely aware of appearance. Lamar, reared in absolute wealth, was utterly indifferent to the visible trappings and signs of success. For much of 1963, the briefcase he used was a battered in-flight freebie from his trip to Dublin on Irish Airlines. Lamar and Hank called each other "Lad," in homage to Stram's Frank Leahy impersonation; they shared a nearly identical passion for games and competition, whether it was golfing at the Dallas Country Club or playing horse in Stram's office, taking turns shooting crumpled-up pieces of paper into a wastebasket.

The weekend before Thanksgiving looked like another normal one for Lamar. The plan for the weekend of November 22–24 was to fly to New York on Friday with Bill and Mollye Adams and Buzz and Dorothy Kemble, take in the Harvard–Yale game on Saturday, then watch the Chiefs play the New York Jets on Sunday.

On that Friday, November 22, Lamar headed to downtown Dallas to work in his office, then met Fort Worth businessman Tommy Mercer and baseball executive Dick Butler for a lunch at the Petroleum Club to discuss the possibility of investing in the Fort Worth Cats, with an eye toward future expansion in Major League Baseball. They were eating lunch when the news broke that the president had been shot. Norma was about an hour outside Dallas, speaking to a Rotary Club about her time in Ireland—her speech was interrupted by the emcee giving the terrible news.

With uncertainty and panic enveloping the streets of Dallas, Lamar and Norma both found their way to Love Field that afternoon, where they decided to carry on with their trip. "Lamar was definitely sad," said Norma. "Everybody was sad, and boy, were we sad it had happened in Dallas."

While Lamar consistently voted Republican, he was mostly apolitical. As a proud Dallasite, he sensed earlier than most what the event would do to the reputation of Dallas. That gray afternoon, the traveling party took off for New York (minus the Adamses, who decided not to make the trip), and they spent a rather listless weekend in New York—both the games they were to attend were canceled. Leaving New York on Sunday morning, Lamar wanted to stop in Washington, D.C. Cobb landed the plane at National Airport and ordered a limo (there were no rental cars available by then), but the snarled traffic that encircled the District prevented them from getting any closer.

The AFL's decision not to play—Foss felt strongly that the league shouldn't play its games that weekend, and on Saturday, the league announced it would postpone the games—was vindicated in the end. By contrast, the NFL had chosen to go ahead with its games. In the harried hours after the assassination, Rozelle had spoken to his college classmate, Kennedy press secretary Pierre Salinger, who advised him that "Jack would have wanted you to go ahead." That may have been, but Rozelle couldn't have anticipated the way the rise of television would alter the rest of the weekend, creating a communal electronic experience that was all the more heightened when Jack Ruby shot and killed Lee Harvey Oswald on Sunday morning, just a half-hour before the NFL's games were kicking off.

(While Lamar would eventually be questioned by the Warren Commission—Jack Ruby had been in the Hunt Oil offices the day before the assassination, driving one of his Carousel Club dancers to a secretarial job interview—the real attention shone on H. L., who had heavily criticized

Kennedy for being soft on communism. The FBI advised him to leave Dallas for the time being.)

With more than a dozen native Texans on the roster, the shock over the assassination was yet another downbeat episode in a brutal season for the Chiefs. The team, beset by injuries and narrow losses, ended the season at 5-7-2.

The overall business prospects were good—the team even turned a slight profit in 1963—but the honeymoon did not last long. Stram would euphemistically describe Kansas City in the 1960s as "not far removed from its frontier heritage," but the truth was something more pernicious. The city, like so many American cities in the '60s, was a victim of white flight to the suburbs and an increasingly dangerous environment around the downtown area. This was particularly true in the heart of Kansas City, sprinkled with a series of mean little bars and dimly lit nightclubs, some of them still under Mafia control. In the spring of 1964, guard Ed Budde was brutally beaten in a bar fight, with one assailant bashing him repeatedly with a lead bolt. After surgery, Budde had a metal plate in his skull, and his return was considered doubtful. A year later, tight end Fred Arbanas was jumped on the street and wound up losing vision in one eye.

Throughout the weeks following Kennedy's assassination, Dallas was rent by recrimination and doubt. As the long, bleak season drew to a close, Lamar was certain of one thing: He'd found his true life companion in the effervescent Norma Knobel.

Back in Dallas over Christmas, Lamar gave Norma a box exactly the same size and shape as the one he'd given her for Christmas a year earlier. She opened it to find the exact same sweater that he'd given her the year earlier—still two sizes too big, since he hadn't yet exchanged it at Neiman-Marcus. She began unbuttoning it, mentioning how much she loved it and that she could wear it over layers and it would be just fine as it was, and then she stopped. As she reached the last button of the sweater, she found one detail different from the previous Christmas's gift: This time, Lamar had attached an engagement ring to the bottom button.

They were married on January 22, 1964, at Norma's parents' house in Richardson. Lamar asked Hank Stram to be his best man, and there was little of the fanfare that greeted his first wedding. On the morning of the wedding, as Hank and Phyllis were driving Lamar to Richardson for the ceremony, Lamar asked them to pull over, so they could stop for a snack at an ice-cream stand.

After the service, the newlyweds took their honeymoon at the Winter Olympics in Innsbruck, Austria. They ran into Dan and June Jenkins on their first day in Austria. Dan was writing about the games for *Sports Illustrated*. He remembered Norma taking the eccentricities of her new life as Mrs. Hunt in stride. "Norma said they flew over in coach," said Jenkins. "Lamar laid down in the aisle to sleep. They lost his luggage, and he went around for two or three days wearing the same thing—a suit, with his tie loose, freezing. I'd say, 'Lamar, there's a store, *there's* a store, there's another store there—I'm sure they've got your size.' He just laughed and said, 'Oh, it'll be here. They say it'll be here any minute.'"

They spent an idyllic week watching the pairs figure skating competition and the men's downhill. They happily braved the frigid days together. On the ski slopes one day, the nearly tee-totaling Hunts finally ordered a drink. "The Austrians had, cleverly, the most gorgeous, blond-haired, blue-eyed, incredibly tall Austrian girls with those tall fur hats in their ski clothes, going around with St. Bernards, with barrels of schnapps around their necks," said Norma.

The best surprise came when they ran into Bills owner Ralph Wilson, who was attending on his own. Early in the Games, news had come back from New York that the NFL had signed a record-breaking two-year, $28.2 million TV contract with CBS—the deal that many NFL owners hoped would spell the demise of the AFL. But just days later, the Jets owner Sonny Werblin shrewdly orchestrated a deal with NBC sports head Carl Lindemann that brought the AFL a $42 million deal for a five-year contract—which would lift each AFL team's annual TV revenue to nearly a million dollars per year, actually narrowing the TV disparity with the NFL. In Austria, the impeccably dressed Wilson and the rumpled Lamar raised a toast (though Lamar's drink may well have been hot cocoa) to the long-term health of the AFL. With the new NBC television deal, the AFL's survival seemed assured. "I didn't hear any, 'Gee, we made it' talk," said Norma. "But they knew they'd taken one gigantic step forward."(Back in Pittsburgh, the Steelers' Art Rooney recognized that the AFL was now around to stay, telling his sons, "They don't have to call us 'Mister' anymore.")

It would have been difficult for the future to be any brighter. Lamar's team had been profitable for the first time in 1963, the shambolic New York franchise that Werblin had purchased had been transformed in a year, and, later in 1964, it would open at the new Shea Stadium, drawing 50,000 fans a game. The Broncos were on the right track and even the Raiders, remade in the image of the former Charger scout Al Davis, had been stabilized. In fact, the battle between the leagues only served to raise pro football's profile. By the fall of 1964, a *Fortune* magazine cover story noted that the game "is wonderfully attuned to the pace and style of American life in the 1960's. To a nation of spectators, it offers an unsurpassed spectacle. In a time of mass education, it is an educated man's game."

The signing of the NBC deal had raised the stakes in the war between the leagues. Though their contract didn't originally call for payments until 1965, NBC advanced five different AFL clubs $250,000 each to help them cover signing bonuses in November 1964, on the eve of the '65 draft. Signing players offered a double advantage, in that it had the zero-sum result of bringing a good player into one league and keeping him out of the other, and it furthered the perception in the press that "the war" was being won.

The entire ordeal brought the AFL owners closer together. Billy Sullivan in Boston was most attuned to the numerous sacrifices Lamar had made, thinking league first and then the fate of the Chiefs. Adams saw Lamar most frequently, though they were not particularly well-matched in temperament—Lamar with his low-key reluctance, Bud barreling into a room. (If any AFL owner was going to get into a fistfight with a member of the press, it could only have been Adams, who did exactly that with *Houston Post* scribe Jack Gallagher in 1966.)

Lamar was perhaps most comfortable with the Bills' Ralph Wilson. They would sometimes eat together during weeks of league meetings in New York. And Lamar appreciated Ralph's fiscal restraint. At Toots Shor's once, Wilson greeted the owner with a bit of kibitzing. "Toots, your prices are outrageous," Wilson cheerfully told him. "I could get a steak like this for half as much in Buffalo."

"Yeah," replied Shor. "But when you finished it, Ralph, you'd still be in Buffalo."

Even Wilson, sensible though he was, couldn't resist poking fun at Lamar's legendary frugality. By agreement, when the owners met en masse in New York, they would take turns picking up the check. In 1965, with Lamar due to pick up the tab for the next meeting, Sonny Werblin and Adams decided the group would eat at 21. Prior to the visit, Werblin had the staff prepare a series of fake menus just for the occasion, in which all the normal 21 prices (already exorbitant) were doubled and tripled. Then, at lunch, the group went around ordering elaborate portions of caviar and filet. At the first sign of Lamar's raised eyebrow, the group fell into laughter and confessed.

But for all the mirth at his expense, the question wasn't one of generosity so much as prudence. "Lamar would always pick up the check," said Dan Jenkins. "But he didn't like being taken advantage of. And he would have friends make reservations for him, not using his name, because he thought people charged more if they knew it was a Hunt."

Those who knew him best understood that some of his most infamous instances of frugality had more to do with the pace of his life than an aversion to spending money.

"He was a spokesman for Hart, Schaffner & Marx," said Jake Cobb. "As a nice gesture, they sent him some beautiful suits. All he had to do was go in and get them fitted. Those suits hung in his office closet for years. He would never take the time to get a tailor. He'd always say, 'I'm going to do that next week.'"

The most notorious instance conflating Lamar's thriftiness with his impatience occurred in New York. At an AFL league meeting, Werblin noticed the holes in his shoes, and Lamar sheepishly admitted he needed to get them resoled.

The next morning, the owners gathered at their conference room and Werblin interrupted the start of the meeting. "My friends, can I just say I have never seen a man so cheap as this," and he pointed to Lamar. "He got *one shoe* soled!"

In the midst of a round of laughter, Lamar explained that by the time he found the shoemaker, it was almost time for him to close. He said he'd have time to do only one shoe.

"So I'll get the other one done the first chance I've got." And of course, he didn't.

Though the joke about Lamar's cheapness was ongoing, the losses the AFL owners absorbed were real, even after the NBC windfall. It was Lamar who, cognizant of the challenges faced in Boston and Denver, pushed hardest for roster limits and prudent spending. Having set out on his own, away from his father, to pursue another business, Lamar was perhaps more committed than most to making sure football was a legitimate business. And one of the definitions of a legitimate business was that it made money.

But for the league, profitability would remain elusive as long as the AFL was battling the NFL. The conflict between the leagues took on tones of the Cold War, full of intrigue, double-dealing, and a layered sense of reality.

In 1965, the NFL established "Operation Hand-Holding," a highly sophisticated "babysitter" program, in which the league recruited salesmen and other business executives to make contact with draft prospects weeks before the draft. "We didn't call them 'babysitters,'" said Rams general manager Bert Rose. "We called them 'NFL representatives.' We put the program into operation in about three weeks. We had about eighty men, about thirty of whom were friends of mine and the rest who were recommended by friends. Almost all of them had the same thing in common: They were sales oriented. They had to be, since we were asking them to sell the NFL to the best pro prospects in the country."

At its most extreme, the babysitting program was equal parts auction, fraternity rush, and velvet-gloved kidnapping. One operation found twenty-seven different players squired away in a hotel in Detroit, and the AFL teams interested in drafting them repeatedly frustrated in trying to get though. In that same '65 draft, the Chiefs had high hopes for signing the dazzling running back Gale Sayers from Kansas. "Sayers, in fact, was married to a girl from K.C.," said Hank Stram, "and he told us he was definitely signing with the Chiefs, when suddenly Buddy Young of the NFL flew into town and simply made off with him." Sayers signed with the Chicago Bears.

Even after losing Sayers, the Chiefs didn't come away empty-handed in the '65 draft, owing in part to a decision Lamar had made a year earlier, when he'd suggested to Klosterman that the Chiefs hire the inimitable Lloyd Wells as an addition to the scouting staff. "The Judge" was an ebullient, sly, ladies' man, a Houston photographer with a long list of contacts, a taste for fine things, and an angle on virtually everything. He had invited Lamar to a black all-star football game in Houston and spoke persuasively about his contacts within the black community. Lamar didn't need to be talked into recognizing the vast reservoir of untapped talent in the black colleges. He'd seen it as far back as the Yam Bowl of his high school days.

Added to the staff, proudly driving around in the red Lincoln with the Chiefs decal on the doors, Wells—the first full-time black scout in pro football—was instrumental in the club's effort to comb the country and connect to players from historically black colleges. Some other pro teams were aware of the talent that existed down South, where the schools in the Southeastern, Southwestern, and Atlantic Coast Conferences remained entirely segregated. But with Wells, the Chiefs were there first and most convincingly, and in the space of a few years, the team selected players from Grambling, Jackson State, Southern, Prairie View, Morgan State, and Tennessee State, all of whom would become pro stars.

That 1965 draft included one of the war's greatest cases of signing intrigue, and certainly its most legendary, the one for Prairie View A&M wide receiver Otis Taylor. At 6-foot-3, 220 pounds, fast, strong, a physical blocker, and a marvelous athlete with dazzling long strides, Taylor was a spectacular glimpse of the future of the wide receiver position. Decades later, Klosterman would say, "When I first saw Jerry Rice, the person I thought of was Otis Taylor." Lamar had personally scouted him as well, catching him in the Prairie View–Wiley College game that he attended, along with Norma and Klosterman, at the Cotton Bowl in 1963.

The Chiefs were confident they would sign Taylor; Lloyd Wells was a friend of the family, had known Taylor since junior high school, and had remained close to him throughout his college years. But on Wednesday, November 26, in a classic case of babysitter subterfuge, the Cowboys descended on the Prairie View campus and invited Taylor and teammate Seth Cartwright away to spend Thanksgiving in Dallas, with handshakes and a kind of pushy cordiality.

While Taylor was being squired away, Wells was down in Tennessee, trying to keep tabs on another prospective Chiefs choice. Klosterman, checking with Taylor as a matter of course, was alarmed when repeated calls to his dorm went unanswered. "So I called Otis's mother," said Klosterman, "and told her that I thought her son had been kidnapped." Wells, having heard from Klosterman, rushed back to Texas and began scouring the Houston area, calling Taylor's mother, his girlfriend, and many of his friends. He learned that Taylor and Cartwright had been taken to a Holiday Inn in Richardson, just outside of Dallas, where they were being watched over by Buddy Young and another babysitter. When Wells tried to go see Taylor, he was recognized instantly, and the Cowboys representatives wouldn't let him through the lobby.

Wells was providing periodic reports to Klosterman, who during one call told him, "Just tell Otis his red T-bird is parked outside the Kansas City Chiefs facility, waiting for him." Later that night, Wells helped Taylor and Cartwright sneak out the back balcony of their hotel room and flew them to Kansas City. The following day, after signing his contract, Taylor joined the Chiefs on a trip to New York for a Jets game on Sunday, November 29, then returned with the team to Kansas City and proudly drove his new red Thunderbird home to Houston.

"The intrigue," Lamar would say decades later, "was marvelous. The public loved it. I loved it."

•

The 1964 season, another injury-marred disappointment at 7–7, was overshadowed for Lamar by the news that Norma was pregnant. Clark Knobel Hunt was born on February 19, 1965, by which time Lamar and Norma had moved to Highland Park, into a handsome white house with four columns in front, at 4231 Armstrong Parkway. It was beautiful, yet sparsely appointed, with a small black-and-white television in the living room, the couple having agreed to furnish it gradually, one room at a time.

By this time, Lamar had grown preoccupied with maintaining his fitness. He'd seen many in his family gravitate toward an egg-shaped middle life: H. L., Lyda in her later years, Bunker, even Caroline. He would never say it out loud, but he fretted over his weight even more than his siblings. On the second floor of the home, Lamar put a five-gallon container from a watercooler. Every day after returning from work, he would sprint upstairs place his spare change in it. "I don't get as much exercise as I should," he once explained to Stram. "I figure I get two benefits at the same time."

He was still traveling plenty, but with the marriage, his new child, and the franchise being more stable, Lamar and Norma lived a life verging on the normal. He spent more time playing what he described as "fat-man football," a regular touch game with some old friends from SMU. He also began coaching Lamar, Jr.'s little league team. He delved into this with customary vigor. He typed up a short playbook, which secretary Jean Finn mimeographed off to distribute to the team. One year, when the team decided to call itself the Mongooses, Lamar found fifty decals of mongooses and carefully affixed them on all the boys' helmets.

For Sharron, by now six years old, he did the most important thing in the world a father could do: He got her and Lamar, Jr., tickets to the Beatles show, September 18, 1964, at Dallas Memorial Coliseum. Lamar, Jr., had already shown an aptitude for music and was taking guitar lessons. Earlier that year, Lamar had taken Sharron to a theater in downtown Dallas to see *A Hard Day's Night*. She would recall him lying on his back in the living room, gently holding her hands as he lifted her up by his stockinged feet, and saying, "Okay, now sing 'A Hard Day's Night' for me!"

They had tickets in the front row, and when they arrived—while the opening act, the Bill Black Combo, had just started playing—there were people in their seats. Rather than confront the squatters, Lamar presented his tickets to an arena usher, and the official cleared the seats for them. When the Beatles opened with "Twist and Shout," Sharron started twisting and Lamar joined in. For Lamar, the concert was an act of parental love. "None of that ever had any appeal for me," he said. "I didn't like the loud noise." His own musical tastes were geared more toward what he described as "romantic music." Others noticed he had a fondness for country crooners in an era when Nashville was moving toward a more cosmopolitan, mainstream sound.

Though his schedule was often erratic, dependent on the Chiefs' schedule and AFL league meetings, he found the time to make it all work. Lamar did not need to explain to Norma that he didn't want to repeat the sins of his own father, who had been an absentee parent in the lives of most of his children. "He spent more time with the kids when he was divorced than he had when we were married," said Rose Mary. Though Rose Mary spiraled dangerously close to a nervous breakdown in the months following the separation, she soon steadied herself and by 1965 remarried to a businessman named John Carr. "Norma was a better wife to him than I could ever be," said Rose Mary. "She was young and pretty and had so much energy. And she liked being out there with Lamar. She was wonderful."

Even under the best of circumstances and with the best of intentions, the divorce had wrenching consequences. Lamar made an extra effort to see his oldest children regularly, but they were less a part of the daily bustle. "After the divorce you just about never saw Rose Mary and Lamar, Jr., and Sharron," said Al Hill, Jr. "I knew where they were—they were over on Walnut Hill—but they really just weren't even around."

Inevitably, of course, something was lost for Lamar in his relationship with Lamar, Jr., and Sharron. "There's a lingering pain that goes with it," said Sharron, who was just three when Lamar and Rose Mary separated. "Even though it wasn't my divorce, there's a piece of your dad that you didn't get. And I always missed that piece of Dad. I always missed that."

CHAPTER NINE

"I BELIEVE WE SHOULD 'COIN A PHRASE' . . ."

It was in 1963, not long after Lamar announced that his team would be coming to Kansas City, when he first met the owner of the city's other big-league sports franchise, the Chicago insurance mogul Charles O. Finley, who'd purchased the Kansas City Athletics baseball team in 1960 and, seemingly, had been trying to move them out of the city ever since.

"This is a horseshit town," Finley told Lamar, by way of introduction, "and no one will ever do any good here." Lamar remained steadfastly cordial, though a bit alarmed. In the months following, Finley subsequently tried to persuade Lamar to join him in moving both franchises to Louisville.

Though he politely rejected Finley's offer, it was true that Kansas City had proved a somewhat tougher sell than he'd expected. After the initial burst of excitement and season-ticket orders, the city had been slow to fully embrace the Chiefs, in part because of the team's disappointing records in 1963 and 1964, but also because Kansas Citians had grown weary and distrustful of Finley and the Athletics, who hadn't enjoyed a winning season since their arrival in 1955.

For their part, the Chiefs had been maddeningly uneven, rather than consistently futile. In 1965, Kansas City fell early to the Raiders but earned a win and a tie in their season series against the division champion Chargers, finishing 7–5–2, in third place in the AFL West. It was a season of discontent, played amid rumors that the team might be considering moving again—the season-ticket rolls had dipped below 10,000—and many Chiefs fans were growing more vociferous in their criticism of Stram.

Some viewed the Chiefs' supporters as overly demanding, but Lamar saw the larger truth: The fans of Kansas City were beginning to care passionately about the team. On the north side of the stadium, right behind the team's benches, the section of stands became known as the "Wolfpack." After a 52–21 win over the Oilers on November 29, the next day's *Kansas City Times* included a story on the clamorous crowd, titled "Wolves Wail as Chiefs Prevail." Two weeks later, on the morning of December 12 in Buffalo, Lamar approved an outline for the team's new season-ticket drive. The Chiefs would embrace the growing involvement of the crowd, and the slogan for the new promotion was "Join the Wolfpack."

That day in Buffalo, the Chiefs fell to the eventual repeat AFL champions, the Bills, and also saw their star running back, Mack Lee Hill, felled by a knee injury. One of the club's early stars in Kansas City, Hill was recruited to the Chiefs in 1964 by the redoubtable scout Lloyd Wells, who signed him for a $300 bonus. In the game at Buffalo, Hill ruptured a knee ligament, and Lamar consoled him in the dank Buffalo locker room as news circulated that he'd likely need to have season-ending knee surgery back in Kansas City.

Hill was notoriously skittish about needles and surgery, but Stram and his teammates persuaded him to get the surgery done quickly, and he was admitted to Menorah Medical Center Monday evening. But Tuesday morning, during the routine procedure, Hill's body reacted to the anesthesia and developed hyperthermia, rising to 108 degrees. Despite frantic efforts to save him, Hill died on the operating table. The call to Dallas with the tragic news—coming just two years after Stone Johnson's death—left Lamar in tears. "I didn't know until, late in the day, Lamar got a call in his office," said Norma. "We just stood there in the kitchen and cried together."

The gravity of Hill's death transcended the fans' complaints about the team's sporadic performance, and changed the tone of the conversation about the Chiefs. Len Dawson's eloquent eulogy at the funeral later in the week served as a testament to the love the team had for Hill, as well as underscoring Dawson's status as the unquestioned team leader. "As terrible as that was, I think the tragedy established a bond between Kansas City and the Chiefs," said Lamar. "Things really began to change soon after."

The team faced another public relations crisis a few weeks later over comments from Don Klosterman, who while in San Francisco for the East-West Shrine Game (where the Chiefs were about to sign USC's Heisman Trophy–winning running back Mike Garrett) breezily implied that the team might move to Los Angeles. Coming on the heels of another Klosterman quote comparing Kansas City to purgatory ("it's not exactly heaven and it's not exactly hell"), the publicity surrounding it exacerbated an already strained situation—prompting another round of rumors that the Chiefs were considering a move—and forced Klosterman's resignation, at Steadman's insistence.

H. L. Hunt (left) in 1932, the year Lamar was born, and Lyda Hunt, in the '40s. "I never heard a cross word between them," said Lamar's sister Caroline.

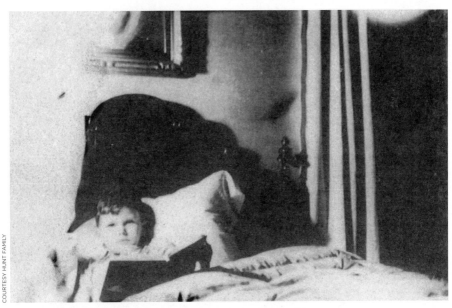

Lamar, aged five, reading in his bedroom at Mount Vernon, circa 1938.

Lamar (center) giving chase to brother Herbert (left), along with Buddy and Paula Rupe, in the Rupe's backyard, early '40s.

Lamar started scrapbooking before he was ten years old. In 1944, he began a new scrapbook on the D-Day Invasion.

While his brothers began early careers in business, Lamar spent his summers getting in shape for football season. One year, Bunker gave him a blocking sled for Christmas.

Lamar with teammate Tom Richey, at The Hill School in Pottstown, Pennsylvania. During his time at The Hill, Lamar became a football star, emulating the man he called his "idol," Doak Walker, who wore number 37 for SMU.

SIXTH FORM

LAMAR HUNT

"Cap," "Herbie," "Kitty,"

"C-Rads"

Dallas, Texas

Lamar's entry in The Hill School Yearbook, *The Dial,* in 1951.

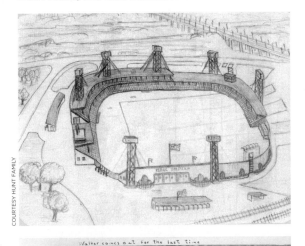

The April 5, 1948, issue of *Life* speculating whether H. L. was "the richest man in the U.S." jolted Lamar, who, in his own words, "had no idea."

Lamar's eye for composition was evident at an early age, as in this sketch (middle left) of a minor-league ballpark he composed at The Hill. He continued scrapbooking throughout his life. In a book devoted to Doak Walker, he carefully wrote on the border (left) about Walker being helped off the field during his final appearance for the Mustangs, against TCU in 1949.

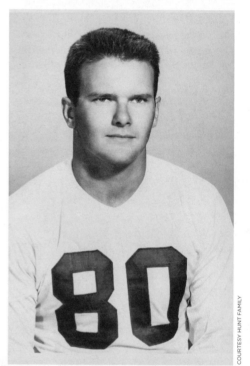

1952 86 87 1953

Southern Methodist University

Students Association Membership Ticket

This ticket is not transferable. If presented for admission by any person other than the one to whom issued, it will be forfeited. If lost, it will not be duplicated.

Lamar Hunt
Signature

TO BE VALID MUST BE SIGNED IN INK

21 22 23 24 25 26 27 28 29 30

11 12 13 14 15 16 17 18 19 20

1 2 3 ○ ○ 6 7 8 9 10

599

VOTED SMU

Lamar would stay at SMU for five years, during which time he'd play football, fall in love with Rose Mary Whittle, join the Kappa Sigma fraternity, and remain unconvinced that he wanted to spend a life in the oil business.

Lamar played four years of football at SMU without ever lettering. To teammate (and future Hall of Famer) Forrest Gregg, he was "one of the guys."

Lamar in the summer of 1955, with his beloved dog Herschel in his lap.

After their January 1956 marriage, Lamar and Rose Mary traveled extensively, including to Las Vegas (above) in 1957 and, after Sharron's birth, to Europe in 1958. All the while, Lamar was languishing at Hunt Oil and pondering a jump into the sports business.

On August 3, 1959, one day after his twenty-seventh birthday, Lamar announced the formation of a new football league, which would in the coming weeks be named the American Football League. After three years spent as a largely forgotten figure in a small office, he suddenly became the center of a national sports enterprise.

The Texans leased a practice field and had a drive-through ticket office at the corner of the North Central Expressway and Yale Boulevard (now SMU Boulevard), the same spot where Lamar had run his Zima-Bat business in college.

Absorbing losses in the early years, the group of AFL owners became known as "The Foolish Club." From a 1961 publicity photo: Billy Sullivan, Cal Kunz, Bud Adams (seated), Ralph Wilson, Lamar, Commissioner Joe Foss (seated), Harry Wismer, Wayne Valley, and Barron Hilton.

At first, the AFL's launch was a battle for publicity. Lamar did whatever it took to raise the profile of the new league, including this 1959 newspaper advertisement, in which he modeled "the first short-sleeved suit shown in Dallas."

The Texan Hostesses, hired to spur season-ticket sales, were trained by the team's broadcaster, Charlie Jones (next to Lamar), and included schoolteacher Norma Knobel (to the left of Jones), who in 1964 would become Lamar's second wife.

The war between the leagues was a constant search for talented young players. Here Lamar officially signs Kansas running back Curtis McClinton, following a college all-star game.

Despite an array of promotions, the Texans played for three years at the Cotton Bowl in front of mostly empty seats. Here Lamar engages in a pregame publicity stunt—a punting competition against a pair of local disc jockeys.

After the Texans won the 1962 AFL Championship Game, Lamar celebrated in the locker room with Sherrill Headrick (69), Hank Stram, and the rest of the team.

In the spring of 1966, Lamar and Norma moved to Kansas City for a few months, to lead a drive that raised season-ticket rolls from 9,550 to 21,000. During that winter and spring, he attended hundreds of functions like this one.

By the mid-'60s, Lamar started dabbling in photography, often going to the sideline to shoot part of the Chiefs games. Here he's flanked by Chiefs general manager Jack Steadman (left) and longtime friend Bill McNutt.

New Year's Day, 1967, after the Chiefs routed the Bills, 31–7, to earn a spot in the first Super Bowl, Lamar joined the team back at a Buffalo hotel banquet room to watch the Cowboys–Packers NFL title game. He sits on the floor next to Hank Stram (both had their ties cut by players in the postgame celebration), with Sharron on his lap.

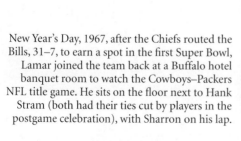

But that was a lone bump in an otherwise remarkable offseason. After emphasizing his commitment following Klosterman's resignation, Lamar worked with the newly formed Greater Kansas City Sports Commission to shore up the Chiefs' season-ticket rolls, and also began talking about the need for a new world-class stadium for the city.

Earlier that December, Lamar had asked Norma if she would consider moving to Kansas City for a few months while the Chiefs worked on a dedicated season-ticket campaign. Subletting a condo overlooking the Country Club Plaza, the Hunts relocated for the winter and spring. Lamar drove to work at the offices in Swope Park, and he went to every Kiwanis Club gathering and Junior Chamber of Commerce meeting he could find, in essence putting the same effort into convincing Kansas City of his commitment as he had in Dallas in 1960.

And to rally support closer to home, he turned the season-ticket drive itself into a form of competition. "We were using some of Margaret and Al Hill's old furniture in our home on Armstrong," said Norma. "The family room was totally full of their old furniture. And he said, 'You know something? If we can sell 20,000 season tickets, we're gonna get new furniture for the family room.' So, I was . . . 'Yes! How fast can we get there?! Work hard!' He knew I was going to think it was wonderful to get new furniture, but that was a goal for him. He had to set that goal, and then he had to reach it. That was what he told himself."

The agency Valentine Radford had pushed for an opportunity to get the Chiefs account, and to launch the campaign, the graphic artist John Martin came up with a stylized cartoon figure of a wolf with long, serrated ears. The pitch was note-perfect, and the execution of the campaign was assured. Offering fans the opportunity to pay for their season tickets with an installment plan at several local banks was crucial, and throughout the off-season months, fans signed up.

By day, Norma strolled along Brush Creek with baby Clark, and in the evenings she accompanied Lamar to many of the events, growing more comfortable with the city and the Country Club Plaza. As he'd done before, Lamar showed an aptitude for convincing people he met of his sincerity. The drive lifted season-ticket rolls from 9,550 in 1965 to more than 21,000 by April 1966. In so doing, the Chiefs finally proved they were in Kansas City to stay. Also, Norma got her new living-room set.

•

On April 4, 1966, in the Chiefs offices on 63rd Street in Swope Park, Lamar was working on the wording of a newspaper advertisement when he received a phone call from the Cowboys' president and GM Tex Schramm. The smart, combustible Schramm had never cared for Lamar, always viewing him as obstructing the Cowboys' growth in Dallas. But on this day, he seemed unusually polite, and asked if Lamar "might be able to come to Dallas to discuss a matter of mutual importance."

Lamar was returning to Texas two days later anyway, on his way to an AFL owners meeting in Houston. He adjusted his schedule to book a lengthy layover in Dallas before continuing to Houston. On the evening of Wednesday, April 6, he got off his plane at Love Field in Dallas and walked to the statue of the Texas Ranger in the terminal's lobby. There, waiting adjacent to the statue, reading a paper, was Schramm. They shook hands and quietly moved to the door, walking into the vast Love Field parking lot, where they sat in Schramm's Oldsmobile in the twilight, and spoke for about 45 minutes.

Once inside, Schramm delivered his message. "I think the time has come," he said, "to talk about a merger, if you'd be interested in that."

"Fine," said Lamar, evenly. "I'm interested."

Schramm made a few things clear: The NFL would want Pete Rozelle to be the commissioner of a merged league; further discussions would have to be confidential, but that the NFL was finally willing to consider a merger in which all existing AFL franchises would be accepted into the NFL. After their discussion, Schramm said he would call Lamar later in the month to talk more specifically about a framework for a deal. Much of the college signing frenzy had died down by April, and it seemed a good time for truce talks.

Lamar continued his trip, heading down to Houston, for the owners meeting. He didn't tell any of his colleagues ("I wouldn't have at that point—there had been negotiations before, and it had all come to nothing, so there was no reason to bring it up at that point") and, in the event, there were more pressing issues.

On April 8, at the AFL owners meeting in Houston, Commissioner Joe Foss resigned (when it became clear that he would be fired by the AFL owners if he didn't). Criticism of Foss had grown steadily over the years, and the success of the NFL's babysitting program, along with the older league's eleventh-hour landing of Atlanta as an expansion franchise (after the AFL had announced it would move to that city), only weakened his position.

For its new commissioner the league elected Al Davis. This was an alarming choice for leaders in both leagues. For starters, Davis was hardly beloved within the AFL. Writing a year earlier in *Sports Illustrated*, Bud Shrake noted that outside of Oakland, "it is not certain where Al Davis would finish in a popularity contest among sharks, the mumps, the income tax, and himself. If the voters were the other American Football League coaches, Davis probably would be third, edging out income tax in a thriller." But still chastened over the results of the '66 draft, the majority of AFL owners decided Davis would be the perfect man to run the league in the event that the war escalated. "There was a feeling that we needed a fighter," said one AFL owner. "Someone who was willing to go eye-for-eye with the NFL." That would happen soon enough. In the short term, Davis began to ramp up the league's own babysitting program, to reach out to college seniors and fight the NFL on its own terms.

On May 3, Schramm visited Lamar at his home on Armstrong Parkway. They sat down together and Schramm outlined a more detailed framework of a deal. The NFL would ask for $18 million indemnity from the AFL but would take all eight teams from the AFL, and would consent to let all the teams remain in their present markets. Later that week, at a meeting in Sonny Werblin's apartment, Lamar first mentioned the proposal to his fellow owners. The group pointedly didn't include Davis on the information. "Al was just starting to put together his own staff at the AFL offices," Lamar said, "and we all knew it could fall through at any moment. If it didn't fall through, well, we were going to be putting him out of a job."

Werblin and Wayne Valley—who would be sharing markets in New York and the Bay Area with established NFL franchises—were both very chilly to the idea, but Lamar succeeded that day in changing the AFL bylaws so a merger could be approved with a two-thirds majority rather than a unanimous vote.

The next news Lamar heard, on May 16, was less encouraging. "Something's happened," Schramm explained over the phone. "The Giants just signed Pete Gogolak." For nearly seven years, the two leagues abided by an unwritten agreement that, while they would compete for incoming rookies through their respective drafts, they would not attempt to sign the other league's veterans. That policy came to an abrupt end when the Giants signed the Buffalo Bills' soccer-style placekicker Gogolak, who had been the second leading scorer in the AFL during the Bills title seasons of 1964 and 1965. In 1965, Gogolak kicked a pro record 28 field goals while playing out the option year of his contract. The Giants' Wellington Mara heard from Gogolak's agent that the kicker was willing to jump leagues and hastily signed him to a three-year, $96,000 contract, the largest ever for a place-kicker. It was, arguably, the single most provocative act of the decade in the war between the leagues.

Anticipating the reaction, Schramm had called Lamar before the news broke to inform him of the signing, and to reassure him that, despite appearances to the contrary, the NFL owners were nearing an understanding, and the senior league was acting in good faith. When the news broke the next day, Al Davis had all the provocation he needed. But since the merger negotiations were going on without Davis's knowledge, there was little that Lamar could do to stop Davis from his own plan of attack. Davis returned that night to the Plaza Hotel in New York and, in a cryptic interview, told the *New York Times*' Arthur Daley, "This is something I've been aware of, and I anticipated the probability. But you don't make threats at a time like this. Our answer will be in action. This is not the time to speak."

"There was no coordinated plan of response," said Lamar, "because there was no plan to begin with. We couldn't tell Al about the negotiations, and he wasn't going to tell us about what he was doing. You'd just hear things. What Al was doing, he was doing on his own."

On one side, Schramm and Lamar were engaged in their negotiations to bring about the terms for a peace. On the other side, Davis, unaware of the truce talks, was waging his response to the Gogolak signing, a guerilla war of retribution on behalf of the AFL that at times threatened to make any peace impossible.

Davis's tactics bore fruit quickly. On May 23, the AFL had its first response. In Oakland, the Rams' young quarterback, Roman Gabriel, met the Raiders coach John Rauch at the Oakland Airport and received a bonus check for $100,000, then signed a contract for four years at $75,000 per year, for a package of $400,000. The deal, announced by the Raiders on May 26, quickly brought a retort from the Rams stating *they* had just signed Gabriel to a contract renewal.

Schramm and his close friend Pete Rozelle realized a deal would need to be struck quickly or Davis's counterattack could further escalate the hostilities. While Schramm and Rozelle secretly convened at Schramm's house in Dallas, Lamar went ahead with his plans and headed with Norma and a group of friends to Indianapolis over Memorial Day weekend, to watch the Indianapolis 500. Buddy Rupe was in Indianapolis with Lamar and found him, in this instance, unusually open. "You're going to hear some things," Lamar said to his old friend. "They're all true, but keep your mouth shut."

Unbeknownst to either Schramm or Lamar, Davis's assistants were working that very weekend on the AFL's next big signing. At Davis's behest, Don Klosterman, by now the GM of the Houston Oilers, started recruiting John Brodie, the 49ers starting quarterback, whose contract was up for renewal. Klosterman had known Brodie for ten years, understood how fanatical the quarterback was about golfing (he'd played two years on the PGA tour), and believed he could be wooed. That Friday, May 28, Brodie headed to Houston, to meet with Klosterman and Bud Adams. After haggling for a bit, Adams wrote out the terms of a contract on a cocktail napkin: "The AFL agrees to pay John Brodie $250,000 a season for three seasons."

Schramm and Rozelle were huddling on specific points of the proposed agreement when Schramm received a phone call from an apoplectic Lou Spadia, 49ers general manager, about the AFL's offer to Brodie.

"And so here it is," recalled Schramm, "we've worked this all out and now we've got the Brodie situation. And so we want to get a hold of Lamar, and he's up in *fucking Indianapolis* at this race! Well, if you've ever tried to find anybody up there, it's damn near impossible. We finally got him, and I told Lamar, 'Look, I can't hold these people together. They're going to get mad and they're going to do something, and if that happens, the merger is gone. You gotta stop this sonofabitch.'"

Lamar had already called Adams and Klosterman, to try to dissuade them from going through with the signing. By now, Davis knew some negotiations were going on between the AFL and NFL owners, but he wasn't aware of the particulars. He was angry at being left out of the loop and convinced that continuing his program would only increase the AFL's bargaining power. Later that night, he called Lamar and explained that whatever was happening, Lamar's bargaining position would be stronger with Brodie signed than it would be without his signature. In this, he was probably right. By now, San Francisco's front office was shell-shocked and resigned to the inevitability of the merger. In the days ahead, 49ers GM Lou Spadia became adamant about retaining Brodie, above all else. "I just want my quarterback," he repeated.

Lamar returned from Indianapolis late the night of May 30, agreeing that there was little choice but to forge ahead, and as quickly as possible. The next morning, he visited Schramm's house. Speaking from five pages of notes he had compiled with Rozelle, Schramm outlined the plan. Writing on a legal pad, Lamar carefully transcribed the specifics. When he finished, Schramm said, "There it is. If you accept, this deal has been approved by every NFL club. If you have to alter it too much, it will blow up."

Lamar flew to New York later that day, to meet with the AFL owners, many of whom balked at the figure of $18 million. "They should pay us," insisted Werblin. But by now, Lamar knew a good deal when he saw one. "I was just beginning to understand the true value of money," he said. With twenty years to pay off the total, the fee amounted to a cost of $2 million per team over the twenty years, with much of the money coming from accrued interest. This paled in comparison to the instantly increased value and revenues for each team in the league, as well as the reduced costs of a stabilized environment with a common draft.

Over the next few days, the negotiation progressed to the fine-grained details of the agreement. Lamar called Schramm back by phone and outlined the twenty-six points with which the AFL took issue, almost all of them involved the wording of the agreements between the two New York clubs and San Francisco and Oakland. By Sunday night, June 5, meeting back in Dallas at Schramm's home, they ironed out almost all of the remaining sticking points. By this time, rumors were increasing in the press and reporters were staked outside both the NFL and AFL offices.

The NFL owners approved the terms of the merger in a telephone conference call on the morning of June 7. That evening, while Lamar was traveling to Washington for more secret meetings, the Patriots' Billy Sullivan sat down with Al Davis and told him he was about to be out of a job. Davis was angry that he'd been left out of the loop on the negotiations, and angry about the terms of the agreement. "I wanted a merger," Davis said. "But I didn't like the terms of the merger. I thought it would be great because we can compete against those guys."

Later that night, in the frantic final hours, Hunt, Schramm, Rozelle, and his aide Jim Kensil converged in Washington, D.C. At the Sheraton-Carlton Hotel, in a suite registered under the fictitious name of Ralph Pittman, the five men spent much of the night banging out the wording for the press release the next day, finally finishing at 3 a.m. Throughout the evening and the next day, the NFL's lead counsel, Hamilton Carothers of Covington & Burling, fielded phone calls from team lawyers, one who asked to vet a copy of the signed agreement. "There is no signed agreement," said Carothers. "It's all just notes, from Tex and Lamar."

The press release came out that afternoon, Wednesday, June 8:

JOINT STATEMENT
NATIONAL AND AMERICAN FOOTBALL LEAGUES

The NFL and AFL today announced plans to join in an expanded major professional football league. It will consist of 26 teams in 25 cities—with expectation of additional teams in the near future.

The main points of the plan include:

-Pete Rozelle will be the commissioner.
-A world championship game this season.
-All existing franchises retained.
-No franchises transferred from present locations.
-Two new franchises no later than 1968.
-Two more teams as soon thereafter as practical.
-Inter-league pre-season games in 1967.
-Single league schedule in 1970.
-A common draft next January.
-Continued two-network TV coverage.

The press conference that day at the Warwick Hotel in New York found Rozelle flanked by Lamar and Tex Schramm. Lamar chimed in when called upon, politely foiling a harangue from Howard Cosell about what might happen with the contracts that NFL players signed with AFL teams. He was humble and genial, but his smile was the most natural and relaxed of the three men. Not seven years after he sat in the back of a congressional meeting room in Washington, D.C, hearing Bert Bell invoke the possibility of a new football league, he and his seven partners would be merging with the National Football League. In doing so, Lamar knew, he had won.

That night, Lamar and Tex shared a plane ride back to Dallas. When they deplaned they again passed the statue of the Texas Ranger.

"I guess this time it's okay for us to be seen together," said Lamar with a smile.

"I suppose so," said Schramm. The two men shook hands and parted.

The weeks ahead were marked by both satisfaction and optimism on the part of the AFL owners. There was also, unmistakably, a powerful sense of vindication for Lamar and all those who'd believed in "The Foolish Club."

A week after the merger, Norma read with satisfaction *Sports Illustrated's* account of the merger, written by the longtime AFL antagonist Tex

Maule. "Would it be okay," she proposed, "if I send a dead crow to Tex—and I'm going to tell him to eat it. Would you let me do that?"

Lamar dipped his head, looked over at his wife, and said, "Nooo." But he was smiling when he said it.

Shortly after the merger was announced, Pete Rozelle appointed a committee—consisting of himself and three owners from each league (the Cowboys' Tex Schramm, the Colts' Carroll Rosenbloom, and the Rams' Dan Reeves from the NFL; Lamar, Ralph Wilson, and Boston's Billy Sullivan of the AFL)—to meet and iron out the myriad details of the coming union. It would take eighteen full months for the merger agreement to be codified, but in the first six months, the group was preoccupied with discussions about the first game between the leagues, which would match the AFL and NFL champions in January 1967.

Plans for the new game had started almost immediately. Rozelle had brokered the compromise that would allow both networks—CBS and NBC—to broadcast the first playing of what was being referred to in the media of the day as "the World Series of football," matching the NFL and AFL champs. As the seven men on the merger committee sat around a conference table in the summer of 1966, exchanging ideas about the schedule, Lamar asked about the timing of the game: "Should there be a one-week break or two before the championship game?"

"Wait," said one of the other committee members, confused about whether he was talking about the league championship games or the new world championship. "Which game do you mean?"

"You know," explained Lamar. "The last game . . . the final game. The *Super Bowl*."

There were smiles all around, and some chuckles. The name had occurred to Lamar one day that summer. The previous Christmas, Norma had given each of the children one of the hot novelties of the day, the Wham-O company's high-bouncing Super Ball, which Lamar, Jr., and Sharron loved bouncing on the driveway and over the house. (More than a decade later, Lamar's recollection of this was quite clear: "My daughter Sharron was six years old then, and she had a ball called a Super Ball, which had incredible bounce. She could bounce it on concrete and it literally would go over the house. She and Lamar, Jr., always were talking about the Super Ball. I don't remember consciously thinking, 'Gee this is going to be a good name for the game.'")

In the weeks ahead, as the group mapped out its plans in a series of meetings, it began informally distinguishing between league championship games and the finale by referring colloquially to the final game as "the Super Bowl."

"But nobody ever said let's make that the name of the game," said Lamar. "Far from it, we all agreed it was far too corny to be the name of the new title game."

In the midst of the committee's deliberations, Lamar began dropping short notes to Rozelle, suggesting changes or innovations, such as a weekly poll of writers, modeled after the AP college football pool, to rank the top 10 teams in all of pro football. It was in one of those letters he sent to Rozelle, dated July 25, 1966, in which Lamar stressed the need to come up with a title game name. "If possible, I believe we should 'coin a phrase' for the Championship Game . . . I have kiddingly called it the 'Super Bowl,' which obviously can be improved upon."

Rozelle agreed there was room for improvement. He wasn't merely unenthusiastic about the term; he actively disliked it. NFL publicity director Don Weiss recalled that Rozelle "just didn't like the word 'super.' Pete was a pretty regular person, but he was a stickler on words and grammar, and 'super' was not his idea of a good word. He thought 'super' was a word like 'neat' or 'gee-whiz.' It had no sophistication."

That may have been true, but "super" was a word that was in the air. The Superman comic was widely popular, and much had been made about the phenomenon of supersonic air travel; in towns around military bases in the '60s, sonic booms were a fairly common occurrence. Lamar also loved expressive, cutting-edge language (during the opener against the Broncos in 1963, he described the 59–7 score to Dan Jenkins as "double unreal;" Sharron would delight later at hearing her father say that something had "freaked me out"), and one family friend remembered that both Lamar and Norma used the term "super" frequently during that era.

Unable to find a novel or catchy name that they were happy with, the committee announced—at Rozelle's strong suggestion—that the game would be called "The AFL–NFL World Championship Game." Even this involved diplomacy, as a few NFL owners resented the AFL being placed first in the order. Rozelle would have liked to call the game "The Pro Bowl," but that title was already taken, since 1951, by the NFL's postseason All-Star game. So the new game's official name would be the AFL–NFL World Championship Game. And almost immediately, people around the country and inside of sports media ignored that and began referring to it as the Super Bowl instead.

The 1966 season began with a 42–20 road win over the two-time defending AFL champion Buffalo Bills, but even before that, the atmosphere felt
different on Lamar's trips to Kansas City. Maybe it was the way the city had
rallied around the team following the death of Mack Lee Hill, or the definitive statement of Klosterman's resignation, quashing all talk about a move to
L.A., or the goodwill generated by the season-ticket drive. For whatever reason, by the home opener on October 2, when some members of the Wolfpack
opened a red-and-gold-striped hospitality tent (called the Wolfden) behind
the north stands, gameday Sundays had become a defining event in Kansas
City. And the Wolfden was the place to be. Beneath banners and pennants,
the six-piece "Wolfden Strollers" band serenaded the revelers.

Lamar, Norma, and their friends often flew in on gameday mornings, but
if the Hunts arrived on Saturday night, they'd routinely be joined for dinner
by Jack and Martha Steadman at Putsch's 210 on the Country Club Plaza. If
it was a Sunday morning flight, they'd land at Municipal Airport just north
of downtown and be at the stadium in less than 15 minutes. After games,
they'd ride over to the Strams' favorite restaurant, Casa de Montez, where the
proprietor would skirt the Sunday blue laws by pouring spirits for Hank and
Phyllis in coffee cups, while the dinner party monitored the late games on a
TV set over the bar.

On November 6, 1966, the 5–2 Chiefs played host to the defending Western Division champion Chargers, their main competitor in the West during
the first part of the '60s. It was not merely a showdown between the two best
teams in the division, and of the dueling martinets Stram and Sid Gillman,
but also a special occasion for the league, marking the first AFL game ever attended by Rozelle. As he sat with Lamar and Norma in the open-air, modified
catbird seat adjacent to the press box, Rozelle was highly complimentary of
the gameday scene—of Bob Johnson riding bareback on the horse Warpaint
after each Chiefs' score, of Tony DiPardo and the Chiefs' Zing Band rallying the
fans throughout the afternoon, and, most lavishly, of the handiwork of Chiefs'
groundskeeper George Toma, who had elevated the routine painting of accents
on the field to an art form. The Municipal Stadium field included a variety of
unique flourishes, from the end zone markings on a sea of Chiefs gold, to the
reproductions of the helmets of the Chiefs and their opponents flanking the
50-yard line, to the ornate yard-line markings themselves, not only colored but
outlined as well, to the candy-striped red-and-gold goalposts. "Your grounds-
keeper is amazing," said Rozelle, and in the days following the game, he would
call Lamar again, and ask if Toma would be willing to work the first champion-

ship game between the two leagues the following January (Toma would supervise the field for the Super Bowl for the next four decades).

Like the game against the Chargers, a 24–14 win for the Chiefs, the season was taking on a charmed quality. Dawson, plagued by injuries in earlier seasons, had fought off a challenge from USC's Pete Beathard and was back to his accurate self; second-year flanker Otis Taylor had become one of the league's most explosive receivers; and rookie running back Mike Garrett added another dimension to the offense, which scored enough to at least disguise the deficiencies of a defense that was aging, undersized, and lacking in mobility.

The Chiefs found out they'd clinched the division title and a spot in the AFL Championship Game on the way back from a Thanksgiving weekend win over the Jets. It was another month before they would walk on the field at War Memorial Stadium against the Bills in the AFL Championship Game, for the right to play the NFL champions. At a booster-club meeting in late December, before a crowd of 1,200 at the Imperial Ballroom in the Hotel Muehlebach, Lamar announced that he was giving Stram a new five-year contract, after which he was unusually open about his own emotions.

"This has been such a great year I hate to see it end," he said. "This has been the most rewarding year of my life. This year our team became successful, we finally became successful at the gate and we finally worked out the merger of the two leagues. It's not often that so many good things happen in one year."

There was a small but spirited assemblage of Chiefs fans who made their way to Buffalo for the AFL Championship Game, including charter season-ticket holder Corky Flynn, a brazen Red Coater in a handlebar moustache who upon the team's arrival persuaded the hotel manager at the Holiday Inn in Buffalo where the Chiefs were staying to remove the "Go Bills" message from the hotel marquee. Flynn was among the few hundred red-clad away supporters that Sunday, blowing his bugle with fervor, rooting his favorite team to victory. With Lamar and Norma bundled nearby in the stands, the Chiefs went out and throttled Buffalo, 31–7, on a chilled, muddy field. Johnny Robinson's key interception in the Chiefs' end zone late in the first half snatched the momentum and sent the team to the first on-field encounter with the NFL.

The *Kansas City Star's* Joe McGuff called the scene in the visitors' locker room after the win "the wildest in Chiefs' history." Lamar had agreed to bring out bottles of champagne if the team won, knowing that it would incur a $2,000 fine from league president Milt Woodard, who had mandated that there be no alcoholic beverages in the winning locker room. Lamar even took part, sticking out his tongue to catch the drops of champagne dripping down his face, happily embracing the players, his tie askew, its end snipped off in part of the traditional postgame celebration. At one point he was scooped up in a big bear hug by the Chiefs' mountainous Jim Tyrer, drenched in champagne and sweat, who asked, "Do you think Kansas City will be happy?!"

Later that afternoon the team gathered in a conference room back at the Holiday Inn and watched as the Packers edged the Cowboys, 34–27. Though there would have been an undeniable allure to facing their old Dallas rivals, most of the Chiefs' squad was glad for the opportunity to face the NFL's dominant team, Vince Lombardi's Packers, which had won the NFL title four times in six seasons.

By then, Lamar's pet term "Super Bowl" had grown in popularity. Headline writers, commentators, and players alike were using the term (the morning after the win over the Bills, the *Kansas City Times* headline read, "Super Chiefs Bound for Super Bowl"). In the weeks leading up to the first game, it was becoming clear that it didn't matter what the league tried to call the game, because "Super Bowl" had already caught on. Networks had taken to referring to the day of the game as "Super Sunday."

The Chiefs arrived in California on January 4, eleven days prior to kickoff. Green Bay arrived four days later, and then only at Rozelle's insistence. (Lombardi had wanted to fly in January 14, the morning before the game, just as the Packers would for any other road contest.) The clear storyline heading into the game—the youthful Chiefs' complex approach against the experienced Packers' meat-and-potatoes attack—was largely hijacked by the boisterous antics of the Chiefs' cornerback Fred "The Hammer" Williamson, who had presented the media with a braggadocio reminiscent of Muhammad Ali. Williamson disparaged the Packers' receivers, predicted the demise of both Carroll Dale and Boyd Dowler, and boasted of his trademark "Hammer Tackle," a swinging arm chop that he described as "a blow delivered with great velocity perpendicular to the earth's latitudes."

Meanwhile, Lamar spent the two weeks before the big game fretting over Williamson's incendiary comments and trying to handle the ticket requests, which came from friends, relatives, politicians, show-business personalities, Chiefs season-ticket holders, and complete strangers. When he and Norma arrived in Los Angeles three days before the contest, they checked into the Beverly Hilton and geared up for the big event. Bunker and Herbert would be there, joined by Dr. Edward Teller at the big game; Hunt Oil landman Mack

Rankin attended with television host Art Linkletter; and part of Lamar's party visited actor Van Williams on the set of *The Green Hornet* (Williams had grown up in Fort Worth and was friends with Buzz Kemble).

As the first Super Sunday dawned, Lamar seemed particularly anxious to his friends, hoping for the best yet fearing the worst. That morning, Steadman was dealing with numerous logistical problems; due to smog, two charter planes full of Chiefs fans flying into Los Angeles for the game had to be diverted to a military airstrip outside the city, and the charter buses rushed to that location to get the fans back to the Coliseum on time. Tension was rife throughout both leagues—Frank Gifford, interviewing his old coach, Vince Lombardi, for CBS, found the Packers' head coach "trembling like a leaf." Lamar was concerned about the performance of his team, of course, but also the publicity fallout from all the unsold tickets. The game would be watched by more than 65 million people, the largest audience to ever watch a sporting event in America. Yet attendance was 63,036, leaving more than 32,000 empty seats; pro fans simply weren't used to traveling to neutral sites.

By the 1 p.m. local kickoff, the setting was perfect—the Coliseum on a sunny January Sunday, the grass field all the more resplendent for Toma's handiwork (including a $3,000 spray-painting it received on the eve of the game). There was, in short, all the grandeur befitting an epic American event: doves, balloons, marching bands, and men taking off from the field in jet packs, just a year after the technology was featured in the James Bond movie *Thunderball.*

After seven seasons of being disparaged by the older league, it was inevitable that the game would feel like a crusade to the Chiefs players. As they stood in the tunnel, waiting to take the field before the pre-game introductions, Buck Buchanan and Bobby Bell were so fired up, they had tears on their eyes.

For a half, fans were treated to a surprisingly competitive game. The Packers scored on their second possession, a six-play, 80-yard drive, but the Chiefs moved the ball as well, marching across midfield on all four of their first-half possessions, as Dawson completed eleven of fifteen passes, employing play-action fakes and Stram's moving pocket to find open passing lanes.

The scene at halftime was tense in both locker rooms as well as in the press box, where the tight score had created a buzz of worry and excitement. NFL employee Buddy Young said out loud what others were thinking: "Old age and heat will get the Packers in the second half." In the Kansas City dressing room, the Chiefs had the look of a team that had been hoping it was good enough and had found out that perhaps it was. "I honestly thought we would come back and win it," said Stram. "We felt we were doing the things we had to do, and doing them well."

In the stands, "Lamar was totally stoked," remembered Buzz Kemble. The Chiefs had more first downs and more total yardage. He was happy but nervous, proud of his team but still worried.

His anxiety was prescient. On third-and-five of the Chiefs first possession of the second half, Dawson rolled back to pass. The Packers blitzed, a maneuver that Lombardi had often dismissed as the "weapon of weaklings." It worked splendidly in this case, as Dawson's hurried pass sailed short and was intercepted by Willie Wood, who returned it to the Chiefs 5. For those standing with Lamar, it was one of the only times they ever heard him curse—Richey recalled him emitting a short "Damn!" when Wood caught the ball. Green Bay scored on the next play, and again on their next possession, and the route was on.

"It was over then," said Jim Tyrer. "They wouldn't respect our run again. Our play fakes were useless. They knew we had to pass, and they just flew to the quarterback." Kansas City never threatened, and by the fourth quarter, Williamson had been knocked out of the game, hammered into submission trying to tackle the Packers' Donnie Anderson, whose pumping knee hit Williamson's helmet. Standing over a prone Williamson, who also broke his arm in the pileup, the Packers' Fuzzy Thurston hummed a few bars of "If I Had a Hammer."

The Packers added another score in the fourth quarter to make the final score 35–10. After the game, Lombardi was peppered with questions about the quality of the Chiefs. Grasping the game ball presented to him by his team, he said, "The players gave it to me. It's the NFL ball. It catches better and kicks a little better than the AFL ball." When asked to assess the Chiefs, Lombardi said, "They've got great speed." Pressed further, he added, "I don't think they are as good as the top teams in the National Football League. They're a good team with fine speed but I'd have to say NFL football is tougher. Dallas is a better team, and so are several others." As silence surrounded him and writers scribbled furiously in their notebooks, a peeved Lombardi added, "That's what you've wanted me to say—now I've said it. But I don't want to get into that kind of comparison."

It was typical of the mindset involved in the game that, afterward, two of Stram's sons went to the Packers' locker room to get Lombardi's autograph. Lombardi patted Henry Stram, Jr., on the head and said, "Tell your dad his team played a good game." Stram took the news from his sons with equanimity, especially after his eleven-year-old, Dale, added, "He said he hoped you wouldn't whip us for going in there." But when notified later of Lombardi's comments to the press, Stram was taken aback. "Did Vince really say we weren't that good?" he asked a group of NFL writers back at the pressroom in the Chiefs hotel. "That we couldn't play at that level? Vince is a friend. Did he really say that?"

Lamar put forward a brave face after the game and was complimentary of the Packers, but said he was proud of his team. In the locker room, most of the Chiefs seemed subdued, almost chastened. The one exception was Buck Buchanan, who'd sacked Starr on the third play of the game and had fought the Packers' all-pro guard Fuzzy Thurston to a draw. "I'm sorry, this team is not 35–10 better than us," said Buchanan in the locker room. "I know it. I want to play them right now."

Later on, when Tex Schramm ran into Norma, he said, "Now you see what we've been living with all these years."

But the wave of enthusiasm for the team in Kansas City carried over into the offseason. In the Jackson County bond election in April 1967, the proposal for construction of a new sports complex passed with a 67.1 percent majority, approving Jackson County's sale of $43 million of G.O. bonds for the construction of two stadiums and a moving roof.

Lamar was still stung by the Super Bowl loss, but as the summer of 1967 approached, there were plenty of other events to occupy his time. One of them was the stadium itself. Across the country, the building boom in stadiums had led to a spate of round, multi-purpose stadiums that could be used for both baseball and football. But in the early stages of the Kansas City push for a stadium, the Denver architect Charles Deaton had called Steadman with a different, revolutionary idea. Deaton argued that by combining many of the stadium service elements in a convertible underground tunnel, it was possible to build two stadiums—one exclusively built for football, the other just for baseball—for not much more than the price of one.

Lamar loved architecture, and stadium architecture best of all. He well understood the appeal of improved sight lines. He'd spent four years watching the Chiefs brusquely treated by the main tenants, the Kansas City Athletics baseball club, experiencing the inconvenience of starting nearly every season with two or three road games (as the A's had priority on Municipal Stadium dates through much of September), as well as the corresponding spate of late-season, cold-weather games. The prospect of a stadium built just for football, with the Chiefs as the sole tenant, was irresistible. The project moved forward with Deaton's design as the template and included a football stadium, a baseball stadium, a rolling roof that could move to cover either structure, and an observation tower that would offer a splendid view of the stadia below and the city to the west. But there was still much work to be done, such as going over specs and dealing with the contractors and city government. Lamar did what he usually did in situations such as this: He worked carefully on the blueprints and chimed in with suggestions and recommendations for the design elements. He left much of the politics and negotiations to Steadman.

Lamar was not yet thirty-five years old. Over the previous year he had solidified the agreement that would expand the universe of pro football. He had named its new signature game and seen his own team play in it. It wasn't merely that pro football was, by 1967, the nation's most popular sport. It also had the soundest economic structure, based on the full sharing of TV revenue among all clubs, a tenet of the early AFL that Lamar had proposed, and that the NFL had later copied. Within a few years, his team would be a full member of the National Football League, playing in the most modern football stadium in the world. Lamar Hunt had engineered his first revolution.

It wouldn't be his last.

CHAPTER TEN

NEW FRONTIERS

On a pristine, sunny Saturday morning in London, July 30, 1966, people across the city awoke with a heightened, palpable sense of anticipation. The festive bustle felt, to many Londoners, like a joyous return to normal, even as it came with an undertow of tension. On that day, national pride would assert itself, with something achingly important at stake, tangible in its particulars but ineffable in its immense gravity: At hallowed Wembley Stadium, England was facing West Germany for the World Cup title.

The contest would surely hew to the British tradition of impeccable sportsmanship, and yet how could an English team face off against a German team in *any* sport within a generation of the end of World War II without there being an extra hint of truculence rooted in the history of the century? That morning, Vincent Mulchrone in the *Daily Mail* led his column by imploring his countrymen, "If the Germans beat us at our national game today, we can always console ourselves with the fact that we have twice beaten them at theirs."

On the very same morning back in the States, Lamar awoke in his house on Armstrong Parkway (he and Norma had moved back from Kansas City two months earlier, the successful season-ticket drive complete). There was exercise to be done and shrubs to be trimmed in front of the house, but on this day, he sat in front of his television set, tuned into *ABC Wide World of Sports*, to watch the broadcast from London of the World Cup Final.

Lamar had not seen a soccer match in three-and-a-half years, since he and Norma had thrilled to the Shamrock Rovers match in Dublin, but he had been following as best he could in the U.S. press the emerging storylines of the tournament—the overdue return of pageantry and frivolity to London, just twenty years after much of the city lay in rubble from the war; the saga of the gifted Pelé of Brazil, who had been hacked and harried mercilessly as the twice-defending world champs were eliminated; the shocking performance of the mysterious North Koreans, a team hidden from much of the build-up to the tournament by the Communist regime from which it sprang; and the rise of the West German team, technically adept but also tightly knit, restoring a measure of cautious pride to its shamed and broken land. It was billed as the "biggest sports event in the world," and this alone was enough to merit Lamar's attention.

That day, as the two sides dueled in one of the most memorable matches in the sport's history, Lamar watched, raptly absorbed in the game's unfolding drama. Remembering it later, he would describe himself as "very fascinated" by the game, "especially by the crowd reaction as indicated by the noise level from the spectators as the game rocked back and forth. I was especially impressed by the internationalism of the game. The *nation* of England against the *nation* of [West] Germany—not the type of thing I was accustomed to seeing in American sports."

What he saw on the field was something he scarcely comprehended—pell-mell running and wild goal-mouth scrambles, a tense, stuttering rhythm to the movement of the ball that sometimes entranced and sometimes confounded, the phenomenon of action that continued in a fluid, uninterrupted siege of 45 minutes at a time. No commercials. No timeouts. No substitutions. All this he saw as a stranger, and at times it was quite unfathomable.

But the sound inside Wembley Stadium, the glimpses of the fans in the grandstand, the packed, raucous chants and cheering and singing in the shadow of the two towers—this was something he recognized instantly. It was the sound of fans transfixed and intent, engaged with the action, riding the events on the field in a surging wave of emotion, antipathy, hope, disappointment, and, ultimately and unforgettably—after two goals for the home side in extra time—triumph. After the game, Lamar marveled at the sight of the English players, marching up into the stands, in front of the queen's box, to receive their world champion's medals.

Lamar was captivated with the excitement and pageantry, and he found that in the days following, he couldn't really shake his fascination with what he'd seen. Over the next several months, he would begin to explore the ways he might transport the game, the atmosphere, and the unique culture of the sport to America.

This goal would preoccupy him, to a great extent, for the rest of his life.

•

From the moment in 1958 when Lamar sat in wonder at the stirring finale of the Colts–Giants title game, he had been focused on finding success with a pro football franchise. The massive effort involved in launching the AFL and running his own franchise had taken precedence over all his other business interests at the time. He still owned a portion of Penrod Drilling and Placid Oil, and there were tax advantages to him keeping a minimal hand in these operations ("he wasn't really involved," said Herbert). He shared an interest in a Dallas apartment complex with his brothers, and he was accumulating other real estate. He owned and oversaw the management of a 72-lane bowling alley, the Bronco Bowl, and had nominally been involved in former next-door neighbor Curtis Sanford's National Bowling League (the Dallas franchise, the Broncos, played their games at the bowling center's amphitheater in 1961 and 1962). Since 1964, he had been a part-owner, with limited involvement, in the Dallas Rangers baseball team, and he was still interested in bringing major league baseball to the city.

In 1966, Lamar was approached about buying a stake in yet another sports enterprise, an expansion basketball franchise based in Chicago. Norma, who had played basketball in high school ("with great mediocrity," in her words), remembered taking a walk with Lamar one day, when he asked her, "What do you think about this investment, in pro basketball?" She encouraged him, reasoning that college basketball was growing in popularity, and the pro game could logically follow, as it had with football. So that summer, Lamar purchased a portion of the Chicago Bulls, an expansion franchise in the National Basketball Association. As a minority owner (with just an 11.25 percent stake in the team), he traveled to Chicago for a couple of games that first season, but he was never intrusive. "You'd see him in the stands occasionally, and he'd be there for some of the board meetings," said the team's first GM, Jerry Colangelo, "but Lamar never meddled. He was just there to support you."

The duties of running the Chiefs, his added responsibility as the founder of the AFL and conduit for its owners, plus the obligations he had for his share of the family's oil and real estate interests made for a daunting workload. All that, combined with Lamar's growing family, assured that he would remain almost constantly busy.

But in 1967, he chose to add to this workload, in dramatic and unlikely ways. The profile of spectator sports was undeniably rising—the massive television audience for the Super Bowl had been just one in a long line of positive factors. Among the millionaires who owned sports franchises in the 1960s, there was a growing belief among a small group that proved quite seductive. Some owners believed that with football and the other major American team sports growing, there could be room for another sport as well.

"I can't say that I heard him say, 'This is why I want to be in the soccer business,'" said Norma. "Lamar, as best as I could tell, wanted to be in *every* sports business. It's all he ever did. It never surprised me when he said he thought another sport was going to be great for America."

Lamar knew he wanted to invest, and sent a note to his longtime friend Bill McNutt. "The day I got a brochure on soccer," he said, "I wrote Bill for his advice. I didn't ask him to invest. He wrote me back in substance that 'this has to be the worst investment I ever heard of. The only one worse would be the Brooklyn Bridge.'" But within weeks, McNutt had agreed to join in the endeavor, trading some of his Collin Street Bakery stock to Lamar for a percentage of the new team, which they agreed to call the Dallas Tornado.

Within six months after the '66 World Cup, two different groups of owners pushed to start major soccer leagues in the United States. Perhaps only in America could a sport that had been dismissed or despised by the mainstream suddenly become the subject of not one but two major start-up efforts. Lamar found himself aligned with Houston's Judge Roy Hofheinz and the North American Soccer League, which earned recognition from the United States Soccer Football Federation and the sport's worldwide governing body, FIFA.

But another organization, the National Professional Soccer League, with backing from some NFL owners (including the Bidwill family in St. Louis and Daniel F. Reeves in Los Angeles), was also intent on bringing soccer to the states. While the NPSL didn't have the official sanction of FIFA, it had something its owners viewed as being far more useful, a national TV contract with CBS. With both groups convinced that the first league to get a product on the field would be successful, the NPSL green-lighted an inaugural season in the spring of 1967, backed by its TV contract with CBS. Faced with that, Lamar and the rest of the NASL group decided they needed to do something sooner rather than later, though they were aware that they lacked a suitable pool of players, as well as the infrastructure to find them in America, where the participation level in the sport was microscopic. In early 1967, the NASL changed its name to the United Soccer Association, USA, to avoid confusion with the rival NPSL, and then set about importing entire teams to play a short season in the summer of 1967, so the league could have some kind of presence to fight the NPSL.

The franchise in Cleveland farmed in the Stoke City club, from England's First Division; Jack Kent Cooke in Los Angeles brought in another English team, Wolverhampton Wanderers; Houston imported Bangu FC Brazil, while Boston brought in the Shamrock Rovers side that Lamar and Norma had watched back in Dublin. After corresponding with manager Jerry Kerr of Scotland's Dundee United, Lamar and Bill McNutt convinced the club to play in America as the Dallas Tornado.

Dundee United had just finished in the middle of the table of the Scottish first division, but they were a team that had played in the European Cup against the likes of Barcelona and Juventus in earlier years. The squad was entirely British, raised in an environment of frigid gamedays when the sun was but a rumor, and in which beer and lager were training-day staples and fish and chips a common pre-game meal. In America, they would have to adjust to a climate that was oppressively hot. "You could tell that they were technically skilled," said one fan of the first season. "But they were *dying* in the heat."

Even as that season was progressing, with the surrogates from Dundee United finishing last in the USA's Western Division, Lamar and McNutt were discussing ways to stock their team for the following season, 1968, when owners were expected to provide their own players for a full campaign.

It was at this point that Lamar received a letter from Canada from someone named Bob Kap. He was a small, round-faced man whose command of English, like his résumé, was extremely sketchy. But in a series of letters and a visit to Dallas, he convinced Lamar and McNutt to install him as the Tornado's manager and, extraordinarily, send him on a worldwide tour over the winter months, playing exhibitions with a handpicked roster of up-and-coming young players. Kap boasted that he possessed the requisite coaching badges from England and had played with Manchester United, and he profited from these claims since none of them, in Dallas in 1967, were easily verifiable.

Lamar had made specious hires at the beginning of the AFL, but because he knew football, he was able to identify his mistakes there much more quickly. The problem was exacerbated in soccer, since he knew so little about the sport. The tour that followed was a fool's errand, though a grand one.

The idea (so elaborately fanciful that no one claimed authorship of it after the fact) was that Kap could recruit an all-star international squad of young and inexpensive young players, take them on a global tour during which he would mold them into a genuinely cohesive unit, and along the way raise enough funds to offset the cost of the tour.

Lamar granted Kap authority to hire a team of young players, time and money to train them in Seville, Spain, and then the itinerary to set off on a 25,000-mile world tour, with stops in Burma, Singapore, Pakistan, and other exotic outposts, all the while scouting for more young players with a taste for adventure. Lamar sent out his administrative assistant, Paul Waters, as an advance man to secure games and set up lodging, and then left the rest to Kap.

The tour began August 22, 1967, in Cordoba, Spain, and ended nearly six months and forty-seven games later, in Papeete, Tahiti. Along the way, the team was fitted out for Stetson hats and cowboy boots, and expected to serve as ambassadors for a country most had never visited.

From all over the world, the contacts poured in. Lamar exchanged regular letters, cables, and telegrams with Waters, who responded with nearly daily updates by telegram: "NO GAMES KOREAN WEATHER TOO COLD PROCEEDING TOKYO PAUL," "LEAVING CALCUTTA FOR BANGKOK THEN RANGOON GAME SCHEDULE UNCHANGED PAUL." Lamar would occasionally respond. On September 20, he wired back, "CONGRATULATIONS TAIWAN, TOKYO, PHILIPPINES. CONTINUE SCHEDULE GAMES EVEN IF YOU EXCEED FORTY. LAMAR."

In August there came from Waters: "AM AT INTERCONTINENTAL HOTEL IN KARACHI HATE BEING REBELLIOUS BUT FIRMLY BELIEF [sic] AFGANISTAN [sic] A MISTAKE. PLEASE RELY MY JUDGEMENT [sic] AWAITING ORDERS. PAUL." Lamar promptly replied, "YOUR REQUEST TO SKIP AFGHANISTAN OKAY. PROCEED TO INDIA. LAMAR."

While the system of player recruitment was entirely haphazard—one of Kap's signees, Frank Randolf, had never played an organized game, and was soon designated by Kap as the team physician, "Dr. Frank"—it also had its highlights. The trio of signees from the Netherlands included Niels Overweg, who would go on to be capped on the excellent Dutch team of the mid-1970s. But his career with the Tornado came to naught. One idle evening during the team's training camp in Spain, Overweg and his two Dutch teammates took turns urinating into Overweg's Stetson. Then, standing on a balcony above the terrace where their coach was enjoying a steak dinner, they poured the contents of the hat onto Kap's head, and then bolted from the scene. The act of insubordination resulted in Overweg's immediate release the next morning (when Kap inspected all the players' Stetsons for evidence).

During the worldwide junket, the assembled youngsters on the team would experience an amazing education, only a portion of it having to do with the sport itself. There were State dinners at several stops, a hotel across the street from a brothel, a shark attack on the Indian Ocean coast in Ceylon (now Sri Lanka), malnourished and deformed beggars on the street in Pakistan. Kap's communiqués from the road, in his fractured English, updated Lamar on the team on the field ("Tornado beat easily this team, but they missed many chances for more goals. Steady improvement, but still far of this what I want from them. Many games team will lose before become solid and good") and off ("Our Spanish is improving. We can order Coca-Cola without major disturbance in the cafes").

It must have appeared to Lamar very quickly that the Kap experiment was going to be a calamity. On September 15, he wrote Kap a carefully worded letter asking him to document his expenses more clearly. "Charles Winn tells me that of the advance of $2,000 ($100 cash plus $2,700 check) which we gave you around June 1, he has received only a very small amount of verified bills from you… In addition, Charles tells me we have advanced a total of $6,100 in Spain and have expense verifications of only $700 or $800 from you."

Even as Lamar was monitoring the progress, and occasionally visiting the team overseas, he was returning to the new football season, unaware that he was about to take up a major battle on yet another front.

•

It was an eventful preseason for the Chiefs. On August 23, 1967, the Chiefs took the field in front of a sellout crowd of 33,041 at Municipal Stadium for their first interleague preseason game, against the Chicago Bears, still coached by George Halas and thus the embodiment of the NFL's old guard. The Bears were an unsuspecting football team caught in the wrong place at the wrong time. Unable to adapt to the frequent shifts on offense, the Bears came unglued in the second quarter, when Kansas City exploded for 32 points. The Chiefs maintained their intensity in the second half, adding 13 points in the last two minutes of the game. On the sidelines, Fred Arbanas was yelling for the team to score 100. The final score sent a message heard throughout the NFL: Kansas City 66, Chicago 24.

After the game, Lamar came to the Bears' dressing room, to share a few words with Halas, a man he'd been following since 1940, when as an eight-year-old boy he'd sat in the library at Mount Vernon, listening to the Bears' stunning 73–0 NFL Championship win over the Washington Redskins, and had become a Bears fan. Though they had been on opposite sides during the formation of the AFL, Halas had grown to respect his young adversary. When he spotted him from across the room, Halas said, "Lamar, have mercy on us. You really buried us." Lamar was, as ever, gracious in victory, allowing as to how the Chiefs were fired up to prove themselves against the older league. But Halas was not bitter; as the coach on the winning end of a 73–0 score, he wasn't about to ask for any quarter from an opponent. "They gave every evidence that they were as good as any team," he told the press. "They were fired up and played with great spirit. They went 100 percent on every play."

In the Chiefs' locker room, a game ball was awarded to Lamar, along with the other three figures who'd received most of the criticism for the Super Bowl loss: Stram, Dawson, and cornerback Willie Mitchell. Many Chiefs of the '60s would remember the game as being one of the most memorable victories in the franchise's history. "That's about as satisfied as I've ever seen Lamar after a football game," said Norma.

It was barely a week after that signal triumph, as the Tornado's global tour was just beginning, when Lamar traveled to Los Angeles, on September 1, 1967, for a return to the Los Angeles Coliseum, to watch the Chiefs face the Los Angeles Rams in a preseason game.

While staying at the Ambassador East Hotel, he had agreed to a meeting with the avid New Orleans promoter Dave Dixon. Even after Lamar decided to move the team from Dallas to Kansas City rather than New Orleans, he and Dixon had stayed on good terms. Dixon had been a talented amateur golfer, had worked as a plywood salesman, and would one day open his own antique store in the French Quarter; what he was, more than anything, though, was a promoter, an idea man who was exceedingly good at selling his ideas.

Many of those in Lamar's and the AFL's inner circle had grown suspicious of Dixon. Jack Steadman never liked the man and still felt a measure of exasperation over how close the Texans came to a move to New Orleans that would have given Dixon a stake in the team. Others in the league felt Dixon was at least partially responsible for the fiasco of the 1965 AFL All-Star Game in New Orleans, when black players were denied service in many establishments, and treated to scurrilous verbal abuse, prompting them to boycott the game, at which point the league decided to leave New Orleans and move the All-Star Game to Houston.

But Lamar retained a good bit of affection for Dixon. The two men shared a boyish sense of the power of "What if?", though Dixon possessed only a fraction of the resources of Lamar. On this occasion, Dixon had a new project in mind, and he made his case with the zeal of the truly converted. He had glimpsed the future of sports, and the future would be . . . professional tennis. Dixon wanted Lamar to join him as a partner in his bid to revolutionize the sport.

The rising tide of television revenue had lifted virtually all boats in the ocean of spectator sports: pro football had led the way, of course, with its frantic bidding among the networks for the NFL and AFL packages. ABC's NCAA football package was growing more lucrative by the year, the quadrennial Olympics telecasts were growing in length and value, the previously ramshackle National Basketball Association was having some success for its "game of the week" on ABC, golf's major tournaments were becoming a staple of spring and summer Sunday afternoons, and the rise of ABC's *Wide World of Sports*—with its dog's breakfast of one-offs and obscure sports, from ski-jumping to cliff-diving to demolition derby—seemed to indicate that a portion of American sports fans were so starved for action that they would watch virtually anything from virtually anywhere.

The future had arrived for spectator sports, with one notable exception. In contrast to the modernization going on almost everywhere else, the world of tennis was still locked in a pristine past of white cotton and ostensible amateurism, a world in which gentlemen and ladies played for the sheer joy of the sport, in which clubs around the world took a paternal interest in the best players, put them up for the week they were in town, and sent them on their way, both sides blandly extolling the virtues of the "purity" of the amateur game.

The reality was decidedly different. Donald Dell was a young player making his way around the amateur ranks for a time in the mid-1960s, and he remembered the unvarying pair of questions that he was greeted with by oblivious rich people at every stop. "The first thing they would ask me is, 'What do you do when you're not playing tennis?' And then, when I told them that tennis was *all* I did, that it was a full-time job, they would always come right back with, 'But how can you make a living at it?'"

The answer to that question was the sport's dark open secret, the "shamateurism" that lay just beneath the game's pristine surface. The best players received cash for appearance fees, for winning tournaments, for giving lessons, and almost all of it was under the table. "We were kept men," said the South African star Cliff Drysdale. For the best players of the '60s, the itinerant existence meant cadging rides to a new city for "a free place to stay, somebody's starry-eyed teenaged daughter to chauffer them about, the chance to actually sign for club sandwiches in the members' lounge."

The only alternative to the kept existence of the amateur ranks was the hard life of the pro tour. The open declaration of professionalism brought immediate excommunication from the game's most hallowed events and institutions—the grass of Wimbledon and Forest Hills, the clay of Roland

Garros, the global prestige of the Davis Cup. "It was so entrenched," said tennis journalist Richard Evans. "This real sort of vitriolic hatred of professionalism, it was quite extraordinary. The old amateur leaders really looked down on the pros as a sort of a servant class. It was absolutely amazing. You would have had to live in the times to understand the vehemence of their opposition to the idea of the pros sullying their country clubs."

So the pros, most of them in a loosely constructed barnstorming tour put together by the great iconoclastic American star of the 1940s, Jack Kramer, rode in station wagons from city to city across America, playing mostly one- and two-nighters, deftly directing their lobs through gymnasium rafters, grabbing a shower and enduring the subpar conditions. One night in the early '60s, the headstrong young Welsh player Mike Davies, who had just turned pro, found himself in a small makeshift room, without bathrooms, lockers, or any other facilities save four barren walls. "Where are we supposed to get dressed?" he asked fellow pro Tony Trabert. The veteran Trabert didn't answer at once, but reached into his tennis bag and brought out a hammer and six-inch nail, which he proceeded to pound into the wall.

"There," said Trabert. "That's your dressing room."

Dixon felt sure that with the right promotion and the right funding, convincing not just one or two but five or six of the top amateurs to go pro at once, the landscape would change, and the world of amateur tennis would have to be opened to the professionals.

Lamar left his meeting with Dixon intrigued. Upon returning to Dallas, he called a meeting with Al Hill, and his son, Al Hill, Jr., who had played on the amateur circuit for much of the early '60s. Lamar knew that Al, Sr., was well-connected—when Kramer had brought his barnstorming pro tour to SMU in the late '50s, he had stayed with Al and Margaret at their house. For his part, Al, Jr., had looked up to Lamar for a long time, climbing on his uncle's back when Lamar was working at the Garden of the Gods during summers in the early 1950s, and, as a ten-year-old, enjoying the spiked punch at Lamar's first wedding reception in '56. More to the point, Al, Jr., was one of the best players in the state of Texas, studying under the legendary coach Clarence Mabry at Trinity University while nearing his degree, and getting a glimpse of the two worlds—the visible one and the secret one—in amateur tennis at the time.

Taking on the entrenched amateur ranks was, on its face at the time, a foolish decision. But Dixon was on to something. Wimbledon chairman Herman David, the quietly competent patrician who'd overseen proceedings at the sport's most prestigious address, had invited a group of professionals to play at the All-England Club that very month, just six weeks after Wimbledon's annual tournament. Though David had not gone on record, the pros invited believed that if the event drew well, David would find a way to make the Wimbledon championships open to all in 1968. It was this potential development that Dixon emphasized in his meeting with Lamar and the Hills.

And it was that promise that finally convinced the Texans to participate. Lamar offered up a 25 percent stake, as did Al, Jr., from his sizable trust. Dixon would control the other 50 percent and, with business manager Bob Briner, operate the circuit from offices in New Orleans. In Lamar's mind, that would be enough. He expected to be a silent partner, as passive in the tennis gambit as he had been for the first year of his minority ownership of the Chicago Bulls.

With the name of Lamar Hunt as cache, Dixon swooped in and signed five of the top amateurs in the game: Australians John Newcombe and Tony Roche, South African Cliff Drysdale, Brit Roger Taylor, and Yugoslav Niki Pilić. Those five, joined by established pros Butch Buchholz, Pierre Barthès, and Dennis Ralston, made up the first WCT touring pros, dubbed the Handsome Eight.

At the same time that Dixon was preparing to launch World Championship Tennis, another investor—former U.S. Davis Cup Captain George Mac-Call—was beginning his own circuit, which he dubbed the National Tennis League. The dissolution of Jack Kramer's tour was plagued by a lack of tennis expertise. Rod Laver, Ken Rosewall, and other top pros chose the proven MacCall, since Dixon had equally specious tennis credentials.

The unintended consequence of the competition between WCT and the National Tennis League, was to further dilute the top ranks of pro tennis. Whereas the best players had been separated by the divide between the ostensibly amateur ranks and the openly professional players, now it was further divided in the pros between the WCT and the NTL.

Even before the group played its first matches, the concussive announcement came December 14, 1967, that Wimbledon would be open to professionals in 1968. That prompted a swift response from the International Lawn Tennis Federation, effectively suspending the English federation from all ILTF activities. But the stricture would not hold. "Wimbledon *was* tennis," said Richard Evans. "And if Wimbledon said we're going to do this, then the ILTF knew the game was up." Soon the other federations rallied in support. In the United States, USLTA chairman Robert Kelleher came up against the same fusty opposition that decried the changes in England, plus an unusually alarmist view of the machinations of Lamar Hunt and the WCT. He held strong at a contentious USLTA annual meeting, and soon the American federation was on board with the English.

Dixon had envisioned a departure from the sport's staid on-court traditions as well. Emboldened by Wimbledon's capitulation, he brought his new stable of players down to Australia in late December. The new era of tennis would begin in a parking lot in Sydney, with the players playing not the traditional 15-30-40-game structure of tennis's long history, but instead a 31-point "pro set" format that owed more to ping-pong (players taking turns serving five points each), with the added variation of a time clock scoring in individual quarters. It was barely recognizable as tennis. From there, the tour would head to the States.

Marketing naïvete ran rampant, and the assumption was made that the ideal place to begin the tour was Kansas City because of Lamar's presence and the deep list of sports fans that made up the Chiefs' season-ticket rolls. Meanwhile, Al, Jr., met with representatives from Sears, who were eager to come out with a new line of sportswear to coincide with the tour's February beginning in the United States.

But the downtown Municipal Auditorium was already booked, so the American debut of World Championship Tennis was held in the Kansas City stockyards, at the site of the American Royal rodeo, where the minor-league Kansas City Blues played their hockey games. It was billed as the future of tennis, and *Sports Illustrated* dispatched writer Frank Deford to cover the opening. What he found was a circus of disappointment, a haphazard outfit that wasn't ready for widespread media exposure. As Lamar looked pensively into the stands at the empty seats, the players were still in the dressing area, trying to fit into the Sears & Roebuck sportswear designed to bring more color into the game (none of the original shorts fit, because the company hadn't made allowances for the muscular thighs of tennis players). Even the players took a while to adjust to the new color schemes. Pierre Barthès, the headstrong Frenchman, took one look at the assigned outfit he was given—a russet and lime combination—and protested to his friend Butch Buchholz, *"Butch, I am not a clown."* The night before the Kansas City final, Deford met up with John Newcombe and Dennis Ralston for drinks at a bar in the city. They were both disenchanted and depressed, convinced that present system, as constructed, wasn't going to work.

In this, they were correct. Dixon's plan was to trot the players out to two tournaments a week (the original March 1968 WCT itinerary called for the players to play two- and three-day tournaments in eleven different cities), but just over two weeks after Kansas City, the entire enterprise was imperiled. Dixon called Lamar and explained that he couldn't continue to suffer the losses. With the entire operation in doubt, the partners agreed to bring the Handsome Eight for a summit conference, at Al Hill, Sr.'s home in Dallas. They were joined by the former touring pro Mike Davies, invited at Buchholz's request, for his expertise in tournament and player issues.

That weekend in March 1968, Lamar spoke to each of the players about their perceptions, then interviewed Davies, and discussed the issue with both Hills and the departing Dixon. Finally, he decided to take over WCT, assuming Dixon's 50-percent stake and shutting down the tour temporarily to reorganize it. While Briner was retained for a time as executive director, the organization's offices would move from New Orleans to Dallas. Lamar recruited the willful Welshman Davies, whose brash confidence grated on some members of the tennis establishment, even as it was engendering loyalty from his peers. Davies joined the tour as associate director, helping provide direction in how to deal with sponsors, tournament directors, idle rich hangers-on, and the numerous logistical details of staging a tennis tournament. Davies was the "tennis guy," but more than that he offered a sense of shrewd wisdom that went beyond what the outsider Lamar (or, for that matter, the twenty-one-year-old insider Al Hill, Jr.) might be able to bring to the table. As the players practiced down at the T-Bar-M tennis ranch in central Texas, the WCT worked on how it might survive the year.

Davies worked to adapt Dixon's model of negotiating rent at each of the venues the tour would travel to, as well as advertising and travel. Famously, on the first leg of the tour, the only purely profitable night came in Shreveport, where the shipping company didn't deliver the Astroturf court by the appointed hour and had to pay a $5,000 guarantee. "It was still pretty bleak," said Lamar's accountant, Wayne Henry, handling the accounts for the tennis enterprise back in Dallas. "We got more money for not playing than for playing."

•

As it turned out, both the soccer and tennis enterprises were floundering at the same time. Though Lamar had seriously considered folding WCT before deciding to go forward with the venture, the nascent world of American professional soccer was, if anything, even more volatile. In 1968, the two leagues merged, with the NPSL and USA coming together to form the North American Soccer League (the original title of the USA, before it changed to avoid confusion with the other league).

The young Dallas Tornado team had emerged from a world tour with a sense of resiliency and growing cohesion. But the squad lacked the experience or technical skill of most of the teams in the league, and it showed, from a 6–0 season-opening loss to the Houston Stars. As the season continued its downward spiral, matters grew more surreal. Ed Fries, the Tornados GM, was the first to go, with Bob Kap given the duties temporarily. On Kap's first day on the job, Lamar's accountant Wayne Henry received a frantic phone call from the Tornado's ticket manager, former football great Tex Hamer.

"Wayne, you need to get down here," said Hamer. "Bob is taking all our records and throwing them out in the dumpster."

Hoping for a literal as well as figurative housecleaning, Kap had jettisoned all the accounts receivables records, season-ticket holders installment plans, and other financial documents. Henry and two other men from the business office hurried to the back of the building and fished the Tornado business history out of the dumpster. The ultimate result? "We found us another general manager pretty quick," said Henry.

The losses accumulated and, at one point, Kap was sent back to Europe to sign more players, and Lamar took over as the nominal manager for a couple of games. "We worked harder under Lamar than we had in weeks," recalled Mike Renshaw, but the results were the same. Finally, when the team's record stood at zero wins, twelve losses, and two ties, Kap was fired as manager and replaced with the English coach Keith Spurgeon.

The move was a tacit admission that Lamar had been hoodwinked by his own manager ("That's Kap, spelled C-R-O-O-K," said one Tornado player).

"It was generally accepted among the small group of supposedly knowledgeable soccer writers and suchlike of the time that Kap was a phony," said the venerable soccer writer Paul Gardner, "if only because no one had ever heard of him in a soccer sense . . . But the fact that he had, apparently, come up with this dopey idea about a team of teenagers functioning in a pro league was further proof of his fraudulent status. Lamar denied being conned, but that was ingenuous."

By the middle of the season, the Tornado was 0-18-3, at which point Lamar conceded, "It is the worst professional athletic team in North America." Throughout the year, the level of apathy around the country was a constant reminder of how difficult it would be for soccer to gain purchase in a landscape already clogged with other historically popular sports. At the 94,405-seat Rose Bowl, the game between the Tornado and the Los Angeles Toros drew 1,251 fans. "When the season ends," Bill McNutt said, "we'll just have to sell the heck out of fruitcakes."

The day of that game, the Toros owner, Jack Kent Cooke, was sitting up in a private box, watching the proceedings. Sitting next to him was a young lawyer from his firm named Alan Rothenberg, whom he had put in charge to keep an eye on the soccer team. But midway through that '68 season, Cooke had already decided to jump ship. Looking down at the field, Cooke said, almost wistfully, "You know this is really a beautiful game." Then, pointing at Lamar on the Tornado bench, he added, "Now, if I was a rich guy like him, I'd stick it out."

At the end of the season, there were abdications everywhere, with many following Cooke's lead. Teams folded from coast to coast, and the North American Soccer League was in shambles. Seventeen teams had entered the season, and each one found that the nation was not ready for a strange sport, in a market glutted with expansion in every one of the other, more established sports.

The experiment had failed, and yet, as he flew down to Atlanta for a postmortem with former Baltimore GM Clive Toye and Atlanta GM Phil Woosnam, Lamar remained determined. Despite the widespread financial failure, Lamar was not ready to concede defeat.

At the time, the league headquarters of the North American Soccer League were in a room off the side of the visiting locker room at Atlanta Fulton-County Stadium. The stars of baseball—Roberto Clemente and Willie Stargell, Willie McCovey and Willie Mays—walked by the room on their way out to and back from the field for Atlanta Braves games. And during the day, amid the antiseptic smells and gameday detritus, Lamar would sit with Toye and Woosnam, and discuss how the sport might be preserved.

After a series of discussions, often over sandwiches on a park bench outside the stadium, the three men arrived at a rough consensus about what soccer needed to make it in America: 1) the best hope was to coerce the game's greatest player, the Brazilian master Pelé, to join the league, and 2) the best hope to sign Pelé was to have a viable franchise in New York City, and 3) the best chance to bring about long-term growth in the game, above and go beyond the initial shock of a Pelé signing, would be to bring the World Cup to America.

Of course, at the time, there was no league to sign Pelé to, no franchise in New York for him to join, and the prospects of a World Cup seemed infinitesimal. But the fact that Lamar had, in the space of two years and despite extensive losses, remained a soccer true believer, was crucial.

"Lamar was always there, as the rock upon which we could rest if it was required," said Toye. "Lamar was the owner. Particularly because Phil and I relied so much on Lamar during those two years when the league was coming back to life. Lamar's focus always, over and above everything else, was the league."

In the end, the NASL survived because Lamar wanted it to survive. The Tornado came back for another season, as did franchises in Atlanta, Kansas City, St. Louis, and Baltimore. The young league of just five teams was largely unrecognizable from its earlier incarnations. But soccer in America wasn't dead yet. The 1969 season would proceed.

In this, Lamar persevered despite the indifference of many of his friends and business associates. Buzz Kemble thought it was a nearly complete waste of time ("just so boring," he complained). Steadman saw in the new enterprise nothing but red ink. Even family members were dubious. "Soccer doesn't fit the American personality," Bunker told *Sports Illustrated's* Bud Shrake in 1970. "The game doesn't have enough climaxes. In baseball you have three strikes, three outs, and so forth, and in football you have first downs. In soccer you're just out there kicking the ball around."

"Believe me, I tried—politely—to talk Lamar out of soccer," said Al Hill, Jr. "His premise was always the same: 'If it's this popular around the world, it can be this popular here.' I thought that was wrong, and I told him that. I said, 'Lamar, look at all the other things that go on in America. In those other countries there's nothing else.'"

His three new enterprises—WCT, the NASL, and the Bulls in the NBA—were all losing money. But after surviving the AFL's shaky early history—the Broncos' vertically striped socks, the weekly rumors of the Raiders' demise, and the folly of the New York Titans—and then seeing how the AFL emerged with patience and resolve, Lamar wasn't inclined to give up on any of it.

During those bleak weeks, when the triumvirate of Hunt, Toye, and Woosnam were merely trying to keep the game alive, Toye spent plenty of time with Lamar, finding him both genial and, at some level, opaque. "Lamar, among many other things, was not the greatest conversationalist, right?" said Toye. "I certainly didn't get the opportunity to sit down, over long, luxurious meals and a couple of bottles of wine, and talk about philosophy and the good of the game, and all that kind of stuff. I mean we met, we talked, perfectly friendly, decent conversations. But they were about what we were about. So I'm not sure why Lamar did it. He *must* have really loved it and wanted to do it, because by God did he put—never mind the money—there was also the immense amount of time he put into it."

So Lamar remained a convert, with his efforts in the U.S. wilderness forti-
fied by occasional trips back to Europe to watch the F.A. Cup finals in England or league games in Italy and Spain. Even as his love for the culture of the
sport deepened, he was beginning to realize just how difficult it would be to
convert the American public. At one point in 1969, when asked how the Tornado was doing, Lamar said ruefully, "You've heard of taking a bath? I think
I'm in for a long swim."

•

Still there was more. In 1965, at a time when the space race was accelerat-
ing, Lamar had read a newspaper piece about the possibility that the city of
San Francisco might consider developing the land on Alcatraz, the notorious
island prison that had been closed by Attorney General Robert F. Kennedy in
1963 because it was antiquated and extraordinarily expensive.

Over the next four years, Lamar and a friend from Dallas, the young entrepreneur Morgan Maxfield, developed the idea for a multi-purpose attraction that would be a monument to the space program, a scenic recreation of
nineteenth-century San Francisco, and a tour stop for those interested in the
history of the prison, which had held Al Capone and other infamous convicts.

The most-discussed aspect of the proposal wasn't the theme park or the
prison tours, but a 364-foot tall observation tower (the exact height of the
Saturn V Rocket that launched the Apollo astronauts into space). Lamar had
loved towers and observation decks his entire life and had enjoyed scaling the
interior steps of the Statue of Liberty, the Washington Monument, and the
Eiffel Tower. After falling under the spell of soccer, he'd studied the site of the
first World Cup, held in 1930 in Montevideo, Uruguay, and the Estadio Cen-
tenario, the stadium built for the event, whose most distinguishing feature
was the 100-meter (328 feet) tall tower that overlooked the stadium and flew
the flag of the winning nation after the tournament.

In the summer of 1969, the San Francisco board of supervisors voted to
approve Lamar's plan, which called for the city to invest $2.6 million to buy
the island, and for Lamar to invest $7 million in developing the area, offering
the city a percentage of his revenue.

As he was preparing to work his way through the legal ramifications, he
called on his old SMU fraternity brother—and frequent traveling companion
for sports road trips—Bill Adams. "We ran into every nutcase in the world
that you could imagine on that deal," said Adams.

Lamar often described himself as naïve, but in this instance his staunch pro-growth optimism and love for spectacle ran headlong against the Bay Area's legendary desire to stand alone and not adhere to the mainstream mores. By the fall, when the board voted to reconsider the development deal, Lamar arrived in a typically conciliatory mode, arguing his case in the face of vehement opposition. "I can only say that I didn't come to San Francisco with the idea of ramming anything down anybody's throat," he told the assembled media after the hearing. "I'm interested in developing Alcatraz because I think it has exciting possibilities as an artistic and financial project."

But inside the chamber, Lamar walked up to the sound of hissing and booing. "That was a true nightmare," said Norma, along for the trip. "By the time you say 'rich Texan' in the *Chronicle* four thousand times, you have a lot of people up in arms."

He would never get the chance to explain himself; two weeks after the development was tabled for further discussion, the board rescinded the deal altogether. It left Lamar perplexed, but those closest to him authentically angry. "It was an open competition and his idea was the best," said Norma. "And then the things they said about him, it was terrible."

The 364-foot tower was never built. Though in 1972, when Alcatraz joined the National Parks system, one of the features was a prison tour, very similar to what Lamar envisioned.

But the fate of Alcatraz was still unknown in the summer of 1969. Lamar submitted the original proposal to the city of San Francisco, and then headed for what amounted, in his life at least, to a rest.

Lamar had been entranced with the space program since its inception, inspired by the sheer audacity of the undertaking, and transfixed by the mountain of detail that was required for each mission. He tracked the missions and made time to watch launches and splashdowns on TV.

But for the historic Apollo 11 mission, he made a point to attend the launch on July 16, 1969. In the observation area, he was humbled by the grandeur of the thirty-six-story-tall Saturn V rocket, and the thundering noise and thrumming tremors of the moment of liftoff, which seemed to encapsulate the best impulses of the awesome power of the military-industrial complex. After watching the launch, Lamar flew to Dallas to prepare for the annual vacation to the Palette Ranch in Wyoming. Even when life was at its busiest, he found time for the family's yearly getaway to the splendor of Wyoming and the Palette, where he first traveled with Caroline shortly after World War II.

The ritual was by now entrenched. They would board the company plane, the eleven-passenger Lockheed Jetstar piloted by Jake Cobb, joined by all

three children and another couple or two—usually Bill and Josephine Mc-
Nutt, often Buzz and Dorothy Kemble, maybe Bill and Molly Adams. Cobb
would consider the luggage the women were bringing along, raise his eyebrows for a moment, then smilingly comply. They would fly into Cody,
Wyoming, then rent a car to drive to the ranch, at the base of the Shoshone
National Forest. En route would be the inevitable stop in Meeteetse, Wyoming,
where the general store in town boasted Lamar's favorite milkshake in the
world. ("Meeteetse was the nearest town to us and it had 450 people," said
Norma. "It had, like, three filling stations and five bars, and a general store,
and I'm not kidding.") And then it was onto the Palette Ranch and the full
respite from his dizzying world.

The days were bristling with activities: volleyball games over a net
stretched across a sloping yard, fishing, hiking, races, contests in which rocks
were thrown over a fence or at a tree. Lamar would spend a few afternoons
sketching out a schedule and then post the order of events for "the family
Olympics." There were ping-pong contests, during which Lamar gave Norma
the nickname of "Stone Mitts" and Dorothy Kemble "Rock Hands." It was a
vigorous leisure—no phones, no meetings, just relaxation, which in Lamar's
mind meant nearly constant activity.

"Playing volleyball was the staple," said Bill Adams. "One year we had a
track meet with the wives—my wife was a good athlete; she'd been a cheerleader for four years. Fishing and hiking every day, horseback riding, walk
down to the creek. Lots of games after dinner. It stayed light up there real late.
More volleyball, throwing rocks over the fence, you name it."

There were no TVs at the ranch, and Lamar's children enjoyed this—there
were fewer distractions all the way around. But on the night of July 20, they
formed a caravan with the McNutts and drove the two hours back up to
Cody, renting two rooms in a motel. In Lamar's room, they huddled around
the television to watch the ghostly black-and-white images of Neil Armstrong's
walk on the moon.

They returned and spent a few more days at the ranch, with Lamar organizing daily games of volleyball and all manner of nightly contests—who could
catch the most fish, who could run fastest around the perimeter of the main
house, which couple could win the mixed-doubles ping-pong tournament.
"He always seemed the most relaxed when he was there," recalled Sharron.

As he sat outside late at night, doing what hundreds of millions of other
people were doing around the globe that week—looking at the moon and
considering that there were actually humans on that distant sphere—Lamar
was seized by the wonder of the world, its infinite potential, and its essential

beauty. He was on the land that Colonel A. A. Anderson described as "the most beautiful I have ever seen," and everything seemed possible.

In the midst of all of it, though—the humbling accomplishment, the unfathomable distance, the beautiful surroundings back on Earth—there was one thought that continued to percolate to the surface. He mentioned it one night as the group was sitting in the stillness of the Wyoming night, looking up at the spray of stars accompanying the moon in the night sky.

"I can't wait to see Marsalis," he said. "Hank says he's looked great."

There were so much going on, in Lamar's world, and the world at large. But in three days, he'd be down in Birmingham, Alabama. The preseason was beginning, the Chiefs were playing, and there was a football game to watch.

CHAPTER ELEVEN

ON TOP OF THE WORLD

To be a professional sports owner in the 1960s was to confront the prickly subject of race in America. Many in sports were breezily confident that, nearly a generation after the NFL and Major League Baseball fields were integrated, sports was setting a societal standard of racial equality. Those who were younger and closer to the games saw a harsher reality of entrenched double standards, glass ceilings, and persistent bias about the capabilities of blacks.

Lamar was hardly a protester in the civil rights movement, but he also was more sensitive than most owners to the plight of the black athlete, and he had taken pains for much of the 1960s to make sure African-Americans were treated equally.

This was appreciated within the team, and yet as the Kansas City Chiefs gathered at William Jewell to prepare for the 1969 season, they did so against a backdrop of protracted racial tension that had enveloped the country for years and had, by then, made its presence felt in the world of sports as well. In the summer of 1968, Jack Olsen of *Sports Illustrated* wrote a celebrated five-part series on "The Black Athlete," one installment of which focused on the racial division among the St. Louis football Cardinals. Weeks after the series debuted, John Carlos and Tommie Smith gave their one-gloved black power salute at the Mexico City Olympics.

No integrated sports team was impervious to the issues of the '60s, but from all accounts, the Chiefs had dealt with the issue with more foresight and tolerance than most clubs. In 1969, they would become the first team in pro football history with a majority of African-American starters. This came six years after the Chiefs were the first pro team to hire a full-time black scout, Lloyd Wells, and two years after they became the first team in pro football to start an African-American, Willie Lanier, at middle linebacker.

Lamar and Hank Stram had set the tone early on: At a time when the Southwest Conference had no black players, the Dallas Texans went out seeking the best football players they could find. The signing of Abner Haynes and the other African-Americans on that first Texans team in 1960 wasn't radical—the NFL's Dallas Texans had featured running back Buddy Young back in 1952—but it still generated its share of hate mail. One note, written to H. L. Hunt and unsigned, arrived at the Hunt Oil offices during the inaugural 1960 season, where the father passed it on to the son, apparently without comment. It read: "Your well known patriotism and contribution to Christianity and Americanism is to be congratulated. I understand your son, Lamar Hunt, is the prime factor in engaging negro football players on the team he owns. Many feel this is an act oc [sic] communism support and hastening the intermarriage of negro [sic] and whites. I wonder if you concur in such actions. If your son wants to sacrifice the white race for a few dollars I imagine it hurts you to see your son take such an attitude."

Haynes, of course, wasn't merely recruited by the Texans, he starred for the team, won the AFL Player of the Year award in 1960, and developed a special relationship with Lamar. "He was a good man, with pure intentions," said Haynes.

Which is not to say that the Dallas Texans were an idyllic oasis. Very early in the team's history, Bunker Hunt began hanging around the team's training camp. While Bunker was not a member of the Ku Klux Klan or any of the other onerous organizations of white supremacy, his views were consistent with many Texans at the time. "You got too many blacks on your team," he told Stram more than once. "You get too many on there, and everything goes to hell."

Stram had seen his own share of prejudice, for both his size and Polish heritage, and he bridled at the suggestions. "Bunker, tell me something—if a black scores a touchdown, does it count? If a black player makes a tackle, does it count? We'll keep the best players."

Steadman was far less virulent than Bunker but had already developed his own preconceptions. In discussing the team's training camp in 1962, he singled out African-American players: "I recommend we only bring in colored players whom we know have the potential of making our squad. I think we learned from our experiment last year that they have very little playing ability and good eating ability."

Lamar had seen too much pain and suffering in blacks that he cared about—most especially the Mount Vernon staff that had helped raise him—

to not empathize with the blacks he knew. But he was not one to lecture, preferring instead a more subtle, often entirely personal approach.

"He'd say, 'Hey, Abner, let's go to lunch,'" said Haynes, "and he'd take me somewhere, and I'd walk in with him, and I could tell that there'd never been a black man served at this restaurant before. But I was with Lamar, and nobody said anything."

The players noticed Lamar's youth, his approachability (well into the '60s, he continued to show up for training camp, stay with the team at a dorm at William Jewell, and occasionally run wind sprints or catch passes in warm-ups). He was still a good enough athlete to engage in these activities without it becoming a source of humor or derision. As importantly, at a time when there was, at best, a patriarchal distance between owners and players, Lamar was unfailingly polite—he helped serve drinks and dinner to the team on flights back from road games. When traveling on the team bus to a hotel for a road game, Lamar made a point of checking his luggage in the stowage compartment along with the rest of the team and carrying his own bags into the hotel.

In the mid-1960s, the Chiefs scoured the country for the best players available, winding up often on campuses of historically black colleges and universities, where Lloyd Wells was a celebrity in his own right.

Back at the team offices in Dallas and, later, Kansas City, Stram set a policy of strict impartiality. "We'll play the best players," he said, "We don't care if a man is purple." More than rhetoric, he refused to play favorites. The summer of the Watts riots in Los Angeles, in 1965, the Chiefs' training camp was marred by a fight between a white player named Doc Griffith and a black player named Ron Fowlkes. Team leaders were heartened when Stram, in response, cut both players.

From the owner to the coach to the scouting department, the Chiefs aspired to an open-mindedness, willing to draft and sign players at positions where they hadn't traditionally played in pro football. One of these was Willie Lanier, the smart, physically intimidating middle linebacker from Morgan State in Baltimore. The Richmond, Virginia, native had decided to travel north to college, rather than stay four more years in the poisoned racial stew of Richmond, and his father drove him through Washington and on to Baltimore on the day that Martin Luther King gave his "I Have a Dream" speech on the National Mall in D.C.

By the time he finished his senior year of football at Morgan State, by winning the MVP of the Tangerine Bowl, Lanier was a self-possessed young man.

One friend of Stram's, who scouted East Coast teams, wrote Hank and told him that Lanier was the best college player he saw that season.

The 1967 NFL draft was held just weeks after the Chiefs' Super Bowl loss, as Stram was focusing on rebuilding his defense. The Chiefs drafted Jim Lynch in the second round, with the forty-eighth overall pick, and fellow linebacker Lanier two selections later.

In a matter of days, Lloyd Wells arrived in Baltimore on behalf of the Chiefs, to present himself to Lanier, informing him he needed to sign a contract—$2,500 bonus, with three one-year contracts for $14,000, $15,000, and $16,000—and that if he didn't sign, he could damn well go play football in Canada. The bluster and patter had worked well for Wells when he was dealing with the raw and sometimes guileless young men from black schools in the Deep South. But with Lanier, he confronted something else—a prideful man who was smart and connected enough to have found out, through calls made by his coach Earl Banks, exactly how much money had been offered to Lynch, selected just two picks before him. Armed with this knowledge, Lanier knew exactly how insulted he should be by Wells's low-balling offer.

Lanier bowed his broad neck, looked deeply into the scout's eyes, and told him, "Firstly, no one talks to me like that. I am a college student, and I'm about to get my degree in business administration. Secondly, you will *not* tell me that I have to take your offer or go to Canada. I will sue you for making that statement. I am done with you here."

The next day, Lanier placed a call to Stram, expressing displeasure with the method of approach that Wells used. There was no direct apology from the scout, but a few days later Wells returned, much more conciliatory, and took Lanier out to a Washington, D.C. clothier, to buy him a new suit of clothes—Lanier remembered the bill came to $286—and more cordially welcome him to the Chiefs family. (It wasn't until after the season, as Lanier was reviewing his 1099 form, that he noticed that the clothes that Wells had bought for him the previous year had been docked from his salary. This prompted another call to the Chiefs, and the matter was settled.)

When Lanier arrived for his first training camp in 1967, he was struck by the atmosphere around the team. "I didn't see any true animosity from a racial standpoint," he said, "which was pleasant and surprising, as it appeared to be a very even, open display of purity and the success of sport, which is a meritocracy. And if you show it and you can do it, you will be accepted for it. I heard about things in other places but it was not like that here. And that was very refreshing because obviously it led to my starting the fourth game of my rookie year. So the numbers spoke for themselves, and the attitudes and relationships of the players. You could have men from the South, men from Alabama, and you would have some from the West Coast, where Huey Newton was gaining prominence, and you had some of us from the East, who were perhaps a little more elitist. But you had all of that coming together, and people got along. People allowed whatever philosophical and political philosophies to be left at the door, and to become part of this thing called the Kansas City Chiefs, and the objective was to win and be better than anyone else and to get to this important step, which was the Super Bowl. I can't really remember any racial strife at all. No error of somebody uttering something that, oops, they apologized for, I mean zero."

What players like Lanier grew to understand, through the turbulent period of the late '60s, was that the Chiefs were, to the extent possible at the time, a color-blind organization, and that started from the top.

"The thing about Lamar," said Lanier, "and I understood this: This was not a social experiment. That was not the issue—that was not what he was trying to achieve. He would say that. It was one of trying to win. It was one of getting talent to be competitive to let you go forward on Sunday and have a chance to win games, which was a purely capitalist view, *which was okay*. But those who deemed themselves as capitalists but who still had hesitancy— they weren't as fully there as they thought they were, because they had let all these other things get in the way of making those decisions."

When he was moved to the starting lineup early in the '67 season, Lanier became the first black starting middle linebacker in pro football history (a fact little noted at the time). By that time, he and Jim Lynch had also become the team's first integrated pair of roommates on the road.

All of that wouldn't have meant as much if the team itself hadn't been willing to overcome long-held prejudices for the sake of a deeper sense of unity. By the late '60s, most of the team spent their off-seasons in Kansas City, many playing on the Chiefs' barnstorming basketball team. In 1968, when Martin Luther King's assassination stirred race riots across the country, Curtis McClinton and Buck Buchanan drove to O.G.'s Lounge, one of the city's black social redoubts, and urged their fellow citizens not to riot. The killing prompted a series of long talks between Lynch and Lanier, as well as other players. Even Jerry Mays—who said, "I'm from Texas, and I know I grew up prejudiced"—admitted the ongoing discussions among teammates helped him understand a problem he'd mostly ignored in the past.

Black players and white alike were united in their impatience with the vanity and excesses of Stram, whom they often referred to as "Little Caesar" or "The Little Man." But they also, to a man, believed their coach to be utterly without prejudice. "There were some people who thought he put form over substance," said one player, "but it was clear, when it came to race, he didn't care about color, he only cared if you could play."

All of which is to say that the Kansas City Chiefs team that reported to the first day of training camp on July 14, 1969, was one of the most cohesive in pro football. Over the ordeal of next five months, it would need to be.

Stram's first directive of the new season was met with much grumbling but little outward opposition. In his initial speech to the team, he said, "Gentlemen, I want to set a few things straight before we get started. Just so there won't be any misunderstanding regarding my policy on long hair and sideburns, I want to emphasize certain requirements, which I expect everyone to adhere to from this day on. There will be absolutely no mustaches, beards, goatees, or hair on the chin displayed by any member of this club. I also want to emphasize that no one will have sideburns longer than the ones I have. Is that understood?" If it wasn't, Stram imposed a $500 fine for any violation of the code (Otis Taylor was fined once, then shaved his sideburns). The Chiefs players were purposeful and determined, still stung by their season-ending 41–6 playoff loss to Oakland at the end of the '68 season.

Lamar rejoined the team down at Legion Field in Birmingham, as they officially began the preseason against the team that had so savagely ended the 1968 season, the detested Raiders. August was only two days old, the regular season was more than a month away, there were five more preseason games to follow and it would be another sixteen weeks before the two teams would meet for the first of two regular-season games. But the rivalry did not allow for complacency. The Chiefs took a 13–7 lead at the half, but fell behind when backup Jacky Lee had a pass returned for a touchdown. The Chiefs rallied to take a 23–17 lead, but when the Raiders rallied toward the winning score, Stram put his defensive starters back in the game to quell the rally. "We had the game won," he explained later. "There was no need of letting it get away at that point." Three weeks later, on August 22, they took an undefeated preseason record into the Los Angeles Coliseum for the third year in a row. In '67 and '68 they'd lost to the Rams, but this time around, they routed George Allen's Rams, 42–14, and did it in front of Richard Nixon, believed to be the first president to attend a pro football game while in office. With wins the following two weeks, the Chiefs finished the preseason 6–0, with four wins over NFL teams. The newspaper *Pro Football Weekly* put the Chiefs on the cover of its preseason kickoff issue, under the headline, "KC Chiefs—Are They Number 1?" Elsewhere in the issue, PFW writer William Wallace predicted the Chiefs would win the Super Bowl over the Los Angeles Rams, though the consensus of the paper's correspondents was that Baltimore would defeat the Jets in a Super Bowl III rematch.

The team certainly looked sharp. Stram had been the most fashion-conscious coach in the pros for years, and the Chiefs expressed his philosophy, not merely in the variety of formations they used but in countless details of their public appearance. When traveling for a road game, the Chiefs wore tailored black blazers and gray slacks, white shirts, and black ties, with the team's logo on the breast of the jacket. In '68, the Chiefs began wearing fire-engine red game pants on the road. The team's offensive huddle formed in a choir alignment, with the five interior linemen standing in the back row, backs to the line of scrimmage, mirroring the positions they would take at the line, the three receivers and two running backs standing in the front row, bending at the waist, all facing the quarterback. In these, and numerous other ways, including the manner in which they lined up for the National Anthem (numerically, most notably in '68 with 5-foot-5 Noland "Super Gnat" Smith, No. 1, in front and the mountainous 6-foot-7 Ernie Ladd, No. 99, in back), the Chiefs exuded a kind of crisp, self-conscious sense of style that was, in both its precision and its vanity, a perfect reflection of their head coach.

For all that, the most important changes were the ones taking place among the personnel, where the porous defense of the first Super Bowl season had been transformed, in the intervening years, into a younger, stronger, faster unit.

Lanier was a key: The even-tempered Virginian exuded a quiet confidence, and while he lacked the theatricality of Dick Butkus, many scouts felt he covered more ground and hit harder when he got there. So hard, in fact, that Lanier often blacked out after making tackles. His frequent concussions and ensuing headaches landed him at the Mayo Clinic in 1968 and prompted him to begin wearing a distinctive helmet with water pockets lining the inside of the shell and wide strip of foam padding bisecting the outside. By the '69 season, Lanier had become a leader of a daunting defense, improved by the acquisition of tackle Curley Culp in a trade with Denver during the '68 season, and first-round draft choice Jim Marsalis, a young master of bump-and-run technique, who stepped into a starting role at cornerback in '69.

For Lamar, in many ways, the season was like so many others. He'd travel to each game and take separate trips up to Kansas City a few times a month. But from his office in Dallas, he'd send numerous suggestions to Steadman, none which trod on Stram's football domain, each meant to rectify or slightly improve an identified problem.

Even while he was becoming immersed in the worlds of soccer and tennis, he still made time to be vigilant about the smallest details with the Chiefs. In '67, he sent a note to the AFL league office, after he noticed that a fair catch by Noland Smith in the season opener at Houston was mistakenly counted as a zero-yard return. In '68, he wrote Steadman to say, "Next year please have George [Toma] shrink the mid-field arrowhead to nine yards in length. As it is now (10 yards) the ends of it touch the two 45-yard lines and this is not artistically pleasing to the eye. I don't want it done this year as it will look messy."

A year later, Lamar was thinking of trumpets. He wrote band leader Tony DiPardo about featuring a heraldry of trumpets at games: "My idea is to have several (number ?) 'Heralds' who would be located on the ramp to signify the emergence of the Chiefs players from the locker room area. They might also 'herald' the start of the fourth period, etc. My idea stems from seeing 'Heralds' in the movies or on TV introducing combatants in various athletic and war contests. They add a note of the spectacular and, I feel, can be an intimidating factor for the opposition." A week later, he wrote a follow-up memo to Steadman, pointing out that the heraldry of trumpets had been blown too soon, right at the end of the third quarter and before the TV time-out. To properly rally the crowd for the fourth quarter, Lamar explained, the heralds should wait until after the TV timeout, in the moments just before the start of the fourth quarter, to signal their charge. "That was typical," said Steadman. "*Nothing* got past Lamar."

After posting a 6–0 preseason record, Kansas City stormed into the season with two easy road wins, over the Chargers and Patriots. But in the second game Len Dawson went down with what was diagnosed as a tear in the anterior cruciate ligament. The recommended treatment, from the Chiefs team doctor and two outside specialists, was surgery that would end Dawson's season. But Stram, knowing what Dawson meant to the team's overall prospects, kept seeking out other opinions, finally finding the St. Louis Football Cardinals' team doctor, Fred Reynolds, who said that there was a chance that, if Dawson immobilized the leg for four to six weeks, he could recover without surgery. Grasping at any possible hope by this point, Stram and Dawson opted for Reynolds' suggestion.

In the meantime, backup Jacky Lee was a capable veteran, a ten-year pro who seemed likely to perform adequately in Dawson's absence. But in the Chiefs' next game, week three at Cincinnati, Lee broke his ankle in a 24–19 loss, leaving the Chiefs to rely on their third-string quarterback, untested second-year reserve Mike Livingston. The defense was superb in response, and Livingston exceeded expectations, piloting the team to four straight victories.

But they missed their leader. Dawson exuded a polished professionalism and outward cool that was the quintessence of quarterback leadership. When lineman Ed Budde was hospitalized after a bar fight in '64, Dawson and his wife Jackie took care of Budde's three children. When Arbanas lost the vision in one eye after being attacked on the street a year later, Dawson spent weeks doing additional passing drills so Arbanas could learn to catch with the use of just one eye. On the field, Dawson was the curt, level-headed commander, moving with unquestioned authority.

After six weeks of rest and rehabilitation, he returned to rally the Chiefs to a win over Buffalo November 2. Two weeks later, he led the club into Shea Stadium just two days after the death of his father and threw three touchdown passes to Otis Taylor in a 34–16 win, before flying to Ohio for the funeral. The Chiefs would lose twice in the last month to the Raiders but would benefit from the AFL's expanded playoff format—which Lamar had been pushing for most of the league's history—in which the second-place team from each division qualified to play the champion of the opposite division in an additional semi-final round of the league playoffs.

It was a week before Christmas when Kansas City headed to New York, for a rematch with the defending world champion Jets, winners of the AFL East. By the time Lamar and his friends walked on the field at Shea Stadium on the chilly, windy afternoon of Sunday, December 20, the green grass of the baseball season—traumatized by Mets fans celebrating their World Series win in October—had given way to a surface that was mostly dirt, some of which was painted. Kansas City held a scant 6–3 lead in the third quarter when a pass interference call gave the Jets the ball at first-and-goal on the Chiefs' 1-yard-line. An impassioned Lanier, atypically vocal in the huddle, rallied the defense to the greatest goal-line stand in team history. On first- and second-down, the Chiefs stopped the Jets running backs cold. On third down, Joe Namath faked a handoff to running back Bill Mathis and rolled to his right, looking for Matt Snell out in the flat. But Bobby Bell hadn't bought the fake and was out in the flat to cover Snell. Under pressure, Namath threw the ball away, and the Jets were forced to settle for a tying field goal.

The game turned right there. Dawson hit Taylor on a 61-yard-pass play on the next play from scrimmage, and then threw a 19-yard touchdown pass to Gloster Richardson on the following play. The Kansas City defense repelled two more drives, concluding the last with a Jim Marsalis interception in the end zone.

The champions were vanquished; walking to the sidelines after the final interception, Namath threw his helmet to the ground in frustration, and the jubilant Chiefs began looking toward a third game with Oakland, two weeks hence, in what would be the final game ever between two American Football League teams.

That game would serve as a fitting end to the league's self-contained history. The Raiders had the league's most valuable player, Daryle Lamonica; coach of the year, the first-year firebrand John Madden; a sizable home-field advantage, and the knowledge that they'd beaten the Chiefs in seven of their eight previous meetings. A sense of dread pervaded Kansas City, where many of even the most loyal fans were predicting defeat. But the Chiefs players felt differently, as though they were being granted a reprieve.

The team stayed at the Mark Hopkins Hotel in San Francisco. Saturday was an exhausting day on its own: Bill Grigsby, the Chiefs radio announcer, was eating at the hotel lounge when NBC's Curt Gowdy sat down with him and confided that the network was getting ready to break a story implicating Len Dawson, among other pro players, in connection to a Detroit gambler named Donald "Dice" Dawson. The usually mirthful Grigsby turned serious, imploring Gowdy to wait until after the AFL Championship Game. Gowdy said he'd see what he could do.

After Grigsby informed Stram, he and Lamar discussed it and decided not to tell Dawson on the eve of one of the biggest games in his life. The NFL commissioner Rozelle, notified of the upcoming report, considered telling Dawson himself. Rozelle phoned Dawson at the Mark Hopkins on the eve of the game but only chatted for a few moments, deciding during the call that it would be wrong to bring it up.

The morning of the AFL Championship Game, Lamar awoke to an unusually queasy stomach. He was normally nervous on gamedays and could be even jittery on the mornings of big ones—the AFL Championship Games, the first Super Bowl with the Packers—but this was something different. "I was scared," he said, "more than I've been before a game."

When he was most nervous on game days, he'd try to do *something*—calculate some statistics, handle a pile of correspondence, find a way to exercise.

On this morning, he walked to the lobby with a huge cardboard placard, which carried an inspirational poem by a girl in suburban Kansas City. He'd received it the day before and now brought it to Stram, and asked him, "Want to show it to the team?" Stram agreed, and they gave it to equipment manager Bobby Yarborough, to put up in the dressing room.

It was an agonizing wait for kickoff. On the field during warm-ups, Lamar and Jack Steadman made small talk with Pete Rozelle and the Raiders' Al Davis. Davis and Lamar were cordial, but there was too much at stake for either man to be relaxed. They shook hands and went their separate ways. Lamar had struggled with the platitudes of wishing other owners "good luck" before a game, resorting to a more honest greeting when exchanging a pre-game handshake with a counterpart. And so he shook Raiders' owner Wayne Valley's hand and said, "No injuries."

That particular good wish was soon dashed. It would be the sort of game that many of the participants would describe later as "a war." Johnny Robinson cracked two ribs on a play; Jim Marsalis left the game with a bruised kidney. Jim Lynch made one tackle with such force that he broke his belt. Lamonica tore tendons in his hand following through on a pass, his fingers caught in the facemask of the Chiefs' onrushing Aaron Brown.

Oakland dominated the first half possession but could muster only one touchdown. Kansas City fought back to tie the game at 7 late in the second quarter. The Raiders spent much of the third quarter in Kansas City territory as well, but couldn't convert. After Emmitt Thomas ran an end zone interception out to the 6, the Chiefs found themselves pinned back deep in their own territory again, facing third-and-14 at their own 2-yard line. In another game, Dawson might have gone with a safe run into the line and punted. But the Kansas City defense had been playing heroically with its back to the wall all day, and Dawson was determined to find a way to reward their effort. Avoiding the rush, he scrambled and threw a high floater from his end zone toward Otis Taylor, who made a spectacular over-the-shoulder catch while tight-roping along the sidelines against double coverage at the 35-yard-line. The Chiefs, emboldened, drove for a touchdown, to go up 14–7 with 3:24 left in the third quarter.

"The Chiefs would be open and flamboyant when they got ahead, but they tended to be a little conservative when the game was tighter and they were behind," said John Madden, then in his first year as the Raiders' head coach. "So that was a hell of a call, and a hell of a throw by Len Dawson. Because that could have turned the game around the other way. That's a dangerous place to throw. Then Otis makes a heck of a catch on the sideline. If we knock that thing down, if we pick it off, we win the game."

From there, the game assumed an aspect of savage desperation. Within a three-minute period in the fourth quarter, there were five turnovers. The Raiders drove down the field, only to be intercepted. The Chiefs, trying to eat some time off the clock, lost a fumble. The Raiders drove again and were intercepted. The Chiefs fumbled a second time, with Oakland recovering on the Kansas City 31. Taking the field again, Jerry Mays said to Buck Buchanan, "Well, maybe we can do it once more, but if they give it up again, they're on their own." Three plays later, Emmitt Thomas intercepted the pass of George Blanda (in for the injured Lamonica) and returned the ball 62 yards to the Oakland 18. Jan Stenerud's 22-yard field goal three plays later gave Kansas City a 17–7 lead that they held until the end.

"That was the greatest defensive game I ever saw in my life," said Chiefs' lineman Ed Lothamar. "You'll never see a greater demonstration of just plain toughness." It was certainly one of the most physical, with Johnny Robinson's broken ribs and Jim Marsalis's bruised kidney leaving both doubtful for the Super Bowl seven days later.

In the locker room after the game, talking to *Kansas City Star* columnist Joe McGuff, Lamar was ebullient, able to rattle off by memory the implications of the big win.

"We have a lot to be proud of looking back over the years we've spent in the AFL," he said. "We've won three league championships, which is more than any other team. Buffalo and Houston won two each, Oakland won one, San Diego and New York won one. That makes us the all-time AFL champion. Hank is the winningest AFL coach and no team won a series from us. Oakland had a one-game lead over us going into today's game but we tied it at 11–11. We also had the best exhibition record and the best record against NFL teams. That's quite an accomplishment."

At the end, Raiders' owner Wayne Valley came to the visitors' locker room to congratulate Lamar, who was his usual deferential self. As the Chiefs team bus prepared to pull out of the parking lot, the players spied the sullen Raiders heading out of their locker room, each carrying the luggage he'd packed for the trip to New Orleans. "That was one of the most satisfying things I've ever seen," said Dawson.

The trip back from Oakland was suffused with a joyous relief—the Chiefs had finally throttled the Raiders, and now would get a chance to redeem themselves from their Super Bowl I disappointment. Even on the flight back,

Lamar was making a list of things he needed to do to prepare for the Super Bowl trip (unlike three years earlier, there would be only a one-week break between the league title games and the Super Bowl, not two). But he put the list down long enough to help serve a special victory dinner to the players on the charter back to Kansas City. There was even a special menu, whose cover depicted a tomahawk buried in a Raiders' helmet.

After consecutive road wins over the defending world champions and the team with the best record in pro football, with a stifling defense that allowed just 13 points in those two games, Kansas City might have been regarded as a formidable contender. Instead, the Minnesota Vikings were installed as a 13-point favorite by Jimmy "The Greek" Snyder. One headline in *Pro Football Weekly* noted that, "If It's a Battle of the QBs . . . Kapp Has It All Over Dawson." Elsewhere in the paper, William Wallace, the same man who'd forecast a Chiefs Super Bowl win in the preseason, now backtracked and predicted a 31–7 Vikings win.

So the buildup to Super Bowl IV played out in eerie parallel to the previous year, with a seemingly invincible team from the NFL being put forth as a heavy favorite, the merits of the AFL entry largely ignored in the calculation. "They're doing it again," warned the Raiders' George Blanda during the week. "They haven't learned a thing since last year. They're underestimating the AFL all over again."

That Tuesday, on the Chiefs' first full day in atypically frigid New Orleans, the news hit. On the NBC Evening News, David Brinkley read the explosive item: "A number of famous names in pro football will be asked to talk to a federal grand jury in Detroit and to tell whatever they know about gambling on sports. The pro football players asked to testify will include quarterback Len Dawson of the Kansas City Chiefs . . ." NBC broke the story linking Dawson and five other pro players to a Justice Department sting of a network of bookmakers, including the Detroit bookie Donald "Dice" Dawson (no relation to the quarterback), whose address book included Dawson's phone number. There was nothing more than that—no evidence of any wrongdoing, no tangible assertion of anything more than a casual connection. But suddenly much of New Orleans, especially the 300 assembled writers and reporters who had descended on the city to cover the game, were buzzing about the implications of the investigation. The report ignited a media conflagration beyond anything seen the year before in Miami, when Joe Namath made his brazen, legendary guarantee that the Jets would win. Rozelle was on a boat in Bimini when the news hit, and he could do little but release a statement from the league office that evening noting that the NFL had "no evidence to even consider disciplinary action against any of those publicly named." But hundreds of writers and reporters were already gathered in New Orleans, confronting a potentially major story with absolutely no answers.

With the media still buzzing throughout the Fontainebleau Hotel, where the Chiefs were staying, it was left to Lamar, Stram, Dawson, and Chiefs' publicist Jim Schaaf to work out a response. Late that evening, the team called a press conference so Dawson could make a statement. "I have known Mr. [Donald] Dawson for about ten years," he said, "and I have talked to him on several occasions. My only conversations with him in recent years concerned my knee injury and the death of my father. On these occasions he called me to offer his sympathy. These calls were among the many I received. Gentlemen, this is all I have to say. I have told you everything I know."

Ultimately, that's all there was to the story. Neither Dawson nor the other players were ever subpoenaed, and all were cleared of any wrongdoing. Rozelle arrived in New Orleans on Wednesday and coolly conducted an hour-long press conference in which he defended Dawson's honor as well as the league's security investigation. But the furor didn't immediately go away, and Dawson was left to face the biggest game of his life under a cloud of suspicion.

For Lamar, the stakes couldn't have been any higher. In the final game before the full merger of the two leagues, he'd be facing off against the Minnesota Vikings, the same team that had abandoned the AFL in November 1959.

That Wednesday night in New Orleans, in the 1840 Room, the private dining room inside Antoine's Restaurant in the French Quarter, Lamar sat with family and friends and spent a few minutes reflecting on what the game symbolized.

"Two things stand out in my mind," he said. "One is the way New Orleans treated the American Football League. The other is the way some of the men who are now owners of the Vikings pulled out on us after committing themselves to an NFL franchise."

Those who knew him best were surprised at his frankness, as he recounted the tale of the Minnesota group's abdication, but they also saw some of the usual whimsy in his eyes as he paused for a moment, then evenly stated, "In looking back on these things, all I can think of tonight is . . ."—he peered to his right and his left, then banged a fist on the table, and said, "kill . . . kill . . . Kill . . . Kill . . . KILL! . . . KILL!"

And soon enough, the entire dining room was matching Lamar's lead and chanting "Kill! Kill! Kill!"

There was a growing sense of confidence throughout the Chiefs' camp. Defensive assistant Tom Bettis spent the week showing the team Minnesota's offensive variations, all modifications on vanilla. The team had seen twenty sheets of offensive formations before their game with the Raiders; they got just four pages with the Vikings (and, as it turned out, they wouldn't need three of those four). On the Wednesday before the game, Jerry Mays walked out of a meeting room and saw PR man Will Hamilton walking down the hall and told him, "If Jan-ski can make three field goals, we're going to win the game. There is no way they're going to score more than a touchdown."

Johnny Robinson, not one for idle optimism, felt the Chiefs could shut Minnesota out. Dawson viewed Stram's game plan as perfectly suited for the opposition. Later in the week, before going to dinner with Lamar, Buzz Kemble cornered Stram at one point and asked him pointedly, "Really—no bull—what do you think?" and when Stram answered confidently, Kemble decided to increase his wager on the Chiefs.

After Lamar and Norma, staying at the Royal Sonesta in the French Quarter, went to sleep to a steady rain, Sunday morning dawned overcast and windy, with dire weather in the forecast. Lamar spent part of the morning at an NFL brunch, with the *Tonight Show* co-host Ed McMahon, whose remarks ran long; Lamar was too gracious to leave during the presentation, but he bolted out as soon as McMahon concluded and headed back to the Royal Sonesta, to pick up Norma.

They collected their things and headed downstairs. Lamar, decked out in the Chiefs traveling blazer, put his hotel room key in his pocket and pressed the elevator button on the fourth floor. After a moment, the door opened, and Lamar and Norma were presented with a pair of tense, alarmed faces, those of Vikings owner Max Winter and his wife Helen. In the spaces between the curt, nervous hellos by all, the two couples rode down the remaining floors in uncomfortable silence. There was no mention of the game, or of the shared history a decade earlier when Winter had abandoned the AFL for the senior league. With a frozen rictus of a smile on his face, Max Winter stared searchingly at the floor indicator as it made its slow descent downward.

After the eternity it took to reach the lobby, the two couples exchanged goodbyes and went their separate ways, with Lamar and Norma heading out to the car driven by an off-duty police officer Steadman had hired to get them to the stadium. As they moved away from the elevators, Lamar's walk grew more relaxed and he cast a brief sidelong glance at Norma. With the barest hint of a smile, he said quietly, "We're going to win today."

She looked questioningly back at him and asked, "How do you know?"

"They're even scareder than we are."

In the locker room prior, the Chiefs were confident and keyed up, but not, in E. J. Holub's description, the "blithering idiots" they were prior to Super Bowl I. Dawson ate a candy bar while looking once more at the game plan in front of his locker. The pre-game buzz among the team revolved around a small addition that Lamar had ordered for the Chiefs uniform, an anniversary patch denoting the ten-year history of the AFL. (The NFL teams had worn patches on their jerseys all year, commemorating the league's fiftieth anniversary, and now, at the behest of loyalist Ange Coniglio, the AFL was finally answering with a tribute to its own history.) "It was incredible to see the reaction of those great players," said Hank Stram. "They were so proud to wear that patch because they cared about the league. They wanted to be first-class."

When the game began, it quickly became clear that while the Vikings' undersized 235-pound center Mick Tingelhoff may have been a worthy all-league selection in the NFL, where he was a quick-footed blocker free to operate in space, he was physically unequipped to deal with the head-on pressure and intimidation of 6-foot-7, 285-pound Buck Buchanan or 6-foot-1, 265-pound Curley Culp, who alternated lining up right on Tingelhoff's nose in the Chiefs' odd-man fronts, largely destroying the Vikings' interior running game. Confused by the Chiefs' triple stack and intimidated by Buchanan and Culp's alternate mauling of the outmanned Tinglehoff, the Vikings were shut out in the first half. And after dealing with the complex offenses of the AFL, the Chiefs had precious little problem with the Vikings basic attack: They ran out of just two formations, and in sixty-two offensive plays from scrimmage, they didn't once shift or start a play with a man in motion.

"Our whole influence was Bambi and the Chargers and the things Sid Gillman was doing, like the Raiders, and the Jets, when you got an arm like Namath; that was our culture," said the Chiefs' Jim Lynch. "The NFL was different. Their culture was the Green Bay Packers. Theirs was, 'Look, we're gonna line up and we're gonna run the Green Bay sweep. And you'd better stop us, 'cause here we come.' "

On offense, the Chiefs double-teamed the Vikings' ends, to prevent them from batting down passes, and in so doing opened passing lanes for Dawson's play-action fakes and short, crisp flares and out patterns. Kansas City drove consistently on the Vikings in the first half, building a 9–0 lead on three Stenerud field goals (the first one from 48 yards out). When the Vikings' Charlie West fumbled Stenerud's kickoff following the third field goal, the Chiefs' Remi Prudhomme recovered on Minnesota's 19, and three plays later, Mike Garrett scored from 5 yards out, and the Chiefs went to the half leading 16–0.

Two weeks earlier, in their first playoff game, the Vikings had trailed the Rams by 17 at the half and came back to win that playoff game. But during the interminable halftime, while the Tulane Stadium crowd was being treated to a reenactment of the Battle of New Orleans that further tore up the spongy field, Grant apparently did nothing to adjust to the Chiefs' tactics, merely advising his team to play better. For a while they did, mounting their one sustained drive of the day, to slice the lead to 16–7.

On the next drive, the Chiefs moved the ball again, converting a long third-down with their third successful end-around of the day to Frank Pitts. On first and 10 at the Minnesota 46, Dawson sensed an all-out blitz and, after a short drop, flung the ball out into the flat just as he was being hit. The pass found Otis Taylor, running a quick hitch pattern, and Taylor did the rest. He broke the attempted tackle of cornerback Earsell Mackbee and sprinted down the sidelines in his long, prancing stride. Karl Kassulke had an angle on him at the 10, but Taylor's juke move and stiff arm left Kassulke on the ground. As Taylor ran to the end zone, he could hear his mother, in the stands in the corner toward which he was running, shouting, "That's my boy!" Suddenly, the Chiefs were up 23–7, and the game was all but over.

Kansas City intercepted three passes in the fourth quarter, and Aaron Brown's tackle of the previously indomitable Joe Kapp sent the Vikings' leader to the sideline, writhing in pain. Minutes later, as the chilled New Orleans twilight subsumed what little sunlight had peeked through the densely packed clouds, the red-clad Chiefs ran off the field, carrying Stram on their shoulders, champions of the world. In the frantic locker room at Tulane Stadium, a crush of reporters came to document the chaotic scene, along with dozens of AFL players and coaches.

Pete Rozelle presented Lamar and Stram with the Super Bowl championship trophy, as the Chiefs' scout Lloyd Wells sat grinning in a window well against the back wall—a spot that placed him in virtually every television shot of the championship podium. Redemption was all around the room. "I knew I went with the right team!" said Bell, who had chosen the Chiefs over the Vikings back in 1962. Taylor, who'd made the key offensive play in all three playoff games, spent the first 10 minutes after the game weeping tears of joy.

Dawson, vindicated both off and on the field, received the MVP award with the same outward calm he'd exhibited all week. Then came the summons to Dawson from Chiefs' equipment man Bobby Yarborough.

"Hey, Lenny, come here," said Yarborough. "The phone—it's the president."

"The president of what?" asked Dawson.

"*The president*," exclaimed Yarborough. "Nixon!"

The short conversation that followed was a seminal moment in American sports and spawned numerous congratulatory calls and White House visits in the decades to follow. It wasn't even the first time Nixon had called the Chiefs that day. He'd rung up Stram that morning at the Fontainebleau, to tell him that he knew Dawson hadn't done anything wrong, and wished the team luck in its game that day. "I don't know if it amounted to a presidential pardon," said Stram. "But it sure made Leonard feel better."

And so the original Super Bowl series, NFL versus AFL, ended in a 2–2 tie and in parity between the leagues that would come together the following season.

"People really thought that the Jets win in Super Bowl III was a fluke," said Steve Sabol of NFL Films. "It didn't really cause people to reassess things. You heard the same thing from everyone: If they played ten times, the Colts win eight or nine. But after Super Bowl IV, nobody was saying that. After that, there was no doubt anymore. You had to grant that the AFL had reached parity. At the least."

Lamar was beaming when he received the Super Bowl trophy from Pete Rozelle in the Chiefs' locker room. Asked by CBS's Frank Gifford to sum up his feelings, Lamar said, "It's pretty fantastic. It's a beautiful trophy, and it really is a satisfying conclusion to the ten years of the American Football League. I want to say especially a thanks to the people of Kansas City. This trophy really belongs to them as well as the organization. This team is Kansas City's."

What he didn't say, in the midst of it all, was how aware he was of the ultimate irony: On the afternoon of January 11, 1970, the American Football League had finally earned the lasting respect it deserved. And at that very same moment it ceased to exist.

That evening, Lamar and Norma joined the Chiefs in a raucous party at the Royal Sonesta, and then watched the replay of the entire game (the live telecast hadn't been shown locally, due to NFL blackout rules). Lamar still wasn't done. With Richey and Kemble and a few others, he walked down to

Jackson Square, where Lamar had them help him up on the statue of Andrew Jackson and his horse. He wasn't drunk, just giddy with triumph.

He neither boasted nor criticized, only reveled in the joy the same way that a million other Chiefs fans were that evening. That night, he received numerous telegrams, floral arrangements, and expressions of love and fellowship from his friends and family, as well as a telegram from his father, which read: "CONGRATULATIONS LAMAR ON YOUR PROUD SUCCESS AND TRIUMPH. BEST WISHES TO YOU AND THE TEAM HL HUNT"

The next day featured an astoundingly large parade in Kansas City. Schools let out, and the streets were lined with fans the last five miles into the city from the new airport, where the team plane had landed. More than 100,000 people congregated on the downtown parade path leading to the Liberty Memorial. It was that moment, finally, when Lamar realized what he had wrought. For the moment, Kansas City was on top of the sporting world. And as he looked out on the throng, and the blizzard of ticker tape, congratulating his coach and his players, he must have felt pride for being the person who had set all that in motion. At the end of a long, bitter decade both the city and the franchise had been greeted with a celebration that was as close as most crowds could ever come to harmonious, unified pandemonium.

After more than a decade of striving, and some moments of genuine, bone-deep doubt, Lamar had emerged in the new decade as the owner of the most successful franchise in football. The ten-year history of the American Football League had concluded in the most satisfying manner imaginable. The Chiefs were the champions of pro football, and they already had a waiting list of more than 10,000 for season tickets.

Lamar answered every congratulatory telegram and letter with notes of his own. He invited his father to the team's new 101 Awards Banquet, sponsored by 101 civic leaders and voted on by 101 members of the national press. He helped design the team's championship rings, awarded to the team that spring.

Then, as he moved forward, turning his attention to soccer and tennis, he must have thought that, perhaps, he might actually be able to do it all, and do it all well.

CHAPTER TWELVE

GLOBETROTTER

In June 1970, Lamar flew to Wimbledon, to take in some matches and get some rest, though even these leisurely days were tightly scripted. WCT had been surviving, losing less money than it had in '68 and '69, but it was still a precarious slog—staging about a dozen tournaments managed by the organization, while farming out some or all of their contract players to other events, so they could play enough matches and win enough money to earn their guarantees.

WCT was nearly finished finalizing details of its buyout of the National Tennis League—George MacCall's endeavor had run out of money—that would see Lamar acquire the contracts of the world's top-ranked player Rod Laver; fellow Aussie veterans Ken Rosewall, Roy Emerson, and Fred Stolle; U.S. legend Pancho Gonzalez, and Spanish clay court specialist Andrés Gimeno. Before he'd left Dallas, Lamar had received a call from WCT executive director Mike Davies, who had already arrived in London on the first week of the tournament, asking for some time to meet. Lamar had grown to trust Davies implicitly—the Welshman occupied approximately the same role with WCT as Jack Steadman did with the Chiefs—but he entered the meeting with no sense of what was in store.

It was the middle of the second week, in the morning before matches had begun, that Lamar visited Davies in his London hotel room. As he settled back in the couch, an animated, beaming Davies presented Lamar with an elaborate, ambitious idea. Just six months after the Chiefs' Super Bowl victory (the Welshman didn't understand football, but he did realize the game's immense importance in America), he had drawn up the blueprints for a regular-season of tournaments, with the top eight finishers qualifying for a championship tournament that would culminate in what Davies described as a "Super Bowl of tennis." Davies had filled up twenty pages of legal paper with his notations, and, as he explained it in detail, Lamar's mind was already working, excited by the possibilities. "We could have weekly standings in the newspaper," he said at one point, and Davies nodded in agreement. Then came the reckoning.

"Now, Lamar," Davies said. "We'd need you to put up a million dollars. I think I could sell at least seventeen of these twenty tournaments, and maybe one or two more, so we'd be mostly covered, but you'd obviously need to guarantee it."

There was more. WCT at that point had twenty-one players in its stable and would need to sign enough contracts so it could start the 1971 season with thirty-two players. Lamar did not say yes that morning in London, but he was clearly captivated with the idea.

He returned to Dallas and sat down with Al Hill, Jr., and they immediately began working on how to structure and present the idea. In the two months between Wimbledon and the U.S. Open, they began working on the details. With Hunt Oil's extensive printing capabilities at the ready, they put together an elaborate brochure with an embossed cover—dubbed "Big Black"—to present at the introductory press conference. Davies was quietly talking to tournament promoters around the world, to see who would want a piece in such a tournament, and lining up stops in the United States, Europe, and Australia.

The announcement was made during the 1970 U.S. Open at Forest Hills, in a temporary tent erected for the occasion—since the United States Lawn Tennis Association would not let WCT use the main clubhouse at Forest Hills. So out on the grounds, with jumbo jets droning by in the La Guardia flight path, Lamar, Al, Jr., and Davies announced the future of tennis: Thirty-two players would compete in twenty WCT tournaments in 1971, and the top eight performers would advance to the WCT Finals, to be played over a week in November in Dallas.

The announcement caused exactly the splash that Lamar and Davies had hoped for, and on Valentine's Day, 1971, at the Spectrum in Philadelphia, the World Championship Tennis "Million Dollar Tour" concluded its first stop, with John Newcombe beating Laver in straight sets, two of them coming on the still-novel 12-point tiebreakers (first player to 7 points, winning by at least 2 points), which had replaced the more arbitrary 9-point tiebreaks of earlier WCT tours, and would soon be taken up by the tennis world at large, from pros to amateurs to weekend players.

The first "season" of the million-dollar tour proved to be a marketing success, and WCT nearly broke even for the first time. After Philadelphia, the tour stopped in fourteen American cities (including both Dallas and Fort Worth), along with Sydney, Rome, Teheran, Bristol, Quebec, Vancouver, Cologne, Barcelona, Stockholm, and Bologna.

Then came the return to Dallas for the finals. On Friday afternoon, November 26, 1971, the day after Thanksgiving (and the epic nationally televised college football "Game of the Century" between No. 1 Nebraska and No. 2 Oklahoma), Rod Laver and Ken Rosewall faced off at Memorial Auditorium in Dallas, with Rosewall prevailing 6–4, 1–6, 7–6, 7–6 to win $50,000, a Triumph Spitfire, and the new WCT Trophy (which happened to be the old Kramer Cup, from the wilderness years, with a new base designed by Tiffany).

It would become clear soon enough that Jack Kramer, who already resented Lamar for the success of WCT, resented him further for reprising the trophy, which had been a prize for a professional team competition, begun in 1961, that was meant to be a pro alternative to what was then the all-amateur Davis Cup. "Well, Kramer can blame me for that, because it was my idea," said Davies. "And when I found out he was mad, I still didn't care—the players bought the trophy in the first place. It was in Kenny Rosewall's garage."

Writing in *Sports Illustrated*, Joe Jares noted Lamar's rising profile in tennis, and his unshowy demeanor in all sports: "Hunt wears a green WCT blazer just like the rest of the help, gives himself second billing on WCT stationery, personally passes out invitations to the reporters on press row and does everything but restring rackets for the 34 men in his troupe."

•

At least tennis was making strides. The North American Soccer League had spent each year of its existence on life support. It had survived the ignominy of just five teams in 1969 and just six in 1970, before the league inched back up to eight franchises for 1971.

Going into the 1971 season, the Tornado made two key personnel changes. Brian Harvey, who'd been one of two remaining players who made the world tour (the other was Mike Renshaw), signed with a club in Australia. In his place came the tall, strong brawler from Liverpool, Tony McLaughlin. "Players like Tony are not allowed any more," said Renshaw. "The game has changed and out-and-out thugs are not encouraged. Tony McLaughlin was a thug of the first order, and he would be proud to be described as such. He was good looking and would have been even better looking if not for a nose broken in several places. Strong in the air and afraid of nothing, he was the ideal teammate, the type of player opponents dreaded."

That year's version of the Tornado had been stabilized by manager Ron Newman, who moved easily into the role of teacher/missionary; when he wasn't coaching his players, he was working tirelessly to spread the word of soccer to a mostly indifferent Dallas. On the mornings of matches, it was Newman who would drive to the exit by Franklin Field and post signs reading "SOCCER MATCH TONIGHT" so passers-by could see. Newman found time to pitch the game to all who would listen, insisting his players do the same—and the Tornados made the rounds, to parks, schools, and youth centers.

The solid, soft-spoken defender Dick Hall was signed in 1971 and went into the lineup in his first game, in Washington, scoring an own-goal in a Tornado loss. Only then did he get to see his new home of Dallas. Hall was still growing accustomed to driving on the right side of the road when he was dispatched by Newman to give away tickets to neighbors. So dozens of Dallasites in the spring of 1971 were greeted with the incongruous presence of a black man with an English accent knocking on their door to invite them down to the local soccer game, offering a few tickets as an inducement.

At the Tornado offices on 5738 North Central Expressway, co-owner Bill McNutt was mostly invisible, since he lived an hour away in Corsicana, but Lamar stopped by frequently, fascinated with both the theory and practice of starting something new. Even more so than with Stram on the Chiefs, he deferred to Newman (he would occasionally ask Stram about player moves, but he was much more circumspect with Newman). On the evenings after games, there were informal receptions at the Hilton Hotel at the corner of Mockingbird and the North Central Expressway, where the players and their wives or girlfriends would mingle with Lamar, McNutt, and their families.

Where Lamar did become involved was with the minutiae of promotion and presentation. When he saw that the players seemed rather indifferent to the playing of the National Anthem before games (it was not a custom in many countries), Lamar called a team meeting to explain the etiquette of the Anthem, and soon the Tornado were grouped in a razor-straight line for the song, just like Stram's Chiefs.

The new team was a blend of elements that was readily adaptable and smart on the field, anchored by center-back John Best, Newman's captain and player-coach on the field.

In 1971, the NASL conducted both rounds of its four-team playoffs with a best-of-three playoff series format. The Tornado traveled to defending champion Rochester to face the Lancers, who'd been the best team in the regular season. The team could have been unhinged in the days before the playoffs. Newman had suspended goalkeeper Mirko Stojanović just days before the game, after the goalkeeper walked off the pitch during practice. But the team rallied around injured goalkeeper Kenny Cooper—who answered to the affirmative when Newman asked him if he was ready to play, though Cooper was still walking on crutches at the time. Cooper played valiantly, and the first game of the series was still scoreless at the end of regulation.

The NASL policy to avoid ties in the playoffs was to play a 15-minute "golden goal" period of sudden-death overtime. But through three, four, five 15-minute overtime periods, neither team scored. At one point, as the succession of overtimes continued, into the sixth extra period, Lamar asked Clive Toye if they should call the game.

"We might be here all night," Lamar said.

"That's fine—we'll make everyone breakfast," replied Toye.

But near the end of the sixth overtime period, NASL commissioner Phil Woosnam had seen enough. He was headed down to the field to suspend the game after the sixth overtime period when Carlos Metidieri kicked the winner past the hobbled Cooper, ending the game at 1–0 in the 176th minute, at that point the longest professional soccer game in history. Said Newman afterward, "It was the only game that I ever remember where both teams celebrated the winning goal."

Dallas fought back, winning the second game at Franklin Field and then returning to Rochester, where they went to extra time once again before Moffat's goal vanquished the Lancers, sending Dallas to the final series against the Atlanta Chiefs.

The championship series began on Sunday, September 12, the day after Lamar had watched the Chiefs travel to Dallas and lose a tight 24–17 preseason game to the Cowboys in front of 74,035 fans at the Cotton Bowl. Against Atlanta, in Atlanta Fulton County Stadium, 3,218 watched the Atlanta Chiefs edge the Tornado, 2–1. Back at Franklin Field three nights later, with the season hanging in the balance, Dallas was dominant, with the Brazilian forward Luis Juracy scoring a pair of goals in a 4–1 victory in front of a decent midweek crowd of 6,456.

The third and deciding game of the NASL Finals was originally to be played on a Friday evening in Atlanta, but weather pushed it back to a

Sunday afternoon, which coincided with the season opener for the Chiefs, who played at San Diego to begin the season. Lamar was torn, but he'd never missed a Chiefs game, and he didn't on this day, deciding to fly to San Diego and keep his streak alive.

Back in Atlanta, it came down to the Tornado's superior offensive fire-power, as well as the daunting presence of their resident English striker, McLaughlin, who influenced the game even though he didn't score a goal. "Manfred Kammerer was scared shitless of Tony McLaughlin," said Bobby Moffat. McLaughlin was a nuisance as a one-off, but in a three-game se-ries, he became a scourge. The classic English striker—moving around in an elbow-slashing fury, leading with his head like someone late for a bar fight—totally overwhelmed Kammerer, and dominated the area. "He owned the 18-yard box," said an admiring Kenny Cooper. In the first half, Mike Renshaw headed in a Phil Tinney cross, and later Moffat scored a second goal, and soon enough the Dallas Tornado were the champions of the North American Soccer League. Lamar got the news on the phone, a nice respite after the frus-trating 21–14 opener loss to the Chargers.

The following Saturday night, Lamar and Norma hosted a gathering for the team and the Tornado staff at their new home on Gaywood. It was a balmy Dallas evening, with a warm glow of shared accomplishment pervad-ing over the evening. Norma was the usual gracious hostess, conquering lan-guage and cultural barriers, providing a tour of the estate and making sure everyone was well-served. Few were served better than McLaughlin. At one point, Lamar stopped by a table where the striker was talking with one of his teammates and, smiling, asked what everyone was talking about. When McLaughlin loudly volunteered that they were talking about "How much *fookin'* money you make," McLaughlin's teammates stood mortified, while Lamar proffered a thin smile, and soon volunteered to fill someone's drink.

Though Renshaw and some other teammates tried to rein him in, McLaughlin wasn't done. Verne Lundquist, the Channel 8 sportscaster, who had covered so much of the Tornado's ascent, was there with his wife before heading back to the studio to do the 10 o'clock news. He was just giving his thanks to the hosts and saying goodbye when an overserved McLaughlin lifted him up from behind and threw him into the pool. Lundquist emerged furious and sputtering, while Norma tried to apologize and offer help.

As Lundquist stormed off in one direction, the movable feast McLaugh-lin headed in another direction, leaving a good part of the party speechless at poolside. At that point Lamar sat down with Renshaw and some of the players who'd been with McLaughlin. There was another moment of pregnant silence, before Lamar pierced it. Smiling at Renshaw, he said, "So, Mike . . . what's Brian Harvey up to these days?"

McLaughlin would never play for the Tornado again.

•

Municipal Stadium in Kansas City, on the corner of 22nd and Brooklyn, was a symbol of many things: a proud if distant heritage of baseball excellence (the Kansas City Monarchs used to play their games there), a signpost of the city's major-league aspirations, and also a monument to a time when cars were less prevalent (the stadium parking lot had only 5,000 spaces).

But by 1971, Kansas City was suffering the urban decay of many American cities, and the team and fans alike were eager for the move to a new facility. The Harry S Truman Sports Complex, located at the intersection of I-70 and I-435, about 10 minutes east of downtown, was being erected, the product of the imagination of architect Charles Deaton. In every way, it seemed, it would be better than its predecessor: Larger, more spacious, cleaner, built just for football, at a more easily accessible location, every seat offering an unobstructed view, and each facing toward the 50-yard-line.

After consistently selling out the 50,000-seat Municipal Stadium, Lamar and Steadman were mindful of the potential of a 75,000-seat stadium. Municipal was old, in a part of town that many season-ticket holders wouldn't travel to except on game days, its amenities poor, its sightlines suited for baseball, not football.

But the small bandbox did have its charms. The Wolfpack, doling out cheers and criticisms, often in equal measure, sat behind the players benches in the north grandstand; Tony DiPardo and the Chiefs Zing Band would serenade the crowd from the corner of the west end zone, and, on the field, the "Sod God," George Toma, was doing his masterful work, maintaining the grass through the fall, painting the end zones in bright gold, making it the most distinctive field in pro football. And on late fall afternoons, after the clock moved back for daylight savings time, the arc lights atop Municipal would give the Chiefs' red jerseys a saturated look that seemed to glow in the fading light. The grass, the mud, the music, the team, the loyal fans—who'd stuck with the team during its down years—made for an unforgettable tableaux.

So 1971 was the last hurrah for Municipal Stadium, and in the opinion of Lamar, Stram, and Dawson, the 1971 team was the best club in Chiefs' history.

Len Dawson was thirty-six but still operating at peak efficiency, a calm, purposeful quarterback who made precious few mistakes. The Chiefs' massive offensive line was mature and adept at both run- and pass-blocking, its running back corps, paced by Ed Podolak and Jim Otis, was stout and reliable. And then there was Otis Taylor. For years, he'd been among the most dangerous receivers in the game, and though he could be brilliant in stretches—he'd made the decisive, game-breaking play in all three postseason games of the Chiefs' Super Bowl run—he'd struggled to put it all together for an entire season, often bedeviled by injuries or Stram's offensive philosophy which, despite all his innovations, still hewed toward a conservative run-first style. But in 1971, Taylor had his best year as a pro, and one of the best years ever by a wide receiver. He played a crucial role in the regular season's pivotal game, a 16–14 win over the archrival Raiders that clinched the AFC West title, and a home game in the first round of the playoffs, where many observers expected the Chiefs to advance to their third Super Bowl in six seasons.

The playoffs opened on an unseasonably warm Christmas Day, as the Chiefs played host to the young, talented Miami Dolphins. Like so many epic games, this one turned on any of a dozen plays, any number of which may have turned out differently and been decisive. After Jan Stenerud's baffling miss at the end of regulation sent the game into overtime, Miami won it in the sixth quarter on a Garo Yepremian field goal, 27–24.

Walking off the field, an exhausted Lanier and his longtime roommate and linebacker partner Jim Lynch were too fatigued to speak. But after having time to reflect on the game, he wasn't haunted. "I left everything I had out there on that field," Lanier said. "That was what pro football was about, that was the game at its best." There were two future Hall-of-Fame coaches and twelve future Hall-of-Fame players on the field that day.

In the Municipal Stadium "owners box" (it was essentially an empty, open-air cement platform near the press box, with a table to place binoculars, programs, and drinks) and folding chairs, six-year-old Clark Hunt—who had been up since 6 a.m. in Dallas—had fallen asleep when overtime started. Lamar had to wake him up after the game, for the glum ride to the airport, and the quiet flight home.

The game left a mark on almost everyone who pledged their loyalty to the Chiefs. The finality of Yepremian's field goal, and the instant extinguishing of hopes that brought the packed stadium to an almost instant silence hit the city with a force that felt almost physical. "It was like the end of the world," said Stu Stram, Hank's son, who walked out with his grim, ashen-faced father on the slightly chilled Christmas evening. "To see the expressions on the faces of the players and the fans, it was the first time I realized the true magnitude of athletics, how it could affect a team and a stadium, and an entire city. It was devastating."

It was an agonizing loss for Stram and for Stenerud. But no one—not Lamar, or Hank Stram, or Jack Steadman, or Len Dawson—could have sensed the finality of the defeat. Lamar was devastated as well, but assumed it was a mere blip in Stram's ongoing record of excellence, and rewarded the coach with a ten-year contract after the season ended. What no one could have realized, after nearly narrowly missing their third Super Bowl in six seasons, is that it would be fifteen years before the Chiefs would make the playoffs again.

•

As soon as Lamar shook off the disappointment of Christmas Day, he was back working on the 1972 Million-Dollar Tour for the WCT, which due to the ceaseless power struggle in the world of tennis, had to be compressed into the first five months of the calendar.

WCT had marched forward despite the politics, and the coup that most changed the landscape came when it was able to negotiate a deal to broadcast a series of tournaments on network TV. Even the '71 final had been picked up on independent stations.

"Lamar *really* wanted a network deal, so we went to NBC and asked them about showing a series of finals," said Al Hill, Jr. "They weren't interested, and said no. And I explained that I needed to bring something other than 'No' to Lamar. So then they said, 'Okay, you can have eight weeks, but then you have to sell the time for the eight weeks. And that way it will prove to Lamar that it can't be done.'"

But Lamar and Davies and Hill were well on their way to identifying the most appealing sponsors for their tennis tour. They brought in the canny negotiator Barry Frank of IMG, and he set about selling the package, ultimately selling every spot. By the time the 1972 final was held—in May in Dallas, at the culmination of a four-and-a-half month spring season that was ideal for capitalizing on the weakest section of the American sports television schedule—it was part of a string of successful broadcasts.

After the rushed Thanksgiving week finale of '71, Lamar and WCT presented a much more focused, professional event in '72. Neil Armstrong had been brought in to be the featured guest at the '71 finals, but in '72, Lamar and Hill looked to Hollywood. James Franciscus, the star of TV's *Longstreet*, was the guest of honor that year, and after six matches narrowed the two finalists, a sellout crowd of 7,800 at Moody Coliseum turned out for a rematch between the Aussies Laver and Rosewall.

Lamar almost didn't get to see the match. That morning, seven-year-old Clark was playing in the back patio of the Gaywood mansion. When he climbed upon one of the large cement urns lining the top of the patio wall, he assumed the pot was anchored. But the urn wasn't secure, and as Clark pulled on the handle, it gave way, sending Clark and toppling to the ground along with the urn, which nearly pulverized his right foot. Lamar and Norma rushed him to the hospital, where the outlook for the boy was originally quite grim, with even the possibility of amputation presented to the parents. By the time doctors had stabilized the injury, and performed their first operation—putting Clark out of any immediate danger—Lamar was able to rush to Moody Coliseum and, still shaken, host the day's event.

It turned out to be a classic, with Rosewall edging Laver in five riveting sets, 4–6, 6–0, 6–3, 6–7, 7–6, with a taut, harrowing tiebreaker deciding it, before a frenzied Moody Coliseum crowd and a record TV audience of 20 million. WCT had arrived, and was big time. The tennis historian Bud Collins would call it the greatest match he ever witnessed. Just four years after starting on an ice rink inside a rodeo barn, WCT had become the most prominent upstart in modern tennis.

Yet for all that success, Lamar found himself once more in a protracted struggle with the tennis establishment. Ahead of the 1971 tournament, Wimbledon's caretakers had been offended when WCT had asked for a percentage of the gate for letting its players enter the regal tournament. Lamar, Jr., flew to Wimbledon with his father in the summer of '71 and saw Lamar bear up with grace and equanimity in the face of withering questioning and critiques from the English press. A columnist in the *Daily Mirror* wrote that "Mr. Hunt should throw a hammer off a cliff—and forget to let go."

The International Lawn Tennis Federation banned the WCT from its tournaments—including the majors, like Wimbledon and the U.S. Open. Barely three years after closed tennis was opened, open tennis had been closed. The recriminations were widespread—Wimbledon chief Herman David charged that Lamar had tried to "take over" the sport, and others on the ILTF board alleged that WCT wanted nothing less than control of the sport. At one point, ILTF president Allan Heyman gave a press conference and argued that Lamar Hunt "did not have anything to give to the game."

This created the most negative press of Lamar's life. "People were convinced that he wanted to take over tennis," said the British writer Richard
Evans, covering the tour at that time. "That was the fear: That he was this
monstrous wild oilman from Texas with bucketloads of money, who wanted
to come in and buy Wimbledon and buy Forest Hills, and buy the game.
And I don't think Lamar ever wanted to do that. He was the mildest, nicest,
most courteous guy you would ever meet. And they treated him like he was
a pariah."

As *Sports Illustrated*'s Curry Kirkpatrick reported in his write-up of the
classic Rosewall-Laver final of '72, "The International group alleges that
Hunt wanted a high percentage of the gate at Wimbledon as well as a piece of
the action on car parking, catering and television, the choice of tennis balls
plus—get this—the introduction of colored shirts. For his part Hunt said he
was using up-to-date business methods, that he only wanted pro tennis to be
a viable institution like other U.S. pro sports and that he had demanded only
reimbursement of air fares."

Even if the truth was somewhere in between (and Lamar had indeed
asked for a percentage of the gross, in exchange for paying for an expansion
and modernization of the Wimbledon locker rooms in 1971) it appeared that
WCT had overplayed its hand, and the headaches that would lead to litigation in the years ahead was the proof.

By April 1972, the two sides eventually agreed to a truce, put forth by
Jack Kramer and Donald Dell, and brokered by USLTA vice-president Walter
Elcock, though not in time to allow for WCT pros to play in the '72 French
Open or Wimbledon tournaments. (Even in the solution there was a sign
of more enmity toward Lamar; the ILTF had called emergency meetings in
the past but couldn't be bothered to do so a month in advance of the French
and Wimbledon, costing WCT players a chance to appear in either.) Missing
Wimbledon infuriated John Newcombe, who was the two-time defending
champion, and he chose not to play WCT in 1973, at least partly because of
his weariness over the politics.

•

Earlier in '72, Lamar had learned that he'd been elected to the Pro Foot-
ball Hall of Fame, becoming the first AFL representative to receive the honor.
On July 29, 1972, after riding on a float incorrectly labeled "Lamar H. Hunt,"
Lamar stood on the steps before the rotunda entrance in Canton, Ohio,

and was introduced by Billy Sullivan. The Patriots owner, remembering the "hundred" times that Lamar had put the good of the league over the good of his team, described him as "our great founding Father, our guiding light, our pleasant leader: the implausible Texan, Lamar Hunt."

Lamar was dressed in a dark suit, with a light-blue dress shirt, a navy tie with a splash of color, and a red carnation sitting high on his left breast. He singled out fellow AFL owners Sullivan, Valley, Adams, and Wilson. "They had a dream on which we worked together, and it was a very tough fight this American Football League, and we were able to achieve a degree of success and I consider them to be among my very closest friends on earth."

Next he talked about the game as a whole. "It's been remarkable luck for me to be involved in which some people call the game of our times. It's been exciting to see pro football grow and develop."

Moving toward the more personal, he made a mention of his family. "My father—from my father I have received the basic desire to invest and build in business and that was the key part of my being here today, I am sure. My wife and children have proved to be very patient sounding boards for ideas and I've come up with all kinds of crazy ones in the middle of the night. But they are always willing to listen."

He named the four staff members who had been with the team since 1960—trainer Wayne Rudy, Stram, Steadman, and assistant coach Bill Walsh. He also singled out three players—Johnny Robinson, who had played in every game in franchise history before retiring at the end of the '71 season, and the two players who'd died while Chiefs, Stone Johnson and Mack Lee Hill.

After giving a nod to the group representing the Wolfpack that was in attendance, he began his conclusion.

"Basically, I just consider myself a fan," he said. "I'm extremely grateful as I stand here before you. I know very clearly that the basic reason I'm here is because the AFL achieved a degree of success. Pro football belongs to the fans and I want to acknowledge this honor in the name of all who contributed to the growth of the AFL and also in the name of the pro football fans of America. Thank you." Later that day, Lamar stood in the stands and watched the Chiefs defeat the New York Giants, 23–17. Barely thirteen years after starting the AFL, just six years after the merger was brokered, less than two years after winning the Super Bowl, Lamar had arrived at the very pinnacle of professional sports. He had a Super Bowl ring; he had been inducted into the Hall of Fame; he was the owner of one of the marquee franchises in America's favorite sport, and the lone tenant of the most modern sports stadium in the world; he had the North American Soccer League champions; and he was the organizer of the most successful professional tour in tennis.

And he was still four days shy of his fortieth birthday.

•

Two weeks later, August 12, 1972, a hot Saturday evening in Kansas City, Lamar and the team reached the culmination of five years of planning, design, budgeting, building, work stoppages, and seemingly interminable politics. But as the newest, most modern jewel in pro football—the 79,451-seat Arrowhead Stadium—prepared to open for its first game, the annual Governor's Cup preseason clash between the Chiefs and the St. Louis Football Cardinals, Lamar was working in the still empty "Gold Suite," his personal luxury box (at that point still just an unfurnished cement box), sweeping up the detritus from the rushed building completion and opening up folding chairs for the visitors who would be arriving shortly.

After Jackson County voters approved $43 million in bonds in 1967 to build the two-stadium structure, Lamar put Jack Steadman on the job of overseeing the building of the stadium. But through it all, Lamar was ever-present, flying up to Kansas City as often as twice a week to walk the grounds in a hard hat, go over blueprints, make further suggestions for improvements. Arrowhead would be one of the first American stadiums without any obstructed view seats; architect Charles Deaton's unique design, implemented by the local firm of Kivett and Myers, required no supporting poles in the seating area.

The fans gave an extended applause to Missouri Senator Tom Eagleton, who'd just withdrawn from his role as George McGovern's running mate on the Democratic ticket, after revelations that Eagleton had received electro-shock therapy during his life. During the game, as the Chiefs jumped to a 24–0 lead over the Cardinals, the fans were transfixed with the animations on the large oval Arrowhead scoreboard. Though it wasn't completely finished at the time of that first game, it was almost unanimously hailed as the next iteration in the development of American sports stadiums.

Lamar built, at his own expense, a two-story apartment behind the owner's Gold Suite, so the family could stay at the stadium on the night before day games, or sleep over after night games.

The Gold Suite provided another repository for some of their antique finds—for the seventeenth-century French stone fireplace that was placed in the living room, the mahogany church pews, and walls full of classic sports drawings and paintings, even a den with a display of vintage sports-themed arcade games.

(After the second work stoppage, the workers finally finished installing the fireplace in the apartment and had placed a piece of cardboard on the mantel, with the written message, "See the 300-year-old fireplace; Adults $5, Children $3." Norma would say, "I think they were just so mad at that thing, at having to put that thing together, it was just unbelievable.")

The suite wasn't completed until the summer before the 1973 season, but it proved well worth the wait. Behind the living room was a football-shaped dining room with a custom-built mahogany dining room table and a football-shaped chandelier. The entry area featured a stained-glass depiction of the first touchdown scored at the stadium, with Ed Podolak eluding a Cardinal tackler.

The luxury extended throughout the stadium, to the team's locker room, which adjoined a wide array of fitness facilities. The building that housed the Chiefs' offices on 63rd Street was 9,000 square feet; in Arrowhead, the locker room and training area alone was 9,000 square feet.

"You couldn't get guys out of the locker room," said Len Dawson. "It was better than some of the places they lived. Carpeted. So different from the facility we had over on 63rd Street. Big whirlpool. You had steam, you had sauna, you had racquetball courts. It wasn't the team that was the important thing; it was the stadium."

At Stram's behest, the Chiefs became even more stylish when they opened the new stadium, wearing shiny red patent-leather game shoes at Arrowhead ("You go out there first and see if they laugh," said George Daney to a teammate before the first game). Stram's sideline attire went from natty to mod, as he wore suits with epaulets, leisure suits, even, most memorably, a tailored one-piece "unisuit" outfit about which Dawson was still laughing thirty years later.

While the parking was more plentiful, the concourses more spacious, the concession stands more abundant and the facilities more accommodating, there was something ineffable lost in the move. The stadium was less intimate than Municipal, the rowdy "Wolfpack" rooting section behind one end zone farther away and less intimidating for visiting teams. In all, the experience was more comfortable but less involved. Hank Stram's son Stu, just entering his teen years, said that with the new move to Arrowhead, "you kind of lost the feeling of football. Everything was so new and lavish."

Like every major new stadium of consequence in the early 1970s, the new stadium featured an artificial surface. Prior to moving to Arrowhead, the Chiefs had been playing on a field supplied by the Kansas City Parks and Recreation Department. With no tarp on the practice field, Stram had been known to take his charges out to practice in the parking lot at the nearby Starlight Amphitheater. That was replaced, in Arrowhead, by a vast, uniform gleaming green carpet and a practice field nearby. Suddenly the team's redoubtable grounds-keeper George Toma was spending his time cleaning bubble gum and tobacco stains on the carpet. "The thing I couldn't figure out," said Bobby Bell, "is when you've got the best grass guy in the world, they'd go to a carpet. I mean, this guy can grow grass in your *pocket*—and they wanted to get turf."

But this was the conventional wisdom at a time when artificial turf manu-facturers were boasting about the increased safety of the artificial surfaces. If everything about the stadium was going to be modern, the field would have to be as well. (The Chiefs sent out a press release noting that the tartan turf field would have the first stadium logo built right into the field—a modern, stylized A.) But experience told the tale. Every week, it seemed, one of the Chiefs' start-ers, Emmitt Thomas or Dave Hill, suffered joint ailments from the constant pounding of the artificial turf. Early on in that first season, several veterans, in Dawson's words, "begged Stram to get some relief from the stuff. All you have to do is get a few burns on that stuff, and have it stay on your elbow, or your knee for a whole season. And in my case, a couple of times, I got blood poison-ing" because still festering wounds would open and, mixed with the chemical compound used to treat the turf, would become infected.

The team was no longer young and hungry. After a decade of sporad-ic bickering and power struggles with Steadman, Stram was now secure in his position, his power largely unchecked (the ten-year contract Lamar had given him in the off-season granted Stram more latitude over the personnel operations). In short, things would be fine as long as the club kept winning.

But the Chiefs fell to an 8–6 record and out of the playoffs in '72, then dropped to 5–9 in 1973. As the losses mounted, Stram grew more irritable. He had created an empire for himself—his elaborate new coaching office featured an opulent fringed couch. Yet he bemoaned the loss of intimacy. Lamar, devot-ing more time to tennis and soccer, remained involved, though now often writ-ing memos to Stram instead of talking with him in person. Stram would grum-ble to his assistants, after the latest note from Lamar, that "this team should change its name from the Kansas City Chiefs to the Kansas City Memos."

Stram, too, had changed. Naturally prideful, he grew more defensive in the midst of criticism, as he waited for the team to assert its natural superiority again. But the team was old, and Lamar was busy—there were fewer games of H-O-R-S-E in the coach's office, fewer victory dinners at Casa de Montez.

"He missed the time with Lamar," said Dale Stram. "He missed his best friend and his best man. Lamar was jetting all over, and had tennis and soccer and everything else. It wasn't the same."

By the 1974 season, as the veteran Chiefs were sliding toward their second straight 5–9 campaign, it was with a growing realization—among the staff and fans alike—that in grasping to return to past domination, Stram had mortgaged much of the team's future (trading four high-round picks in the '73 draft, including giving the Chicago Bears a first-round draft choice for thirty-year-old lineman George Seals, who played two years in Kansas City without winning a starting job). Other trades were simply perplexing. In '74, Stram traded Kansas City's first-round draft choice in the '75 draft along with disaffected defensive tackle Curley Culp for John Matuszak, then well on the way to earning his reputation as a player that most teams simply couldn't control. Matuszak, after being caught with a woman in the team whirlpool at Arrowhead, played part of two seasons with the Chiefs before they let him go. Meanwhile, Culp put up four more Pro Bowl seasons for Houston.

On Monday, November 25, 1974, the day after a lopsided 33–6 loss at Cincinnati left the Chiefs with a 4–7 record, Lamar convened a private meeting at Arrowhead with various Chiefs boosters and prominent civic figures to discuss their laments. He had asked each to talk about the image of the Chiefs, and as the business leaders and supporters went around the room, a clear trend emerged. Dutton Brookfield, longtime Chiefs booster and the first chairman of the Jackson County Sports Authority, claimed that Stram's arrogance and sense of entitlement had become a problem, and that two golf clubs in the city didn't want him. The lawyer Irv Fane complained that his firm couldn't give tickets away now, not "even to secretaries in the office." He went on to add that the perception was that Stram was down on his players.

Joe McGuff, the *Star*'s flinty columnist, spoke last. He said the team's reputation was as an organization that was efficient but not warm. Steadman's reputation, he said, was "of a mean, tough S.O.B.—an overly sharp businessman."

After the lunch, in a more private setting, the men cited other petty instances—Stram parking his car in spaces reserved for others, the story of Brookfield and Stram nearly coming to blows over an argument during a racquetball match, the growing reputation that Stram cheated at golf.

Summarizing later in a memo to himself, Lamar noted "almost all present expressed personal, individual liking for Hank but grave concern as to his personal behaviour [sic] as it relates to the image of the organization."

The Chiefs won one more game under Stram, snatching the Governor's Cup from the Cardinals in St. Louis, and then closed with a dispiriting 7–6 home loss to the Raiders (in front of a crowd of just 60,577—Arrowhead hadn't been sold out since the season opener) and then a 35–15 regular-season final loss at the Vikings. Lamar asked Hank to dinner after the game that evening, but his old friend was too distraught.

Lamar was getting criticism from all sides, none more so than from Steadman, who at the end of the season gave him a clear ultimatum: Either he or Stram had to go, because they couldn't work together any longer. By then, Lamar had agonized for weeks and come to the conclusion that it was time to replace the only head coach he'd ever had.

For someone who despised any sort of conflict, this was a confrontation that Lamar particularly dreaded. Steadman would have been more than willing to give the news, but Lamar knew that this was something he'd have to do himself. Stram was in San Francisco, scouting players at the East–West All-Star Shrine Game, when Lamar reached him by phone.

"Oh, lad," said Lamar, using the nickname that he and Hank often used for each other, "this is a very sad day in the history of the Kansas City Chiefs. I've decided to make a coaching change." Lamar said he was flying out to San Francisco to discuss it with Hank personally, and they met that night, at 8 p.m. at the Embarcadero Center.

When they saw each other that evening, Lamar said, "I write better than I talk," and asked Hank to read a letter he'd composed first. In it, Lamar strained to recap his reasons for making the change:

> To say the least, this is a difficult memo to write. After a lot of thought, I have reached the conclusion that I need to make a change in the Head Coaching position of the Chiefs. This decision is not based solely on the drift of our record in the last three seasons, but more completely on (1) an analysis of the circumstances surrounding the entire operation of the franchise; (2) the public outlook toward the organization and its future fate; and (3) consideration toward the position of you yourself in the coaching profession.

As he detailed his reasons in a firm but conciliatory tone, Lamar emphasized the long rebuilding period ahead, speculating that it would be best for the both the team and Stram himself to part at this time.

In short, considering the human and economic factors, I believe now is the intelligent time to make a change. I certainly do not consider that you have been fired. You, overall, have been a fine coach—your record proves that—and I'm sure you still have that ability. Rather, I would look on this as an opportunity for a fresh start, and I'm sure you will probably go on to bigger and better things.

After Stram read the letter, they talked further, but soon it became clear that no matter how sad and apologetic Lamar was, he had made up his mind. Hank asked to hold off on an announcement until he could get back to Kansas City to tell his staff, and Lamar agreed.

Back in Kansas City, with Lamar deeply saddened by the encounter, Norma stepped in the breach and called Hank herself, to tell him how sorry they both were that it had come to this.

"You'll always be The Coach," she said to Hank, and he replied, "Well, the first time I saw you, I know you were the No. 1 draft choice." They laughed, wished each other the best, and rang off. On December 27, Lamar called a press conference and announced that Stram had been removed.

Then came the task of replacing the only coach he ever had. Lamar had not interviewed for a head football coach since the fall of 1959, so early on in each interview, he apologized for being "out of practice" at performing interviews. He was joined in nearly every instance by Steadman and Jim Schaaf.

The day after the Stram announcement, Lamar called several friends, including Bud Wilkinson. The former Oklahoma coach gave his top recommendation to Michigan's Bo Schembechler but also gave special commendations to Nebraska's Tom Osborne ("Almost saintly in his outlook," Wilkinson told Lamar, "Pirates' crew—with missionary at the helm"), though he remained somewhat skeptical about Osborne's ability to adapt to pro players. On New Year's Eve, Lamar spoke with Sam Blair, *Dallas Morning News* sportswriter, about his opinion of the people on Tom Landry's Dallas Cowboys' staff. Blair recommended former Cowboy halfback Dan Reeves, pointing out that, as a player, Reeves had been the one non-quarterback on the offense who knew every player's assignment on every play.

He interviewed nearly a dozen candidates, but on January 15, he spent two hours and 45 minutes interviewing the San Francisco 49ers assistant coach Paul Wiggin, who'd played under Paul Brown and Blanton Collier in Cleveland. Lamar's notations from the meeting were extensive: "Used to feel facial hair control important—no longer," "No restrictions on talking to the press," "*Hire people based on their ability to relate to others* (knowledge is secondary)."

In the end, what clinched it for Wiggin was the sense of unpretentious-
ness and intellectual self-security. After fifteen years of Stram's innovation
and vanity, Wiggin seemed less complex and more approachable. At the press
conference, Lamar spoke very forcefully about Wiggin's unassuming ways
and his personal rapport with his players.

And as he returned to the road for the latest WCT extravaganza, it was
with the sense that his football team was, if not back on the right track, at
least no longer perilously out of control.

•

The offseason would not be free of concerns. In Medford, Oregon, Woody
Green, the Chiefs' star rookie running back who had been one of the bright
spots of the '74 season, was charged—along with the New York Jets' Rich
Lewis—of the rape of a sixteen-year-old girl.

It was an unsavory charge in a remote area of Oregon that would be heard
by an all-white jury. But Lamar had met with Green, and he came away convinced that the player was innocent. What happened next would resonate
with many of the Chiefs veterans for years to come.

"I'm not sure how the question came to us to go," said Willie Lanier, who
was asked to be a character witness. "Lamar requested it. I knew Woody, but I
didn't know Woody *well*. I knew that he was a decent person as far as I'd been
able to observe. But I went because Lamar asked. If Woody had asked me, I'm
sure I would have said no. My relationship was with Lamar."

Jan Stenerud and Ed Podolak were also asked and called to the stand as character witnesses, and Lanier, sitting in front of the all-white jury and an all-white
audience—in fact, as the only black face in the room not being charged with a
crime—couldn't help but think of the movie version of *To Kill a Mockingbird*.

"The thing that I saw Lamar do," said Lanier, "is extend his arm around
Woody Green's shoulder in the lobby of a courthouse and express, 'We're
going to do everything we can to help you,' which I thought was more than
magnanimous. He could have been one to send a high-priced attorney to
take care of this uncomfortable issue. I can't speak for him, but it was very
uncomfortable for me; highly uncomfortable. But he maintained presence
over the time of the trial. I felt that just the presence in a situation like that,
when he could have just written the check, was huge."

On September 5, 1975, the jury came back with a verdict of not guilty, and
Green returned to the Chiefs (a knee injury would later shorten his promising career).

At times, Lamar's belief in his players—or anyone else for that matter—could border on the naïve, as the case of Bob Kap's world tour certainly proved. But at his core he adhered to a devout belief in redemption. The same summer that he was dealing with Woody Green's rape case, he received a note from the former Chiefs' player Gene Thomas, who had been traded from the team during the 1968 season after bringing a loaded gun into the Chiefs' training room at Swope Park and taking an angry, wild shot at Jim Tyrer. In the letter from Thomas, the player asserted that after bouncing around the Canadian Football League, he'd been leading a very Christian life ("I haven't even been out to Buck's Lounge in four or five months"). Lamar sent a note over to Paul Wiggin, mentioning the history of instability but asking him to give Thomas a tryout. The running back had lost a step in seven years and wasn't ultimately signed, but he ended his pro career knowing that he'd had more than a fair chance in Kansas City.

It wasn't simply in football; the intense loyalty to his own players was a theme that would run through Lamar's life. In 1968, having been in Dallas for just a few months, Mike Renshaw of the Tornado was driving home with two teammates in his powder-blue Triumph TR4 when he struck a child running across the Harry Hines Boulevard. The boy was instantly killed, and a traumatized Renshaw waited for the police at the scene; he was brought to Dallas police station where he spent part of the evening in jail. When he got the news, Lamar sent his lawyer, and later he and Norma journeyed to the jail to pick up Renshaw.

"Lamar and Norma took me to their home, and I spent the night there," said Renshaw. "They were fantastic, through an extraordinarily difficult time in my life. I *still* have nightmares about that. But I'll never forget Lamar being there, and helping me."

For reasons like this, Lamar engendered a fierce loyalty in many who played for him, one that went far beyond a few brief conversations, and tapped into a deeper kinship.

"I keep going back to the fact that Lamar was quiet, but Lamar had a lot of resolve," said Lanier. "Lamar was quiet, but he had a lot of determination. Lamar's quiet, but he was going to make it happen. I was somewhat similar. In its own way, when you think back, on how sometimes minorities were defined as being 'uppity.' It was no different for Lamar. Anyone who struggles to achieve an outcome when they are denied something, that does not appear equal, is on the same footing, regardless of what words were used. Because I think back, on Lamar and I, that was the same thing he was facing."

CHAPTER THIRTEEN

"YOU WANT TO ACCOMPLISH THINGS"

While WCT was a rising presence and an artistic success in the mid-'70s, it was still only barely profitable, a function of the vast guarantees paid to players to get them under contract. (Lamar had negotiated a $1 million deal to sign Arthur Ashe, brokered with Ashe's agent, the former player Donald Dell—who would recall, in the midst of a marathon, past-midnight negotiating session, Lamar taking a break to fire off ten quick push-ups, as a way to keep himself fresh.)

By 1973, though, WCT's place seemed secure; it had carved out a niche of about four and a half months in the first half of the year, coinciding nicely with the football off-season. And very quickly, the annual Finals Week in Dallas became the stuff of party legend. One of the staples of the week was an outdoor cocktail party for press from around the world, hosted by the Hunts at their new Gaywood home, and over which Norma Hunt presided with an assured sense of gracious inclusion.

"She was a great partner for Lamar because Lamar tended to be quiet," said Jack Steadman. "And he would ask her to tell something to someone. And Norma was, oftentimes, the life of the party. And Lamar really enjoyed that."

"When you think of the different worlds she had to move in," said Richard Evans, "the soccer and the football and the tennis and the oil and God-knows-what-else Lamar was involved in. We used to see this every year, this batch of British and French tennis writers used to turn up, there was probably about a dozen of us. And as we arrived at the house, she'd greet us all by name. I thought, '*Girl, you do your homework. Or else she's got the most astounding memory.*' She knew who was married and who wasn't, and the whole bit. That was Norma: the ultimate charming hostess."

"I certainly did my homework," admitted Norma, and there was plenty of it to be done. Even with the WCT's success, Lamar was an outsider in the tennis world, but here he was vying for a foothold in a hidebound sport whose leaders often blamed him for the larger revolution of professionalism. In the face of that opposition, and in the volatile environment of the emerging world tour, the rise of WCT occasionally had the frantic feeling of the Oklahoma land rush. By 1973, there was a pair of thirty-two-man tours going on, in parallel eleven-tournament seasons for which the top four finishers in each group qualified for the final, won that year by Stan Smith over Ashe. In 1974 and 1975, that grew into an eighty-four–player organization, with three different tours, and a dizzying amount of logistical headaches.

In the end, it was too much too soon for the tour. "I never understood why Lamar insisted on growing it so fast," the agent Barry Frank would say later. "It just became diluted."

"I think it was the reality of the market," said Ivan Irwin, the lawyer who served as a key assistant to Lamar in WCT. "You had to sign players before somebody else did. We signed an awful lot of players. Those were crazy times. I was traveling all over the world to tennis events, with Al, Jr., usually. It wasn't any trouble to sign the players—they all wanted to sign. It's pretty hard to manage something that size."

By the mid-'70s, Al Hill, Jr., was spending even more time traveling than Lamar. He wasn't yet thirty, just ending a marriage, and spent part of the period dating the model Cheryl Tiegs. "It's difficult about Al," said Richard Evans, who covered much of the WCT's itinerary. "He was very young—I suppose I could say immature—to start with. He was very much the rich kid having a great time. But he served a good purpose, quite apart from the fact that he had financial clout through his family. Al was around a lot. And it was good that he was young, because he was the same age as the players, and he could relate to a lot of the players, and I think many liked him and enjoyed his company. Others found him a little too *'Let's go off to a nightclub and have some drinks and a good time and a party.'* He was just a little immature. But as he grew up he became more influential and more serious."

"I think Al turned out to be very important," said WCT staple Cliff Drysdale. "He really rose to the occasion."

Lamar and Al agreed that at least one of them should make an appearance at every tournament, and to do that required a punishing travel schedule for both men. Very early on, Al, Jr., had sensed the disappointment on the part of tournament hosts and sponsors when he was the one there to represent WCT management instead of Lamar. In response, he asked Lamar to get more in-volved: "I said, 'Lamar, I need you present. Not just running the show from Dallas, but I need you here.' And he was very good about taking a more active part in the running of WCT."

That required a real commitment from Lamar, who was already ridicu-lously busy. The WCT was in Tokyo and Denver one week in '75, and then Charlotte, Houston, and Stockholm the next. Lamar went, and WCT was stabilized because of his attention and presence, but those gains came at a price—Lamar was gone more, away from the Chiefs, away from the Tornado, and away from home. "We were on the road one time," said Al Hill, Jr. "I don't even remember where, and Lamar said, 'I'm not going to be around to see my son born.'"

Norma was pregnant with their second child in 1976. By November 21, when Daniel was born, Lamar was back in Dallas, but that was an increas-ingly rare occurrence; he spent more than 200 days traveling each year in the period from 1974 to 1976.

Norma had grown more comfortable (in a way that Rose Mary never was) with the reality that her husband would be almost constantly in motion. He frequently made it back to the city for an important event—Lamar, Jr.'s flute recitals or football games, Clark's soccer matches—but then he'd be off again. "And he just loved it," said Norma. "He loved hard work. He thrived on it. So I was happy for him. Heavens, if this is what makes him happy, then great. You always hear about women who say, 'Oh, my husband is just gone too much,' and that's a difference in personalities, I guess. A lot of people need to have their spouse with them. And some people, maybe more independent people, can handle that a little better. We always talked on the phone. If you couldn't figure out what to do with the children, you could just call him up and say, 'What do you think about this?'"

In the midst of that travel schedule, Lamar seemed caught in a never-ending quest for more productivity. He wrote notes to himself, mapping out his days, admonishing himself to find the time (and at other times, trying to discipline himself; more than one to-do list included the item, "Go to bed by 10:30.")

By the early '70s, Lamar had taken up jogging, much against the protesta-tions of his more dormant, chain-smoking traveling companion Bill McNutt, who used to proclaim, while taking a deep drag on a cigarette and watching Lamar run past, "He's going to exercise himself to death."

Years later, Clark would explain to his half-brother, Lamar, Jr., "You know, it wasn't just *you* that he was gone a lot of the time for." It was said not with a

trace of bitterness but rather a sense of understanding. Those who loved Lamar came to understand that his was not a body comfortable in repose. And
they also recognized his commitment to be there whenever possible.

After Lamar, Jr.'s high school football team went undefeated in 1974, Lamar presented him with a scrapbook of the team's exploits. "He had taken
the time to clip out *everything* from it," said Lamar, Jr. "From school newspapers, the regular Dallas papers, he laid it all out."

"What we all, I think, would unanimously say about Dad was, he was present, but he was preoccupied," said Lamar, Jr. "I lived in another house most of
the time, so there wasn't the daily contact, but I think even Clark would echo
there wasn't a whole lot of hands-on guidance and stuff. Dad I think was just
consumed with his activities, and it wasn't out of selfishness, because he was
a considerate person. But I think he parented—whether it was Sharron and I
because we were in another home, or Clark and Daniel where they were, live
and in color every day—the same way. It was how he parented, which was
distant, very hands-off. I can remember calling him once because I needed a
car, and he said, 'Well you have some money of your own, why don't you use
that?' And I was like, 'Really? I didn't even know.'"

A week after Clark's horrible foot accident the morning of the '72 WCT
Finals, Lamar bought his bed-ridden son a half-dozen baby ducks and another half-dozen baby geese. "We raised them in the bathtub in the house,"
said Norma. "Only Lamar's mind could have thought of that. I'm a clean
freak, so I definitely would not have." When the ducks and geese became old
enough to fend for themselves, Clark—still in a wheelchair—led a parade
out to the backyard pond, where they were released.

That summer, Clark finally got out of the wheelchair and began his rehabilitation, with Norma still taking him to weekly visits with the vascular
surgeon, trying to get the wound to heal. It was around then that Lamar, in
the front cadre of American recreational joggers, had the idea that his son
should start training to run in the eight-mile Thanksgiving Day Turkey Trot,
since 1968 held on the shores of White Rock Lake.

Norma was initially dumbfounded.

"Run in the Turkey Trot?!" she said. "This child is barely walking, and you
want him to run in the Turkey Trot?"

"Yep, we're gonna do it."

"Lamar, when I tell his doctors that you're going to do this, they are going
to tell me no way," said Norma.

"You're not going to tell them," he said, gently. And so she didn't.

That Thanksgiving, Clark was not yet eight years old, but he'd already developed some of his father's resolve, along with a stoic resistance to pain. On the second half of the race, he was in tears. But they finished, with Clark the youngest runner to do so.

•

On Nov. 29, 1974, H. L. Hunt died. The family patriarch had created a vast empire, but he had not been especially close to the children of his first family in later years.

What had been whispered about in certain social circles—the truth that H. L. Hunt had fathered three families, all during his marriage to Lyda—now became a matter of public record.

"Any dysfunction there might be," said Norma, "that was something that Lamar never talked about. I'm not saying he didn't think about it. He might have. But it's just not something that he ever would have said anything to me about his father."

This, too, proved a painful jolt to Lamar. After H. L. married Ruth Ray in 1957, Lamar had reluctantly conceded that her children had been fathered by H. L. But Lamar didn't want to talk about it. And though Frania Tye had met both Margaret and Hassie, her existence wasn't common knowledge within the rest of the family. "We never talked about it," said Margaret decades later. "We *still* never talk about it."

Shortly after H. L.'s death, when news of Frania Tye and the "third family" became a matter of public record, Lamar was crushed. He called Lamar, Jr., in college at the University of Cincinnati, and apologized to him for his grandfather "bringing shame on the family." He also delivered a tearful apology to the sixteen-year-old Sharron, who was shaken by her father's outpouring of emotion.

"The first time I heard my father cry was on the phone to me," said Lamar, Jr., "when my grandfather's will was being probated, and this other family stepped forward. There was a bunch of splash of news, and he was embarrassed by that—'I'm sorry you have to go through this.' But I really now look back and think, I think he was mainly crying for himself, because when you're a grandkid, you're really pretty removed from grandpa's shenanigans."

It was left to Ray Hunt, H. L.'s prized son with Ruth, to inherit Hunt Oil, and sort out the awkward multifamilial puzzle. H. L.'s last will had given much of his estate—that which was not already tied up in trusts for H. L. and Lyda's children—to Ruth, and divided the rest equally among his children with both women (but had excluded Frania Tye and the children he had with her).

For Ray, at Hunt Oil, there was a sense that his stoic loyalty had been vindi-cated. Not all of the "first family" had been warm to him—Margaret was often dismissive, Bunker was at times plain rude. Among the most noted exceptions was Lamar. "He was never anything less than warm to me," said Ray Hunt.

Though some of the first family was bitterly disappointed by the terms of the will (as well as H. L.'s stipulation that any child who protested it would be cut out of the will entirely), Lamar seemed to take it in stride. For their part, his children were most disappointed that the Palette Ranch no longer belonged to the first family but would now be controlled by Ruth and Ray.

"I thought he should have made more of a point about making sure we could still visit there," said Sharron. "But he didn't. It wasn't like Dad to rock the boat."

•

To those on the outside, the presence of the Dallas Tornado and a North American Soccer League franchise in football-silly Dallas remained an anomaly.

What was going on in Dallas, because of the Tornado, wasn't easily visible from the outside, but it was real nonetheless. When the Tornado debuted in the summer of 1967, there couldn't have been a more difficult outpost to try to sell the world's game. The players who were imported were, for the most part, paid a flat rate of $75 per game. Yet attendance was poor, and the initial investment—especially the around-the-world tour—was significant.

But Lamar hadn't been the only one touched by the '66 England–West Germany final at Wembley. On the same day that he was watching at his home, the thirteen-year-old Kyle Rote, Jr., was with friends, watching the match elsewhere in Dallas. Rote's father was the Hall of Fame football player, who starred at SMU and then went on to a distinguished pro career with the New York Giants. By the mid '60s, he had retired and was working with Curt Gowdy, as the expert commentator on the AFL's Game of the Week for NBC, a job that some of his friends in the NFL viewed as tantamount to treason.

Kyle, Jr., was blessed with his father's athletic skills and was building a promising career as a three-sport star at Highland Park High School. Rote and his friend, Rocky Davis, lived to play games, and when they saw the '66 World Cup final, they were moved by the athleticism and the intricate geometry of the passing game. Their enthusiasm quickly bumped up against the reality: There were no soccer balls to be had in Dallas; in fact, there wasn't a sporting goods store in the state that sold them. But they persevered, ordered away from Soccer Sports Supply, on First Avenue in New York, and were playing a rough approximation of the game by the middle of August, even forming their own team, which they dubbed the Black Bandits. Rote appealed to the Dallas Parks board to get a third soccer field (there were only two in the city at the time, both used largely on weekends by the Mexican-American community), for their burgeoning Dallas Independent Soccer League.

Over the coming years, Kyle Rote, Jr., and his friends would belong to the first broad wave of Dallas youth who grew to understand and love soccer. And the Tornado players—Mike Renshaw, who had been on the original Tornado world tour of '67–'68; the goalkeeper Kenny Cooper; the defenders Bobby Moffat and John Best—all conducted hundreds of instructional clinics around the city. In high school visits, Best would stand in front of the students and ask anyone to take the ball away from him without using their hands. When the inevitable football player would lunge and try to kick the ball away, Best would dribble it away, demonstrating that the sport of soccer valued skill over size. Rote and his teammates saw those early incarnations of the Tornado—first the Dundee United visitors in '67, then the first "true" Tornado team, culled from the world tour, in '68. They marveled at the ball control and the stamina—always the stamina.

After starting college at Oklahoma State as a highly recruited football player in '68, Rote eventually transferred to Sewanee, the University of the South, on a soccer scholarship, and by 1972 he had been signed by the Tornado—by virtue of NASL's first college draft, which itself was an idea of Lamar's, designed to increase interest in the league during the offseason, just as it had for pro football.

As the '73 season began, the Tornado was playing at Texas Stadium, trying desperately to draw fans. In Rote they had an established name adept at a skill that supposedly eluded most American players: heading the ball. Fast and more broadly built than most of his foreign counterparts, Rote showed an affinity for getting prime positioning in the unstructured chaos of goalmouth scrambles, and a gift for finding open teammates. His 10 goals and 10 assists won him the "NASL Scoring Title" (another Lamar idea, computed the way the National Hockey League computed its scoring leaders, with two points for each goal and one point for each assist).

In the finals that year, held at Texas Stadium, Philadelphia scored two late goals to win, 2–0, but the game wound up as the first soccer cover in the history of *Sports Illustrated*, with Atoms' goalkeeper Bob Rigby batting a ball away from the charging Rote under the headline "Soccer Goes American." Edwin "Bud" Shrake's story covered the game, but it was the lead to *SI*'s "Letter from the Publisher" that hinted at the beginning of a revolution:

> Lamar Hunt had extra lights turned on in Dallas' Texas Stadium last week so *Sports Illustrated* photographers could better shoot the pro soccer finals in color, but it is unlikely that he expected the pictures to show an upset of his Dallas Tornado, which is what happened. We can only hope that he was cheered by what the Philadelphia Atoms' victory implies about the state of the sport in America. The astonishing success of a team that has consistently started more U.S.-born players than any other in the league, under the direction of the league's only American-born coach, is the most heartening sort of evidence that soccer is alive in this country and very well indeed.

While the final was a loss, the impact of the Tornado in Dallas could already be felt. There had been eleven amateur teams in the city in 1967. Just over five years later, there were 1,170 teams, more than 25,000 people playing soccer in Dallas.

So Rote's star was on the rise already when he traveled to Boca Raton, Florida, in February 1974 as a late addition to the second made-for-TV athletic competition called "The Superstars" (similar to what Lamar had envisioned with the Bronco-thon of the '60s), which he proceeded to win. (Rote would go on to win three Superstars titles in four years, interrupted only by football's O. J. Simpson winning in '75.)

That generated even more publicity and left Rote—as the rookie-of-the-year and the league's leading scorer —in a good bargaining position as the '74 season neared its kickoff. Though he and Lamar remained cordial, Rote held out for a better contract (he had earned $1,400 playing for the Tornado in '73). Rote and Lamar each negotiated on his own behalf and wound up staying up late the night before the Tornado opener against St. Louis. After a negotiating session that ran past midnight, Lamar finally found a way to make a deal work, supplementing Rote's athletic pay with more marketing and promotional work around the Tornado office. After they'd all shaken hands, Lamar accompanied Kyle and his wife, Mary Lynne, down the elevator to the ground floor, when Lamar thought of one other thing.

"Oh, I forgot to say," he added, "we need to make sure that we agree that this contract must be confidential."

"Don't worry, Lamar," said Mary Lynne. "We're just as embarrassed about how little you're paying Kyle as you are."

The problem with the NASL, beyond the style of play and the difficulty with the seasons (conflicting, as they did, with the international soccer schedule, which was dominated by fall-through-spring leagues), was the lack of a culture. Curious Americans who tuned into a game on TV or ventured to a contest live, were seeing the game on the field, but missing entirely the flavor of the soccer experience in the stands.

The fields and stadiums were also poorly suited to the sport. In 1972, the Tornado moved their home games to the Cowboys' Texas Stadium. Though it provided a major-league address, it was a horrible place to play soccer.

"There couldn't have been a worse venue for it because that semi-roof that they had didn't let air come into the stadium," said Norma. "You would sit there and your clothes would just be drenched. So there's no breeze at all and it's a hundred degrees. I don't know how the players stood it."

"And then, you couldn't see your passes," said Bobby Moffat. "The crown on the center of the field was so large, that when you passed sideline to sideline, you sometimes couldn't see what happened to the ball."

Like Lamar, Rote had been astonished during his visit overseas to see the game he'd loved in an entirely different context, in an environment in which it was absolutely essential. "What was haunting about that trip, in a good way, was the chants, which were not led by a cheerleading squad, which erupted organically, and the passion and the loyalty and, yes, the drunkedness and all that, but also the total not just ignorance about American sports, but . . . they couldn't care. They didn't know who Tom Landry was, and they didn't know who Roger Staubach was, and they couldn't care."

Lamar, trying to sell a grand sport to an apathetic public, struggled with the question of how best to do it. During one of the planning meetings at the Tornado offices, Ken Cooper suggested the unthinkable, uttering a thought that many of the English-born players shared but none dared to say: "What if Americans just don't get it? What if we need to change the game to suit their tastes?" It was one moment where Lamar seemed particularly forceful. Sitting next to Cooper, he gently placed his hand on Cooper's own and firmly stated, "Kenny, we must play the game the rest of the world plays."

Unsuccessful at re-creating in America the fan culture that was so central to the soccer experience, Lamar did the next best thing: He brought American journalists to the World Cups in '70 and '74 to show them the real thing first-hand. The '74 contingent included respected columnist Blackie Sherrod, as well as announcers Verne Lundquist and Tom Hedrick. "Blackie cared as much about soccer," said Lundquist, "as I care about log-rolling. But he decided to go." When the journalists arrived, they were greeted with hand-drawn signs of welcome from the Hunt and McNutt children.

Lamar believed that when the journalists saw the game played at its highest level, they would better understand and appreciate it. "Here's where it didn't work," said Lundquist. "I saw Blackie's lead one day, after West Germany had played Poland, and he showed me the copy, because he was chuckling to himself. His lead was: 'Scoring at will, West Germany ousted Poland by a score of 1–0.' So, that was probably not what Lamar was hoping to see in the Dallas newspaper."

Those trips were particularly enjoyable for Lamar, because World Cup summers meant no responsibilities beyond being an avid fan, and he made it a point to visit as many of the World Cup venues as he could, to study the stadiums and the unique traits of each. In one public square in Germany, the nine-year-old Clark, fully recovered from his 1972 mishap, joined the family in watching German youths play a game in which guests tried to kick a soccer ball into the small target holes in a simulated goal. "There were some teenage boys hanging around, and I could see that they were having some degree of difficulty doing it," said Norma. "And so it finally got to be Clark's turn. And he stepped right up there and the first ball he sailed it straight through like a rocket. And I saw the teenage boys look at each other, and I could hear them say, 'Americanski!' They couldn't believe that an American even knew what a soccer ball was." The Hunts and the McNutts were game travel partners, hitting shopping sites, museums, and restaurants among all the soccer games, with Lamar tabulating the number of Michelin stars they could accrue from the restaurants visited during the stay.

And along the way, he closely monitored the response of the American journalists he'd brought to see the event. Upon his return to Dallas, he clipped and saved the acerbic Sherrod's straightforward, largely respectful report from the final, in which West Germany defeated Holland: "The bedlam after the German triumph was unbelievable, the triumphant parade around the field perimeter, the hugging and kissing by adult men, the deafening roar of partisans. V-J Day in San Francisco was comparable, but a distant second."

While in Germany, Lamar had dinner with Clive Toye, by now the general manager of the NASL's New York franchise, the Cosmos, who continued to work on a project that he, Lamar, and Phil Woosnam had discussed as early as 1969: the crucial objective of trying to coax Pelé (now retired) to come to play in the United States as an emissary for the game.

It was a year later when the deal finally came through, and Pelé debuted on a nationally televised game, against the Tornado, broadcast on CBS. That game featured the world's greatest player squaring off against America's best-known player, Rote, in front of a sellout crowd at Randall's Island, New York. If you squinted, you could see the makings of a path forward for U.S. soccer.

Then again, as always seemed the case with the NASL, there was a dose of reality: The nationally televised spectacle wasn't even a league game but instead a hastily arranged friendly, apart from the NASL's regular-season schedule, not counting in any competition. And the Tornado had played a game the *night before* in San Antonio. The Tornado players were just glad to be there, on the same pitch with the legendary Pelé, but it didn't change the humble existence of most NASL franchises or, barring a game in which Pelé was playing, the scant attendance.

Lamar reveled in the publicity for the league, and another *Sports Illustrated* cover that week, while expressing worry to partner Bill McNutt about the dubious advisability of signing other big-name players (in the same week, the Boston Minutemen signed Portuguese legend Eusébio), who lacked the same stature in America as Pelé.

He was right to be worried. There were sellout crowds when the Cosmos played around the country. That, combined with the frequent requests among investors for expansion teams and Woosnam's messianic zeal for the game, led some to feel that success had arrived.

But Lamar was one of many in the NASL who was still skeptical. Despite the headlines and the infusion of new investors, he knew that the NASL was going to be a work in progress, and that Pelé's reception didn't necessarily signal a sea change.

"It was like bringing the Beatles over for a concert," said Paul Tagliabue, then a lawyer at Covington & Burling, handling some of the NASL's casework. "It wasn't your own local singers. It was perfectly clear that in the inner-city, no one knew what a soccer ball was."

•

From his office on the twenty-ninth floor of the First National Bank Building in downtown Dallas, Lamar presided over a group of holdings that were increasingly diverse and complicated. He owned the Chiefs and also

had the largely ceremonial title of President of the AFC, though it did require his attendance at all NFL league meetings. He also owned the Tornado
and was a key executive in the nascent NASL. He had WCT, along with two
emerging tennis-related real-estate ventures, the Lakeway World of Tennis in
north Austin and the Peachtree Tennis Resort in Atlanta, as well as a chain of
WCT teaching academies across Europe. Though he had in 1971 divested his
interest in the Dallas–Fort Worth Spurs minor league baseball team (selling
to the owners of the Washington Senators, after they moved the franchise to
Arlington to become the Texas Rangers), he still held his minority interest in
the Chicago Bulls of the NBA (and, since the team was still losing money, he
continued putting up more money during the nearly annual capital calls, to
keep the franchise solvent), still owned the Bronco Bowl bowling complex
and entertainment center (whose amphitheater, originally built for the de-
funct National Bowling League, had become a popular small concert hall for
touring acts), and still had real-estate interests in Texas.

At the beginning of the '70s, sensitive to not wanting to be viewed as an
absentee owner, he invested heavily in land 10 miles north of Kansas City,
building the Worlds of Fun amusement park, which he based loosely on Jules
Verne's *Around the World in 80 Days*. While Steadman oversaw the project
on a daily basis, Lamar became keenly involved in the details. From the back
lot of MGM Studios, he purchased the riverboat "Cotton Blossom" (featured
in the 1951 movie *Show Boat*) and had it moved to Kansas City, where it became a hub of the amusement park, serving as both gift shop and restaurant.
There was also a lemonade stand called "Lamar's Libations" (and, eventually,
another stand called "Norma's Funnel Cakes"), and an emphasis on musical
theater and stage shows.

On the same parcel of land he purchased for Worlds of Fun was a limestone mining interest, which he took over. (In the years ahead, the mining
would leave underground space, which was turned into an underground
business park, Subtropolis.) In addition to all this, there was his portion of
the family's oil and gas business, and various other family holdings, such as
his stake in the chain of Shakey's Pizza Parlors.

No rational person could expect to remain on top of all of those matters
at once, and the effort to do so began to wear on Lamar. The travel was nearly
constant; his devoted secretary, Jean Finn, worked longer and longer hours. Lamar himself had less time for the fine-grained detail that he loved focusing on.

Finally, around 1975, Lamar decided to seek more help. First, he designated a greater role for his longtime friend and traveling companion Bill Adams,

with whom he had stayed close since the SMU days. Bill and his wife Molly frequently joined Lamar and Norma for Chiefs games, Cotton Bowls, and Palette Ranch vacations, and Lamar had asked Adams for some help during his interest in Alcatraz. Now, Lamar reached out to Adams again. His old frat brother was a fascinating mixture of homespun charm and flinty sophistication, and Lamar wanted him to help manage his side projects, citing the litigation in tennis, the two tennis resorts in the states, and the academies in Europe. Adams first balked, telling Lamar that what he needed was two more secretaries, then signed on when Lamar assured him that Adams would have the authority to fix the problems or dispose of them.

"I ended up with more projects than I knew what to do with," said Adams. "Lamar was not a hands-on person with most of these things. He'd just kind of look at me. He wanted me to get him out of them. Lamar, basically, was a dreamer and a builder, and I was a man to put out fires, and run his projects."

The accountant Wayne Henry, the Arkansas State graduate who'd moved to Dallas and worked his way up the ladder as an accountant for Hunt Oil, was moved to a newfound position in 1975, working as Lamar's personal financial assistant, trying to bring more cohesion to Lamar's varied enterprises.

"His interest was more in the field of sports and games," said Henry. "Buying and selling leases, and the rest of the things in the oil business, he pretty well relied on us to put stuff in front of him that needed to be signed."

Adams, as well, noticed that the regular oil business did not capture his friend's imagination. "He didn't have any numbers that were fun," Adams said. "The idea of exploration excited him a bit, but not any of the rest of it."

•

In July 1975, the franchise began its first-ever training camp without Hank Stram as head coach. "We're Comin' Back" was the promotional slogan featured on advertising, schedule cards, and media guides, heading into the 1975 season, with a depiction of Charlie Getty, the second-round draft choice out of Penn State who'd earned a starting spot in his rookie year of '74.

But by the time Paul Wiggin's tenure began, the talent on the Chiefs was in decline. The defensive greats—Lanier, Bell, Buchanan, Emmitt Thomas—were all into their thirties, some of them well into their thirties. "People said, 'Why don't you replace those guys?'" said assistant coach Vince Costello. "But that was the problem—we had nobody who could beat them out."

A series of poor trades and barren drafts in the later Stram years had left the team with a dearth of young talent. Len Dawson, who agreed to stay on for one more season, was forty years old at the start of the 1975 campaign; Otis Taylor was thirty-three; and the key players in the offensive line, perennial all-pros Jim Tyrer and Ed Budde, were thirty-six and thirty-four respectively.

Just as importantly, many of the players left were an amalgam of malcontents and head cases. George Seals, who'd been acquired from the Bears for a first-round draft pick, retired to work at the Chicago Board of Trade. Lamar, at William Jewell for his annual training camp stay, performed his annual ritual of guessing the cuts and found he was hard-pressed to come up with the final forty-man roster, not because there was so much competition, as in the past, but because there was so little depth.

Wiggin was well liked and the Chiefs played hard for him, but there was not enough talent to make up for all that had been lost. Lanier and Lynch retired together after the '76 season, and in '77, the Chiefs got off to another woeful start, winning just one of their first six games. That October, Lamar wrote a four-page letter to Steadman, stating, "I do not believe Paul can cut the mustard." He surveyed the team's shortcomings and reasserted his personal fondness for Wiggin, but concluded, "I have no doubt we will continue to make mistakes on the elementary stuff like two minute offense, conservation of timeouts, ten men on the field, etc. I believe quarterback handling is beyond his comprehension (and desire) and I am convinced that he will let the entire season go by before he would take the step to make a change . . ."

After the team looked flat and dispirited in a 44–7 loss to the Cleveland Browns October 30, to drop to 1–6, Lamar reluctantly fired Wiggin, replacing him with assistant coach Tom Bettis. The response to the Wiggin firing was instant and voluble. Those who knew Wiggin well felt it was unfair. After the crying on the fourth floor, in and around the coaches' offices, on Halloween morning, there was a vituperative reaction in the press.

Feeling bereft after the press conference announcing Wiggin's firing, Lamar drove to Wiggin's home to apologize personally, and to further explain himself. It had worked with Stram, but on this night it didn't work. "My wife tore into him and he didn't handle it at all," Wiggin said. "He got up, walked away and left. She just wanted to know why. Simply, the repetitive why. 'Why you, Lamar? The guy who put together the AFL. The guy who had the guts to hang in and stick to his principles. Why you?' Lamar didn't say anything."

Lamar left and, in the weeks ahead, withdrew further. He was stunned by the vehemence of the opposition, writing a two-and-a-half–page letter to the *Star* columnist Dick Mackey, who had charged in a column that in the wake of the Super Bowl win, the "Chiefs became an egotistic, almost arrogant organization." The jabs, some diplomatically hidden, others more open, were directed at Steadman. Even his friend, Lamar's lawyer Jim Seigfreid, conceded that Steadman "could be pompous." Bruce Rice, the veteran sports director at KCMO-TV who had been on the Chiefs radio broadcast crew and was a member of the Chiefs board, wrote to an outraged booster, "One other thing, Don . . . we seemed to reach a point . . . some time ago . . . when an organization which was built on a very 'personal' basis . . . has, for whatever reason, become 'impersonal.' This is the hole in the dike."

Tom Bettis, hired to be interim coach to replace Wiggin, was a loyal soldier and a longtime Chiefs coach, but after an initial win over the Packers, the team returned to its losing ways, so by the end of the season, Lamar and Steadman were convinced it was time to make another change. Toward the end of the '77 season, Lamar and Steadman and Jim Schaaf made the rounds again, this time interviewing an even wider range of candidates, as Lamar was looking for someone with whom he could develop the personal rapport that he'd once shared with Hank.

Lamar decided that he'd overcorrected in going for the simplicity of Wiggin. The two coaches he'd most wanted—Miami's Don Shula and Washington's George Allen—were both unavailable, so he returned to a candidate he'd passed on three years earlier. It was Marv Levy, the learned, avuncular coach who had been among the first special-teams coaches in the NFL and had gone on to coach the Montreal Alouettes to two Grey Cup victories in the Canadian Football League. The Chiefs had first interviewed Levy in January 1975 (he was recommended by George Allen) at a Los Angeles hotel. Nearly three years later, he sat down for another interview, on December 4, 1977.

Levy was a literature major who quoted Eisenhower ("Morale is built by victory in battle"), and he seemed both civilized and approachable. Lamar liked him, and he decided he'd found a man who was equal parts erudite and tough, who made no empty promises, but who clearly knew how to build a winner. On December 20, 1977, Levy was announced as the new coach of the Kansas City Chiefs.

And then Lamar headed off to deal with the other problems: the lagging attendance of the Tornado, the question of how the 1978 World Cup would affect the NASL season, and the latest round of recriminations and battles between WCT and others vying for control of the booming professional tennis business.

Things were so hectic and so fraught that Lamar didn't even make it to the 1978 World Cup, with threats of kidnapping and civil unrest persuading him that he shouldn't go. His sister Caroline was traveling in South America that summer and took in the final, though she cared not a whit for sports. Watching on TV, as the sea of confetti rained down on the bedlam of the Estadio Monumental in Buenos Aires, where Argentina beat the Netherlands 3–1 for the World Cup, Lamar longed to be there and might have also wondered if he'd ever be able to import that culture of soccer love to the United States.

•

By the late '70s, Lamar's public persona was becoming more clearly defined. In the press clippings of this era, he was the mild-mannered eccentric who flew coach and was constantly in motion. In a 1978 feature story for the *Kansas City Star* magazine, Lamar was humble and introspective, recalling gaining weight (he estimated he had added thirty pounds) and finally realizing that his time was limited. "I can remember when I was, say, 22, 23 years old, and I don't recall a feeling of urgency to do anything. There were things to be done. But now, as I'm getting older, I guess I feel I'm getting closer to the end of the line. And you want to accomplish things."

His mornings at Gaywood featured light breakfasts—often just a slice of grapefruit with a sprinkling of sugar—and, when he was up early enough, an hour's work in the yard ("the one thing I do best in the world is clip the bushes," he would tell Norma), before driving Clark to the St. Mark's School and then heading into the office.

"So he worked that gardening in, which he absolutely loved," said Norma. "But he was very specific about what he liked: This was not the guy who likes to go out and dig in the soil season by season and put in flowers. That's not Lamar." At the Gaywood estate, Lamar developed an affinity for the delicate, precise craft of shaping the property's forty-four Yaupon Hollies. "He called them being 'poodled,' trained into fanciful shapes. Not anything specific. The trees always told him what shape it wanted to be in—so he listened to the tree. He would trim it in incredible shapes. Not so extreme as you might have seen in the Japanese gardens —these were much more free flowing, very modern, sculptural looking."

Lamar was an inveterate listmaker and record keeper. Each day would include an exercise notation of R (two-mile run), T (tennis), or W (his extended walk through the 11 acres of the Gaywood estate, shears in hand). In his daily exercises of still-dips, knee-lifts, and trunk-twists, he would endeavor to do ten of each, but often did one extra, for good measure. Self-denial didn't work as well. For a time, he stopped reading the comics, but this struck even him as draconian, and soon he was back to his regular daily helping of *Peanuts*, *B.C.*, and *The Wizard of Id*.

He would be greeted at the office by the redoubtable Jean Finn, who was the keeper of Lamar's schedule and his cash, withdrawing money downstairs at the First National Bank so he would have funds for his trips and other outings. She would say in 1982 that, in twenty years, "I've never seen him lose control."

Into the office, he'd spend a short time reading the paper before diving into his correspondence and solving problems.

With the Chiefs, he continually made an effort to stay out of his coach's way, though he corresponded regularly with Steadman about his thoughts on the coaching staff and team's performance.

And, when he had the time, he zeroed in on fine-grained details. His preoccupation with symmetry was evident. After a 1978 game at Arrowhead, he wrote Steadman, "the 'NBC' signs (and ABC and CBS whenever appropriate) should be placed equal distance between our Chiefs' logos on the wall. They were off center."

The Cowboys' success was vexing for someone as competitive as Lamar. By the late 1970s they were Super Bowl champions and had been dubbed "America's Team," and, at times, he seemed to be responding to everything Tex Schramm did. Writing Steadman in '78 about game production for the coming season, he noted, "I'm convinced we don't need to go 'sleazy,' and what do we really accomplish if we (un)dress our girls like the Cowboy cheerleaders? Let's be unique . . ." To that end, he suggested implementing gameday routines like "a 48-girl circle around the Arrowhead emblem for the National Anthem," or developing "a full stadium 'K'—'C' yell (each side of the stadium doing one letter) . . . I know a good cheerleader can, with help from the band, pull this cheer out of the crowd."

But the deeper lesson was that the crowd's involvement sprang organically from an involvement with a winning team. By 1979, as the crowd continued to dwindle (the 12,000-person waiting list for season tickets was now a distant memory), Lamar was always seeking a way to rouse the crowd and placate the media. He wrote Steadman, "How about the Chiefs sending a box of candy to the wives of our media list next Valentine's Day—with some type of no-serious, fun message? Something like: 'Take heart—it's only five months and two days until football training camp starts. We will need your husband back then because we are going to have a great season. (Signed) Kansas City Chiefs.'"

While Lamar was casting about for ideas to promote goodwill, Steadman was fretting the bottom line, growing increasingly arch and defensive. After the dismal '77 season, he wrote a letter to Kansas City business leader and longtime Chiefs supporter Dutton Brookfield, all but demanding help ("the finest football stadium in the world is going to be half empty or worse during the 1978 football season unless the business leaders of this community take action to get a successful season ticket drive going . . .") and exhibiting an epic misunderstanding of the nature of the draft and the team's sterling history of selections and signings in the '60s ("[b]ecause of our No. 2 drafting position, we should have the best draft in our history this May.").

Yet for all the worries and concerns, Lamar was living a life that hewed almost exactly to his wishes—it was both hectic and exciting, with just as much glamour as he desired. At Norma's fortieth birthday party in March 1978, Lamar had Howard Cosell tape a message, broadcast to the birthday revelers. Cosell assessed Norma thusly: "Exquisite beauty, but a woman who too early handicapped herself by marrying beneath her own status . . . doomed her to the task of ad sales for nonsensical women's organizations and a lifetime of sitting on hard stadium seats."

The dominant image of the couple during this era was of Norma as the supreme hostess, the warm, bubbly outgoing presence that helped draw Lamar out of his natural shell. She dutifully joined Lamar for most of his outings. "I never met a game I didn't like," she once said. "I can't say the same about banquets." Lamar already loved antiques when they met, but with Norma by his side, they became serious collectors, of both art and antiques. In 1979, when Lamar and Norma were in New York, they became fascinated with the story sweeping the art world, of American artist Frederic Edwin Church's lost masterpiece *The Icebergs*. Found in the home of a late English railroad tycoon, it was put on auction through Sotheby's in a fall sale.

Seeking a greater profile for the Dallas Museum of Art, Lamar spoke with Norma about bidding for the painting and giving it as an anonymous donation to the museum. They had been in New York shortly before the auction, and had run into Harry Parker, the director of the DMA, at lunch. Afterward, Lamar and Norma were somewhat circumspect. "We were looking at each other saying, 'My God, do you think they're going to bid on it?'" said Norma. "You certainly don't want to bid against them—you're getting ready to give it to them, you know?" Lamar and Norma were not in New York for the bidding, but they knew exactly what it would mean to the Dallas Museum of Art, even then publicizing a fundraising drive to build "A Museum our City Can Be Proud Of."

On October 25, 1979, Sotheby's Madison Avenue office was the site of Auction 4290, "Nineteenth- and Twentieth-Century American Paintings, Drawings, Watercolors, and Sculpture." As the auction began, all eyes were on item No. 34, *The Icebergs (The North)*, Church's lost classic.

Bidding began at $500,000 and went in increments of $50,000, topping $1 million in less than 30 seconds. By the $2 million mark, only two anonymous telephone bidders remained, one of them Lamar. At $2.4 million, the Sotheby's president and auctioneer John Marion departed from the $50,000 sequence and asked if either bidder was willing to go to $2.5 million. Lamar did so, and then there was silence on the other line and, after the inevitable "going once, going twice . . .", Marion announced the sale to the anonymous bidder, for a price of $2.5 million, far outstripping the price paid for any other piece of American art (the previous record had been George Caleb Bingham's *The Jolly Flatboatmen*, which brought $980,000). In less than 3 minutes and 30 seconds, the deal was done, and the Hunts owned a five-foot by nine-foot painting that would become the talk of the art world.

Just days later, Lamar called Dallas Museum of Fine Arts director Harry Parker and inquired whether he would be interested in displaying *Icebergs* as an anonymous loan. The museum made the announcement November 7, at a time when much of the art world—and beyond—was still speculating about who the buyer was. Norma and Lamar were there to appreciate the painting at the opening, and their beneficence was by then an open secret among Dallas society (and the newspapers, since the *Dallas Times Herald's* art critic Bill Marvel reported on November 8, the day after the museum's announcement, that Lamar was the likely benefactor). An apocryphal story began to make its way around the city that the Hunts only donated it because it proved to be too big for the room in their home where they intended to place it.

When asked whether he was the donor, Lamar took his typically diplomatic tack, taking pains not to be dishonest. "I know it sounds funny, since I'm in a business as public as professional sports, but our collecting is very private. I will say that we're tickled to death that it's in Dallas. I think something like that is great because works of art become available to great masses of people."

Lamar was forty-seven years old, still running every day, pursuing all of his interests, vying to restore the Chiefs to their past glory, to keep the NASL alive and to keep WCT relevant. He loved his work and loved his play, and the two were inextricably bound.

In the years ahead, he would continue these endeavors, but what he couldn't know, on that festive November night when he appeared at the museum opening with Norma, was that his whole world would soon be imperiled for the most mundane of reasons: With all he was doing in his chosen field of sports, he still occasionally went along, at times absent-mindedly, with some of his brothers' business ventures.

At Super Bowl IV in New Orleans, Lamar walked the field with NFL commissioner Pete Rozelle beforehand (above left), and celebrated in a jubilant locker room as MVP Len Dawson (above right) took a call from President Nixon afterward. The next day featured a joyous victory parade in Kansas City that Lamar would later describe as the most memorable day of his life.

The Chiefs played for nine seasons in the aging yet cozy Municipal Stadium (above). In August 1972, they moved to the palatial Arrowhead Stadium (right), which redefined the possibilities of a football stadium.

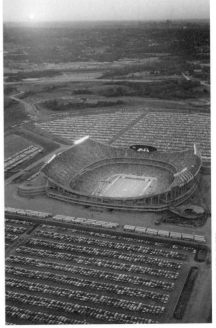

A few days shy of his fortieth birthday, Lamar was inducted into the Pro Football Hall of Fame. Patriots' owner Billy Sullivan (left) hailed him as "Our great founding father, our guiding light, our pleasant leader: the implausible Texan, Lamar Hunt."

By the early '70s, more of Lamar's time was devoted to World Championship Tennis. The 1972 WCT Finals in Dallas featured a classic match between Ken Rosewall and Rod Laver. Lamar almost missed it after Clark's accident that morning.

Lamar didn't merely preside over the tournaments, he also oversaw every aspect of them, from putting up flower arrangements courtside to sweeping the courts after a rainstorm.

Much of the mid-'70s found Lamar traveling the world, often with his nephew, Al Hill, Jr. (left), trying to run dozens of tennis tournaments.

The main part of the expense of running WCT was signing players to contracts, which offered large guarantees to top-ranked marquee players such as Arthur Ashe (above right).

One of the crucial factors in the success of WCT was executive director Mike Davies, a former pro player himself, here conferring with Lamar during a mid-'70s tournament.

In the early, struggling years of the North American Soccer League, Lamar's two main allies were commissioner Phil Woosnam (above left) and New York Cosmos general manager Clive Toye.

The first "homegrown" Dallas Tornado team, in 1968, with Lamar and Bill McNutt flanking the squad in the back row, and erratic manager Bob Kap—soon to be fired—front and center.

Lamar photographed around the time of his fiftieth birthday party in 1982 (his T-shirt reads "The Yard Man is Trim Fit and 50"), with siblings Bunker, Caroline, Margaret, and Herbert. By the end of the decade, much of the family's fortune was wiped out in the silver crisis.

"I just got tired of losing," was how Lamar described his decision late in 1988. Jack Steadman cleared the way for Carl Peterson (left), the team's new president, CEO, and general manager, who hired new coach Marty Schottenheimer (right).

Lamar with Jack Kemp and Carl Peterson at the Berlin Wall, before the 1990 preseason game in Germany against the Rams.

Lamar and Norma on the subway in New York City. "I never met a game I didn't like," she once said. "I can't say the same thing about banquets."

Lamar at the May 15, 1999, opening of Crew Stadium, the first soccer-specific stadium in the United States, with Clark, Norma, and Daniel.

In 2004, Lamar celebrated on the field with the Wizards after they won the U.S. Open Cup, the venerable club knockout competition that had been renamed in his honor.

In 1990, Lamar began constructing the "30-year history wall," which became the "31-year history wall" by the time he finished it. It was his child scrapbooking writ large, and in 2002, he updated it again. Chiefs PR man Bob Moore recalled "hundreds of memos" exchanged as Lamar meticulously planned for the construction of the wall.

Lamar with his four children—(from left) Sharron, Lamar, Jr., Clark, and Daniel—who were the benefactors of the Arrowhead Trust.

Late in the game: Lamar (with Norma and longtime friend Buzz Kemble in the background) left the hospital to attend the MLS Cup on November 12, 2006. Major League Soccer president Mark Abbott (foreground) sat with him for a chat before the game, and recalled him as being in a "very reflective" mood.

CHAPTER FOURTEEN

THE CRISIS

For much of the nearly quarter-century that Lamar had been out of college, he had gone his own way. He remained in the Hunt Oil offices, at the Mercantile Building in the '50s and '60s, then moved with his father and his siblings to the new First National Bank Building in 1965. At the beginning of the '80s, he'd already planned to join his brothers after they completed the construction of Thanksgiving Tower, on 1601 Elm Street, when the fifty-story skyscraper opened in 1982.

He remained an equal partner, with his siblings, in Placid Oil, and a partner with Bunker and Herbert in Penrod Drilling. There were still tax reasons for him to invest some time and money in oil exploration on a regular basis.

But the picture that emerges of the Hunt brothers in the '60s and '70s is one of Bunker and Herbert acting in concert on many business deals, while Lamar journeyed out on his various sports endeavors. The explanation that Bunker had given Bud Adams when Adams asked why Lamar wanted to meet him in the spring of 1959—"I don't tell Lamar my business, and he doesn't tell me his"—remained largely true.

"I don't think there's any question but Lamar went down a totally separate path from what Bunker and Herbert were doing," said Ivan Irwin, Lamar's SMU classmate who served as outside counsel for WCT during much of the '70s and '80s. "Bunker and Herbert were very much wrapped up in oil and gas, and while I'm sure Lamar Hunt Trust Estate had some investments in oil and gas, and certainly through Placid they had investments, I don't think Lamar ever paid any attention to the oil and gas business. He had other people doing that for him, but I don't think he was ever interested in it. He was really, really wrapped up in sports. He got so wrapped up in it, you wonder how in the world he had time to do anything else."

Lamar was friendly with his brothers, dined with them at the Petroleum Club occasionally, but he had quite intentionally followed his own path. When Bunker had offered to invest in the Texans in 1960, Lamar had politely declined. He did convince Herbert to stand in as a part-owner of the Tornado in '67, though only to avoid the dual-ownership rules the NFL was putting in place at the time. In 1973, when Bunker put Lamar up for a 5 percent stake in the George Steinbrenner–led syndicate that was purchasing the New York Yankees, Lamar demurred (he was already hearing enough criticism from other owners for his involvement with the NASL). He shared little of Bunker's interest in horse racing; while Bunker for a time owned more thoroughbreds—over 700—than anyone else in the world, Lamar owned none. And while Herbert's real-estate holdings grew extensively, with significant property in Arizona, Lamar focused largely on the area in and around north Kansas City, where his Worlds of Fun and, later, Oceans of Fun amusement parks were located.

Bunker hewed more closely to his father's political stance than anyone else in the family, while Lamar remained mostly bored by politics, a solid Republican, but someone with little passion for the minutiae of policy, and dedicated to a more inclusive view of patriotism. (This was true in sports as well. Although he dutifully served on NFL subcommittees when drafted by his peers, he didn't seek them out, and he was minimally involved in the politics of the United States Tennis Federation, to his detriment, some of his longtime allies said.) He had friends on both sides of the political spectrum, and his views on race were, to put it gently, far more evolved than Bunker's.

So in the '70s, while Bunker and Herbert were growing fascinated with the soundness of silver as an investment and a hedge against inflation, Lamar generally agreed in theory but remained focused on sports. His friend and former AFL star Jack Kemp, by then an aspiring young U.S. Congressman from Buffalo, had begun arguing the merits of the gold standard—and the value of a hard currency that could withstand all manner of market fluctuations.

It was well into Bunker and Herbert's buying spree, in which they bought over 40 million ounces of silver bullion, that Lamar grew interested enough to invest himself, though not in concert with his brothers. This came against the explicit advice of his lawyer, Jim Seigfreid, who at one point in the late '70s sat down with Lamar and said, "I don't think this is a good idea for you. And I know you have a lot of trust in Bunker and Herbert. I'm not going to stop you; I *can't* stop you. But I'm going to tell you it's very dangerous." Lamar responded as he usually did, thanking Seigfreid for his advice but maintaining his interest nonetheless. And as the price of silver rose in the late '70s, from a historic low of $1.25 per ounce to the otherworldly highs of $20 and then $30 and then $40, Lamar joined in on the investments. By the end of the decade, at his brothers' behest, he had purchased millions of dollars of silver on his own.

On January 21, 1980, the Hunts and Steadmans were in Honolulu, for league meetings and the Pro Bowl. Jack and Martha Steadman were sitting at dinner with Norma that evening, when Lamar walked in late, ashen-faced. He'd just learned that Comex, the New York commodity exchange commission, and CBOT, the Chicago Board of Trade, had both initiated severe restrictions on purchases and sales of silver. As Lamar sat down to dinner, he said, "Comex changed the rules. I think we're in trouble."

It turned out to be far worse than that. Silver, which had increased to a preposterous $50 an ounce on January 17, began free-falling, to $34 an ounce just days later, and all the way down to $21 an ounce by mid-March. Bunker and Herbert's losses were immense—as much as $2 billion by some estimates—but the larger problems were yet to come. What Lamar had gotten himself into, by following his brothers, was the biggest full-scale silver crisis in modern history, and one that threatened the entire family fortune.

Margaret was furious at the brothers for putting the entire family at risk, and Norma felt much the same way. As the pressure mounted in the weeks ahead, Lamar found himself regretting his involvement. On a trip to Kansas City, he sat down with Seigfreid and began a discussion by saying, with a mirthless laugh, "Jim, I wish I'd listened to you before."

The loan that allowed the Hunts to remain solvent resulted in the family mortgaging Placid Oil—Herbert and Bunker required more than $50 million to cover their positions, while Lamar needed a fraction of that, $5.5 million, to cover his own investments. Even that didn't end Bunker and Herbert's calamitous misfortune, or Lamar's involvement in it. The ride would be a perilous one, and though many people were advising him to separate himself from his brothers' predicament—and though his involvement was probably minor enough that he might have been able to extricate himself—it was never a question. The Hunt brothers stood together. The repercussions and the lawsuits would drag on through the decade and seemed to mark virtually everything Lamar did.

"The Silver Crisis" would just about span the decade of the 1980s, a nearly endless procession of meetings with lawyers, negotiations with banks, and unpleasant sit-downs with government officials. The days burned away from Lamar, drew his energy, and left his brothers as caricatures of public ridicule. Through it all he was reminded, on a daily basis, why he had chosen a life based on something other than turning a large fortune into a larger one. During the crisis, the *New York Times Sunday Magazine* did a cover story on the brothers, in which a Dallas historian remarked, "There is something about being a Hunt: You're never rich enough." That may have been true for Bunker and Herbert, but it decidedly wasn't for Lamar. While Bunker was making a play for the biggest oil field in the world in Libya, Lamar was busying himself with flower arrangements on the morning of the WCT final and working on the wording of mailers for Tornado season-ticket holders.

He had possessed the same means and options as his brothers, and he had chosen an altogether different course. But now, with the brothers paying a million dollars a month in legal fees, and with their debt to banks growing at a rate of six figures per day—with a billion more in bank debt than the liquidation value of their assets, his entire life's work was in jeopardy.

And throughout the ordeal, Lamar continued to go to the office every day, tried to answer every piece of mail, saw every Chiefs game, got to every tennis tournament and soccer match he could. At home, after Clark left for college at SMU, Lamar and Daniel would spend time up on the third floor of the house, playing marathon ping-pong contests. The games would continue.

Norma, as worried as anyone over what the ordeal meant to her husband and all that he'd worked for, didn't hear a single instance of complaint.

"It just wasn't in his nature to dwell on anything negative," she said. "So he moved forward."

He lived by Lyda's words: *We do not collapse.*

•

After the disappointment of the Paul Wiggin years, the Chiefs began anew under Marv Levy. He was a calmly assured presence, willing to take a deliberate path toward improving the Chiefs, starting with a stout defense, to better keep the team in every game, and then working to fill in the missing pieces on offense.

Progress was slow, both in the standings and at the gate. After a 4–12 opening season, Levy's Chiefs went 7–9 in '79 and 8–8 in 1980. The fans had grown disenchanted with the team's persistent failure in the '70s, and they were slow to return. In those first three seasons, the Chiefs drew more than 70,000 fans to a home game just four times.

The Arrowhead Stadium of that period was still a magnificent edifice, but one that already seemed antiseptic and out of step with the times. The vast parking lots were spacious, with room for more than 20,000 cars, but there was little activity to speak of prior to games (fans from nearby colleges were used to tailgating, but it was not a common practice in Arrowhead, which included no bathroom access in the parking lots and precious few garbage receptacles). Inside the stadium, the staff in 1980 were still wearing remnants of the early–'70s mod looks: double-knit leisure suits with polyester neckties for the male ushers, long skirts and white boots with fringed vests for the female "usherettes."

Levy's Chiefs in 1980 had begun 0–4, then turned around to win four straight games, only to alternate losses with wins the rest of the way. The scrambling Clemson quarterback Steve Fuller had been taken in the first round in 1979 but wound up losing his job to the lightly regarded Bill Kenney, who showed an admirable toughness and more accuracy on deep passes. In 1981, with Kenney taking most of the snaps, rookie running back Joe Delaney running for 1,100 yards, and a young defense anchored by a strong secondary finding its way, the Chiefs started 6–2 and took first place in the AFC West, with a rare road win at the Oakland Raiders. But they lost five of their next seven games, wound up mired in a quarterback controversy between Fuller and Kenney, and finished third in the AFC West, just a single game behind San Diego and Denver. They did beat the Colts in the season finale for their first winning season in eight years.

Over the years, Lamar and Levy developed a rapport. One summer, Marv and his wife Dorothy traveled to France and went to the Louvre, where they attempted to match Lamar and Norma's "record" of walking through the entire museum in 56 minutes. "Despite a valiant effort on our part, Dorothy lost concentration under pressure and stopped too long at the *Mona Lisa*," Levy wrote, "and we had to settle for a 58:16.4. I'm sure that the experience we gained will help us next time."

But the era of Lamar making weekly visits and having regular dinners with his head coach were long gone. With Lamar's hectic schedule being what it was, the daily oversight of the football side of the organization—which historically had been Lamar dealing with the head coach—moved to Jack Steadman. He had been with the franchise for two decades, had a strong understanding of the finances of running a franchise, and remained resolutely loyal to Lamar.

Steadman's manner was more stern than Lamar's, and many in the organization felt as though he overstepped his bounds. Lamar would evaluate his coach's personnel decisions after the fact, but he would never presume to recommend which player should be drafted beforehand. According to Levy, Steadman was different, pressuring him to draft offensive skill position players in the draft, and then pressing him to start the highly publicized Fuller over Kenney in the 1981 season. "Jack was so imperious, he was hard to like," said one longtime Chiefs employee.

For his part, Steadman took seriously his role as the chief financial officer of the team, and he had concluded years earlier that any commercial success would follow on-field success. With this reality a given, as well as Lamar's fierce competitiveness, it was Steadman who felt responsible for putting a winning team on the field.

The 1982 season looked like a decisive year for Levy—just as the 1966 season had been for Stram—and after a hard-fought 14-9 road loss at Buffalo, the Chiefs had come home and defeated the three-time division champion San Diego Chargers in their Arrowhead opener. Then came the 1982 NFL Players Association strike, and all the momentum and continuity that had been built up by Levy in the four-plus years dissipated.

In the coming weeks, the offices at Arrowhead took on a haunted aspect. The coaches remained at work, all revved up with nowhere to go. Coaching secretary Ann Roach saw the staff spend their days in a directionless funk. "They'd come in the office anyway," said Roach. "I don't think their wives wanted them at home."

When the team returned, there was a residue of dissension, both between players and management, but also among the team itself. (The strike lopped seven games from the schedule, and five of those would have been home games for the Chiefs.) They returned with three road games and a home game against the Raiders, all of which they lost. The NFL had expanded the playoffs to sixteen teams but it didn't matter: Kansas City was 1–5, its season effectively over.

By then, Lamar was agonizing over the prospect of yet another coaching change. On the morning of the December 19 Chiefs–Broncos game in Denver, he began drafting a letter to Steadman, unusually bleak in its tone. "We are possibly in the worst position that the organization has ever been in," he wrote. "There are a lot of factors involved in that—the major one being the after effects of the strike, which I believe place the entire business in the most jeopardized position it has been in since the failure of the [New York] Titans late in 1962."

After acknowledging the slow growth of the team under Levy, and the steady disappointments of the strike year, Hunt came to the coaching staff. "I think Marv is a good, basic coach, but I think he is not capable of making the big breakthrough." Lamar cited a number of factors, including the team's inability to win as a favorite, Levy's "lack of exterior toughness," the uneven handling of quarterbacks.

"My belief is that we need to consider a coaching change—*if we can bring someone in who has a proven track record.*" Lamar's list was a short one: 1) Don Shula, 2) George Allen, both proven coaches who were already under contract. The third choice was the former Cowboys assistant John Mackovic, about whom he wrote, "I've never met him, but reputation, heightened by his outstanding performance as a head coach at a really 'sick' college (Wake Forest), put him in the 'proven' category . . . Mackovic, of course, would have to prove himself to the public and the players. There would be a degree of risk with him." In conclusion, he stated, rather hopefully, that "if a change is to be made, I would envision asking Marv to 'ask for a change of duties with the organization,' which may or may not be acceptable to him as he may choose to continue to coach elsewhere. He does not deserve to be fired and I would hope that if we went that route that it could be handled 'at his request,' or with some type of 'mutuality' agreement."

This was wishful thinking. Lamar still went to every game, but he'd not spent the time with the team or conferred with his coach the way he had in the past. The decision was made, in spite of the Chiefs winning two of their last three games, including a season-ending 37–13 rout of the playoff-bound New York Jets in front of a record Arrowhead low turnout of 11,902 people. When Steadman told him of the decision the next morning, Levy was calm but defiant. "You're making a big mistake," he said. When Steadman pressed further, asking Levy if he'd be willing to resign, Levy said, "Why would I want to do that? I've done a good job, and you're wrong to fire me."

The Chiefs came out of the 1982 season seeking to hire their fourth different coach in less than a decade. The new man was John Mackovic, the Cowboys' assistant who had been heavily influenced by his time under Tom Landry, both in his insistence on a passing-based multiple offense and, less fortuitously, in his commitment to remaining an unemotional character presiding above the fray, removed from his players and unemotionally directing the team. (For his part, Mackovic said he'd *always* been unemotional; but his detachment, after some time on Landry's staff, was even more pronounced.)

The 1983 draft would be one of the deepest in NFL history, as six quarterbacks were taken in the first round, starting with No. 1 draft choice John Elway being drafted by the Baltimore Colts, who subsequently dealt him

(Elway insisted he didn't want to play for Baltimore and used the leverage of his baseball career to threaten to not sign at all) to the Denver Broncos. With the seventh pick in the first round, the Chiefs—fully committed to drafting a quarterback—were looking at a draft board that included five other quarterbacks with first-round grades. They were Todd Blackledge, who had quarterbacked Penn State to a national championship in 1982; Ken O'Brien, a raw prospect out of Louisville; the mobile Tony Eason, who'd led Illinois to a Rose Bowl; Jim Kelly, the strong-armed passer who had helped revive the University of Miami program; and Dan Marino, the preseason Heisman favorite who'd suffered a disappointing year at Pittsburgh and had seen his pre-draft stock drop in the wake of a persistent rumor that he smoked marijuana.

While Elway was almost unanimously considered the best quarterback prospect, there was a great deal of disagreement over who was second best. With all five available when the seventh choice in the draft came, the Chiefs knew that much of the next decade of their franchise's fortunes would be dictated by the selection.

In the draft "war room" where Mackovic, Schaaf, and Jack Steadman stood with scouting director Les Miller and Lamar, the new head coach felt that Blackledge was the right man to pick (Levy, who had spent some time looking at the same question before his exit, had strongly preferred the other two Pennsylvania-bred quarterbacks, Marino and Kelly).

Before the team even reported to training camp, the franchise suffered another trauma, as running back Joe Delaney—who'd been instrumental to the team's rise in his rookie year of '82—died while trying to save some children in a swimming hole in Louisiana. While Delaney's death had nothing in common with the Stone Johnson or Mack Lee Hill's tragedies, many longtime members of the organization couldn't help wondering if the team was somehow cursed.

After a decade and a half of stability under Stram, the Chiefs had been reeling ever since. But by the end of 1982, it wasn't merely the team that was in trouble—the entire NFL was embattled. On Friday, May 7, 1982—nearly two years after Al Davis announced his intention to move the Oakland Raiders to Los Angeles, only to have the NFL reject the move—a district court jury in Los Angeles brought back an all-too-predictable verdict in favor of the Los Angeles Coliseum Commission and the Raiders. In the aftermath, the NFL directly filed an appeal of the verdict, and both parties prepared for another trial, to decide damages.

Discussions of the implications of the Raiders' victory were still in the news four days later, on May 11, when a new professional football league announced its formation in a festive press conference at 21 in New York City. The United States Football League was the brainchild of Lamar's longtime friend David Dixon, who had been arguing for the merits of a spring football league for more than a decade. With Lamar's help, Dixon had even made a presentation to NFL owners at an annual meeting in 1973, to use a spring league as a developmental league. From that germ of an idea, and a survey of attitudes about sports that showed a strong public interest in football even during the spring, the USFL got off the ground.

With his brothers' calamity in silver, Lamar was already destined to spend much of the next few years in meetings with lawyers and business analysts. But the sum total of the first players' strike (with another in the offing), Al Davis's challenge to the NFL, and Dixon's start-up of the USFL ensured that there would be plenty of time spent in law offices and courtrooms for football as well. And that wasn't the end of it—by the end of the '70s, the NASL had filed suit against the NFL (with Lamar ruefully noting he was paying legal fees on both sides), and World Championship Tennis had gone to court with the Men's Professional Tennis Council and the International Tennis Federation. Lamar would muse later in the decade that in the '80s, he seemed to spend most of his waking hours giving depositions.

•

In the midst of these crises on multiple fronts, Lamar's public face in the 1980s was different. His hair, growing more sparse, was now often parted in the center, combed back. He'd taken to more modern tortoise-shell eyeglasses, with exceedingly large frames. His running kept him slender, but he looked more worried than anything else. Sitting in Dallas for a WCT press conference in 1983, he seemed visibly nervous, sweating, absently tinkering with a piece of paper or a Dr Pepper cup as he answered questions about the WCT's lawsuit with the International Tennis Federation. He had never been slick in front of the media—it was one of his charms—but for the first time in more than twenty years he seemed visibly uncomfortable.

This was understandable. For the first time in his professional career, his employees could see visible signs of stress. He was not irritable or snappish. He continued to preface all requests to secretary Jean Finn or others with a tentative "Would you mind . . ." or "If you get the chance, could you . . ." But he was quieter than usual, fell even further behind in his correspondence (by the mid-'80s, there were entire offices on the floor that was given over to stacks of Lamar's ongoing letters), and often looked haggard, even as he continued his health regimen.

"He had a vision there of maybe losing everything he had," said his long-time financial aide Wayne Henry. "That really bothered Lamar, I think—that everything could get away from him."

The additional time he spent on the unpleasant matters of the silver cri-sis—depositions, testimony, long strategic meetings considering arcane tax matters and plausible exit strategies—was a drain on his energy, whereas spending time on the sports he loved had always seemed to give him energy.

In 1983, Lamar hired Thom Meredith, the bright, jovial sports marketing executive who had worked as the director of public relations for WCT for two years, after jobs in the NFL and NASL in the '70s. As Lamar explained it, he wanted Meredith to serve as his administrative assistant and help with his voluminous correspondence, drafting letters for which Lamar didn't have time and Jean Finn didn't have energy.

So Meredith was hired to draft replies to much of Lamar's correspon-dence and to field the bizarre queries that had only grown in volume since the Super Bowl win and, again, after his father's death.

Rich people get plenty of unsolicited mail, as do famous people, and rich famous people get the most of all. And so he replied to people who wrote ask-ing for funds to start educational institutions that "will make us independent of the kingdom of Saudi Arabia;" he replied to people who either claimed to be or claimed to know illegitimate children of his father; to people who were as close to being crazy as made no difference; to people who sent letters on round stationery, with football formations on the bottom and nonsensical lists of educational institutions and pharmaceuticals on the top; to women who either didn't know or didn't care about his marital status and wanted to date him; to a man marketing a "synthetic solar power plant;" to a man who claimed to have passed a lie detector test proving that he could take any team in professional sports and raise its winning percentage to 70 percent or more; and to a man who asked for $180 million to build a "movie museum and parking garage" in rural Mississippi.

"Lamar tried to answer every letter he received that was signed," said Meredith. "Even the cranks. He felt that if someone signed their name, that person deserved a reply."

Around the office, when Lamar could break free of his obligations with the silver crisis, he moved from one office to another in his work, often sitting up in the largest conference area not being used that day. There he would write out longhand whatever correspondence he had, then hand over the paper and its miniscule longhand script to secretary Jean Finn whom, armed with her magnifying class, would read it and type it up.

What did not end, despite the distractions, was his mastery of minutiae. One time in the early '80s, Lamar presented WCT director of communications Rod Humphries with an itinerary for a trip the two would be taking from Dallas to Houston, to check out the specs of The Summit for an upcoming WCT tournament. Humphries, knowing Lamar's attention to detail, noticed that the projected travel time from Houston Hobby to the Summit was three minutes less than the projected travel time for the return.

"Ah, Lamar, look here, you've made a mistake," he said slyly, pointing out the discrepancy.

Lamar peered down at the sheet, then explained that, "No, I checked—at that hour of the day, it will take us a little longer to return to the airport." And so it did.

•

Soccer was the first to go.

The North American Soccer League's last chance to save itself might have been the league's Long Term Strategic Plan, conceived by a committee at the apex of Pelé's popularity in 1977–78. With Lamar in the group, along with Jim Ruben of Minnesota and Steve Danzansky from Washington, D.C., the committee strongly recommended a policy of slow growth, shoring up the league's weak links before going forward.

But on the other side of the equation, expansion franchises were going for $3 million, and with sellouts at Giants Stadium, and a national TV contract, new money was lining up for a shot at the NASL.

So the admonitions were ignored. The lure of cash was too strong—especially to many of the franchises that were either barely solvent or struggling. That period of edgy optimism pervaded at the beginning of the 1978 season, as the league grew from eighteen to twenty-four teams, accompanied by rumors that Henry Kissinger would be named the league's new commissioner (false), and that the new franchise in Colorado, the Caribous, would sport fringed jerseys (true).

In his memoir *A Kick in the Grass*, Clive Toye recalled a meeting in which it became clear that there was a new order; the conservative suits of previous meetings were no longer common. "Rock stars, their agents and managers, middle-aged men with open shirts, hairy chests, dangling gold medallions and rings to match. Lamar . . . looking around the room, commenting drily: 'We have a different looking league.'"

There was even a period, in 1977, when the league considered granting an expansion franchise to boxing promoter Don King, who in one of his usual volleys of bombastic rhetoric, argued that the NASL could rescue itself by making King and Muhammad Ali co-owners of a new franchise called the Montreal Shuffle, which would play its games at Montreal's cavernous Olympic Stadium. "Of course, Don King wanted the NASL to *give him* the franchise," said Paul Tagliabue. "So my recollection is that didn't get very far."

The subsequent death of the NASL was protracted and agonizing: After the 1977 season, St. Louis, a cornerstone of American soccer even well before the city provided a majority of the starters on the 1950 U.S. World Cup squad that shocked England, couldn't compete and the franchise sold to a group in Anaheim; an expansion team was awarded to Hawaii and lasted one season, before moving to Tulsa. Only once since its inaugural year in 1967 did the league have the same lineup of teams in consecutive years. At a meeting in 1981, on the verge of a vote to post a bond for the next season, Calgary owner Nelson Skalbania and Edmonton owner Peter Pocklington sat together and conferred long enough to settle on an agreement to merge their two franchises, which they drafted on the back of a pack of cigarettes.

Fifteen seasons of the Tornado in Dallas had yielded a bustling youth soccer scene, but not much of a fan base for professional soccer. Lamar and Bill McNutt had, it seemed, tried everything: They'd recruited the best players they could find from England and South America; they'd launched the first American superstar, Rote; they had spent a small fortune in promotion, had Crazy George in the crowd pounding on drums and Dick Berg's running promotions from monkeys on the goalpost to dancers on the sidelines in the mid 1970s. Along the way, the team had played in small stadiums, renovated medium-sized ones, and in large ones, and attendance was lower the fifteenth season than it had been in the first. So after the 1981 season, Lamar and Bill McNutt finally surrendered, deciding to merge the Tornado into George Strawbridge's Tampa Bay Rowdies franchise.

"It wasn't like they were getting out of the business," said Bob McNutt, Bill's son. "They were just going to take a new direction [co-owning the Tampa Bay franchise] that made more sense economically. I mean, my goodness, the amount of money they pumped into that, particularly Mr. Hunt. Their decision came at that point in time when the logic of, *You played as a kid, you'll come buy tickets as an adult*, it became evident that that was not happening. When you're two years out, or three years out, you can always say, 'They're going to start coming.' And they just never started coming."

By the end of the 1984 season, only two teams—the Minnesota Kicks and Toronto Blizzard—had posted the necessary bond to move into the next season, with even the Cosmos abdicating. Clive Toye, who had been around since the early days, was by now the league president, and he helped preside over the death knell. Lamar sent a consoling note.

It would be hard to know how much money Lamar lost in his time in the North American Soccer League, but suffice to say that while his family (especially Clark and Daniel) grew up loving the sport, and a few friends (like Tom Richey) shared his enthusiasm, most of the people in Lamar's life did not share his love for the game, disagreed with his commitment to it, and were glad when the NASL went out of business.

The situation in tennis wasn't much better. The tenth WCT Finals had been held in 1980, opening the new Reunion Arena in downtown Dallas. But a year later, WCT split from the Grand Prix tour, to run its own twenty-two–tournament schedule. The infighting that had marked much of the first decade of the open era returned—the ATP used one set of computer rankings, the WCT used a different computer system, and by the end of 1982, the WCT was crippled by its war with the Men's International Professional Tennis Council. The MIPTC had outflanked Lamar by making it prohibitively difficult for some of the world's top players to compete in WCT events.

On January 21, 1983, the WCT filed a complaint in New York federal court, seeking an injunction against the Men's International Professional Tennis Council, which ran the rival Grand Prix tour. On November 10, the two sides announced a settlement, in which the WCT could operate seven tournaments, again under the aegis of the Grand Prix.

It was a hollow victory. Lamar slashed his staff and reduced the WCT schedule from twenty-two tournaments to only nine, with just five a year later. The WCT would limp along for the rest of the decade, but Lamar had long ago lost the power that he'd once had with the players.

Some observers felt that he could have controlled the entire world of tennis if he'd chosen to be more ruthless in the early '70s. Others felt the game's ultimate evolution—in which the players took control of their tour, the way golfers had in the formation of the Professional Golfers Association tour—was inevitable.

"To me, the whole thing was the Establishment versus Lamar," said Rod Humphries, who worked for nearly a decade for Lamar. "And the players playing the two of them off against each other. And in the end, the players won."

•

When he hired John Mackovic, Lamar noted that he was looking for someone with "external toughness," but in Mackovic he found a practitioner who sometimes put expressions of toughness above all else. A trim man with golden-brown hair, not a strand out of place, he was distant from his players, other staffers in the building, even his own coaches.

The Chiefs team that had been built for four straight years before the strike year of 1982 took a major step backward in 1983, going 6–10. In the preseason of 1984, Mackovic handed a list of cuts to Bud Carson, the respected defensive coordinator who'd helped coach the Steeler dynasty of the '70s. The list included at least three players that Carson had hoped to start for the Chiefs, and from that the disagreement deteriorated. One day in August, the Chiefs' defensive players showed up for a meeting only to find no coaches in the room. Then Mackovic presented himself and told the players that Carson had quit, news that they greeted with barely concealed derision. Officially, Carson resigned over what he and Mackovic agreed were "professional differences." As one player put it, "Yeah, well, the 'difference' was that Bud didn't think John knew anything about defensive football."

Though they improved to an 8–8 record in '84, they took another tumble in '85, starting 3–1 before suffering through a seven-game losing skid, culminating in a 31–3 loss to San Francisco. By then, media speculation was rampant and many in the Chiefs' increasingly alienated fan base were calling for Mackovic's ouster.

The next day, Lamar released a statement saying, "There is great emotion that goes into the preparation and conduct of a season and we, like the fans, are very deflated at our current status. The Chiefs are struggling at the moment and I'm sure John Mackovic, his assistants, and the 45-man squad want to do everything possible to turn things around in the remaining five games. We are working in that direction as a total organization. I do not believe in votes of confidence in the middle of a season. They inevitably are distorted or misinterpreted and we would prefer to wait and evaluate the season as a whole."

Later in the season, after the team split its next four games, Lamar called a press conference. There was one game left, at home against the Chargers.

"In many ways, we have been disappointed in the visible community support, as seen through attendance, and we have missed the intangible life that that brings a football team," he said. "This has been most evident by contrast when we play AFC West opponents on the road."

He evoked the catcalls of twenty years earlier, when rumors were commonplace that the Chiefs were moving. "The answer then," he said, "was 'Baloney!' Following that 1965 season, which was also very disappointing, everyone—fans included—committed to the project. The result was six consecutive years where the organization produced the fourth best won-loss percentage in pro football, won the AFL twice, and won the Super Bowl. That success, in turn, helped build the greatest sports complex in the world, and at the time the highest season-ticket sale in pro sports history."

Declaring "we remain committed to John and his staff," Lamar also moved to take some of the heat off of Steadman. "So that there is no confusion on the part of our players, coaches, or the public, I want to reiterate that general manager, Jim Schaaf, has direct responsibility for all day-to-day football operations, which includes coaching, scouting, and player personnel."

Finally, he reiterated his own commitment. "Back to 'square one,' and really as a beginning point, I am challenging myself to put it on the line, to be a forceful catalyst to *help* make this organization the best in pro sports. Just as in the past, a lot of my efforts necessarily have to be on the league level. But, I'll promise, you are going to see the Kansas City Chiefs back in a position of prominence. Because of what it says on the stock certificate, as well as the number of years I've spent in pro football, I have the advantage of not needing accolades or job security. Nevertheless, I assure you, from a career standpoint—I have no matter of greater importance."

The '86 team started strong, with a competent offense (with quarterback Bill Kenney beating out the uneven Blackledge as starter), a stout defense, and an absolutely maniacal special teams group, paced by special teams coordinator Frank "Crash" Gansz, the Chiefs marched to a 7–3 start, before a three-game losing streak, punctuated by a galling 17–14 loss to a rebuilding Buffalo team that would finish 4–12 under their new coach, Marv Levy.

Just days after that loss, with the team standing at 8–6 and its playoff hopes diminishing, Lamar had already considered sacking Mackovic. Weighing the pluses and minuses of his coach, Lamar gave Mackovic credit for being "bright" and having "high ideals regarding make-up of squad." But he gave him minuses for being "uncommunicative to a fault (with everybody)," "lacking in single-mindedness of purpose toward winning," being "unable to instill great loyalty in associates," and having "unrealistic appraisal of sense of accomplishments (wanting contract extension last year)." Writing to Stead-man on December 11, Lamar offered, "I do not believe John has what we need. His people skills (lack of communication ability) is such a flaw that I can't see his being able to consistently lead."

His two solutions were very old and very new: The first was George Allen, and the second was special-teams coach Frank Gansz. "He has never been a head coach," wrote Lamar, "but in my 27 years' experience he strikes me as the best head coach 'prospect' I've seen. He is a born leader of men. Charis-matic, etc. An outstanding person."

But the Chiefs won the next week, to go to 9–6, and then traveled to Pitts-burgh, on December 21, where they needed a win to make the playoffs. The game would go down in Chiefs lore as one of the team's greatest, and un-likeliest, victories. With Kenney out due to an injury and the Chiefs' offense sputtering in the face of the Steelers' defense, it was left to the Chiefs' de-fense and specialty teams to make the difference, and they did, accounting for two blocked kicks and all three touchdowns in a 24–19 victory that sent the Chiefs to the playoffs for the first time in fifteen seasons.

While Christmas was unusually sweet, the bubble burst three days later, when the New York Jets trounced Kansas City, 35–15, in a playoff win that was seldom in doubt.

But the aftermath of the game brought up an even greater schism, as Gansz resigned—he'd felt that he would be given a greater role in coaching and claimed Mackovic reneged on the promise—and then, in a nearly unprec-edented development, a group of players asked for a meeting with Lamar.

"I started getting calls, from Deron Cherry, from Bill Maas, from others," said kicker Nick Lowery, the team's player representative. "So I called Lamar and I said, 'I think we need to talk.'"

Lamar traveled to Kansas City and, along with Steadman, met Lowery and several of his teammates at Lowery's house. "There was definitely a lot of dislike in the locker room for John," said one longtime Chief. "He talked a great game. He talked so much about the relationship with the players. But it wasn't really there."

It was highly unusual for players to have input on the hiring and firing of coaches, but the Chiefs' players expressed their support for Gansz as well as their opposition to Mackovic. It was what Lamar needed to hear to con-vince him to make a decision he'd been considering for months. As Stead-man would put it later, talking to Lowery, "this was just the last snowflake in a long blizzard." By the end of the day, Lamar had fired Mackovic.

"The chemistry of an organization is an intangible that is crucial to its success," he said in a statement announcing the firing. "My evaluation is that our football team is lacking that ingredient. There is no perfect formula for becoming the best in pro football. We'd all like to think we have the right answers. In this case, I have to make a judgment, and I have reluctantly concluded that a coaching change is necessary at this time."

It was a calculated risk, and one that Lamar was quite certain would backfire on him if the team didn't win. In little more than a decade, he'd gone from owning a franchise with only one head coach to being the owner of a team whose leadership seemed in more or less constant flux. And he knew the game well enough to know that if Gansz wasn't the right man, he would be the one blamed for it.

"The thing that people really didn't understand about Lamar," said his friend Tom Richey, "was how much he hated to lose. He was gracious and always a good sport, but it just ate at him."

Against the backdrop of the Chiefs travails, Lamar was still dealing with the fallout from the silver crisis. But inside the house, "it was just never discussed," said Clark. Lamar didn't want the children to worry, so he more or less ignored it when the topic came up.

In the '80s, Clark Hunt had graduated from high school at St. Mark's in Dallas, a star in both soccer and football, and followed his father to SMU (though he would wind up in the athletic fraternity, Phi Delta Gamma, rather than his father's Kappa Sigma). Clark had spent a week with the SMU football team before deciding he was far better suited for a career as a soccer player. Once he got back into soccer shape, he was a three-year starter for Coach Schellas Hyndman at SMU. He graduated as the valedictorian of the class; Lamar, beaming, said he got his smarts from Norma, and his pride in Clark's accomplishment was enough to assuage the pain of the school's fall from grace, and the 1987 "death penalty" for repeated recruiting violations that shut down the football program for two full seasons.

In 1987, Lamar and Norma had sold the Gaywood mansion for an estimated $12 million to Gene Phillips, the CEO of the financial services company Southmark, and moved to a smaller, though still impressive, home in Highland Park, on Arcady, across the street from the Dallas Country Club. It was a more manageable property—Clark was out of the house by then, and Daniel was already eleven years old—and significantly less expensive.

But there were still grave doubts about whether Lamar could emerge from the ordeal with his holdings intact. The most pronounced threat was the trial by the Peruvian mining company Minpeco against the Hunt brothers, asking for treble damages of nearly a billion dollars.

Though Lamar was ostensibly standing trial along with his brothers, he was represented by his Kansas City lawyer, Jim Seigfreid. Seigfreid had made a nervy ploy early on, calling the judge, U.S. District Judge Morris E. Lasker, and explaining that he would like him to meet Lamar personally. In a private meeting in Lasker's chambers, Seigfreid and Lamar showed up, sat down, and chatted. Siegfreid explained the unusual nature of how the Hunt brothers did business—each essentially a separate, autonomous partner, though they split the costs of the company's overhead equally—and argued that while Lamar was in the wrong, he had gone along unwittingly.

And then, as the trial played out, he worked to see that Lamar never testified. The verdict of guilty was handed down in August 20, 1988, with Bunker and Herbert found guilty on all charges, and Lamar ruled guilty on all charges save—significantly—racketeering, since it was determined he had not acted in concert with his brothers.

Still, it was a dire scene outside the court room, and in many family members minds the end of the Hunt dynasty as they'd known it. After consoling his brothers, Lamar adjourned with his own advisers, and the first question came from Steadman: "What do you want to save?"

Both Bunker and Herbert wound up filing for personal bankruptcy to avoid paying the judgment. But Seigfreid had persuaded Lamar that doing so guaranteed nothing but further litigation. "I don't know how we're going to do it," Lamar said at one point, "but let's try."

In this, they succeeded. In a 10-minute public hearing on October 20, 1988, Lasker allowed for Lamar to settle his portion of the Minpeco suit, and he vacated the judgment against him. Afterward, Seigfreid handed Minpeco's lawyers a check in the amount of $17 million. It had been a long and torturous process, but now Lamar was through with it. He had already decided what he needed to do next. Seigfreid had given him a way to survive the lawsuit.

And over the previous year, Jack Steadman—finally—had given him a way to rescue the football franchise.

•

Frank Gansz was a handsome, inspirational figure, beloved by players. But even he couldn't avoid the same fate that had befallen Levy five years earlier. On September 21, 1987—just two games into his tenure as the Chiefs' new head coach—the NFL Players Association went on strike again, and pro football faced its second ruinous work stoppage of the decade.

By this time, Lamar had grown resolute. He wasn't one for poisonous rhetoric, and he continued talking publicly about hoping that the two sides could find common ground. But he belonged to a majority of owners who felt the league needed to continue playing games, with replacement players.

The third week's schedule was cancelled, and then the replacements came in. Some teams had hedged their bets, lining up replacement players knowing that the day could come. But the Chiefs under Gansz didn't have that kind of preparation. They took the players they could get, and promptly lost all three replacement games.

For the second time in six years, a promising season would dissipate in the acrimony of labor unrest. "I think everyone felt good about the direction we were going," said Gary Heise, the Chiefs public relations director at the time. "We had the excitement of a new head coach, the players were excited going into the season. The strike had a huge, huge impact. I believe many of the players came back with a different mentality."

The team lost seven straight after the strike was over—they were 1–10 when they shocked Detroit on Thanksgiving Day at the Silverdome. Lamar knew there was no way—after firing Levy following a strike year, and the quick hook for Mackovic, after a playoff year—that the Chiefs could contemplate another coaching change, but the time had come for a sea change, and Steadman recognized it before needing to be told.

On Christmas Eve 1987, Steadman drafted a memo to Lamar. "Because our 1987 season has been such a disaster," he wrote, "I have spent a lot of time studying and thinking about our total Chiefs operations." After analyzing the 1987 season, the difficulties with the strike and with Gansz, he concluded, "The change I am proposing is a very difficult one for me because it affects Jim, who has been one of our most dedicated and loyal employees. It could also affect my status with the Chiefs, depending upon what it will take to hire a top football executive, who we are confident has the experience and knowledge necessary to turn our football operations around."

What Steadman was proposing was "the hiring of a vice president of football operations who will have full authority over our entire scouting, coaching, and field operations . . ."

Steadman allowed as how some candidates might only be willing to come to the team as president, "In which case I would have no problem moving full time to Hunt Midwest, which is demanding more and more of my time anyway."

Steadman's first candidate was Dick Vermeil. His second was the aging George Allen, and his third was USFL executive Carl Peterson, "an ex-coach who has a reputation of being an outstanding talent evaluator, was with a winning program with Vermeil and the Eagles, and did the best job in the USFL with the Philadelphia Stars."

In conclusion, Steadman was blunt. "Frankly, you are tired of losing, I'm tired of losing, the public is tired of losing, and in my opinion, the only way that we have a chance of regaining public confidence and support is to change the way we run our football operations."

The change would not come for another twelve months, after the Chiefs posted their second consecutive four-win season under Gansz, a miserable 4-11-1 campaign most noteworthy for the protracted fallout of a *Kansas City Star* investigation into inconsistencies between Gansz's talk about his time as a pilot in the Air Force and his actual résumé. By this time, the criticism in Kansas City had grown so intense that Heise compared Gansz's media appearances that year as being "almost like walking to a torture chamber."

For fifteen years, Lamar had resembled a general always fighting the last war. In place of the resplendent trappings and vanity of Stram, he had hired the resolutely down-to-earth, even humble, Wiggin. To escape from the vague generalities and bland rah-rah of Wiggin, he'd hired the cerebral, detail-oriented Levy. Judging Levy to be too graying and methodical, he'd hired the tough, imperious Mackovic, only to find him distant and at times cold to both player and staff. That brought about the hiring of the non-stop emotionalism of Gansz. And now, after two seasons—during which Lamar spent much of the time defending Gansz, defending Steadman, and defending Jim Schaaf—the time for incremental change was over.

Steadman fell on his sword December 8, announcing his resignation at the same time that it was announced that Jim Schaaf would not return as general manager.

The loyalty of Steadman's gesture cannot be underestimated. In 1960, it was Steadman who helped stanch the flow of red ink with the nascent Texans; in 1963, it was Steadman who'd moved his family to Kansas City, to represent the franchise on a daily basis. From 1967 to 1972, it was Steadman who had run interference for the protracted efforts to win approval for and build

Arrowhead. And throughout all that time, he had cheerfully (too cheerfully for some) played bad cop to Lamar's good cop.

Those closest to Lamar felt that unless Steadman had offered to leave, Lamar never would have fired him. "Loyalty is not something he took lightly," said one longtime Chiefs executive. "After what he and Jack had been through together—after all the flak Jack had taken, some of it for Lamar, and some of it just because of the way Jack was—there is no way he would have fired him, even as bad as it had gotten."

And it had gotten increasingly bad. On ESPN, the rapidly growing cable channel whose Sunday night highlights package was becoming a staple for NFL fans—Lamar included—announcer Chris Berman had spent almost two full years referring to the bumbling team from Kansas City as "the Chefs." Lamar was never one to curse out a TV set, but every bit of lost respect, every investigative piece about Gansz's war record, every empty seat at his beloved Arrowhead, weighed on him.

"I just got tired of losing," he said.

On December 4, as the Chiefs were winning for just the fourth game of the season, a 38–34 victory over the New York Jets, a figure sat nearly alone in one of the empty luxury boxes, watching the dismal but now familiar sight of the half-empty Arrowhead Stadium, with just 30,059 fans in attendance.

Carl Peterson—who preferred tailored suits and mirrored shades—did not look like anyone's traditional picture of a football general manager. But beneath the polished exterior, he was a brainy football lifer, who'd received his doctorate in kinesthesiology from UCLA and worked first as an assistant coach and later as the personnel director with his close friend Dick Vermeil on the Eagles teams of the 1970s. A few years later, in the United States Football League, Peterson built the Philadelphia Stars into the league's dominant power, going to all three championship games and winning the last two. After the USFL folded, Peterson went into business in Philadelphia and waited for the right NFL offer to come. By the end of 1988, Lamar was desperate for winning, and ready for a seismic change.

On December 19, the day after the Chiefs' seventeenth non-playoff season in eighteen years and a season in which the Chiefs' eight home games had been played in front of more than a quarter-million empty seats, Lamar introduced Peterson as the new president, general manager, and chief operating officer of the team. With Peterson's new job—he would occupy Steadman's old office—Steadman moved to the Hunt Midwest offices downtown, where he became the Chiefs' chairman of the board.

The firing of Gansz, Steadman's departure from Arrowhead, and Peterson's arrival marked a symbolic end to Lamar's most trying decade. Norma noticed a more relaxed figure by that Christmas. On January 1, 1989, Lamar made his annual weigh-in, the source of year-long competitions that he had with Buzz Kemble, and registered a deceptive 180¾, which he noted with scrupulous honesty in his personal log was not entirely accurate "(sick – 188 real wt)".

But he'd done more than just survive. He had managed to remain outwardly upbeat through much of the discouraging decade. In disposition and worldview, Lamar fit William James' definition of someone blessed with healthy-mindedness: "I mean those who, when unhappiness is offered or proposed to them, positively refuse to feel it, as if it were something mean and wrong."

No one saw this more clearly than Norma. "He was such a positive person that he was always looking to the future and thinking positively about the next thing he was going to do," she said. "He just really remained in a good mindset about almost everything. He was really amazing. So I didn't feel that *he* felt in turmoil. He always believed that the sun was going to come up tomorrow. He was the ultimate Scarlett O'Hara."

Three months later, on April 4, 1989, he settled the last of his silver-related lawsuits. It was now time to separate his financial interests from his brothers, and Lamar did so by forming the umbrella company Unity Hunt. In contrast to the six-letter words beginning with P, he chose Unity to symbolize himself and his four children. Having witnessed the tension between H. L.'s families, Lamar was determined that Lamar, Jr., Sharron, Clark, and Daniel would feel equally loved, equally cared for, and on equal financial footing. The company would handle all of Lamar's interests. One of the keys to staying out of bankruptcy was his decision, at Steadman and Seigfreid's behest, to sell Hunt Midwest (the real-estate, amusement park, and mining interests based in Kansas City) to the four children, transferring that asset to the next generation, while at the same time generating the cash out of their trusts to help him pay off his settlement in the Minpeco case.

The president and CEO of the new company was Jim Holland, a serious-minded engineer by trade who had developed a specialty in running conglomerates. Though Holland had a background in football (he had once worked for Bud Adams's KSA Industries), at Unity Hunt his focus was on the conventional business side, so that Lamar could focus on sports.

It would be an oversimplification to say that the money he made from his family's oil properties had allowed him to be adventuresome in sports for three decades, and that now the sports ventures would have to fund themselves. But there would be less margin for error in the future, and more pressure on his sporting properties to perform. He'd made one other important decision during the decade, deciding to hold on to his stake in the Chicago Bulls, despite some of his advisers urging him to sell what had been a traditional money-loser.

"He didn't have the freedom to do some things that he'd been able to do in the past," said his financial assistant Wayne Henry. "Tennis was still going then, though soccer was over. He still had the Chiefs. We had lost Penrod Drilling [and would later sell Placid Oil] . . . and those had been throwing off some cash. The realization was that we were going to have some crunches."

Coming out of "the silver crisis"—the family would refer to the ordeal by those words for decades to come—Lamar was humbled, shaken, and considerably less wealthy, but unbowed. Paul Harvey, on his nationally syndicated show, said "Some people say the Hunt Brothers have lost their shirts; they're just loosening their neckties." It was a little more severe than that, especially for Bunker and Herbert, but as Lamar emerged from the long decade, he could look forward to a life that was substantially similar to the one he had enjoyed prior to the silver calamity.

In spite of Lamar's unsinkable equanimity, the trial inevitably left scars. Margaret, particularly, was furious at Herbert and Bunker for what she viewed as an obviously foolish ploy. Norma, always protective of Lamar, was similarly disappointed in his brothers. "She blames them for what happened to Lamar," said Jim Seigfreid. "And I've got to agree with her in many respects. He got sucked in on it."

But through it all—the torched decade of embarrassing headlines, bankruptcy threats, lawsuits, two players' strikes, countless depositions, the demise of soccer, and the marginalization of tennis—Lamar had never lost that sense of belief that a better time was just around the corner. And now, less than three weeks after finalizing the silver fallout, he felt himself turning that corner. On April 22, he flew to Kansas City, so he could spend the weekend at Arrowhead, for the 1989 NFL Draft, intently watching Carl Peterson begin to rebuild his football team.

CHAPTER FIFTEEN

RENAISSANCE

Around the younger Peterson, Lamar was revived, working alongside someone who brought an entirely fresh perspective to both the game and the business of football, a young man's maniacal work ethic, and a more recent history of success. The morning of their first draft, before Peterson used the fourth overall pick to select Derrick Thomas, the personable and highly motivated linebacker out of Alabama, Lamar was in the Chiefs' draft room, laughing with the rest of the men when Peterson said, "Okay, let's get this right. If we're drafting this high again, we're all going to be out of a job."

The tanned, restless, and ultracompetitive outsider, Peterson took the lofty titles of President, General Manager, and Chief Operating Officer. Despite his economic and marketing experience, Peterson brought a blend of talents uniquely suited to the modern game. After building the Eagles team that went to the Super Bowl under Dick Vermeil, he'd moved to the Philadelphia Stars of the USFL, where he constructed from scratch the team that dominated the league. Previously, most "football people" dealt with football alone and left business concerns to an administrative staff. But Peterson was part of a new breed that, following Tex Schramm's trail-blazing example with the Cowboys, thrived at both.

The changed mood in Arrowhead was profound, as were the necessary physical alterations—Jack Steadman vacating his regal office inside Arrowhead to take up space at an office in downtown Kansas City, where he could often be seen dining (usually alone) at the bustling Italian Gardens restaurant and adjusting to his time out of the limelight. Lamar had dealt with Steadman on a daily basis for nearly thirty years, and he continued to remain close to him even after the move. But it was now Carl Peterson's show.

Lamar gave him wide latitude and Peterson used it; he commissioned some market research studies during that spring of 1989 and discovered what Lamar had long sensed but couldn't quite articulate: The existing fan base was an aging, dispirited lot, insisting not on instant success or playoff spots but rather a sense of credibility. Two demands stood out: Make the team respectable, and don't change the announcers (radio host Bill Grigsby was a Kansas City staple, and Len Dawson—still doing the nightly newscast at 6 and 10—was the single most beloved athlete in Kansas City sports history).

Rather than making any boasts or empty slogans, Peterson developed a series of TV commercials, shot in gritty black and white, that showed players working out in preparation for the new season, and closed with the phrase, "No Promises, No Excuses." He also made the rounds, with players, season-ticket sales executives, and other team reps, throughout Kansas and Missouri, but also Nebraska, Iowa, Arkansas, and Oklahoma, covering much the same ground Lamar had back in 1963 when he was making his case for the Chiefs to be "not just Kansas City's team, but mid-America's team."

Peterson's first choice as head coach, his close friend Vermeil, turned him down. He was casting about for other candidates when one of the best coaches in the NFL suddenly became available. Marty Schottenheimer had just led the Browns to their fourth straight playoff season, and his '88 season was particularly impressive in light of a plague of quarterback injuries. Yet after the season, Browns owner Art Modell and Schottenheimer had clashed over his assistants, and he resigned. Within days, Peterson hired Schottenheimer and began to stabilize that crucial position. Where the Chiefs had been through five coaches over the previous twelve seasons, Schottenheimer would man the helm for the next decade, the longest tenure other than Stram.

The Chiefs had been casting about for nearly two decades, looking for a coach who could return the franchise to its glory days of the 1960s. In Schottenheimer, they found a man who was certainly not slick but who exuded an undeniable authority and got results. His teams were smart, tough, aggressive, and fundamentally sound.

"The best way to realize success in the National Football League," Schottenheimer said at his introductory press conference, "is to expect it." There were no moral victories for Schottenheimer. After the Chiefs fought to an epic 10–10 tie with his old team, the Cleveland Browns, missing a victory by two missed field goals by the usually reliable Nick Lowery, the flight back to Kansas City was deathly silent. "I thought Marty was going to throw Nick off the plane," said one Chiefs staffer. Schottenheimer's fundamental approach and Teutonic resolve worked as well in Kansas City as it had in Cleveland, and the results were nearly instantaneous: The team went 8-7-1 in 1989, barely missing the playoffs, then went 11–5 in 1990, advancing to the postseason for only the second time in nineteen seasons.

Schottenheimer soon developed an almost reverent affection for Lamar. Like so many others, he was struck by Lamar's humility. One day, early in his tenure as the Chiefs' coach, Schottenheimer was sitting in a meeting with Peterson and scouting director Whitey Dovell in Dovell's office. Without a word, Lamar ducked his head in the door, then sat down on a chair near the door. After a few seconds and a natural break in the conversation, he asked the men, "Pardon me, do you mind if I intrude?" before asking a question about the merits of a particular player the team was scouting.

And like the best football coaches, Schottenheimer didn't just change the personality of the team but its character as well. His teams did things right, playing sound, bruising defense and conservative, ball-control offense. For the first time since Stram's heyday, Lamar and Chiefs fans felt the team's heightened discipline and rectitude were reflected in its onfield performance.

The change in culture on the field was matched by one off the field as well. It wasn't just the wins in Arrowhead that were different; Peterson helped transform the gameday experience, encouraging tailgating outside the stadium, adding rock music at key intervals (becoming one of the early teams to pump the opening chords of the Rolling Stones' "Start Me Up" prior to kickoff), as well as moving the team's radio contract to an FM rock station that would bring a younger audience, in recognition that both football and rock music were now part of the same modern American mainstream.

In the Chiefs' offices, the personality was already changing. When the new vice-president of administration Tim Connolly, one of Peterson's hires, showed up for his first day of work, there were several people missing from the office. Connolly asked about his staff and was told they were in a Bible study class that met each Monday morning. Connolly found the meeting, walked into the room, and summarily told the attendees that while he respected what they were doing, there were no longer going to be extracurricular meetings on company time.

"It was a dysfunctional place," said Connolly. "Lamar was unbelievably loyal. There should have been major, major changes long before they happened."

While the moves could be wrenching, there was also a sense of flinty Eastern professionalism that was transplanted to the Midwest. The dated costumes of ushers were scrapped and replaced. The colt Warpaint was cast aside for the new mascot, KC Wolf. And the cheerleaders' costumes were updated (at a considerable savings on fabric). Peterson changed the culture without disrespecting the team's history. The Super Bowl trophy the team won remained on the first-floor lobby outside the elevators, a constant reminder of the team's past, and its future goal. An organization of former players, the Chiefs Ambassadors, were formed, as a liaison to the past, and another method of community outreach. Watching from Dallas, visiting Kansas City frequently, Lamar loved it all. In place of the queasy sense of worried hope that pervaded much of the past twenty years, he now shared much of Schottenheimer's quiet, purposeful confidence.

The team's season-ticket base of 26,000 in 1988 grew within four years to more than 71,000, with a waiting list of 15,000, and the Chiefs would lead the league in attendance six times during the '90s. By opening day of the 1991 season, when the Chiefs played in front of a sellout crowd of 74,246 in beating the Atlanta Falcons, 14–3, the entire gameday experience at Arrowhead had changed. Arriving with everything from $4.98 disposable burger grills to full pig-on-a-spit roasters, Chiefs fans raised pre-game tailgating to a kind of culinary performance art.

By then, the old guard of Chiefs fans, many who'd parked their cars in residential driveways close to 22nd and Brooklyn in the Municipal Stadium days, had been joined by a new breed, often younger professionals, many of whom lived across the state line in the affluent residential developments of Johnson County, Kansas. What both groups shared was an intense, somewhat thin-skinned pride in their city, the almost quaint notion that it mattered, a great deal, what people thought of the city.

On November 6, 1991, the Chiefs played host to *Monday Night Football* for the first time in eight years. For a city that had always been self-conscious about its sense of big-league status and had resented being overlooked the previous season, when the Chiefs went to the playoffs, it was a coming-out party. Derrick Thomas, driving to the stadium from I-70 east of the city, came up over the rise and got his first glimpse of the stadium—lights already on in the late afternoon and clouds of barbecue smoke emanating over the hill. "I smelled it before I got there," Thomas said. "It was amazing."

Lamar flew in that morning, joined by the regulars Richey and Kemble. He had been particularly excited before that game, reveling in the crowd outside the stadium and the electricity inside. That night, Thomas would terrorize the Bills' left tackle Will Wolford, and the Arrowhead crowd would rock the stadium, as the Chiefs rolled to a 33–6 win over the defending AFC champions. Lamar, cheering from the open-air suite, provided high-fives to his family and friends. Tony Dungy, then an assistant on the Chiefs' staff, would call it the loudest crowd he'd ever heard. (When Dungy returned home that night, he had a call from a neighbor exclaiming, "Tony—*we never sat down!*")

The confluence of success on the field, confidence in the front office, a terrific stadium experience, and smart marketing were coming together to make Arrowhead the place to be in the 1990s, just as Municipal Stadium had been in the late '60s. The city was in the throes of a second honeymoon with the Chiefs. What the team meant to the city was no less real for being so ineffable. As Mike Davis, a Kansas City attorney put it, "you'll never get 100,000 people together because you bought a Van Gogh at the Nelson Gallery. Sports is the principal unifying force in the metro area."

Outside the stadium on game days, the parking lot became a haven for tailgating and barbecuing, while inside the raucous crowd developed an intimidating reputation, its volume and intensity often marring opposing teams' on-field communications—with John Elway and the Broncos' offense whistled for seven false-start penalties in a 1993 Monday night game. The Chiefs and Arrowhead had become a social magnet, the games serving as a cohesive, mobilizing event that occurred with less regularity in disparate modern societies. "Without the Chiefs and the Royals," said Kansas City Mayor Emanuel Cleaver, "we'd be Omaha . . . Wichita . . . Des Moines."

As the season-ticket rolls increased, Lamar took an even deeper interest in the profile of the Chiefs fans. He began tracking how many different states they came from. And as the dismay of the '80s receded, he began to find a renewed sense of sanctuary at Arrowhead. Flying in the night before the game, the family might stop at Stephenson's Old Apple Farm restaurant, with Lamar always savoring the apple fritters, then head to the stadium. For Norma, the pristine view out of the family's Arrowhead apartment—of the lit field in an empty stadium—had always evoked for her memories of *Eloise at the Plaza*. Lamar, if anything, loved it even more. Weather permitting, he'd head down to the field with one of the children to kick the football around. And as the sense of occasion surrounding game days grew in the '90s, so did the sense of promise on the eve of a big game.

Even in the grim years of the '70s and '80s, Lamar would often jog the two miles around the perimeter of the sports complex early in the morning, before the gates opened. He still went through his paces in the '90s, but now added more leisurely strolls, walking the grounds a couple of hours before kickoff, interacting with fans.

And his focus returned to its previous levels of acuity. His reading was voracious and no error was too small to correct. Prior to a Chiefs–Broncos game in 1992, the *Dallas Morning News* ran a small note in the midst of a capsulized game preview noting that Elway had thrown 24 touchdowns and 10 interceptions in his career against Kansas City. A day later, Lamar wrote *Morning News* sports editor Dave Smith to note "the Elway touchdown and interception numbers were reversed in the News' 'Preview' . . . I know these numbers seem strange, especially since the Chiefs have such a hard time beating Elway . . . No reply needed—just wanted to make sure y'all had the numbers correct for the future."

Over more than a year during 1990 and '91, Lamar began pulling some old files and memorabilia from his early days in the AFL, and bringing them to Kansas City during game weekends to sort through them. By the middle of 1991, he had covered the floor of one room of the apartment with pictures, decals, old pennants, and pages from game programs, all the while sifting through additional boxes of pictures and files of old programs. He'd decided that he wanted to assemble a collage celebrating the franchise's 30-year history. By the time he finished it, the "30-year history wall" had become the "31-year history wall," required a graphic designer for consultation, and contained two banks of video screens with highlights of the team's greatest triumphs. Lamar invited all the team's employees for a small ceremony at the unveiling, featuring brief remarks from a Chiefs player from each decade of the team's history. "Hundreds of memos went back and forth on that project," said Chiefs PR director Bob Moore. It was one of Lamar's scrapbooks writ large, and was put on display in the foyer of the Chiefs' indoor practice facility, where a new generation of players could get a sense of the team's history.

Maybe it was being rid of the silver crisis and all its accompanying worries. Maybe it was being re-energized by Peterson and the ascendant football team. For whatever reason, Lamar—who always cared passionately about the team—seemed more fully engaged than he had been for decades.

At the end of the 1992 season, the mother of Chiefs' defensive back Kevin Ross died. In the days leading up to the team's playoff game, Ross returned to Camden, New Jersey, to attend the funeral. He was in the back, waiting for the ceremony to start, when one of the pallbearers came to him and said, "Hey, Kevin, guess who's here? Your *owner.*"

As Ross walked out he saw, in the back of the church, Lamar, who had flown out unannounced, rented a car, and come to the memorial service.

"I will never forget that as long as I live," said Ross. Afterward, as Lamar and Ross embraced, he emphasized to Ross that he was in the thoughts of everyone in his "Chiefs family." And then he was on his way.

The same was true of past Chiefs' greats as well. When Buck Buchanan was dying of cancer, Lamar came to his south Kansas City home and sat in the kitchen, answering the phones for three days, then traveling with Buchanan's widow, Georgia, to find a burial plot. (His penchant for symmetry existed in all matters; he picked out matching headstones for Buck and Georgia.)

•

By 1989, Lamar was in his late fifties, even as he had a young son who was only a teenager. Those in the family noticed a kinship between Daniel Hunt and his father. Just as Lamar had been the youngest of a big, boisterous family and had grown up after that family's most formative events, so it was with Daniel. Quiet, arguably more sensitive than his siblings (just as Lamar had been), Daniel showed an affinity for art, scouting out the family's Sotheby's catalogs when they'd arrive in the mail. By Daniel's eleventh birthday, Lamar was bragging to friends about walking into the Chicago Art Institute and hearing Daniel correctly spot, from across the room, a painting he'd never seen before as a Van Gogh.

By the summer of 1989, after two years in the internship program at Goldman Sachs, Clark had returned to Dallas and began working for Unity Hunt as well. Working around his father for the first time, he quickly noticed one thing: Given the choice, Lamar would spend "about 120 percent" of his time on the sports field.

But Clark, resolute, serious, purposeful, athletic, was every bit his father's son. He was welcomed by many of Lamar's aides because, though he shared his father's love of sports, he was also more practical and far more sophisticated about money.

With both Lamar, Jr., and Sharron, Lamar continued to make a concerted effort to include them in work and play, both business projects and family vacations. When Lamar, Jr., got married in 1981 and Sharron in 1987, Lamar constructed elaborate collages of their lives—from young pictures swimming, vacations, school photos, old notes—in a monument to be displayed at the wedding receptions.

Lamar, Jr., was the one family member who actually moved to Kansas City, playing in the Kansas City Symphony. Sharron had been the most rebellious, going through a slow maturation process and a failed marriage in the 1980s. Even as she recognized his loving intent, his only daughter felt as though she couldn't truly reach out to her father.

"A lot of the dialogue with my dad was very superficial, unfortunately," Sharron said. "He wasn't a person that would go very deep with me on stuff.

And if I would try to draw him out sometimes, he would globalize the answer. He would deflect. He didn't get in depth on stuff."

By the early '90s, Sharron needed for Lamar to get deep. Living in Florida, where her first marriage had ended, she'd begun another relationship that had ended poorly, and felt herself cut adrift. In May of 1991, she decided she was ready to move back to Dallas, and she asked Lamar to come help her. He flew out and they drove a U-Haul and her car from Jacksonville back to Dallas.

"Dad, of course, starts planning," said Sharron. "He says, 'We are going to trade drivers every 75 miles, because it breaks it up.' So he would drive my little car, and I would drive the truck. Then he draws up one of his little schemes—you know, the stopping points. So he calculated that we could stop in Tallahassee and get a motel room and watch part of the Bulls playoff game. So we timed it where we stopped in Tallahassee at a motel, and they didn't want to rent us a room, but the manager, of course, recognized Dad, and said, 'Come in my office and watch the game.' So we ordered burgers in from the restaurant there and watched part of the Bulls game. When you have a rock star for a father, you can go into a motel in Tallahassee and the guy is going to know who he is."

Two years later, Sharron married again, more happily this time; her husband, David Munson, was also from a well-to-do family. And by then, she had come closer to making her peace with her father's strengths and weaknesses. "I felt closer to him in some ways," she said. "He was a hard person to get close to, though. If you asked him something he wasn't comfortable with, he just wasn't going to answer. If it was painful or difficult for him to respond, he just wouldn't respond to me about stuff."

•

Just as Lamar was emerging from his daunting decade of the '80s, one of his most cherished loves—American soccer—was also revived. Back in 1983, the United States had pushed hard to be the host of the 1986 World Cup (Colombia, originally chosen to host, had withdrawn from the role in 1982) but had lost out to Mexico. A year later, when the NASL died, the sport as a commercial property was left for dead.

But nearly two decades of zealotry and youth soccer had bred a solid network, and on July 4, 1988, the United States was awarded the host nation's role for the 1994 World Cup. At the time, even Lamar thought it was "a bit crazy" that a country that had proved itself so apathetic toward soccer might actually be hosting the world's biggest sports event. But he had remained an avid fan, not just for the World Cup, but also amateur events, like the Dallas Cup and SMU's soccer games, as Clark starred on a team that would reach the NCAA quarterfinals in both his junior and senior seasons (and Lamar would miss a half-dozen Chiefs games—more than he'd missed in the team's entire history before—to watch his son play soccer).

On November 19, 1989, when UCLA grad Paul Caligiuri scored a goal to lift the Americans over Trinidad and Tobago, the USA qualified for its first world cup in forty years. Lamar, after flying back from the gripping 10–10 Chiefs tie with Cleveland, saw the goal in his living room.

As soon as FIFA announced the schedule for the 1990 World Cup in Italy, Lamar began surveying his schedule, to see how many games he, Norma, and Dan could attend (Clark and other family and friends were coming later). On one legal pad, he began making an elaborate chart, calculating how many games—and museums and antique stores—they could take in, while getting to the maximum number of stadiums.

In addition to the McNutts, 1990 would mark Buzz and Dorothy Kemble's first World Cup visit, and knowing Kemble to be a soccer agnostic, Lamar worked hard to make sure he would see the best the game had to offer. Two months before the tournament began, he composed a four-page handwritten note preparing Buzz for the quarterfinal he was slated to see at Stadio Artemio Franchi. He'd ordered them the Category 3 tickets, explaining, "I do not believe there is a significant difference in where one sits at a soccer game . . . these prices are all pretty well shocking as it is!"

"It is very difficult to theorize on who the opponents will be in this game," he wrote, "except by looking at the 'seedings' which would indicate it might be Brazil vs. Belgium. If so y'all will be seeing the #1 most attractive style of play over the last 25 years or so (Brazil)."

Lamar, Norma, and Dan left for Italy on American Flight 66 (flying coach, per Lamar's custom), taking the overnight flight to Madrid and then making a connection in Milan. They attended eight different games over the fortnight of the group phase. Once the single-elimination portion of the tournament began, the itinerary became even more ambitious. June 24 began in Turin, as they watched a matchup of former champions, with Argentina eliminating Brazil, 1–0. As the game ended, they raced for the rental car and drove the 90 miles on the A4 to Milan, for West Germany's 2–1 win over the Netherlands, in the rematch of the '74 final. Two days later, the Hunts and McNutts were in Verona, for Yugoslavia's 2–1 upset of Spain in extra time, then headed south to make the kickoff for England's showdown against Belgium, won by the

English on David Platt's late volley in the 119th minute, just seconds before the game was to go to penalty kicks.

Years later, Daniel would tell Bob McNutt that that he loved traveling to World Cups because on those trips, his father was just a fan—still avid, still fascinated with stadiums and fans and contacts, but without a financial and administrative stake in the proceedings.

They were at Stadio San Paolo for Argentina's semi-final elimination of host Italy, with Diego Maradona converting the telling penalty kick. Lamar and his group were sitting near his old NASL comrade Clive Toye. "He was sitting a row behind me and to my right," said Toye. "And in front of him was this well-known Argie character, seen at so many games, thumping away madly and loudly on this bloody great drum. Not quite the same as sitting in the best seats in the house."

A day later, on July 4 in Stadio delle Alpi in Turin, the Hunts and McNutts watched the rematch of the '66 final, with West Germany eliminating England on penalty kicks. Even the stultifying final between West Germany and Argentina, which featured another red card for the defending champs, and the Germans winning on a late penalty kick, offered a sense of gravity and occasion, as Lamar watched Franz Beckenbauer—who had captained the West Germans to the Cup in 1974 before coming to NASL to play for the Cosmos—now managing the world champions.

It was leaving the final on that day in Italy that Lamar articulated what almost every American in attendance had been thinking: "Can you believe, in four years, this is going to be in America?"

It was a month after Italy 1990 when Lamar finally surrendered to the inevitable, and shut down World Championship Tennis. The enterprise, so essential to the growth of the professional game in the late '60s and early '70s, had become marginalized early in the '80s, and withered steadily through the rest of the decade. It was not so much a failure of marketing as it was a function of time.

"He fulfilled a crucial role," said Mike Davies, "but then the players took over, and the role didn't need to be filled any longer."

The announcement came in August 1990, when Lamar and Al Hill, Jr., called a press conference after the Tournament of Champions at the West Side Tennis Club in Forest Hills. There was no combativeness or resentment at the press conference, only Lamar and Al's agreement that the time had come. "The decision to terminate operations was a business judgment based on the realities of the economics in sports marketing," said Al, "as well as the difficult circumstances of an independent company operating a group of high-quality tennis tournaments on a financially viable basis."

For weeks after the announcement, the letters poured in—from Cliff Drysdale and John Newcombe, Arthur Ashe and Rod Laver, Stan Smith and other pros—all expressing regret about Lamar's departure from the tennis scene. Arthur Ashe offered a note of caution ("A friend of mine used to say that 'Some people can't stand prosperity.' Pro tennis may come to that if it doesn't watch out"). Frew McMillan congratulated Lamar on the WCT imprimatur that became the template for the modern tennis tournament ("Stylish, with grace and handsomely rewarding. They were the role models which successors have rarely equaled"). Stan Smith wrote that he "will always consider you and you[r] organization as the founders of our modern professional game."

Perhaps it was the fact that after more than a decade of uncertainty, he was able to return to his passions. Maybe it was the optimism from the first season of the Peterson-Schottenheimer regime. For whatever reason, Lamar seemed less gutted about the demise of WCT than he had about the end of the Tornado and, later, the NASL.

For Adams and Wayne Henry and those in the inner circle, the measure was necessary to stop the financial bleeding. Although Al, Jr., recalled some modest profits, the perspective was less rosy from where Wayne Henry sat. "I don't remember a profitable year," said Henry. "I don't want to dispute what Al said. But it was the prize money and the appearance fees and all the player contracts, that was why it never really made any money."

The tennis world had turned its back on Lamar, but it wouldn't take long for that to change. In 1993, he was inducted into the International Tennis Hall of Fame, an honor that left him, in his words, "flattered, honored, and flabbergasted, if those words go together."

•

For the NFL, 1993 was a watershed year. It brought about the long-awaited Collective Bargaining Agreement between the league and its players, one that had been years in the making. "My father was so glad that period in the league's history was over," said Clark, "and he recognized how important the salary cap was in terms of competitive balance."

At the end of the '92 season, after a stifling 17–0 playoff loss to San Diego, the Chiefs were again wrestling with the same problem they'd faced since Len

Dawson grew old: They were without a first-class quarterback and hadn't been able to develop one through the draft. But the prospect of free agency and the salary cap meant that player movement would be accelerated, that football GMs would become more active, like their baseball counterparts.

In San Francisco, the 49ers had been harboring two all-pro caliber quarterbacks in Joe Montana, with four Super Bowl rings already to his credit, and the talented understudy Steve Young, who seemed more than ready to take over for the aging Montana. The advent of the salary cap meant that, even if they'd wanted to, the 49ers couldn't keep both. And in the spring of 1993, Peterson called Lamar to tell him that the team might have a shot to trade for the already legendary Montana. The window of opportunity was dangerously small: Montana was already thirty-six, and he'd missed all of the 1992 season with an elbow injury. But reports were that he was healed, and the prospect of bringing Montana's quarterbacking magic to Kansas City was irresistible.

The trade, when executed, prompted an unprecedented outpouring of anticipation and excitement in Kansas City. Montana was back on the cover of *Sports Illustrated*, next to the headline, "Kansas City, Here I Come," and the team announced it would install the West Coast offense in 1993, to maximize Montana's value.

It led to a season for the Chiefs that was unlike any that had ever preceded it. For the first time since the early 1970s, they were one of football's marquee teams, among the national leaders in merchandise sales, prime-time TV appearances, training-camp visitors, and road-game attendance. The offseason trade for Montana and the free-agent signing of outcast Raiders star Marcus Allen further cemented their reputation as a potential Super Bowl team.

As the Chiefs were marching to their first division title in twenty-two seasons, Lamar made even more midweek trips to Kansas City, to work on ticket marketing campaigns and to finalize plans for the Chiefs' pavilion, a gathering spot for banquets and other functions.

The week before Christmas, the Chiefs rallied after a sluggish performance against San Diego, pulling out a 28–24 win. The following Sunday, they sat Montana in a 30–10 loss to the Vikings, but they clinched the division title anyway.

On January 8, 1994, Arrowhead played host to just its second home playoff game, with Montana rallying the Chiefs late against the Pittsburgh Steelers, tying the game on a late drive that featured a fourth-down touchdown pass to Tim Barnett. Next, they traveled to Houston to face the Oilers, the hottest team in football with an eleven-game win streak. As Lamar sat in the Astrodome, next to Norma and Tom Richey, he watched Montana and Allen, and the Derrick

Thomas–inspired defense rise up to sack Warren Moon nine times, forcing five fumbles, as the Chiefs rallied from a 10–0 deficit to win 28–20. The Chiefs had won three league titles in the AFL years, but since the merger they had yet to play for a conference championship, which since 1986 had carried Lamar's name.

"We didn't have to say anything that week," said Marty Schottenheimer. "Everybody knew what we were playing for."

Montana was at the apex of his rock-star status, and so the entire week before the game, Lamar and the team faced a media blitz unmatched by any game since Super Bowl IV. Kansas City was giddy. Never mind Red Friday; the city was bedecked in red throughout the week. Radio stations were playing the novelty song "The Schottenheimer Polka," and Montana sightings were being reported on radio and TV.

When the game started, though, it was a reminder of how crucial home-field advantage could be. Buffalo gashed the Chiefs defensive line early, setting up Jim Kelly for an early touchdown pass to Andre Reed. In the last minute of the first half, the Chiefs trailed 20–6, but were driving for a score to narrow the margin to a touchdown. On second down and goal at the Bills' 5, Montana found running back Kimble Anders free over the middle, and hit him in stride near the end zone. But the sure-handed Anders bobbled the ball, and it was intercepted by Buffalo's Henry Jones.

Lamar had seen thousands of football games in his life, and he knew what the turn of events meant. But he put on a brave face at halftime, visited briefly with Ralph Wilson, and then went back to the second half. Three plays into the third quarter, Montana was knocked out of the game, sustaining a concussion, and the Chiefs—nearly a quarter-century since their last Super Bowl—were to be denied again, as Buffalo eased to a 30–13 win.

And just that quickly, the months of momentum and excitement and promise dissipated.

"Always in the locker room, win or lose, Mr. Hunt would come down and say something to each player," said Kevin Ross. "But this time, I walked over to him, and I apologized, and gave him a hug. It was the only time I ever saw him cry."

As the team boarded the plane for the flight back to Kansas City, somber and defeated, Marty and Pat Schottenheimer sat in their usual spot in the front of the team charter. Before the plane took off, Lamar reached out and touched Schottenheimer's shoulder and said, "Don't worry—we beat them worse at our place than they beat us at their place."

"I didn't know whether to punch Lamar in the face or kiss him on the mouth," said Schottenheimer. "But I appreciated what he was trying to do."

•

By the early 1990s, Jean Finn was working on thirty years as Lamar's secretary, executive assistant, personal banker, chief of staff, and gatekeeper. "She did not let anybody speak directly to Lamar that wasn't absolutely necessary," said one Hunt staffer. "You had to go through Jean; even his children spoke to Jean. And she made the decision whether they could speak to him or not." Norma would breeze straight through to the office, of course, and after returning to work for the company, Clark often strode right in. But almost everyone else went through Jean Finn.

In the midst of the broad range of responsibilities, she also continued doing the small jobs she'd begun for Lamar decades earlier. One of her duties was to keep track of how the original AFL franchises were doing since the merger. "If we are doing good, I tell somebody about it," Lamar said. "If we aren't, then I wait and let somebody ask me first."

Like Norma and the children, and many of his closest advisers, Finn had grown protective of Lamar, and she was often suspicious of and standoffish to newcomers. But she'd learned not to lecture him. Many afternoons in the early '90s, after putting in five to six hours of work, Lamar would emerge from a conference room with his weathered satchel, stop by Jean's desk to pick up tickets and cash, and rush out to meet Norma and catch a plane. If he did that two or three times a week, it usually meant that it was spring, and the Bulls were in the playoffs.

One of the pleasures of the late 1980s that kept Lamar going through the endless court cases and meetings with the IRS was the rise of his basketball team. The Bulls, for which Lamar continued to be silent minority partner, had fallen on hard times by the mid-'80s. In a league in which it was much, much easier for a team to make the playoffs than in the NFL, the team went through a period of seven seasons where they qualified for the postseason just once.

Then, on June 19, 1984, they selected Michael Jordan of North Carolina with the third pick in the NBA draft, and the franchise's fortunes were transformed. It didn't come instantly, but with Jordan leading the league in scoring, Lamar started to travel to Chicago occasionally. By the time the Bulls reached the finals for the first time, against the Lakers in 1991, Lamar was out from under the bonds of the silver crisis. That year, when the Bulls won their first title, the spring was dominated with frequent trips to Chicago.

Carl Peterson remembered a game when Lamar invited him and his new wife, Lori, to see a game with him and Norma. They were joined by Daniel but had only four tickets together on courtside. Carl volunteered to take the odd ticket, but Lamar wouldn't hear of it. He said he'd go up first and they could change at halftime. But of course he didn't tell anyone else where his upper-deck seats were. And he didn't come down at the half. "It became clear to me that he was just as happy up there in the nosebleed seats as he would have been at courtside," said Peterson.

As the Bulls titles piled up in the early '90s, even Bulls executive Steve Schanwald noticed that Lamar had never actually met Michael Jordan. There were opportunities to do so—quiet afternoon shootarounds, or jubilant locker rooms—but Lamar was always aware of streaks, and, after the second title in 1992, he grew superstitious and decided he didn't want to wreck another streak.

"He absolutely would not do that," said Norma. "The boys would think, 'Oh, this is my chance'—if Dad would just go over there with me and say something like—totally unlike him—'I was one of the original owners of the Chicago Bulls.' But he wasn't even about to do that. That was a true superstition with him. Because otherwise he would have loved meeting Michael Jordan, I know."

When Schanwald offered again to make the introductions one evening, as the Bulls were chasing a third straight title, Lamar demurred. "I wouldn't want to jinx him, or me," he said, half-jokingly. But only half.

Though he no longer had tennis to occupy his time after August 1992, Lamar found another avenue for work. He had accepted the calling to be a full-time unpaid volunteer chair of the Dallas organizing host committee, along with Jim Graham.

Lamar had worked diligently on Kansas City's behalf to be one of the host cities for the '94 World Cup, but Kansas City was passed over in favor of other cities (the lack of direct international flights from Europe was a big problem), one of them being Dallas.

Graham had met Lamar in Italy in 1990, while he was working, as president of the Dallas Parks and Recreation Board, to represent the Dallas Bid Committee. After Dallas was named one of the nine cities to host World Cup games for '94, Mayor Annette Strauss asked the two men to co-chair the committee. They were instantly faced with the timeless problem of all host committees: A whisper of a budget, the governing body FIFA trying to off-load as many expenses as possible on the city government, and—in this case—a city government that was mostly ignorant of, if not outright hostile to, the effort.

"Nobody at Dallas City Hall knew what it *was*," said Graham.

The key point of the preparation was a 27-hour-long negotiation at Graham's office, with Hunt and Graham representing the Dallas host committee; FIFA, trying to deflect as many expenses as possible; and the City of Dallas, intent on doing the same.

For a magazine profile highlighting the Dallas effort, Lamar said, "My interest in the game today is primarily as a volunteer, and as a parent," citing Daniel's games at St. Mark's. But Lamar was too excited to be coy. When the reporter asked him how many games he'd see during the World Cup, he laughed and said, "If I told you how many games I'm going to, you'd think I was a lunatic!"

Bob McNutt, Bill's son and one of the only people that Lamar allowed to call him "Mr. Hunt," had made a suggestion before the '94 World Cup. "Wouldn't it be great," he suggested, "if we found a way to get to all nine venues?"

Lamar was captivated with the idea, and he freed up time in his schedule. The World Cup in '94 would again involve intricate planning. On the weekend of June 18–19, they met at 5:30 a.m. to fly from Love Field to Pontiac Airport in Detroit, where they caught a van to the Silverdome. It was the group stage game, with the USA facing Switzerland. The Silverdome was the only domed stadium used for the World Cup. Per FIFA rules, it meant that the stadium had to cover its artificial turf with trays of natural grass. When the Silverdome crew did so, they created a massive greenhouse effect and, on a summer day that was already hot, inside the non–air-conditioned stadium, the Hunt "traveling squad" of nine was subjected to the same sweltering conditions. Clark would remember the day feeling like "a moist oven." Dan Hunt, eighteen years old, was concerned about Bill McNutt—smoking all the while—succumbing to the heat. After the game, Lamar speculated that it would be "another hundred years" before anyone of Swiss extraction came to the States again. Lamar's group, wringing wet, got out of the dome and caught their charter from Detroit to Teterboro airport in New York, and arrived by van in the first half of the Italy–Ireland match at a teeming Meadowlands, then flew on to Washington, D.C. for a late dinner at the Prime Rib, before catching games at RFK Stadium the next two days.

One stop in '94 was in Foxboro, Massachusetts, where the Patriots' new owner, Robert Kraft, was also a soccer fan. As a member of the NFL's finance committee, Lamar had interviewed Kraft when he was applying to buy the Patriots earlier that year. Since then, the two had developed a friendship. At one of their first meetings, Lamar had congratulated Kraft on "the greatest logo in all of sports," the lobster with an extended claw holding a tennis racket that was the emblem for the Boston Lobsters, of the 1970s era World Team Tennis.

Kraft had noticed Lamar's quiet authority at NFL meetings, but at the World Cup he first had a sense of his relationship with fans.

"We had the old Foxboro stadium," Kraft said. "And we had 5,000 chair seats, with backs, and the rest was like a high school stadium, just metal benches. So we saved him seats, and he came to my office, and we had all the fancy folks from FIFA and everything. And we said, 'We've got these seats for you,' but no, he wanted to sit in the end zone with the real fans, which were the traveling foreigners."

This would be noted over and over by the soccer community. Everyone else on the World Cup Steering Committee wanted Category 1 seats, the premium midfield boxes. Though Lamar ordered Category 1 on a few special occasions, he was more than happy with Category 2 and Category 3 seats. Lamar's frugality certainly factored into the equation, but there was also his attraction to the supporters' culture at international soccer matches, which was somewhat muted among the dignitaries and other VIPs in the Category 1 seats.

Back in Dallas, on July 9, Lamar eagerly awoke on the morning of the last match of the tournament to be played in Dallas. After breakfast, he and the family drove to Fair Park for a pre-game function under a mammoth tent at Fair Park. Then it was the short walk over to the stadium. Fifty-five years after he'd watched his first Cotton Bowl football game; forty-two years since he'd sat on the bench, and played sparingly, for SMU; thirty-four years since he'd walked on to the field as the owner of the Dallas Texans of the new American Football League; and twenty-four years after he'd watched his Kansas City Chiefs take the field against the Dallas Cowboys as the world champions of professional football, Lamar climbed the bleachers at the refurbished Cotton Bowl to watch Brazil face Holland in the quarterfinal of the World Cup.

The House That Doak Built had been transformed, with more than 10,000 Brazilian fans chanting and singing, and nearly as many Dutch followers, dressed in their trademark orange, swaying in the midday sun.

Lamar remarked to McNutt that both teams were wearing their "change strips"—Brazil in its rarely seen blue jerseys and white shorts, the Netherlands wearing orange shorts and white tops in the Texas heat. After a scoreless first half dotted with real scoring opportunities, the game caught fire in the second half, with Bebeto sending a sharp cross that Romário volleyed into the net just a few minutes after the break, followed 10 minutes later by Bebeto breaking clear, sidestepping the charging Dutch goalkeeper to slot home the second goal that seemed to kill the game. But less than 2 minutes later, Dennis Bergkamp grabbed one back for the Dutch. Then, in the 76th minute, with Holland still calling for a handball, they equalized on a swerving corner headed in by Aron Winter. There in Dallas, where the Tornado had vanquished because of public indifference, the Cotton Bowl was pure bedlam, and fans were watching the best match of the '94 Cup. Branco's free kick in the 81st minute, darting around the wall and just inside the far post, put Brazil back up on top and sent the crowd back over the top. Afterward, lingering, still listening to the incessant din of the Brazil fans, watching the distraught Dutch supporters exiting slowly, Lamar was giddy with the moment, telling Richey it had been one of the greatest games—of any sport—to be played at the Cotton Bowl.

Ten days later, he and the family were at the Rose Bowl in Pasadena, for a final being seen by half a billion people around the world. Afterward, Lamar and Norma and the family sat in the stands, reveling in Brazil's win in penalty kicks. It was the completion of a remarkable month of soccer, with every ticket to every game having been sold. And now in a suburb of Los Angeles, the same city where in 1968 he'd staged an exhibition soccer match viewed by 1,200 people, Lamar was one of 104,000 to watch his second-favorite national side, Brazil, win their fourth World Cup.

As the Brazilian captain Dunga held the trophy aloft, Lamar snapped pictures. He could be seen, on the cover of the next week's issue of *Sports Illustrated*, on the far right of the frame in a blue dress shirt, with a camera over his face, shooting the same scene from behind as photographer Simon Bruty was shooting from in front.

•

It had already been a good football season, even before it started. After Lamar spent nearly a quarter-century pushing for it, the NFL finally instituted the two-point conversion rule, giving teams the option of running or passing for two points on the conversion after touchdown, instead of just kicking for one. Lamar had pushed for it during the merger committee meetings in the late 1960s but couldn't convince his NFL counterparts to try it. Now, in 1994, the competition committee voted it in. Lamar was roundly congratulated by the other owners after the announcement.

That fall, Lamar reveled further in the Chiefs' home-field advantage and relished the aesthetic change that he'd become convinced Arrowhead needed: the move to a natural grass field. The last remnants of the antiseptic Arrowhead were washed away with the carpet (but not before individual pieces of the Arrowhead turf were cut up to be sold as souvenirs). With the tailgating outside, the smart, engaged crowd inside, playing outdoors and on natural grass, the stadium had finally become, in the words of one writer, "the perfect place to watch a football game."

Lamar thrilled to Joe Montana's final season as a Chief, including a 24–17 win over his old team the 49ers early in the season, and a stirring Monday night duel in Denver, when he bested the late-game heroics of John Elway with a late drive of his own, and the go-ahead score with 7 seconds left. At the end of the year, the Chiefs once again fell short. They had been to the playoffs for five consecutive years, but they could not quite get over the hump.

Financially, the picture had drastically changed. In 1992, after the team sold out its games for the entire season in the preseason, the NFL's rich new TV contract came into play, and the team's local and regional marketing began to bear fruit, Lamar sat down for the annual meeting, in which the Chiefs would report record profits in the history of the division.

"I thought it was going to be this huge deal," said Tim Connolly. "We'd made more money in one year than the franchise had in 17 years combined. But Lamar didn't celebrate, and he didn't gloat—he just smiled and said, 'Okay,' and we moved on to the next thing. It's when I realized, finally, it wasn't about the money."

"It wasn't just that it wasn't a big deal," said Peterson. "It was that Jack Steadman was in the room, and Lamar didn't want to look like he was celebrating at Jack's expense."

Not merely financially but also artistically and spiritually, there was every sign indicating that Lamar was back. His Chiefs were succeeding, his twenty-five-year investment into the Bulls was starting to yield dividends both competitively and financially, he was out from under the onerous weight of the lawsuits of the previous decade, as well as the long run of losses from soccer and tennis investments. He was a healthy, engaged, spirited sixty-two-year-old man, and he'd already accomplished more than he could have dreamed of. After the chaos of the '80s, it seemed entirely understandable that he enjoy the relatively calm prosperity of the '90s.

Of course, that's not what happened. Because, in the end, he had one piece of unfinished business, and he had been quietly steeling himself for one more grand challenge.

CHAPTER SIXTEEN

"HAVEN'T WE DONE THIS BEFORE?"

In the hallways of Unity Hunt, the subject was strictly avoided, though for much of the early to mid-'90s, the air was pregnant with it. Lamar's wife, his children, his closest friends, and financial advisers all chose not to talk about it, though each was aware of the prospect, and most viewed it with trepidation, if not outright dread.

Yet the people who knew Lamar best also knew, deep down, that it wasn't going to go away.

The central promise that the United States Soccer Federation made to FIFA to get the World Cup to the United States for 1994 was that it would, after a decade without a major, first-division club soccer league, rebuild one to start sometime around 1994. In the rush to build the infrastructure to host the World Cup in '94, the USSF's vow to start a new league wasn't forgotten, but it became a lower-priority item.

Mark Abbott, one of the other lawyers at United States Soccer Federation President Alan Rothenberg's firm in Los Angeles, volunteered to put together a business plan for the new league. Abbott had been a soccer lifer, who'd played the sport in youth leagues growing up in Bloomington, Minnesota, and been a ball boy for the Minnesota Kicks of the NASL. The key to Abbott's proposal was its vision of the league structure as a single entity. Individual owners would operate the teams, but the contracts that players signed would be with the league, and so the league's salary cap would be mandated by the league.

On November 14, 1993, while Lamar was in Los Angeles for the Chiefs–Raiders game, he met with Rothenberg to discuss the upcoming World Cup, and Rothenberg left him with a copy of the confidential document, "Major

League Soccer, L.P., Business Plan and Confidential Memorandum," circulating to a few prospective investors.

Just over two weeks later, the day after the Chiefs beat Buffalo to move their record to a division-leading 8–3, Lamar was back in his office in Dallas, completing his detailed review of the prospectus, which he returned.

"Typical of Lamar," said Rothenberg, "he didn't just give it a cursory reading. He made an exacting review, with all these notes, and Post-its. It was amazing." The five-page letter included thirty-five references to Post-it flagged notes inside the proposal, as well as Lamar's conclusions.

In the main, Lamar gave the sort of fine-grained examination that was the product of thirty-five years of pro sports experience, commenting on the proposed schedule:

> The number of regular season games needs to be an even number. It is impossible to have an equitable schedule with an odd number (27 would mean 14 at home and 13 away—or vice versa—which would not be equitable)

Lamar also weighed in on the proposed salaries that were projected to average $70,000 ("I really believe the compensation for a 5-month soccer season should logically be considerably less than this because they can't produce the revenue to justify these types of salaries"). He stressed the value of the U.S. National Team, and the prospect of annual series with the Mexican and Canadian national teams; he also spoke of the appeal of the Canadian market, suggesting the desirability of at least a couple of Canadian franchises.

One of the tenets of Abbott's plan was the value of stadiums built expressly for soccer. While Lamar was in favor of this idea, he took issue with the prohibitive cost estimates, both in terms of specific expense ("two service tunnels 400 feet apart connecting to the field—not necessary") and aesthetics:

> . . . as designed—field could be overly wide—looks like the first row is 40 feet outside the soccer touch line, which if I calculate correctly, means the first row would be 73 feet from the football sideline. I appreciate that the design is primarily for soccer, but I can't envision why 40 feet would be needed for row one to the touch line and this will definitely make the stadium less useful for other events.

Lamar passed a copy of the prospectus and his comments to Clark before returning the material to Abbott, and Clark was struck by the unifying principle that animated Lamar—the search for competitive balance. "Twice there were references to equality of play," Clark said. "He talks about 'building a system that gives all teams a chance to be successful,' which is clearly something he believed in, that ties into revenue sharing in the NFL, ties to a cap in the NFL, which you were getting about this time. Plenty of people may have been of the mindset that we're better to have a system like the English Premier League or Major League Baseball, or the NASL, where you had the Cosmos. My father was always of the opinion that you have a much stronger league if you've got an equal chance to win."

Lamar was clearly intrigued. "Please don't take any of these comments negatively," he wrote to Abbott in conclusion. "My soccer experience is so influenced by the nightmare of the NASL of overpaying foreign players who were no real help in developing young American players—that I can't see repeating that mistake." And then, in the end, he emphasized his central point once more: "It's a game, and the attractiveness of the league will be based on the evenness of competition."

Through it all, and even after the meeting in Los Angeles later in the fall in which he sat down with Rothenberg, Lamar's professed position was one of a fan, not a potential investor. "He wasn't outwardly talking about getting involved," said Clark. "This was just helping Alan get this thing together, because it was part of what was required for the '94 World Cup is that we bring back Division I soccer, the deal with FIFA. He was just assisting that."

It wasn't lost on anyone in his inner circle that the sixty-two-year-old patriarch, working for two years as an unpaid volunteer coordinator of the Dallas Host Committee effort, was having a terrific time. Those closest to him noticed both his absorption into soccer and his punishing schedule. Like a lot of executives nearing retirement age, Lamar felt a sense of urgency to increase his output, to get more done while he had the time.

By late 1993, when the new executive assistant Susie Stephens was hired to help the ailing Jean Finn with Lamar's workload of correspondence, Lamar had three different offices on the nineteenth floor stacked with papers. "At one time, on a daily basis, he would exercise and walk and that sort of thing," said Stephens. "But it seems like, as he got older, all he did was work. It was like he didn't want to take any time at all away from his work time."

"He stopped doing the yearly assessments at the Cooper Clinic," said Lamar, Jr. "He used to love that—it was the greatest thing in the world; he'd train to get in shape for the physical. When soccer started up again, though, all that changed. And then it turns into pursuing the MLS, and he got completely off regular exercise."

All that would seem significant later. For the time being, in the mid-1990s, Lamar's friends and associates merely marveled at his otherworldly reserves of energy.

•

As he mulled a return to soccer in the summer of '95, Lamar made his annual trip to River Falls, Wisconsin, where the Chiefs had based their training camp since 1991. Just as he had in the '60s at William Jewell, Lamar came to River Falls and stayed in the dorm for a few nights, watching practice, pointedly not interrupting the coaches, and taking notes, ranging from the entirely personal (he would keep his own running list of which players he thought would make the team and which would be cut) to the practical, like sending memos to his staff, with ideas about better ways to reach the growing throng of Chiefs fans who would show up in Wisconsin to watch their team.

He would "scout" his team like any other fan, talking up to his friends (but never the coaching staff) the merits of some rookie or free agent. With Joe Montana retiring after the '94 season, expectations were low heading into '95. Peterson had signed another 49er quarterback, the little-known Steve Bono, to replace Montana. Conventional wisdom had the Chiefs, absent Montana, falling to last place in the AFC West. But six years into Schottenheimer's regime, he and Peterson had built a franchise that was bigger than any one player. From the first month of the season, the team's chemistry felt special. After going on the road to beat Seattle in their opener, the Chiefs battled the New York Giants, with Bono leading a late rally after an ineffective game and the Chiefs winning in overtime. A week later, against the arch-rival Raiders, James Hasty, the newly signed free agent, picked off a pass in overtime and returned it for a touchdown, sparking a massive, celebratory dogpile in the west end zone.

By the sixth game of the season, a Monday Nighter against San Diego, when the Chiefs won their third home overtime game of the season—Tamarick Vanover taking a punt 86 yards to the same end zone where Hasty had finished off the Giants—Arrowhead was becoming known as "the loudest outdoor stadium in football" and the site of an inimitable gameday experience.

On that Monday night, walking out of Arrowhead with Norma, Lamar was stopped by an ebullient, red-bedecked Chiefs fan, who pressed a five-dollar bill into his hand and told him, "Mr. Hunt, you are *not charging enough* for the entertainment you're providing! I want to give you some more money." At first,

Lamar cheerfully demurred, but the fan insisted, and Lamar finally relented. He was delighted by the gesture, and flashed the bill with the story to friends and family over the next week.

The Chiefs had the best defense in the AFC; they had a 13–3 record, and to open the playoffs, they drew the lightly regarded Indianapolis Colts, who'd qualified on the last week of the season, with a 9–7 record.

But game day dawned a bitter 11 degrees, with a wind-chill of minus 9. Bono, who had played so well during the season, was horribly ineffective, going 11-for-25 and throwing three interceptions. The Colts took a 10–7 lead in the third quarter, and kicker Lin Elliott missed his second field goal of the day to begin the fourth. With the defense playing heroically, the Chiefs got the ball back, but after Bono's third interception of the day, Schottenheimer sent in backup Rich Gannon who marched the Chiefs down the field, only to have Elliott's third field goal attempt of the day—from 42 yards out—miss.

After a season of promise, the frigid crowd and Lamar went home deflated.

"It was horrible," said Tom Richey. "So quiet up in that suite. Lamar was always very good in those situations—he'd go down and console the players. But you saw how much it got to him later."

Later in the evening, sitting in Peterson's office, Lamar would ask the same question: "Is there anything I can do to help?" Peterson did what he'd been in the habit of doing since his days in Philadelphia: He ordered every member of the coaching staff out of the office for a week, to get some distance and perspective on the season.

Lamar would do the same and then, invariably, return to Kansas City in late January or February, curious but never prying, eager to sit in and hear the talk on the team's draft plans.

•

Throughout the mid-'90s, as the Chiefs' fortunes began to rise and the value of the franchise continued to increase, Lamar worked with Jack Steadman and the rest of his business team at figuring out how to best set up a succession plan. He'd seen other NFL families that had to give up their franchise, which were now valued in the hundreds of millions of dollars, after the passing of their patriarch.

The succession plan, devised by Steadman and Lamar's lawyer, Jim Seigfreid, called for each of his four children to eventually own 24.5 percent of the team, for Norma to have 1 percent and for Lamar to retain 1 percent. The neat mathematical equation meant that the gift taxes that each child would face—while still severe—would allow them to move forward, knowing the club would remain in the family.

It also, in a way, provided the financial stability that emboldened Lamar to undertake one final grand gamble, which began in earnest in 1995.

"It really wasn't until after the World Cup," said Clark Hunt, "which was so successful, that I think caused another lightbulb to go off in my dad's head to say, 'Hey, I think it might be time to give it another go.'"

Lamar had passed along the start-up prospectus to Clark, who since returning from his time at Goldman Sachs had become his most trusted adviser. But in this instance, he was undeniably on his own. In the conference room on the nineteenth floor of the Thanksgiving Tower, where he took his papers and files so he could spread out, he summoned Clark and broached the subject. "I remember sitting there with him," said Clark. "Instead of talking about this from a theoretical standpoint, he started talking about it as something that maybe we should think about getting involved with." Clark, Norma, and even the youngest, soccer-loving Daniel, were all reticent, none more so than Clark.

Clark had grown up playing the sport and loving it; soccer was in his DNA in the same way that his father grew up unabashedly in love with football. But like so many other members of his family and associates, Clark had "grave reservations" about the venture. His father had been keeping a break-neck schedule, was still working his way out of the calamitous losses of the '80s.

"Having recognized what a bad financial ordeal the NASL had been for him," Clark said, "and after a bad financial decade for him, he was back in good shape financially."

Among his other closest business associates—Jack Steadman and Carl Peterson in Kansas City, Bill Adams and Wayne Henry in Dallas—there was a unanimity against getting back into soccer.

But it was also clear, to everyone from Clark and Norma to his new secretary, Susie Stephens, that the prospect of returning to soccer was energizing to Lamar.

"He was really pumped," said Wayne Henry. "It was something he really wanted. When Lamar made up his mind about something, it was very difficult to get him to think differently. There were times when we made decisions to do things when he was the only one at the table comfortable with doing the thing under consideration."

Peterson disliked the prospect of having another tenant share Arrowhead, crowding the schedule, disrupting the unique daily flow of a football team's schedule. But he also realized his boss was an unabashed lover of the beautiful game.

"I can remember Carl being very . . . thoughtful . . . in his discussion with my father about it, because I think he could tell that my dad was set on doing it," said Clark. "And Jack was seeing it through a different lens, which is we've just spent ten years putting the struggles of the North American Soccer League and World Championship Tennis, the silver crisis, behind us. Do you really want to do this again, financially?"

In the fall of 1994, Lamar called a meeting of Hunt Sports to outline what he was considering. "I can remember going into a meeting, sitting down, and all of us—all of us—pleading don't do this, don't do this, don't do this," said Lamar, Jr. "You know, he would listen, he wouldn't fight back much, he wouldn't participate in the heat of the exchange. And then he'd go do what he wanted to do. And that was kind of how he was."

Lamar responded the way he usually did when confronted with united opposition to a decision that he felt was right. He smiled, he told his friends and employees that he appreciated their opinion, but he remained resolute, and announced that the project would move forward. Concluding the discussion that day, Lamar said, "I think we agree that the time is right to go ahead."

Norma had loved the game for decades but fairly dreaded seeing her husband returning to the business. When he told her he'd decided on it, she merely sighed, smiled wanly, and asked, "Haven't we done this before?"

It would took more than a year of negotiation, but Lamar finally signed on as an "investor-operator" for the 1996 launch of Major League Soccer, joined by Patriots owner Robert Kraft and the Denver mogul Philip Anschutz, among others.

"The biggest issue we tackled was getting the costs to what we felt were sustainable for a start-up league," said Clark. "Of course, soccer-specific stadiums got junked at this point because there wasn't enough money in the budget to tackle that. The other thing we were struggling with was getting enough franchises."

The consensus was that the league should begin with ten teams, but without enough owners to sign on, three of the MLS franchises were designated "league-run" franchises. To make it work, Lamar took on two franchises—

one in Kansas City, where the team would play at Arrowhead, and another in Columbus, Ohio, in which the city's mayor, Gregory Lashutka, guaranteed 10,000 season tickets for an MLS team.

Around the offices of Unity Hunt, the joke was "Lamar has solved his estate-planning issues."

As Abbott had envisioned, the league purchased and managed all player contracts, but licensed teams would invest $5 million to be "investor-operators."

The only things as unwieldy as that euphemism were the team names themselves, rolled out in October 1995. On the rising tide of legitimate soccer fandom in the United States, the league chose to emphasize nicknames that sounded canned, stilted, and self-consciously edgy, as though MTV were starting a sports league.

The names and logos had been conceived by apparel manufacturers Nike and Adidas, who had contracted to supply the league's uniforms. The San Jose team was named the Clash; the Tampa Bay club was called the Fusion. Dallas was the Burn. The Columbus franchise run by Lamar would be called the Columbus Crew, with a marketing campaign that was a natural ("the hardest working team in American sports"). But Kansas City, Lamar's second home, a city keenly self-conscious of living down its past, a city that stridently wanted to distance itself from all vestiges of its no-longer-apt reputation as a cowtown . . . Kansas City's new soccer team was given the nickname of "Wiz."

The response was swift and severe. A research study conducted for the franchise by the Kansas City media research firm VML, held in January of 1996, included several dire points about the initial response to the name. In the survey, 54 percent of respondents had a negative response to the team's name. When listing conclusions, the marketing firm noted "WIZ name is a marketing disadvantage (team nicknames should at least reach indifference in a name; high percentage of [market] holds strong dislike for name").

The Wiz name had been the brainchild of the marketing arm of Adidas, but Lamar went along reluctantly. "I think Lamar's love of musical theater got him in trouble there," said Norma. "I think he saw *My Fair Lady* on Broadway five times." It proved to be a concession the entire family would come to regret. "It was just an all-around bad idea to let the apparel companies name the franchise," said Clark.

Very early in the first season, the team's lawyers were contacted by the New York organization "Everybody Loves the Wiz," an electronics firm. The name was a titanic negative but also indicative of Lamar's naïvete. When a reporter asked him years later if he had been aware, when the name was unveiled, that "wiz" was slang for urination, Lamar sheepishly admitted that he had not been.

Lamar and the family were in San Jose for the first game in league history, on April 6, 1996, in front of a sellout crowd of 32,000 at Spartan Stadium. A week later, at Arrowhead, the Kansas City Wiz debuted, with multi-colored uniforms including blue shoulders and sleeves, a gold stripe, three thick red strips per the Adidas logo, and a smaller blue and green stripe. The team's star was Preki, who had been a star for the Tacoma Stars and St. Louis Storm in the Major Indoor Soccer League of the '80s. The original plan treated the Wiz as a new company, which contracted with Arrowhead and the Chiefs to use their facilities.

The first season, fresh off the success of the '94 World Cup, had been positive. "I remember we were all very excited about the attendance levels, because so many of the franchises came out of the gates very strong, and the attendance was really above what we projected," said Clark Hunt. "And the financial results were either in line or perhaps better than what we'd projected. So there was a little bit of feeling of euphoria. Still a loss, because of all the start-up costs. But the attendance numbers were really encouraging. They didn't last, but they were encouraging."

The team—the nickname had mercifully been changed from "Wiz" to "Wizards" after the first season—practiced on the same fields where the Chiefs once practiced, behind the old Chiefs' offices in Swope Park, with coach Ron Newman (returning to the fold after coaching Lamar's Dallas Tornado twenty years earlier) occasionally being allowed to bring his team to Arrowhead for game practice, though both Peterson and Schottenheimer, while mostly cordial to the soccer interlopers, were fiercely protective of the venue.

Arrowhead was, even then, some twenty-five years after its opening, among the most beautiful stadiums in all the world, and when packed to the last row of the upper deck for a Chiefs game, the atmosphere could be mesmerizing. But for soccer, with the top level cordoned off, and only 15,000–20,000 fans in the lower bowl, the stadium lacked both intimacy and atmosphere. And once again, Lamar found himself trying to explain away his inability to replicate the unique culture of soccer in a stadium ill-suited for those purposes. The lower bowl seated about 33,000, and with often less than half of that section filled, the effect was baleful. "It felt empty," said Clark Hunt.

As in Dallas in the '70s, there had been a small contingent of soccer true believers who began following the team, at both home and away games, forming a spirited supporters group. But not enough. The numbers went down in 1997 and were even worse in 1998. "We ultimately made the mistake of having the league-run franchises," said Clark. "First of all, the league appointed very capable executives to run each franchise, but it was not the same thing as having a dedicated owner with a personal stake in the team working 20 hours a day to try and make the franchise work. Secondly, it was a huge financial drain. Every franchise was losing money, and then you had to add up the additional losses of the league-run clubs and divide it among the remaining owners."

The Wizards had an additional problem. They did not feel particularly welcome at Arrowhead. Peterson, focused on the Chiefs being a competitive, commercial, and artistic success, was not eager to have another tenant inside Arrowhead, or soccer markings on the football field, or another team practicing on it. John Wagner, heading the Hunts' soccer efforts in Dallas, noticed that there seemed to be no special relationship between the Chiefs and Wizards. "Wasn't it amazing that we couldn't get anything done?" said Wagner. "It was like they were dealing with a completely unrelated company." Even outside of Arrowhead, the tension was becoming apparent. "It was clear that Carl didn't care about [soccer] at all," said MLS commissioner Doug Logan.

By 1998, the Wizards' ticket base was dropping, and the team was dealing with diminishing returns. A preseason mailing of 21,000 pieces netted a grand total of thirty-eight adult and seventeen youth ticket orders, resulting in a loss of $8,000. In the halls and cubicles of Arrowhead, where many of the team's administrators were stationed, staffers wondered how long it could go on.

After the disappointment of ending the 1996 season with a three-game losing streak that knocked them out of the playoffs for the first time in six seasons, the Chiefs bounced back in 1997, adding wide receiver Andre Rison to the team, in one of the club's richest free-agent signings in history, and replacing Bono with yet another former 49er, the gangly Michigan quarterback Elvis Grbac. The result was perhaps Schottenheimer's best team, which scored more points and allowed even fewer than the '95 squad.

The season was marked by a wire-to-wire race with the Denver Broncos, and Schottenheimer's nemesis, John Elway. In the regular season, Kansas City won a crucial game at home, with Pete Stoyanovich connecting on a 52-yard field goal as time expired, lifting the Chiefs to a 24–22 win and into a tie for first place in the AFC West.

But in the Chiefs opening playoff game, with the two best teams in the AFC playing again at Arrowhead, Elway got the measure of Schottenheimer once more, prevailing 14–10. In the locker room, there was the anguished stillness that greets the end of any promising football season, of strong men weighing the yield of six months of intense, daily effort and sacrifice. But deeper in the bowels of Arrowhead, in the coaches' offices, there was a scene that Lamar would later describe as one of "profound sadness." Wives weeping, coaches looking distraught and shocked, unwilling to accept that a season's work was over. And, in the center of it all, Marty Schottenheimer, absolutely devastated.

Walking into that, weighing the anguish his coach felt, Lamar knew that Marty was feeling all the worse for what he had failed to provide.

On the Hunt plane home that night, there was an almost stifling quiet. "Lamar wasn't a bad loser," said his friend Tom Richey. "But he was a hard loser." On that trip, the family and friends sat quietly in their seats, while Lamar, crushed and alone, stared out the window into the darkness.

It was the second time in three years the Chiefs had lost a home playoff game. They had been to the playoffs seven of eight years in the decade, and they'd come up short again. At the press conference, Schottenheimer had looked beseechingly out at the Kansas City media and asked, "Guys, what am I doing wrong?"

"What made it so hard," said one longtime Chiefs employee, "is that Marty and Carl and everyone, really, wanted so bad to win one for Lamar. And you knew Lamar appreciated that, but he just wanted them to win one for themselves. He felt so bad for Marty."

•

While Kansas City had been a logical place for Lamar to launch his venture into soccer, Columbus, Ohio, was entirely different—a city in which he had no history, whose stadium problem was even worse than Kansas City's. While the Wizards were playing in front of 60,000–70,000 empty seats at Arrowhead, they were at least keeping their rent in the family. The Crew played their games at the fabled, and enormous, Ohio Stadium, the 93,000-seat stadium on the campus of Ohio State University, known as the Horseshoe. In addition to the vast seas of empty seats, the quality of play suffered, as the field was just 59 yards wide, a full 11 yards shy of world standards.

In 1997, Ohio State announced that it would begin extensive renovations on Ohio Stadium in 1999. After the 1998 season, the Crew would have to leave the stadium for at least two years. Thus began a race against time, as Lamar searched for a way to find a new home for the Crew, so he wouldn't have to move the team out of Columbus, either temporarily (while Ohio Stadium was being refurbished) or permanently.

On May 6, 1997, the voters of Columbus rejected Issue One, which would have built a downtown sports complex, including a hockey arena designed to bring an NHL expansion team to Columbus, and a soccer stadium for the Crew. Lamar was the most prominent among a group of investors in the former effort, though the defeat of Issue One seemed to abort the city's hockey prospects altogether, and left Lamar still desperately seeking a permanent soccer facility.

"We didn't really have a Plan B," Lamar said. Moving quickly into action, Lamar and general manager Jamey Rootes began casting about for a community that would help build a stadium. That lead them to the nearby city of Dublin, Ohio, located just north of the stadium. A financing plan was proffered, and the Crew started making plans. But typical of the naïvete that occasionally plagued Lamar, he thought the agreement was done. In fact, it had to be put on the ballot in a referendum. In February of 1998, Lamar flew in for one final push. On the evening of February 10, Lamar and Rootes were up in Dublin when the returns from the voter referendum came in—the voters had narrowly rejected the proposal.

Rootes was driving Lamar back to his hotel in downtown Columbus. The car was mostly quiet as they drove back, and they decided to stop at a McDonald's, as they hadn't eaten anything since lunch. Throughout the silent drive, Rootes was contemplating whether it was more likely that his boss would try to move the franchise, or give up and fold it altogether.

They walked into the McDonald's and, after placing their order, Rootes went to get condiments. As he sat down, he looked around for Lamar. He finally saw him over by a wall, looking intently at a large map of Columbus.

He walked over and asked, "What are you doing?"

"Oh, I'm just trying to figure out," said Lamar calmly, "where else we can build this soccer stadium."

Providentially, just a few days later, an opportunity arose, with land from the Ohio State Fairgrounds offered at no charge. The Ohio State Fairgrounds was, in retrospect, an ideal site. "I feel kind of dumb we didn't find it earlier," said Lamar, "because I think it's the best of all sites."

The parking lot and access roads were already in place. The land could be had for free. But there was one large catch: There would be no funding support for the stadium itself.

At that point, Lamar told Clark, "I'm going to make the financial commitment and get it done. I have to do this for the Crew to succeed."

That meant Lamar was going to commit to pay the entire cost of the building effort, something in the neighborhood of $25 million. (It would eventually be $30 million.) It would be the first soccer-specific stadium of its kind in American history. And the only question, in the minds of many, is whether the league would still be around when it opened.

"He had the deal cut at this point with the Ohio Exposition Center," said Clark. "And he wasn't worried about the timing, which in retrospect, he should have much more worried about, though that came a little bit later, once we got into the design phase."

And Clark's reaction to his father going even further out on the MLS limb?

"I was concerned," he said. "I'll phrase it that way. I was concerned. But he was determined to get the stadium built. He had the vision to recognize that soccer-specific stadiums would be the linchpin for the long-term success of the league."

It wasn't as though Lamar was exclusively interested in soccer during this period, though it often seemed that way. In fact, he continued casting about for other sports interests, but none of the other efforts came to fruition. There was a modest bid for the Kansas City Royals in 1998 that was turned down by the team's board of directors, who'd set a $75 million asking price. Lamar's bid, in partnership with the utility Western Resources, was for $25 million up front, and another $27 million, contingent on improvements to Kauffman Stadium. The board rejected the bid and, two years later, longtime Wal-Mart CEO David Glass (a member of the board himself) bought the team for $96 million.

Over the same period, the effort to bring an NHL franchise to Columbus wound up in the courts. After Issue One failed in 1997, John H. McConnell, head of the steel company Worthington Industries and part of the investor group that included Lamar, cut a side deal for an NHL expansion team that left Lamar out of the equation entirely. Lawsuits and countersuits ensued, leading to little more than more legal fees for Lamar. "He wasn't pleased about the hockey situation," said one longtime aide. "But he also didn't obsess about it the way he did with football and soccer."

The spring and summer of 1998 marked another absurdly busy period for Lamar. He was flying to games in both Kansas City and Columbus, and was back in Kansas City for the '98 NFL Draft. On June 9, before leaving for the World Cup, Lamar signed a twenty-five-year lease for the Crew at the Ohio Exposition Center, for a stadium that he still needed to build.

The summer of 1998 marked the third year of existence for MLS, and the first time the league would have to deal with a World Cup season. It was a desultory showing for the American team—which was eliminated in the group phase, without so much as a draw—but a festive time for Lamar and Norma, who made it to all ten venues and stayed in their all-time favorite hotel, the Hotel du Cap d'Antibes in the south of France.

On July 7 at Marseille, they saw the rematch of the '94 classic between the Netherlands and Brazil, with Brazil advancing on penalty kicks. They were in Paris for the emotional final, with the French hoisting their first World Cup, outplaying Brazil. Lamar was too good a sport to feel too bad about his team losing, and, after the match, he and Norma and the family strolled down the Champs-Élysées, with a million jubilant French.

Lamar was sixty-six years old, absurdly active, traveling more than a hundred thousand miles a year by air. His life was, even for a calm, positive man who was fit and active, unusually stressful.

After the end of the World Cup, Lamar and Norma stayed over a few extra days in Paris. One day, after a lengthy lunch at another Michelin-rated restaurant, they went on yet another antique shopping foray. That day, walking on a Paris street, he became suddenly, violently ill. After pausing to regain his bearings, he rushed back to the hotel with Norma, both sensing it meant trouble. She demanded he see his doctor at once when they returned to Dallas, and Lamar consented to do so.

The news, once they returned to the States, was not good. The initial diagnosis, confirmed after a biopsy, was that Lamar was suffering from an advanced case of prostate cancer and had perhaps as little as two months to live. Lamar and Norma left the doctor's office and drove home. Both were shocked, but she was initially livid at the coldly pessimistic forecast.

"The first diagnosis was *so* negative," said Norma. "I just thought, you have to give him some kind of hope."

Within days, and after dozens of phone calls, Lamar was in Houston, at the office of Dr. Christopher Logothetis, prostate cancer research chief at M.D. Anderson in Houston. In this instance, Lamar hit it off with the Greek-American Logothetis, the men's natural optimism feeding off each other. After another battery of tests, Logothetis was much more positive, telling Lamar, "If you do what I ask, we can get you twenty years."

It was exactly what Lamar needed to hear. He now discreetly passed on the news to his children, adding the rosiest possible prognosis. And then he did what anyone who knew him by then could have predicted. He continued working, told no one, and moved on with it. He had a stadium to build. At the end of the year, he took a two-week vacation in the Caribbean, taking a break to return for the Cotton Bowl.

"He didn't change much at all," said Sharron. "Still ate hamburgers at lunch. Still kept his schedule, still traveling."

The news finally came out in January, before the annual trip to the Super Bowl, where Lamar's appearance would have prompted the talk anyway.

Shortly before then, he told a few of his employees about the prognosis. In Columbus, he walked into general manager Jamey Rootes's office to give him the news and, in the next breath, assure him it was nothing at all to worry about.

"It was kind of a contrast," said Rootes. "So, you get this news and then—nothing noticeable changes."

He'd take his chemotherapy treatments, wearing down deeper into each cycle, but, almost without fail, he would leave the clinic in Dallas and return to the office in the afternoon, sapped and sickened, but getting back to work nonetheless.

When feeling particularly bad, he'd consent to trips to see Dr. Logothetis at M.D. Anderson, but even then, he flew commercial, loyally taking Southwest's service to Houston Hobby.

"I don't think he fully comprehended it, what he was facing," said Susie Stephens. "Because by that time he was so heavily involved in his soccer. His soccer teams were going, he was building his soccer-specific stadium. I mean, soccer became his lifeline. That was it. And it was just an annoyance to him to be bothered with all this other stuff."

It had been a difficult autumn. In Kansas City, the Chiefs were imploding. In the tenth year of Schottenheimer's tenure, the squad was talented but lacked the unity of a typical Schottenheimer team, and still seemed haunted by previous playoff setbacks. In a Monday night game at home against Denver, Derrick Thomas became unhinged, incurring three unsportsmanlike conduct penalties in a single drive. After the game, Peterson—aghast at the performance—apologized to Lamar, as did Thomas. The team suspended Thomas for a game, but the year ended on a sour note, and Schottenheimer resigned a few weeks after the end of the season. It had been a glorious decade, but the '90s would end with the Chiefs still falling shy of their goal to return to the Super Bowl.

Even as the year was ending in disappointment in Kansas City, Lamar was back on the job, visiting the construction site in Columbus with Crew general manager Jamey Rootes and stadium manager Mark McCullers. As the construction crews were excavating the giant boulders underneath, and setting them aside for removal, Lamar walked by one day on a site inspection and stopped.

"I never realized the glaciers came this far south," he said, seemingly to no one.

Rootes and McCullers looked at him quizzically, and Lamar hastened to explain the distinctive features of the glacial rocks that had been unearthed.

"These are wonderful," he said. "Don't carry these away. Let's use them for landscaping." Over the weeks ahead, the Crew staff was treated to multiple sketches and renderings of the proposed parking lot, and how the "rock gardens" could be incorporated into the design.

The first shovel dropped August 14, 1998. On May 15, 1999, just 278 days later, Crew Stadium opened. The United States had its first soccer-specific stadium.

That day, with the New England Revolution, owned by Robert Kraft and his family as the opponent, and a full assortment of big and small names in attendance (the boxing announcer Michael Buffer, of "Let's Get Ready to Rrrrumble" fame, who had been contracted to fire up the crowd at some big Chiefs games, was called in, did his shtick, and fairly mangled a couple of the names in the Crew starting lineup), Columbus beat the New England Revolution, 2–0.

Lamar, his face orangeish and his head bald after radiation and chemotherapy, was wearing a baseball cap, working his way around the stadium. As he made his tour, finding minor problems and major, he'd pull his small notebook out of his pocket and write down a few more notes in his microscopic hand.

That afternoon, as he sat during the long traffic jam out of the stadium, his mind was already whirring around what was next. The bigger question was whether a stadium could save a league. Attendance was dipping, TV ratings were stuck at the microscopic level, and many of the millions of devout soccer fans in the United States made it almost a point of pride to ignore the league entirely.

Later in the summer, Robert Kraft called Lamar to float an idea that had been on his mind for weeks. Discontent had been growing among the MLS board with commissioner Doug Logan, but there had been no open revolt, and, given the problems the league was facing, there had been no obvious replacement candidate. But now Kraft had one in mind,

"What would you think about Don Garber?" he asked Lamar.

Garber was a shrewd, hard-working executive whom both Kraft and Lamar had been impressed with, for his work—sometimes in vain—for NFL International, the arm of the league that was trying to sell the NFL's European development league, NFL Europa.

There had been a growing feeling among the owners that MLS had become stagnant, and that at least part of the problem was Logan's lack of leadership. While Lamar had initial reservations—he didn't like to help one of his enterprises by hurting another—he was persuaded that Garber was the right man for the job and could do more good running MLS than NFL International.

With both Lamar and Kraft behind the idea, they spoke to Phil Anschutz, the Denver businessman who'd gone to the World Cup in 1994, fallen in love with the sport, and, by 1999, invested in a second team (the Chicago Fire) to go along with his original franchise, the Colorado Rapids.

"There was a cocktail party in the Coca-Cola museum in Atlanta," said Garber. "This was the March NFL league meeting in 1999. Lamar and Bob approached me and said, basically, 'What do think about being our commissioner?' By the end of that weekend, I was essentially traded. Over the next few months, I met with Phil Anschutz and Alan Rothenberg."

Logan had learned of the planned coup while on vacation in Mexico, and he hastened the matter by abruptly resigning.

In a sense, Garber had spent years working on the very task that MLS faced: taking a wildly popular game and importing it to a harsh land that knew little of its culture. Garber, who'd started his NFL career with Properties, the merchandising arm of the league, had been hired by Paul Tagliabue in 1992, to bring more cohesion to the league's numerous international efforts.

It didn't take long for Garber to seize on the donut-like paradox that MLS was facing: the most fervent soccer fans in America—the ones who planned their summers around World Cups, who rose early on Saturdays to follow their European teams (whether by satellite or short-wave radio), and who scoured international newsstands for copies of English titles like *FourFourTwo* and *When Saturday Comes*—were almost unanimous in their contempt for MLS. The biggest sins, according to the true believers, were not the counterintuitive scheduling or the Second Division level of play, but the casual ways in which the game's rules had been subverted. Clocks counting down from 45:00, rather than up; shootouts to end draws in the regular season. It all had to go.

Though Garber was no soccer purist, he quickly grasped that the culture that everyone in the league was trying to create couldn't be attained by a game that was significantly different than the one played in the rest of the world. "It was a mistake, the concept of 'Americanizing' soccer," Garber said. "The core value was lost."

At MLS Cup '99, the league made the announcement that its rules would change to more closely conform to the international standard. "We would play the same game as the rest of the world," was how Mark Abbott put it. "Fans could come and get the authentic soccer experience."

At one time, Lamar had been among the forefront of those who flirted with new rules, both in the NASL and MLS. But by now, after more than thirty years of watching Americanized soccer mostly shunned by American soccer purists, he was ready to try it the other way. And he was among the first to point out what could be gained by being able to translate "the authentic soccer experience" to the United States.

In a way, this was the missing ingredient that almost all of the NASL and the first four years of MLS had lacked. But if the supporters groups that were springing up—Local 103 in Columbus, The Inferno in Dallas, Section 8 in Chicago, The Cauldron in Kansas City—could make an impression, perhaps that would be a way to bring more casual soccer fans on board.

What Garber noticed in his early talks was Lamar's consistency and resolve. "He's so focused," he said. "When there's an issue at hand, he does not get distracted by any noise whatsoever. His message was simple: We need to get people who are committed to our clubs, and slowly go about growing our overall fan base. It was all very fundamental—blocking and tackling—Lamar was never up in the clouds. He was not a guy that showed any fear or trepidation or regret. An eternal optimist. It was one of his defining qualities."

It was a quality he would need in abundance in the years ahead.

CHAPTER SEVENTEEN

FINAL SEASONS

On Sunday, October 15, 2000, the Chiefs were at home against the Raiders, playing in front of their eighty-ninth consecutive sellout crowd, 79,025 fans at Arrowhead Stadium. It was the eighty-third meeting between the two teams, and the first one that Lamar would miss. He was neither ill himself nor tending to anyone who was.

Instead, he and Norma were at RFK Stadium in Washington, D.C., for the MLS Cup, watching his Wizards play the Chicago Sting for the fifth MLS championship. It had been nearly thirty years since one of his soccer teams had played for a league title, and this time he wasn't going to miss it.

While keeping tabs on the Chiefs' narrow, 20–17 loss to Oakland, Lamar cheered the Wizards on to a 1–0 win over the Chicago Fire, with goalkeeper and team MVP Tony Meola making ten saves, including three in the game's waning moments. In the victorious locker room, Lamar was asked to compare the MLS Cup win to Super Bowl IV. "There the sport was established," he said. "That made everything even, 2–2. This is a different battle. The battle here is against the bill collector. Here, the battle is to sell tickets."

Soccer found itself in a curious position in the American sporting landscape at the beginning of the new century. The power of the global game was beginning to assert itself on the American audience. Fans were following the fortunes of their favorite European and South American club teams on the Internet, on premium satellite subscription channels, even by short-wave radio. The success of the Women's World Cup and the high profile of the '99 U.S. Women's National Team (voted Sportswomen of the Year in *Sports Illustrated*) increased interest in the U.S. Men's National Team as well, and provided proof that soccer was beginning to make inroads in the famously indifferent U.S. market.

Yet at the same time, Major League Soccer was losing money, struggling to find investors, and spending much of its time defending itself from a players' lawsuit challenging the legality of MLS's single-entity structure. Rumors abounded that if the owners lost the lawsuit, they would respond by simply shutting down the league. But on December 11, 2000, in a Federal court in Boston, a jury ruled in favor of MLS and the U.S. Soccer Federation, determining that the league was not an illegal monopoly. That afternoon, the league's investor-operators flew en masse to Colorado, for a weekend at Phil Anschutz's Eagle's Nest ranch, to reconvene and consider the future of the league.

The mood of the weekend was more relieved than celebratory. Garber and Abbott presented the owners with a five-year forecast that was spectacularly grim: All of the league's franchises were losing money, the three league-run franchises, without the strong guiding hand of a true owner, were losing even more money, necessitating even greater annual capital calls. Garber's numbers projected that the business would not improve in the short term, and if the league were to succeed in the long term, the owners who stayed would need to invest even further in MLS. In Garber's words, the owners would need to "double down."

Out of these tense meetings came one glint of marketing genius that Garber presented as a possible way through. Prior to the meeting, Alan Rothenberg had called Garber, to let him know that the German company InFront, which held the TV rights to the 2002 and 2006 World Cups, was having trouble selling those rights in America. It occurred to both men that if the MLS bought the rights to the tournament, it could then package *those* rights along with a slate of MLS games, to ensure the league retained a viable presence on national television.

It wasn't only the World Cup rights. The representation of U.S. soccer was about to be open again, after a long association with IMG. And the Mexican national team, wildly popular in America, was seeking a more lucrative, pronounced presence in the States.

It made sense for MLS and the United States Soccer Federation to work together. Dr. Robert Contiguglia, the head of the USSF, was friendly with Lamar (earlier that year, the USSF had renamed its domestic cup competition The Lamar Hunt U.S. Open Cup), and USSF vice-president Sunil Gulati had worked as the deputy commissioner of MLS. What would emerge out of these early discussions, over the course of the following year, was the marketing partnership Soccer United Marketing (SUM), which put MLS and USSF in close quarters but which also used the World Cup broadcast rights for 2002 and 2006 as a way to maintain a presence for the MLS on national TV.

But all of that was still on the drawing board in Colorado. Lamar was not openly emotional, only very intent on the process, though by then, Garber felt he knew where Lamar stood. "I knew just by looking in his eyes," said Garber. "I knew he was going to be in."

If he needed another reason to justify his long support of U.S. soccer, he would find it early in 2001. In the weeks leading up to the February 28, 2001, World Cup Qualifier between the United States and Mexico, to be played at Crew stadium, Lamar tried to prepare his staff for the arrival of the fiercely loyal Mexican fans: "Be forewarned that this crowd will not be like any we have ever experienced before, and they will not necessarily be interested in the niceties of normal stadium protocol." For years, the United States had felt like a visiting team playing Mexico on American soil, but this would be different: A game in the Midwest, with a pro-American crowd, and hostile weather conditions. When the game started, on that night, it was "as cold as I've ever been," said Garber. Mexico's Cuauhtémoc Blanco, taking the field in gloves, was visibly shivering on the field before the kickoff. The United States marched to a 2–0 win in front of a raucous pro-American crowd. "He took so much pride in the U.S. whipping up on people in Crew Stadium," said Daniel. "That brought him so much joy and happiness."

But the 2001 season found more sobering numbers for the league: Attendance was flagging, television ratings were dismal, and the league's profile was virtually nonexistent. Outside of the twelve MLS markets, one was hard-pressed to find highlights about games on ESPN, a story about the league in *Sports Illustrated*, or discussion of the teams on sports talk radio.

And then, on 9/11, everything came to a screeching halt. Lamar was in Columbus and instantly thought of Daniel, who had been working in New York City for a high-tech firm near Ground Zero, but was unharmed. MLS shut down its games for more than a week, and attendance fell even further when the league resumed play. Through a series of promotions and discounts, Crew Stadium did manage to sell out the MLS Cup that year, with Dwayne DeRosario's extra-time goal lifting the San Jose Earthquakes to a 2–1 win over the Los Angeles Galaxy in front of a crowd of 21,626.

A board of governors' meeting held at the MLS Cup that year was particularly dire. "We're going to lose Tampa and we're going to lose Miami," confided Garber to one colleague. "I'm 95 percent sure that these two aren't going to make it."

The tone of the meeting was urgent, preoccupied with questions of survival. "The first thing we had to establish was who was willing to stay in, because there were definitely some owners who'd had enough," said Clark. "And we lost [Miami owner] Ken Horowitz about that time. Also, there was a recognition that the league-owned teams had to go away."

By this time, Phil Anschutz also owned multiple franchises, having started with the Colorado Rapids, then subsequently purchasing the Chicago Fire, D.C. United, and the Los Angeles Galaxy. Robert Kraft, who had begun with the New England Revolution, had agreed to operate the San Jose franchise as well, but by the end of 2001, he was doubting his investment.

With the league's future in the balance, the men involved—Anschutz and his assistant, Tim Leiweke, Lamar and Clark (along with John Wagner, who oversaw the Hunt Sports soccer franchises), Robert Kraft, and Garber and Abbott from the league office—began discussing what it would take.

At one point during the meeting, while chewing on his favorite prop, an unlit cigar, Anschutz said, "Throughout my business career I have frequently made investments that seemed counterintuitive at times—that seemed pretty desperate for the business involved. And those have been the ones that generally have worked out the best for me." At the time, Anschutz agreed to continue exploring possible solutions. But much was left unsettled, and other investor-operators were blanching.

Daniel Hunt, twenty-five, by now freshly returned to Dallas from his stint in New York, was invited by his father to listen in to the league conference call on November 29, 2001. That afternoon, Daniel sat in Chiefs' executive Denny Thum's office inside Arrowhead, a few hours before the Chiefs–Eagles primetime Thursday night game. What he heard was extensive bickering, and the New York owner Stuart Subotnick announcing he was out of the league, along with confirmation that Miami was dropping out as well. Many assumed that Subotnick capitulation was the final element in the league's demise.

After the call, a slightly dazed Daniel looked at Clark.

"Welcome, you've just been on your first—and last—MLS conference call," said Clark.

At the MLS headquarters in New York, Garber hung up the phone from the same call, looked at Abbott, and said, "That wasn't very fun." But even in those gloomy circumstances, he sensed that the core partners—Lamar, Anschutz, and Robert Kraft—would find a way through. "I just knew those men too well; I knew they wouldn't quit."

Robert Kraft and his son Jonathan were done running two franchises, and perhaps done altogether. "I really wanted out," said Robert Kraft. "But Lamar—he was the opposite of a bully. He was collegial, and he appealed to a higher calling. That was what made him special. He was so pure emotionally, that you knew if he was invested in something, you wanted to be along for the ride. So we stayed along for the ride."

Anschutz had the deepest pockets, but he didn't want to be the only one reaching into them. He bought the New York–New Jersey franchise from Subotnick, and he was willing to take over the San Jose franchise, giving him six of the league's ten surviving clubs. But he would do so, he said, only if Lamar would take over a third team, the Dallas franchise, which had been run by the league.

In December, Lamar and Clark joined Anschutz and Leiweke for dinner in New York, and soon got down to the central question.

"I remember it well," said Tim Leiweke, the president of AEG. "Phil said, 'Lamar, I'll do it—I'll take the sixth team. But only if you take the third.' Lamar almost choked right there; I don't think it required the Heimlich, but it was close."

Now Lamar vacillated. The route he took to the decision was circuitous, and included discussions about shutting down the Wizards and moving financial support to the league-owned Dallas Burn or, alternatively, shutting down the Burn until a soccer-specific stadium could be built. Lamar and Clark and John Wagner worked through any number of other possible solutions, one of which would have ceded a controlling interest to Dallas businessman Tom Hicks, who owned the Texas Rangers. (At one meeting, Lamar waited for Hicks, who never showed.) A month later, Hicks and George Gillette bought a controlling interest in one of the most venerable clubs of all, the legendary Liverpool Football Club in England. It soon became clear that if Lamar was going to take over the Dallas team, he was going to have to do it on his own.

Once again, Lamar's head was telling him one thing and his heart was telling him another. "I told him that it was a risky investment for him financially, just in terms of stretching," said Clark. "On the other hand, for the league to go forward, it was important for him to do."

It was lost on neither Lamar nor Clark that a good part of the reason the other owners were still involved was out of their respect for him. Anschutz, originally somewhat pessimistic at the beginning of the meeting at his ranch in December 2000, had been swayed then by Lamar's determination. "I remember Phil at one point in those discussions being skeptical that we had something that was worth taking forward," said Clark, "to swinging the other way 180 degrees, to being enthusiastic, to being willing to pick up six franchises contingent on us picking up a third, because that was sort of the key to it. Once he got Lamar's agreement on that, then we went forward."

"I think we were all concerned," said Anschutz, "and I'm sure we were all worried a bit about this. I don't think the investment, if it had gone totally sour, would have put Lamar or Bob Kraft or myself out of business. But still, we had substantial money at risk."

But by the fall of 2001, this had become something more than just a financial question—it was one of willpower, as well. Norma had already partitioned her own finances from Lamar's, so her financial interests were not directly involved. "I'm the last person that he's going to talk to about how things are not going right," Norma said. "Because I had already said, 'Why are you doing this? Do you really want to do this?' I just think there's a whole lot of that that I never heard."

Much of the family's soccer interests were part of the Arrowhead Trust and would belong to the four children in the succession plan. But by then, even some family members had seen enough. "I tried to opt out," said Lamar, Jr. "I just said, 'I want out of soccer. I can't take these losses.' But Dad just said, 'Don't worry, I'll cover it for you.' And at that point, I just gave up. You sort of had to say, 'Well, it *is* his money; he can do with it whatever he wants.'"

And so he did. Lamar called Anschutz, late in 2001, and told him he would take on a third club, the Dallas Burn (which within a year would be rebranded with the more traditional-sounding FC Dallas). Anschutz had six teams, the Hunts had three, and Robert and Jonathan Kraft had the tenth club. Seven years into the new era of American soccer, there were three owners left. But they were, to the league's way of thinking, the right three.

"Lamar and Phil and Robert sticking in, and not being willing to give up and say, 'We lost,' was remarkable," said Garber. "Absolutely incredible. It would have been so easy to throw in the towel, and everybody would say, '*Finally!*,' as opposed to 'What are you doing?'"

On January 8, 2002, the league announced it was contracting the two Florida franchises and extending its contract with ESPN; the league also announced the formation of Soccer United Marketing, which by then had secured the television rights to the 2002 and 2006 men's World Cups and the 2003 women's World Cup.

When Norma got the news of Lamar adding a third franchise, she was, in Clark's words, "not super-excited" about it. It wasn't merely that soccer was a major time and cash drain. It was that her husband was nearing seventy, still going through treatment for cancer, and was showing no signs of slowing down.

"I think Norma got to a point where she realized that he was going to do what he was going to do," said one family friend. "She knew him better than anyone and I really, truly believed that no one could talk him out of it. Nothing she could say or do was going to change anything. Nothing *anybody* could say or do would change anything."

"This was something he wanted to do," said Sharron. "And he was going to do it, and people had begged him not to. I remember feeling like he just wanted to succeed because he believed in it, and he had been right before about stuff, and I hope it succeeds this time." For Lamar, Jr., his father's impulses went deeper than that. "He liked being the underdog," he said. "And with the AFL, he'd created something out of nothing. In a way, he spent the rest of his life trying to repeat that accomplishment."

Just as Lamar had developed a deep loyalty to the men with whom he started the AFL, so did he come to identify with his MLS counterparts, most notably Anschutz. Both were sons of oilmen, both shied away from the most visible trappings of wealth, and both desired a sense that they were part of something greater than mere wealth-building.

"This league certainly needed support financially," said Anschutz. "I owned six teams, which was *nuts*. But it had to be held together financially. I lost a lot of money, but I didn't really get into this to make money, per se. I didn't realize that I would lose as much money as I did, but, anyway. I don't think Lamar ever looked on this as a financial thing for him, in terms of a return. I would guess he probably looked at his football team that way. That's my impression. I don't think he looked at this as a financial equation, although with the losses, when you had to be supporting all these multiple teams, I'm sure that weighed on him, just like it weighed on anyone. But he was never in it for the money."

Through the course of the protracted negotiations, starting at Anschutz's ranch at the end of 2000, throughout 2001, and into 2002, the league made a series of crucial decisions, none more important than the creation of Soccer United Marketing, which would work in concert with the U.S. national team, as well as the Mexican national team, to try to capitalize on the interest in international soccer within the United States. Its first initiative was promoting the upcoming World Cup broadcasts on ESPN with an MLS tie-in. The marketing arm of the league printed up a series of ads designed to look like movie posters, billing the coming arrival of the "MLS Strike Force," and featuring pictures of MLS stars DaMarcus Beasley, Josh Wolff, Brian McBride, Landon Donovan, and Clint Mathis. Not all of them were pure strikers, but the message was unmistakable: The players had all thrived in MLS, and in the summer of 2002 they would form the backbone of the Bruce Arena–coached U.S. team that traveled to Asia for the World Cup. "Ready to take on the world for their club and country," read the subhead.

•

During much of his adult life, Lamar had owned one or two teams; by now he effectively owned four—the Chiefs and the three MLS teams—with a passionate interest in a fifth, his Bulls. He had also become very active in the efforts of SMU to resuscitate its athletic program and build a new stadium (Gerald J. Ford Stadium, which opened in the fall of 2000) to replace the pre–WWII era Ownby Stadium. Though he remained a mostly silent partner with the Bulls, he was directly involved, especially in ticket sales and other fan-related areas, with each of the other teams.

By the late '90s, another assistant, Kathy McDaniel, was hired at the office to help with the crush of correspondence. But the stacks continued to mount. "He writes the memos faster than we can read them," was the line repeated often at Arrowhead and in Columbus. In Dallas, picking up a head of steam, Lamar would sit in the large conference room, write a memo by hand, and place it on top of the letter he was replying to. Then he would move one chair over in the empty conference room and proofread an earlier letter, make any necessary fixes, or, if there were none, sign the letter; then he'd move to the next spot and sketch out rough notes for a speech, or inspect a publicity mailing, or examine the blueprints for a new stadium addition. At five or six or seven chairs in the conference room he'd have a new task, and he would work his way up and down the rows, proofing, composing, revising, and then his assistants, Susie Stephens and Kathy McDaniel, would come in with freshly typed copies, new printouts, new memos, and it would go on and on.

His schedule, even with chemotherapy and radiation treatments, remained punishing. More than once, coming in for a morning meeting after flying in from Columbus or Kansas City, he would succumb to fatigue, and simply doze off during lengthy financial reports. "He didn't mean to," said Susie Stephens, "but he'd just become totally exhausted."

He'd take lunches on the fly, sometimes with Daniel or Clark but often by himself. Where he once preferred a tuna-fish sandwich on white bread, he'd gravitated by the late '90s to Sonny Bryant's Bar-B-Q, in the basement of Thanksgiving Tower, where he could josh with one of the employees, a die-hard Mexican-American soccer fan, while ordering his inevitable barbecue beef sandwich, fresh apple, and Dr Pepper or Diet Coke for lunch. This wasn't merely where he went on typical days, it was where he brought important guests—NFL league counsel and executive vice president Jeff Pash dined there with him, as did Garber. (His other favorite go-to spot was Rose's, the burger joint near SMU where he'd eaten for decades—he would occasionally bring out-of-towners there, but for time and convenience, he most often preferred staying at Thanksgiving Tower.)

He spent almost no time behind his own desk, in his office strewn with pictures and memorabilia. His favorite room was a small conference room with a round table—Stephens took to calling it the Round Room. "That was his main area," she said. "He liked to sit in there, look out the window, make his calls. He wanted to be doing something all the time."

There were still tasks associated with the rest of his business, but he did those reluctantly. Jim Holland, the CEO of Unity Hunt who oversaw the organization's non–sports-related entities, took to calling Lamar "The Great Procrastinator." Even the monthly management meetings became a chore. Lamar was invariably late. Holland began referring to it as "Hunt Time," and he grew vexed waiting for the chairman of the board to show up for the meeting until, finally, Lamar told him to start without him.

"He did spend time on other businesses," conceded Lamar, Jr. "Because those businesses—oil and real estate—they made money. But if it was up to him, he would have spent every minute and every dollar on sports."

Through his bout with cancer, the pace for going to other games—those not involving teams he owned—had slackened somewhat. Lamar and Norma still made it out to the Ballpark in Arlington a few times a summer to see the Texas Rangers, though the rise of frequent pitching changes had become, in Lamar's words, "one of my pet peeves." He was a fan who craved action, and he grew restless during the numerous stops and starts in the later innings. More often than not, by the seventh or eighth, Lamar and Norma looked at each other and agreed they were ready to leave.

In football, he continued to focus on matters that struck him as essential to competitive balance (a fair rotation of Thanksgiving home games had been a long preoccupation) and—just as his peers Rozelle and Schramm had advocated—putting the game in its best light.

"I've got one football rule that I despise," he told a writer in 2003, "and I hope before my dying days, it can change, and that's that we allow the kneel-down at the end of the first half and at the end of the game. I mean I cannot believe that. And you talk to people individually and they say, 'I agree, I totally agree.' But then the coaches get in the act, and they say, 'Oh, no, when you're ahead, you deserve the chance to kill the clock. You deserve to win the game if you're leading.' And you can hear on *Monday Night Football*, Al Michaels says, 'They'll kneel it down here. They've got a couple of kneel-downs.' What a horrible way to end a national telecast, to have announcers telling people you're going to kneel it down." Lamar would bring it up at meetings, both formally and informally, but he never found an apparatus for proving that a team wasn't trying to advance the ball.

Nearly 70, he remained attuned to the fine details, none of which were too small. After the 2001 Super Bowl in Tampa, Lamar wrote a letter to NFL Commissioner Paul Tagliabue, noting that in the Super Bowl XXXV program, "the pages devoted to players' pictures contained the head shots of only 36 players for both the Giants and Ravens. Also, there were no photos of the assistant coaches for either team. . . . I would suggest that it would be an extremely high priority to include the photos of the entire playing and coaching staffs of the two teams in future year's Super Bowl programs. . . . I can only imagine the disappointment of a player or a coach who makes it to this game and has no picture."

Two years earlier, during a game against San Diego at Arrowhead, he noticed that on the team-produced flip chart distributed throughout the press box, there had been a small error. A little-used Chiefs' cornerback named Juran Bolden was listed on the depth chart correctly, and also on the team's alphabetical roster, but his name was missing from the numerical roster. After Lamar wrote a note to the Chiefs public relations director Bob Moore, and followed it up with a phone call, Moore sent a note to Carl Peterson evincing equal parts amazement and exasperation. "It happened once! Once!," wrote Moore. "I mean Bolden?? Really!!" Peterson replied to Moore with the rhetorical question that many had asked: "Does he miss *anything*?"

At home at Arcady, Daniel was out of the house, and Lamar and Norma had the place to themselves. Their routine changed little. After clearing the plates from dinner, Lamar would head to his favorite room in the house, the family room, with its comfortable off-white couch, brightly lit end table, and large wooden coffee table.

There he would settle, with iced tea or a Dr Pepper, and unsheathe his briefcase, writing out more longhand letters, flagging newspaper articles to copy, with a look list for the sequence of recipients. He would sit and work for hours, beneath a Thomas Moran oil of the Grand Canyon that was Norma's favorite, with more Moran originals and a variety of antique bronzes lining the tables and walls. If there was a game on, it would be on the big-screen TV in the corner, over the bronze of a leaping Michael Jordan that he'd bought for Norma one Christmas. He'd watch and cheer for the Bulls or a football game. But through it all the work continued.

"He loved work," said Norma. "Work, play, pleasure, and fun were all the same word to him."

By the beginning of 2002, the health signs were good. Lamar's cancer was apparently in remission, and he was eager for a month-long adventure in Asia. The 2002 World Cup would be the first to be co-hosted by two countries, with South Korea and Japan sharing the duties. Each country would hold matches at ten different venues, making for twenty stadiums overall.

As Lamar scanned the schedule over the spring, cross-checking the dates with an atlas, he devised a way that he could travel to all twenty venues. Norma had, adamantly, begged off. She had grown more adventuresome with her own interests and had recently bought a vineyard in California, and she was working to settle in there. At any rate, she was not a fan of Asian cuisine, and the thought of a journey to all twenty different cities in a month held no joy for her. The ailing Bill McNutt's World Cup days were over, though his sons would join Clark and Daniel in Asia after the group phase. So Lamar flew to Asia alone. "It was one of those things," said a Hunt staffer, "where he didn't really tell anyone. The family all assumed he wouldn't go, and by the time they found out he was going, it was too late to stop him or go with him for the whole thing."

The USA's opener was in Suwon, about an hour from the main USSF hotel in Seoul. Lamar happily joined a surprisingly sizable large contingent of U.S. fans, U.S. soccer dignitaries, U.S. military, and friends and family of the team in Seoul. The game was against world power Portugal, which featured reigning player of the year Luis Figo.

Lamar arrived at the stadium early as always and, with his small notebook in hand, circled the grounds, jotting down observations about the lucid, multilingual signage, and the orderly manner in which the crowd was led to their seats. Once inside the stadium, he found his seat, with some boisterous U.S. supporters, not far from the FIFA VIP section, where the rest of the U.S. soccer dignitaries were sitting.

Prior to the kickoff, MLS president Mark Abbott asked USSF General Secretary Dan Flynn to explain to Lamar that there was a seat for him in the VIP area. A few minutes later, Flynn reported back, "I get the impression he'd just as soon sit out there." Abbott sent him back but Lamar, ever gracious, was steadfast. He was happily ensconced in the regular seats. Abbott soon relented, and he went over to sit with Lamar.

What transpired that day barely registered on the radar of most American sports fans, but to longtime followers of soccer, it was stunning. The Americans, who'd performed wretchedly at France '98, jumped out to an early lead less than five minutes into the game, then added another when Landon Donovan's cross veered off the mark and over the Portugal goalkeeper, into the net.

Then came the third American goal, a header by Brian McBride, a stalwart performer on the Columbus Crew, about whom Lamar had once joked "no one should be allowed to be that handsome." As the stands shook with the surprisingly partisan pro-American crowd, Lamar had "tears in his eyes," according to Don Garber.

And there, amidst the chants and the flag-waving, the sight of "Uncle Sam's Army" blowing horns and cheering on the Americans, Lamar saw what he had first imagined thirty-six years earlier, in his living room in Dallas while watching the '66 World Cup final: *This was something different. This was nation versus nation.*

Portugal would rally, and score two goals, drawing within one before the United States hung on for a 3–2 win that jolted the soccer world.

"How great is this?!" yelled Abbott to Lamar in the din.

"This is the best thing since the Chiefs winning the Super Bowl!" Lamar shouted back.

After cheering the U.S. team out for a curtain call and exchanging congratulatory handshakes and hugs with hundreds of longtime U.S. soccer supporters, Lamar caught a ride back to Seoul on the Nike bus that was transporting USSF personnel and sat next to an IMG agent named Brad Hunt—no relation—who was at the tournament coordinating a possible deal with the CBF, the Brazilian Soccer Federation. Back at the hotel, Lamar invited Brad Hunt and Brad's son Brian to dinner, and they ate in an ebullient daze, contemplating how important the victory was for soccer in the U.S. During dinner, Lamar mentioned that he was hoping to visit all twenty venues, and Brad volunteered that he also was planning to go to tiny Jeju Island to see Brazil play China.

"I have a ticket for that game, but I don't have lodging yet," said Lamar. Brad invited him to stay with him and his son, and Lamar said he would take his number and get back to him.

It was the perfect start to a World Cup trip. But then, days later, at a train station in Seoul, Lamar sat his briefcase down to take a picture, focused for the shot and snapped, and was putting his camera back in his pocket when he real-ized that his briefcase—with his passport, credit cards, reservations, and, sig-nificantly, more than $10,000 worth of World Cup tickets—had just been lifted.

The phone rang at Susie Stephens's home at 2 a.m.

"Have you got a pencil?" Lamar asked.

She got her glasses and something to write with, and Lamar explained that he wanted her to call Dale Young, the Chiefs' treasurer in Kansas City, and have him send money. He wanted it handled through the Chiefs, so that no one in his office in Dallas would be alarmed. (Trying not to worry the family was a recurring theme. "He was just unruffle-able about stuff like that," said Sharron. "I found out about it later, and I actually said, 'Dad, what was that about?' But it wasn't a trip-breaker for him. He lost all his money and lost all his tickets. And he just went on with his trip.")

To the extent that someone could take something like that in stride, La-mar did. After seeing USSF president Bob Contiguglia and his wife, Georgy, at the last group phase game in Daejeon, Lamar shared his tale of calamity, but then invited to take the couple out to dinner after the match, adding apologetically, "but we have to stay at the hotel, and I only have a $200 limit."

New tickets were purchased, more cash was wired, and Lamar continued on his journey, meeting up with Clark, Daniel, and the McNutts in the days ahead. They brought good news from home.

For the small band of diehard American soccer fans back in the States, the month went by in a sleep-deprived haze of astonishment and gratitude, fans seeking each other out, staying up late (2:30 a.m. EDT kickoffs) to watch the afternoon games in Asia, and getting up early (6:30 a.m. EDT kickoffs) to watch the late games.

Among the survivors of the MLS endeavor, there were knowing smiles throughout the month. It wasn't merely that the USA team was exceeding all expectations, it's that they were doing so with the "MLS Strike Force" of Landon Donovan, DaMarcus Beasley, and Brian McBride leading the way.

The day before Brazil was set to face China on Jeju Island, Lamar called Brad Hunt, explained that he'd struck out in his hope for lodging, and said he'd gladly take Brad up on his offer.

When Lamar arrived at the hotel in Jeju, Brad and his son Brian were already in their room, with two queen-size beds, and a foldaway cot that had just been delivered.

"Lamar, you can take one of these beds," said Brad, "and Brian will sleep on the foldout."

"Oh, no," said Lamar, "I'm the guest. I'll be fine on the foldaway."

There was much back-and-forth, but Brad insisted, and Lamar finally re-lented and put his bags on one of the queen-size beds.

The three went to the game together, saw Brazil win to punch its ticket into the round of 16, and returned to the hotel for another dinner. Brad said he was going to stay to meet the Brazilian delegation, but Lamar said he was tired, and he was going to go to sleep.

Hours later, when Brad returned to a darkened hotel room, where Lamar and Brian were both asleep, he quietly slipped in and went to bed. In the middle of the night, he heard loud snoring coming from the foldout. He got up in the dark to jab his son and ask him to be quiet. But the figure he jabbed wasn't his son. Lamar, in the end, had insisted on sleeping in the foldout and now sat up to ask, "I'm sorry, was I snoring?"

Brad, mortified that he'd woken up Lamar, allowed "Just a little," and apologized.

For Lamar, the tournament, the itinerary, and the people offered the perfect fan's experience. The U.S.–South Korea game, in the group phase, provided a daunting wall of sound. "That was the greatest atmosphere I've ever felt at a sporting event," he related to one reporter. "Part of it was the stunning stadium in Daefu, but it was mostly the fans. I've seen Kansas City Chiefs fans dressed in red, but I've never seen anything like that—the whole nation was dressed in red."

For the second time in three World Cups, the United States had qualified for the knockout phase of the tournament, the round of 16. This time, the Americans faced their arch-rival Mexico, in Jeonju, and emerged with a com-prehensive 2–0 win, with goals from McBride and Donovan, and another large contingent of American fans saluting the team at the end of the match.

By June 20, Lamar's traveling party reached Ulsan, where the next day the United States would face one of soccer's greatest powers, three-time world champions Germany.

"I just remember seeing the German national team walk through the ho-tel that night," said Clark. "And thinking how big they were. I wasn't used to seeing a soccer team look that imposing."

The next day, the Americans acquitted themselves well, losing to Germa-ny, 1–0, in one of those games that soccer fans live and die with—a glaring handball on the line that would have equalized going uncalled. "My father was so very proud of the way the U.S. played in that game," said Clark, "and the entire tournament really. After dedicating the better part of 35 years to promoting soccer in the United States, it was extremely satisfying for him to see our national team competing with the world's best on the biggest stage. It was a special moment for all of us to see him so excited."

Back home, with the sensation of the American team, things finally started to change. "People began to get it on their radar screens here," said Phil Anschutz, "that, hey, this is a sport, that the world, particularly Europe, has always thought—and perhaps still think—that Americans somehow can't figure out how to play this sport. We've had to deal with that for years. But that began to go away."

Lamar's summer ramblings weren't complete. Shortly after returning from Asia, Lamar left for a five-day, four-night trip to the old Palette Ranch. Lamar, Jr., had arranged it, calling Ray Hunt to see if he could rent it to celebrate his father's seventieth birthday (typically magnanimous, Ray agreed to the terms, then never sent Lamar, Jr., a bill). Lamar and Norma hadn't been there since 1978, and the return was a nostalgic trip through time, of fishing and horse-riding and volleyball games.

It was also the summer that Clark and his wife Tavia had their second child, which they chose to bestow with Norma's maiden name, Knobel. "Alas he is 'Knobel' (Norma's maiden name), instead of 'Noble,'" Lamar wrote ruefully to Al Hill, Jr. "This assures that his name will be among the most misspelled in history."

•

After Marty Schottenheimer left following the 1998 season, the Chiefs hired defensive coordinator Gunther Cunningham to be head coach. Cunningham built a remarkable personal rapport with his players, based on his melding of old-school language and temper with new-school sensitivity and compassion. He was intense and nearly successful, but he never did recover from the agonizing season-ending loss to the Raiders in '99 (the Chiefs surrendered a 17–0 lead at home, and the defeat cost them the division title and a playoff spot) and the death of Derrick Thomas, from injuries sustained three weeks later in a car accident. In 2000, with a roster weighed down with aging veterans and a hangover from the death of Thomas, the team lost five straight in the second half to sink from the playoff race. On Sunday, December 24, 2000, the Chiefs played their poorest game of the year on the last day of the regular season, losing 29–13 to an indifferent Atlanta squad. The next day, a grim Cunningham spent Christmas morning in his office, arriving at 5 a.m. to begin a systematic review of the season.

Within two weeks of Cunningham's somber Christmas siege, Carl Peterson had fired Cunningham and coaxed his friend Dick Vermeil out of retirement. Vermeil's arrival had about it the whiff of a last stand for the coach and, with Lamar nearing seventy, perhaps for the owner as well.

Lamar and Vermeil had been friendly throughout the '90s, when Vermeil would annually visit training camp, and worked as a color commentator on the Chiefs' preseason telecasts. In his previous coaching stops at Philadelphia and St. Louis, Vermeil had dealt with two particularly mercurial owners, Leonard Tose and Georgia Rosenbloom. But in his first two seasons coaching Kansas City, Vermeil bonded with Lamar, most frequently at the informal Sunday postgame gatherings in Vermeil's office, when the coach and his wife Carol were joined by the rest of the coaching staff and their spouses. "Lamar and Norma always stopped by," Vermeil said. "And I think it really became something he enjoyed, and looked forward to sharing in that environment. I asked him to come to a team meeting at one point, and he said, 'Would that be okay?' And then he started to coming to our Saturday team meetings whenever he was in town."

Most Sundays after a game, Lamar would stand at the back of the room during Vermeil's postgame press conference, then wait until after he'd flown back to Dallas before calling Peterson, often at about 10 p.m. "Am I calling too late?" he'd ask Peterson, and then they'd talk about the Chiefs game that day, as well as the other games around the league. Occasionally, Norma would want to get on the phone as well, to ask Peterson about a player, or a guest in the suite, or some element of the gameday presentation. If she was on for more than a couple of minutes, Lamar would remark, upon returning to the line, "As I've said, Norma's always going to win the time of possession."

In the summer of 2003, in the Chiefs locker room, Vermeil put up a huge poster of the team's goals for the 2003 season, which featured a photograph of the founder, displayed prominently.

"I saw Lamar the day after we put it up," said Vermeil. "He walked into the locker room, and he saw the sign, and he looked at it . . . and smiled a bit and looked at it some more." Vermeil sensed that Lamar was too shy to thank him for it, or do anything to call attention to it—but that he appreciated it nonetheless.

Lamar turned seventy-one two days before the first preseason game of the 2003 season, a Hall of Fame game clash with the Green Bay Packers, in a Canton full of Chiefs fans (Hank Stram was finally being inducted into the Hall of Fame).

The campaign had a charmed quality to it. Vermeil had built a remarkably adept offense, around the dynamic running back Priest Holmes and solid quarterback Trent Green. In the home opener, the Chiefs came out in a version of the choir huddle, a tribute to Stram. (Green threw an interception that was returned for a touchdown, but the Chiefs went on to rout Bill Cowher and the Steelers, 42–20.) It was a season whose early weeks were marked by the dazzling performances of punt- and kick-returner Dante Hall, who returned kicks for touchdowns in an NFL-record four straight games.

But the season also brought the prospect of major surgery. That fall, after another invasive round of procedures, Lamar wrote a letter to his old college friend Phil Jones, reluctantly explaining that the doctors were doing more tests and then, evoking their college adventures, added, "They haven't found my *Senoj Gland* yet; I think they're going back in." The cancer had returned, and now Lamar's oncologist, Dr. Christopher Logothetis, strongly recommended removing the entire prostate.

It was surgery that had to be done. Lamar, characteristically, planned the procedure so as to work around the football season in which it was occurring—scheduling it right before a run of two nationally televised games and a bye week, so that he wouldn't miss any games while recuperating.

On October 13, the day after the exhilarating overtime win over Green Bay and the day before the surgery, Lamar and the family met down in Houston. They all went out to dinner at the Great Seafood Company—Lamar wasn't allowed to eat, but he reveled in being surrounded by his wife and children and friends. He had said all he needed to say to everyone in his family, remaining unfailingly positive. "He acted like he was going in to have a tire changed," said Sharron. But the reality was grave: A daylong surgery to remove his prostate and anywhere else the cancer may have spread. The family congregated the next morning in the waiting room. And for 13 hours they waited, receiving periodic reports from Dr. Logothetis on the successful surgery.

Three weeks later, he was back in Kansas City for Lamar, Jr.'s second wedding and two games at Arrowhead, appearing full of cheer though more frail than before. Even as recently as the summer of 2003, he'd moved at a wispy pace, constantly going forward; but now he seemed gaunt and halting, though clearly as determined as ever. Lamar, Jr. and his new wife, Rita, held their wedding reception Saturday, November 8, at an Arrowhead banquet room. The event fell on the same day, coincidentally, as the Wizards' MLS conference semi-final game against the Colorado Rapids. So Lamar stayed for much of the reception, then quietly walked over to watch the conclusion of the Wizards' game, along with barely 10,000 fans. The next day, he was back at a sold-out Arrowhead, as the Chiefs beat Cleveland to move to 9–0.

Lamar loved keeping track of players, but ever since Doak Walker he'd had a special fondness for all-purpose backs, and as the season wore on—even in his hospital bed recuperating from surgery—he kept track of Priest Holmes's progress during games, tracking him in the yardage race and on his record pace of touchdowns scored.

On November 16, the team lost its first game, to Cincinnati, and the doubts began to creep in about the team's postseason prospects. Defensive coordinator Greg Robinson favored complex schemes that were designed to camouflage weaknesses. His system had helped the Broncos win two Super Bowls, but as the season progressed in Kansas City, the Chiefs were proving themselves increasingly vulnerable. Kansas City bounced back with wins over Oakland and San Diego, and stood 11–1 heading to division rival Denver on December 7. On that day, the growing fissures in the defense burst apart in a 45–27 loss. Two weeks later, they were blown out of a nationally televised game at Minnesota. "It was like seeing a bad movie again," said Carl Peterson. "You could see the players had lost confidence."

The Chiefs finished 13–3 on the season, and for the third time in nine seasons, that record had earned them one of the two byes into the divisional round of the playoffs.

It had been, even by Lamar's high standards, a remarkable season for football. But the playoffs came with a sense of dread, as the Chiefs' defense would be asked to play host to Indianapolis and All-Pro quarterback Peyton Manning.

Playoff football elicits a distinctive kind of desperate intensity on the part of fans, a unique coagulant of hope and dread that Lamar knew well. There is a sense of breathless near-panic that can overtake those involved—players, coaches, and fans alike—as the prospect of a full season of work faces the mounting possibility of sudden extinction.

Lamar had known that feeling before, on Christmas Day 1971, and on numerous occasions with Schottenheimer's Chiefs. But while the Chiefs teams of the '90s seemed to be trudging from station to station, trying to carve out scant scoring opportunities with the smallest margin of error, the Chiefs of 2003 were something else entirely. They had scored nearly 500 points during the regular season, and with Trent Green's passing ability, the threat of tight end Tony Gonzalez, and the irrepressible Holmes, the team offered a wondrous display of offensive firepower.

It was the defense that had everyone worried that day, especially with the Colts coming to town with their own offensive array. The game opened in a dire fashion, as Manning marched the Colts 70 yards down the field to take a 7–0 lead. The Chiefs responded, only to be stopped at third-and-goal from the 3-yard line, forcing a field goal. The next time KC got the ball, they were down 14–3, and the rest of the afternoon felt like a frantic game of catch-up.

Lamar, from the Gold Suite, refused to get discouraged, and the afternoon proved to be a wild gambit of emotions. Trailing 21–10 late in the first half, the Chiefs appeared to score a touchdown on a Green pass to Gonzalez, but the tight end was called for offensive pass interference, and when Morten Andersen missed a 31-yard field goal attempt, the halftime mood was restless, with Lamar urging his guests to keep hope alive.

The second half began with the Chiefs receiving the ball, and, on the second play from scrimmage, Holmes found a crease in the Indianapolis line and burst into the open. It looked for a moment like he might take it all the way for a touchdown, but he was caught by the Colts' David Macklin, who ripped the ball out of his grasp, and the Colts marched back down the field, kicking a field goal for a 24–10 lead.

The Chiefs got a favorable kickoff return from Hall and executed a businesslike, eight-play, 55-yard drive that made the score 24–17. But up in the Gold Suite, and throughout Arrowhead, there was the sense of worst fears realized. Indianapolis, behind the masterful Manning, responded with another exasperatingly easy seven-play touchdown drive, taking a 31–17 lead. At that moment, with much of Arrowhead teetering on the edge of despair, Dante Hall took the ensuing kickoff and returned it 92 yards for a touchdown, and the third quarter ended with the Chiefs down by just 7 points, prompting one of the all-time scenes of jubilation inside the Gold Suite.

The Colts scored early in the fourth quarter, to go up 38–24, and though the ensuing drive—seventeen plays for 76 yards—saw Kansas City narrow the gap to just 7 points, there was only 4:22 left in the game.

Perhaps the dominant image of the game was one of the Chiefs' historically superb offensive line, anchored by perennial All-Pros Willie Roaf and Will Shields, coming to the sidelines after leading the offense on a long drive, and then, only minutes later, wearily picking up their helmets—like factory workers facing a second shift—and heading out to the sidelines to do it all over again. The final score was 38–31. Neither team punted.

Lamar did not weep—he comported himself in public with remarkable equanimity—and he told his team that there would be another day. But the strain—on a crying Vermeil, on a devastated Peterson—was there for all to see. And the family's flight back to Dallas was one of near complete silence.

Lamar was an optimist to his core—he had been faced with a dire prognosis, overcome many adversities, and bravely wrestled cancer to a draw for five years. But even he, staring into the black void of an empty January sky, might have suspected that he would never again get to see his football team come so close to another Super Bowl.

•

The recovery from the prostate removal was slower and more involved than his recuperation after previous surgeries, but by the spring of 2004, Lamar was moving about slowly and steadily with the help of his cane. His friends, family, and employees continued to marvel at his productivity, and he would need that energy, because he was dealing with stadium issues on three fronts.

After possibilities in Arlington and McKinney had fallen through, funding for a new soccer-specific stadium in the Dallas area was finally secured in 2003, when the Hunt Sports Group announced a partnership with the city of Frisco, 28 miles north of Lamar's office in downtown Dallas. The location wasn't ideal, but it was a solution, and Lamar was as determined as he'd been in Columbus to find a way to get a soccer-specific stadium built in the area. The complex partnership would include not only the main stadium but a vast complex of seventeen surrounding fields, in a 145-acre complex jointly operated by the Hunt Sports Group, the Frisco Independent School District, and Collin County.

During one of Don Garber's visits to Dallas to mobilize support for a new stadium, a meeting ran long, and Garber became convinced he'd miss his flight.

"Don't worry," said Lamar, "I've got it covered." He and Garber, accompanied by John Wagner and Abbott, climbed into Lamar's red Jeep Cherokee and headed toward the DFW Airport. When they encountered the inevitable rush-hour traffic jam, and Garber and Abbott started discussing their contingency plans, Lamar knifed over to the shoulder and accelerated through the breakdown lane, kicking up gravel at 70 miles per hour, while the passengers grasped onto doorframes and seatbacks for support (and also mortal fear—Lamar was never a good driver to begin with). As he wheeled them up to the terminal entrance in the nick of time, Lamar smiled and wished them a good day. Another game won.

Attempts to get a similar soccer-specific stadium built in Kansas City had failed, and with the Wizards continuing to play at a mostly empty Arrowhead, the problems of scale and atmosphere remained acute. Lamar remained convinced that Kansas City could support an MLS team with the right stadium, but he grew discouraged. After extensive discussions with potential investors in San Antonio and Louisville, Lamar remained hopeful of finding an investor in Kansas City. In the fall of 2004, he announced the team would be put up for sale and that he hoped to sell to a buyer or investment group that would keep the team in the city.

Just months earlier, at a guest house in Napa Valley, where Norma was working on her vineyard, Lamar slipped heading downstairs and broke his hip. He had been bed-ridden for periods during the fight with cancer, but this long convalescence in California was an adjustment, leaving him physically immobile for the first time since his broken leg at the Hill School. The injury prevented him from some of the personal lobbying he wanted to do on behalf of his third—and arguably most important—stadium project; funding to refurbish the Truman Sports Complex, where many of the amenities that had made Arrowhead state of the art in 1972 were antiquated in the new century.

After the initial failure of the Bi-State Referendum to renovate Arrowhead in 2005, Lamar rallied support for a two-part vote, to be held in April 2006. That spring, voters in Jackson County approved a 3/8-cent sales tax to raise $425 million in improvements to the Truman Sports Complex, with $250 million slated for Arrowhead Stadium, though they rejected further funding for a retractable roof that would have brought a Super Bowl for Kansas City.

"On the night of the vote, we had a party to celebrate the approval of the lease agreement," said Clark. "He was delighted to win approval on the sales tax, but it was definitely bittersweet because we lost the rolling roof, which had been a dream of his for almost 40 years at that point. The NFL had gone to unprecedented lengths to help us win support, not only guaranteeing a Super Bowl in Kansas City but actually awarding the community a specific game without a formal bid of any kind. Cities spend millions of dollars just putting together a bid for consideration. It gave him great comfort to know that Arrowhead would be the home of the Chiefs long after he was gone, but he was pretty disappointed that it would be without the rolling roof."

Within the boardrooms of the NFL, Lamar's stature had steadily grown over the decades—the option of a Kansas City Super Bowl was the most visible proof of that. Tagliabue relied on him as a thoughtful consensus-builder in the '90s, just as Rozelle had in the '70s and '80s. He was a good listener, avoided the backroom politicking favored by many of his contemporaries, and remained attentive and essentially unreadable—or, in Colts' owner Jim Irsay's words, "Spock-like"—in meetings. Tagliabue noticed that in most matters of debate, Lamar spoke rarely, and when he did it tended to be toward the end of the discussion. His opinion had been decisive in getting the league to finally approve the two-point conversion option, passed in 1994. But most of his work was quieter, such as when he worked with Dan Rooney in securing a smooth realignment when the league grew to thirty-two teams in 2001 (a move that was in contrast to the seemingly endless series of meetings and negotiations before the realignment in 1970).

Lamar was consistently friendly, though not overly social with his fellow owners. Though diametrically opposed on many policy questions, he and Cowboys owner Jerry Jones were neighbors, living not far from each other in Dallas. Lamar still made a great show of—and took great pride in—the "Preston Road Trophy," a somewhat homey bauble he created, that would reside at the home of the winning owner of the most recent Chiefs–Cowboys game.

During Super Bowl weeks, he was a constant presence, though often deferential, choosing instead to focus on Norma and her Super Bowl attendance streak (she was believed to be the only female to attend every Super Bowl game) rather than his own seminal role in naming the game. On other occasions when the owners congregated, Lamar tended to spend time with Ralph Wilson and Dan Rooney. Among the newer guard of owners, he was closest to Robert Kraft, with whom he'd developed an abiding friendship, both in the NFL and in MLS. After league meetings, Kraft would notice Lamar, inevitably carrying his battered black leather satchel, stopping by the refreshment table at the back of the boardroom, putting two bottles of water and a soda in his bag for later. "Well, we paid for it," explained Lamar, "I might as well take it."

On August 6, 2005, Pizza Hut Park opened in suburban Frisco, with FC Dallas drawing 2–2 with the New York-New Jersey MetroStars. Typically, Lamar didn't merely bask in the congratulations, but spent weeks prior to the opening constructing a collage of the franchise's history for display on one of the interior walls of the stadium.

A couple of months later, in November, Lamar traveled to Mexico with Daniel, on the occasion of Daniel's twenty-ninth birthday. They were visiting the Mexican soccer club Pumas de la UNAM, to discuss possible partnerships with FC Dallas. When they deplaned at the airport in Mexico City, they were met by a pair of armed bodyguards whom Daniel had hired for the trip, prompting Lamar to fret at one point about what the added security must have cost.

"Well, dad," said Daniel, "we don't want anybody to take you."

"If they do," said Lamar with a rueful smile, "they can have me. Don't send money."

Lamar had to go in for more surgery on December 21, making Christmas 2005 less festive, and the Chiefs just missed the playoffs in Dick Vermeil's final season. As the new year dawned, Lamar was finally acknowledging his physical limitations. "I don't think I'll be making it to Weltmeisterschaft this year," Lamar wrote to Bob McNutt at the beginning of 2006, begging off returning to Germany for the 2006 World Cup. "My long walking days are over."

So Clark and Daniel went with friends to Germany for the 2006 World Cup, though they made a private pact that if the United States reached the semifinal stage, "we would get a plane to go get him, and bring him to the game." It wasn't necessary, as the United States crashed out in the group phase, but Lamar went to Pizza Hut Park for several World Cup viewing parties that summer, still moving with his cane, still tending to the small details, still filling out his World Cup bracket as the tournament progressed. "We talked to him a lot when we were in Germany," said Daniel, "and every time, the message was, 'I'm so glad you're over there getting to do this. Your streak is alive.'"

For all the discouragement that he faced in connection with soccer, Lamar had begun to see signs of growth. The soccer-specific stadiums were a crucial element, allowing the culture of the game to develop organically in Columbus, Los Angeles, and Dallas. A month after the World Cup, he wrote Phil Anschutz to congratulate him on being inducted into the Soccer Hall of Fame. "At times, I almost get 'cocky' about where the game and league stand today," he wrote. "I guess none of us should ever become 'overconfident', but—by gosh—I feel like we are all getting ever closer to 'success' however the public and media want to and are willing to describe it."

One other sign of the sport's growing success were that some of Lamar's football peers were growing aware of it. Some even began to view his pioneering efforts for soccer in a different light.

"What he did was wrong for the prospect of pro football," said one longtime NFL owner. "He was instrumental in bringing soccer to the U.S. He then challenged the rule that you couldn't have cross-ownership, and he won that. Probably for America, it was a good thing. For pro football, I thought what Lamar did was disloyal to his football partners."

But this was a minority view. Robert Kraft, for one, also owned a franchise in MLS. And most NFL owners still couldn't be bothered to worry about the soccer league. "The only thing I ever heard from owners is, 'What an act of futility,'" said Paul Tagliabue.

As early as 1984, Lamar had been pushing to get Kansas City on the docket as a traditional Thanksgiving Day game host (the Chiefs had played host to games on Thanksgiving Day in the last three seasons of the AFL) or, failing that, to at least open up the rotation of the games so that other teams could share in the competitive advantage of hosting a game on a short week and then getting three extra days of rest late in the season. At the 2006 annual meetings, the owners voted to add a package of games for the NFL network, debuting with a Thanksgiving night contest. They awarded the host of the first game to the Chiefs, with a round of applause.

Tagliabue himself had decided to retire, noting the death the previous year of the Giants' Wellington Mara, and being well aware of Lamar's own declining health (from the periodic medical reports Lamar quietly forwarded to him). "I felt that it was the end of an era," said Tagliabue, "and it was time to step aside." Just weeks later, Tagliabue named Lamar as a member of the search committee to find his replacement. Before the summer, declining health had forced Lamar to opt out, with Clark taking his place on the committee that recommended longtime NFL employee Roger Goodell.

But Lamar still made the league's quarterly meetings. "He was always there, always smiling, never complained," said one league executive. "But you could tell by the end of 2005 that he was getting weaker."

Later in the summer of 2006, Lamar was asked by a writer in California to write about the best day of his life. His reply was both optimistic and sentimental.

"I'm going to take the liberty to split your request into two answers," he wrote.

> My 'Best Day' is *yet to come*, because I look forward to the challenge of upcoming projects, always with the knowledge that there are solutions for everything. I look on tomorrow as the 'Best Day' opportunity.

Regarding past experiences—particularly related to sports:

> My 'Best Day' from the past was January 12, 1970, the day after the Chiefs
> had won Super Bowl IV. It specifically relates to the 'Victory Parade' and
> 'Celebration' through the downtown area and on to the Liberty Memo-
> rial in Kansas City. Thousands of fans had congregated to be part of the
> event. The Chiefs winning the game the day before was fun, but seeing
> the reactions of the fans was the icing on the cake for my 'Best Day.'

He then closed the letter by thanking the writer for "letting me share these two thoughts with you."

That summer, he visited Lamar, Jr., and his new wife, Rita, on Father's Day. Lamar, Jr., presented him with a Jerry Garcia–designed tie, in Chiefs colors, which Lamar promised he would wear (and did) to Chiefs games. But his frailty was striking. That evening, after his father left, Lamar, Jr., said to Rita that he feared that his father would not be alive on Christmas.

The 2006 Chiefs' season began poorly, with quarterback Trent Green suffering a concussion in the season-opening loss to the Bengals. But first-year coach Herm Edwards plugged in journeyman quarterback Damon Huard, and the Chiefs remained on the fringe of the playoff hunt. Lamar was growing quieter, even as his ties—red-and-gold, often with a Native American theme—grew louder. Moving with some effort, he still relished the moments on the field. One of the signature pictures of his later years showed him at Arrowhead during a rainstorm, multicolored umbrella over his head, small smile on his face, the very picture of a man in his element, exactly where he wanted to be, doing exactly what he wanted to do.

But by the fall of 2006, those around him sensed his frailty. The people who'd known him so long made it a point to thank him for all that he'd done. Before a game one day, Len Dawson stopped by his suite and shared a few words of gratitude, which Lamar deflected with the usual mixture of grace and self-deprecation.

"I think he was just shy," said Dawson. "Hank knew him as well as anyone, and Hank used to say to me, 'Lamar is different.' Anyone who stops on the way to his wedding to order ice cream, well, he's different. Lamar was just different."

In late October, Lamar invited his old friend, teammate, and frat brother John Marshall, and his wife Elizabeth, to the Chiefs–Seattle game. Afterward, Lamar led Marshall down to the Chiefs' locker room. "He was using a cane," said Marshall, "but I had two artificial hips and I couldn't keep up with him."

Down in the locker room, Lamar introduced Marshall to some of the players, and then held his hand tightly when Larry Johnson led the team in a
postgame prayer.

On November 12, 2006, Lamar was released from the hospital just in
time to serve as host of the MLS Cup, which returned to Pizza Hut Park
for the second year in a row. The game matched the Houston Dynamo,
owned by Phil Anschutz, with the New England Revolution, owned by the
Krafts. "He somehow managed to convince my mother and the doctors to
let him out of the hospital to attend the match," said Clark. "He was pretty
sick by then, but he wasn't going to miss the Cup. It was a great match. The
stadium was sold out and both teams' supporters had traveled and were
singing and chanting. He had a big smile on his face the entire time because
he knew how far the league had come and that the future of soccer in the
U.S. was secure."

That day found Lamar in a particularly philosophical mood. Moving
slowly with his cane, he sat down in his chair, a blanket on his lap, and called
MLS president Mark Abbott over. "He was very reflective," said Abbott. "He
talked a lot about how far the league had come."

A week later, he was up in Arrowhead again, as the Chiefs faced the Raiders. The family flew in that morning, for what became the sixth straight
Chiefs win over the Raiders, sealed by Jarrad Page's end zone interception.
Afterward in the Gold Suite, Lamar thanked Buck Buchanan's widow Georgia for coming, and she promised him another peach pie the next time he
was in Kansas City. Then he took out his copy of the NFL standings, adjusted
the win-loss records with the day's results, moving the Chiefs to 6–4, and
speculated that the Chiefs still had a shot to make the playoffs.

The next night, Lamar was back in Dallas, where Norma and the family had rented out a movie theater to celebrate Daniel's thirtieth birthday.
They watched *Casino Royale*, with Lamar gamely trying to stifle his persistent cough, then went to dinner at Mi Cocina with a group of friends and
family. "You could tell he was really struggling, but he never complained,"
said Daniel.

The following morning was the day of the Unity Hunt Thanksgiving luncheon, the one annual office gathering in which employees would bring their
spouses and children. The office was bustling that morning, but Susie Stephens could tell early on that her boss was suffering. "He just had looked terrible for such a long time, so frail and pale, but never complained," she said.
"Never. By that time, he was just worn out."

He strained to cheerfully make it through the luncheon, but right afterward, he agreed to let Daniel drive him to the hospital, where he was admitted with a collapsed lung. After tests were taken and the doctors conferred, word was discreetly sent back to the family. There was no longer any point in rushing him down to MD Anderson for further treatment. The end was near.

Two days later (after Daniel himself was admitted to the hospital, on the same floor as Lamar, with a bleeding ulcer), Clark and Tavia flew to Kansas City to stand in for Lamar, first at the Country Club Plaza, to turn on the lights for the ceremonial Thanksgiving evening tradition. And then at Arrowhead, where the Chiefs played host to the Broncos.

Lamar was in his hospital bed, unable to watch because the NFL Network was still not available on the Dallas cable system available at the Presbyterian Hospital. He did get new NFL commissioner Roger Goodell on the phone, eager to hear what Goodell thought of the scene in Kansas City (it was the first Chiefs game he would attend as a commissioner, and beforehand he was treated to a tour of the Chiefs' "42-year history wall," which Lamar had updated in 2001).

That evening, Sharron called Lamar's hospital room from her home and put the phone down in front of the television, so Lamar could listen to the television broadcast. At halftime, he hung up so he could call Peterson, but then he got back on the line with Sharron to listen to the second half.

And there, at seventy-four years old, listening through the static-filled phone line to the sounds of his favorite team, he could imagine himself far away, up in Kansas City, lost in the luminescent light of a night game, the swelling roars that greeted the action on the field . . . and he was not that far from where he'd been in 1940, in the library at Mount Vernon, head pressed close to the wooden base of the radio, listening to Kern Tips and Graham McNamee and Bill Stern broadcasting the big games, transported to a more vivid and perfect world.

American sports had changed dramatically in his lifetime, and he must have taken some special satisfaction from helping to change it. But that night, hip throbbing, breath coming with effort, face sallow and eyes deep-set, he still smiled when he heard Dante Hall running a kick back for a touchdown.

"You just realized at some point," said Lamar, Jr., "that this time he wasn't coming out."

His condition worsened—by early December, the disease began to ravage his internal organs, and he was paralyzed below the waist—and soon the family began a vigil. Norma would sit by him all day long, returning home to sleep and shower, and then be back the next morning.

One day, in early December, Norma left for a moment to get some food, and the phone in the hospital room rang. Lamar reached over to pick it up and answered with a faint "Hello."

"Lamar? It's Bobby—I thought Norma would have answered."

Nearly forty-five years after they'd first met, Bobby Bell was calling. They talked for a few minutes. "And he wanted to know how *I* was doing," said Bell.

At one point, after a long vigil, Clark said to Lamar, Jr., "You know, this is the longest period of time I've ever been alone with my father."

The NFL was holding a meeting in Dallas in early December, when Bills owner Ralph Wilson phoned Norma and asked if he could visit Lamar. Lamar was weak, his body hooked up to a network of tubes and machines, preparing for an MRI, as Wilson came to his bedside. Wilson recalled that it had been nearly forty-seven years ago that they'd first met, then he leaned over his old friend, took his hand, and said with a smile, "Lamar, this is Ralph. How did I let you get me into this whole mess?"

Lamar looked up with a wordless smile, moisture welling up in the corners of his eyes, and took Wilson's hand. A moment later, the two men— partners, competitors, friends—said their last goodbyes.

Later that day, after the MRI, as the nurses were wheeling Lamar back to the convalescing room, Daniel was the first to see him. His father, voice raspy and weak, implored him, "Don't let them do that to me again."

Dozens of his dearest friends and family members came by. Even Rose Mary returned, with Norma's blessing, to tell Lamar she still loved him. Carl Peterson came and shared a private moment of gratitude as well. At one point, Sharron sat by his bed and sang "On the Street Where You Live" from *My Fair Lady*, a song Lamar had sung to her when she was a toddler. Through his oxygen mask, he gently sang the chorus back to her.

In the final week, he would slip into and out of consciousness. One day, Daniel and Bill Adams were sitting in his room. Lamar had drifted off, and they were making small talk, discussing rookie quarterbacks, and Adams brought up the Broncos' rookie passer, but neither Adams nor Dan could remember the player's name.

"Oh, yeah . . . ," said Dan, the name on the tip of his tongue. "What is it?"

From the bed, Lamar's voice suddenly emerged, weak but clear: "Cutler," he said.

Over the last few days, traffic increased, each of the children felt as though it was nearly impossible to spend some time alone with their father. "I didn't really have a meaningful conversation at the very end," said Sharron, "because everyone was in and out of the hospital room every few minutes. It was kind of hard. That's kind of how it was during his life."

As the end drew near, they each gathered to pay their last respects. On Sunday, December 10, Lamar, Jr., had been in Dallas for days and had to return to Kansas City for work.

"Dad," he said. "Are you ready?"

"I can't imagine my life turning out the way it did," Lamar said. "Yes, I'm ready."

Lamar, Jr., kissed him on the forehead and left. Later that night, preparing to fly back to Kansas City, Lamar, Jr., called Sharron, remarked on their father's serenity and gratitude, and said he realized he would never see his father alive again.

A day later, Lamar was alone with Clark and had the chance to convey his most fervent wishes.

"I've worked hard to create some businesses that I think are really outstanding," he told Clark. "I know you're going to do a great job looking after them. I'd like to think that I had some ability myself, but I know you'll do fine."

It was time for unequivocal statements, and Clark didn't blanche. "I will do my absolute best," he promised. "And I'll work as hard as I can."

Lamar nodded. He knew as much. There was just one more thing.

"Please make sure," he said firmly, "that your mother goes to the Super Bowl. I don't want her to break her streak."

Clark promised his father he would. Having received that assurance, he drifted back off to sleep.

Two days later, on December 13, 2006, Lamar Hunt died.

EPILOGUE

So many years, so many lives touched. And when the news hit, they all thought of the last time they'd seen him. For one of the people whose life was shaped by Lamar—Kyle Rote, Jr.—it had been a couple of years earlier, getting on a plane in New York.

From his early twenties, Rote had envisioned a life in sports beyond his playing career, and he had found success as an agent. In the course of his decade with the Tornado and working with Lamar, he'd internalized a few habits. Lamar worked during flights, so Kyle worked during flights. "Lamar's always doing paperwork," said Rote. "He always carried paperwork, so if he got stopped or delayed, he could be productive. Don't waste precious time on an airplane, when they can't call you, no one can interrupt you, you get a lot of quiet time, use it—that was his philosophy as best as I could tell." And it had become Rote's philosophy.

He had amassed more than 6 million miles in air travel, so while upgrading to first class was always a possibility, Rote usually saved those for occasions when he traveled with his wife and children. He had learned over time that he could often get more done in a row to himself in coach rather than sitting next to someone in first class.

On this day, boarding a flight in La Guardia, Rote had a coach ticket and hadn't decided yet whether to upgrade. As he boarded the 707 jet, he noticed that there was plenty of room in first class.

"So I get on this plane, and it's going to be about a two-hour flight, and as I just get to the end of first class, I'm now surveying coach to see where there's space. The row that I've got is toward the back, and it's supposed to have only me in it, and it's a 2-3 configuration, I remember that very clearly. As I get to the coach section, I see, not three rows back, on the two-seat side, in the B seat on the aisle, Lamar's sitting there, and next to him is a very large, overweight woman. And already, they have pulled up the armrest between them."

Lamar was, in Rote's memory, "squinched up," and was wearing the Lamar Hunt Uniform: gray slacks, blue blazer, red-and-blue striped tie, light blue long-sleeve dress shirt, and loafers. Rote walked up and greeted his friend and longtime employer. "Lamar!" he said, and Lamar looked up, smiled, and the two men exchanged greetings, talked for a moment about Clark, and their respective families.

The attendants were closing the doors to the plane by now, and before moving back to his seat, Rote told Lamar, "Hey, I've got a complete row of three in the back, and if you want, feel free to come on back and we can talk a little bit more."

Lamar thanked him graciously, and with that, Rote moved on toward his seat.

"And, it didn't take me more than four or five rows walking back, and I wasn't even close to my row yet, but I already *knew* he would never come back," said Rote. "And the reason he would never come back is because he did not want to embarrass the lady sitting next to him, and make her feel uncomfortable that she was maybe too heavy or too fat, and that maybe he left because of that."

In the days following Lamar's death, friends and family would talk about his vision and his drive, his accomplishments in sports, his innovations, the opportunities he gave people, and his deep love of games. But what would remain with many of those who knew him was that simple, ineluctable fact: In a graceless age, Lamar Hunt was a man of steadfast decency.

"I cannot imagine having played pro sports for any entity other than Lamar and the Hunts," said Willie Lanier. "I don't see how it could have worked. I say that, because I know I have a somewhat different mindset and approach to things. I tend to clash pretty quickly at times. But with Lamar, it was based on mutual respect, and it just worked."

"With other owners, after the game they would summon you to their boxes," said Pat Schottenheimer, Marty's wife. "With Lamar, he would stop by and visit the coaches. Entirely different."

All the rest was important but that quality, and perhaps that alone, would have been enough. That was why, after memorial services in Dallas and Kansas City, it took Norma fully nine months to finish writing thank-you notes for each and every sympathy card, each and every heartfelt note, each arrangement of flowers, each person who wanted her to know how her husband had touched another life.

For his four children, the absence was acute, felt at the most obvious times—World Cups, Bulls' playoff runs, the grand reopening of the renovated Arrowhead in 2010—and also at less obvious moments, when they found themselves repeating some endearing quirk of his that they'd experienced long ago. Sharron, on the road with her children, would introduce a car game to pass the time. Clark, in the midst of his hectic schedule, found a way to coach his son's Little League team. More than five years after Lamar's death, each of the children would occasionally encounter someone they were meeting for the first time, who would tell a variation on the same story: "I met your father once, a long time ago, when I was a *nobody*. And he was so nice to me."

•

H. L. Hunt's legacy was the fortune wrought by his play on Daisy Bradford No. 3 and the empire he built with it. There are statues celebrating his life at the Thanksgiving Tower in Dallas and at the East Texas Oil Museum in Kilgore. But in the main, he is remembered today largely for his bigamy and his eccentricity. When Daniel Yergin's 800-page *The Prize: The Epic Quest for Oil, Money, and Power* was published in 2001, winning the Pulitzer Prize for general nonfiction as the definitive history of the oil industry, H. L. Hunt merited but two small mentions. His exploits were considerable at the time, but his long-term impact was limited.

By the time of his death, Lamar Hunt's boyhood worry—that he would never be remembered as anything other than just another of H. L. Hunt's sons—seemed preposterous. He'd launched the most successful upstart league of the past century of American sports. In football, the AFC Championship Trophy continued to bear his name. In soccer, the U.S. Open Cup, the oldest annual team tournament in American sports, had been renamed in his honor. He was in the Pro Football Hall of Fame, the International Tennis Hall of Fame, and the United States Soccer Hall of Fame, along with a score of others. Majestic bronze statues of Lamar were erected outside of Arrowhead in Kansas City, and the soccer stadiums he built in Texas and Ohio. But his impact went far beyond monuments.

To understand all that he had accomplished, it was useful to remember how humble and provincial the American sports industry was in the late '50s. The games, even then, were a vital part of the leisure time of a group of spirited, youthful-minded people. But in 1959, one could walk down a street in virtually any major city in America, and see no evidence whatsoever of the existence of spectator sports in the country. Relegated to a few pages in the back of most metropolitan newspapers and a corner of the newsstand, sports constituted a kind of secret society out in the open, operating on the fringes of American life. The biggest effort of sports marketing in the '50s focused on simply letting people know when the games would be played.

By the time of Lamar's death, sports had breached the walls of mainstream culture, and insinuated itself into the daily fabric of American media, discourse and popular culture. One could quibble over high ticket prices and the sense of entitlement among modern athletes, but the importance of the *culture* of sports was formidable, offering a precious sense of common ground in the increasingly Balkanized, niche-driven, narrowcast America of the twenty-first century.

America's most popular sport, pro football, owed much of its robustness and stability to his vision. At the memorial service in Dallas, Paul Tagliabue pulled Colts owner Jim Irsay aside and said, "Now, it's your generation's turn." Lamar's fellow owners recognized it as well.

"Lamar was a visionary," said Jim Irsay. "When we're playing games on the Moon or Mars, they ought to think about Lamar Hunt, because he's probably in his dreams seeing a retractable dome, with the right ventilation to keep everyone breathing."

•

The area around White Rock Lake is full of houses today. The empty lots that Lamar used to traverse on his way to the Lakewood bus line have been filled in. There are still sailboats out on the lake, and cyclists whiz by on the bike path that goes in front of Mount Vernon. But to drive up to H. L. Hunt's old mansion today is to see a change in Dallas. Football is still preeminent— Cowboys' decals on many of the cars, SMU and Highland Park schedules on the restaurant walls. But there's more evidence of another movement: Round dotted balls in front yards in nearby Highland Park, practice goals with netting, pylons for cone drills, and dozens of signs reading, "WE SUP-PORT OUR LADS SOCCER."

The change is seen well beyond the view from Mount Vernon. In Colum-bus and Frisco, north of Dallas, are the first and third ever soccer-specific stadiums ever built in America, and in Kansas City, where Lamar had pa-tiently waited for a local buyer, Livestrong Sporting Park, a $200 million fa-cility, opened on June 9, 2011, and instantly became, in the words of *Sports Illustrated*'s Grant Wahl, "a facility that can legitimately claim to be the finest soccer stadium in North America."

The soccer-specific stadium boom was just one in a confluence of fac-tors—World Cup ratings, Gold Cup ratings, European Champions League ratings, the popularity of the English Premier League on American televi-sion, the continued widespread popularity of the game as a participant sport, the stellar crowds enjoyed by traveling teams like Barcelona FC and Manchester United on their summer tours of the United States, and the slow, but unmistakable signs of growth of MLS—all pointing to a reality that would be true well before it was widely recognized: soccer was becoming the fifth major professional team sport in the American spectator sports landscape.

Books could be written about the sport's slow climb in America, but the story couldn't be told without Lamar's indefatigable advocacy, faith, and work on the game's behalf. He had found a second act to his grand American life, and the implications of that, of soccer's growth in the American marketplace, were just beginning to present themselves.

"Well, there's no American soccer today, without Lamar Hunt," said Don Garber. "His contributions and experiences from the early days of the NASL through the formation of Major League Soccer, and the guidance on key decisions, the sport is what it is today largely because of Lamar's vision. I don't think Phil Anschutz would have come into the league if Lamar wasn't a key supporter."

"He deserves a lot of credit," said Anschutz. "He deserves *the* credit. He was a great partner, he was the kind of guy you want to have as a partner. There are plenty of guys who are in sports leagues that are, I'm sure they're nice enough guys, but you wouldn't want to be their partner, even though you might have to be. Lamar was different."

The key, in the end, was not just Lamar's boundless faith but also his unquenchable patience. He took the long view. "I have no doubts that it will be a major sport in the United States," Lamar had said of soccer in 2002. "I'm probably not going to live to see that day because Americans are a little afraid of getting interested in something at which they're not very good."

He had brought America's Game to more cities than even the caretakers of pro football could have imagined. He helped drag tennis, despite its own vehement opposition, into an age of open prosperity. And thanks to Lamar Hunt, the Beautiful Game had finally taken root in America. Yet, in 1999, when *The Sporting News* released its list of the "100 Most Powerful Sports Figures of the Twentieth Century," Pete Rozelle placed first, followed by Judge Kenesaw Mountain Landis, ABC's Roone Arledge, Branch Rickey, and Marvin Miller. Lamar was ranked seventeenth, right below longtime NCAA chief Walter Byers and just ahead of sports and broadcasting mogul Ted Turner. As celebrated as he was in his lifetime, his own quiet, retiring manner had left him underrated.

The rankings took note of his contributions in football and innovations in tennis and soccer, but they were perhaps blind to his deeper and more profound effect on American sports.

Asked to articulate his worldview once, Lamar said, "I really feel strongly in the equality of people, though not necessarily in ability. Some people can run faster than others, some people are smarter than others."

If there was a theme to his life—beyond a love of sports, a gently reckoned optimism, and avoidance of personal conflict—this was it. From the fall of 1959, when he made sure that the first AFL draft was essentially a blind draw to protect the newer franchises ("we recognized it would be terribly unfair if some teams had a huge advantage in scouting") to the end of his life, when he was still arguing for a more equitable rotation of Thanksgiving Day home games in the NFL, this impulse animated him. At virtually every turn, from the beginning of the AFL to the zenith of the NASL to the formation of MLS, he argued and worked for a philosophy and league rules and structure in which any possible financial advantages, for him and others equally wealthy, would be obscured by mechanisms that guaranteed overall competitive balance for all franchises in all markets.

Don Garber would remember, after moving to MLS, the emphasis that Lamar put on equality of opportunity. "Lamar believed that you can't have a league that's driven just by big markets," Garber said. "You know, you've got to be successful in every market. Small markets have to succeed, they have to matter, they have to be competitive, their fans have to believe their teams can win, and have an opportunity to lift that trophy, just like fans in New York, LA, Chicago and other markets can. That model of equality and parity was a big part of Lamar's views of what professional sports require to succeed."

One can trace the concept of revenue sharing—the single most important aspect of the long competitive balance in the NFL—back to Lamar's airline stationery that launched the AFL. (If you want, you can trace it back farther, to the egalitarian audacity of Bill Veeck. But even if you do so, you'd have to grant that without Lamar, the practical viability of the idea may well have died with Veeck at baseball's 1952 winter meetings or with Branch Rickey on the drawing boards of the Continental League in 1959.)

Sports businesses around the world are Darwinian environments in which a bare fraction of teams have any kind of hope to compete. In the Scottish Premier League, either Celtic or Rangers has won the title every year since 1985. In the English Premiership, the top division of English football, only four clubs have won the title since 1995. The same is true throughout much of the world.

By contrast, sports in America—the land so often criticized for runaway commercialism and ugly avarice—stood as both the most lucrative sports market in the world, and among the fairest. Some of these mechanisms, such as the NFL draft, were in place before Lamar started the AFL. But his genius came in an understanding that competitive balance required fairness in both playing rules and in economic structure.

It started in 1960, when he pushed through equal television revenue sharing for all eight original AFL teams. The success of that plan, and the reality that every team in the AFL made more in TV revenue than nearly half of the teams in the established NFL, finally pushed the older league to adopt the same system a year later. When television revenues mushroomed in the '60s and exploded in the '70s and beyond, pro football alone had a financial structure that helped to guarantee competitive balance. And when the league finally adopted true free agency in the '90s, it was with a salary cap, another mechanism that Lamar staunchly supported.

The structural realities of the NFL—teams sharing equally among television revenue, teams constricted in their spending by an artificial cap, accompanied with a salary floor, so that every team had to spend the money to be competitive—would inform the formation of MLS. During the '90s and the '00s, every other league in American professional sports was trying to construct a system that moved closer to the NFL model.

As the broadcaster Bob Costas wrote in 2000, "baseball owners are still fighting today over things that football owners settled 40 years ago." Major League Baseball would move closer to the NFL model in the '00s; the NHL would soon follow suit. And in 2011, in the midst of the lockout that threatened the NBA's season, none other than Michael Jordan, by now the owner of the Charlotte Bobcats, said, "We need a lot of financial support throughout the league as well as revenue sharing to keep this business afloat. . . . For us to be profitable in small markets, we have to be able to win ballgames and build a better basketball team."

In every case, the rhetoric of collective bargaining was informed by the principles that had first guided Lamar in starting the AFL, and later had been applied to all of pro football. Without fanfare, he had pulled off the most audacious of revolutions, not in any single sport, but across much of American professional team sports as a whole. It wasn't just that he built, directly or indirectly, so many stadiums and playing fields. It was that, all along the way, he worked to make those playing fields more level. He had successfully interjected the doctrine of fairness into the business of American sports.

•

Lamar, Norma, Clark, and Tavia were at a party in the early 2000s in Aspen, where Clark and Tavia often vacationed. At one point, a group of guests were gathered on the patio, engaging in the aimless but comfortable after-dinner chat that marks a Saturday evening of good food and good company.

Someone brought up a fabulous vacation to a distant island, and described it as "my favorite spot in the world." And then that became the subject, and the small group of revelers went around the circle, each person citing his or her favorite place in the world.

"Lamar, what about you?" someone asked. "What's your favorite place in the world?"

The question required no extended reflection. Lamar knew his answer, and smiled as he replied, "Arrowhead."

He had been around the world, spent millions on fine art, eaten at many of the world's most celebrated restaurants, stayed in the most luxurious hotels, and spent time at exotic locales, looking at the world from countless breathtaking vistas. His favorite place was a football stadium.

None who knew him could be surprised. He'd spent a childhood conjuring up visions of packed stadiums from agate box scores, and later realized those dreams in ways that even he couldn't have conceived. What, after all, could be better than building an apartment *inside your own football stadium?* On the eve of games, as Norma went over final preparations for the next day's Gold Suite gathering, Lamar and his children often headed down to the field at Arrowhead. There was a sideline-to-sideline punting game that Lamar invented, where contestants tried to kick it as far across the field as they could, while keeping the ball as close as possible to the yard line they were kicking from. Those games, and their variations, could last into the evening. With the lights glittering down on the sacred space at the heart of the empty bowl, Lamar and his family and friends would *just play.*

Lamar Hunt's triumph was not merely that he loved games and stadiums and sports, and so many of the same things that he'd loved as a twelve-year-old. It was that he loved those things in the same way. An arch pun in a sports story, a good-natured yet wholly serious competition with Buzz Kemble over their respective weights, an eye-catching gimmick in a halftime show. It was a life in sports, not merely a livelihood; it was his connection with the world around him and, to a great extent, the way he viewed that world.

Always, at the heart of it all, were the games themselves. This, too, made perfect sense. If you'd grown up in a privileged world where your house was every bit as big as your imagination, with deer grazing in the backyard and a lake in the front, if you felt loved by but somewhat disconnected from your parents, and not privy to many of the whispered secrets of your older siblings, if you grew up realizing you would have more money than you might ever know what to do with, and this caused some people to stare at you or treat you differently, wouldn't you want to avoid that attention? Did Rita Hayworth like talking to strangers about her beauty? Did Einstein enjoy discussing his own intelligence? Lamar Hunt didn't dwell on money.

Nor did he dwell on pain—on the sadness of his lobotomized brother; the sudden, unimaginable loss of his mother; the stubborn will of his father, whom he was proud of and ashamed of at the same time. He never mastered a way to talk about these things, or his own divorce or, later, about the divorces of his two oldest children, or the financial self-destruction of his brothers, or his own illness.

These things surely troubled him. But he found sanctuary where he always had: It was in the tumult and boisterous goodwill before a big game, on a sunlit day or under the lights at night; sitting beneath a scorer's table courtside or looking out from the distant remove of a grandstand seat. His refuge was in the stadiums and arenas, where for two or three hours, he was swept up in the beauty and urgency and brilliant promise of the moment. Amid the clamor and excitement, the differences felt so acutely elsewhere in the world melted away, and people flowed together across race, class, and even language and nationality.

There, as a face in the crowd, Lamar Hunt was at home.

By the end of his life, much of America was right there with him.

ACKNOWLEDGMENTS

I was ten years old and growing up in Kansas City in 1973 when it first dawned on me that a man in Dallas named Lamar Hunt was responsible for some of my favorite things about my hometown, including the Chiefs, Worlds of Fun amusement park, and the Shakey's Pizza on Old 40 Highway. I first met him twenty-five years later, while beginning work on a book about pro football called *America's Game*. During the five years it took me to write that book, he was endlessly patient and accommodating.

So my first thanks are to Lamar's family—his widow, Norma; and his children Lamar, Jr., Sharron, Clark, and Daniel; as well as Lamar's siblings, Caroline and Herbert; and his nephew (and World Championship Tennis co-founder) Al Hill, Jr. They are a private family, and yet they graciously accommodated my many intrusions and my endless questioning. They also consented to let me write the book I wanted to write; although the family reviewed the manuscript to clarify points and correct errors, they neither altered nor censored any of my reporting. While I know there is material in here they would have been more comfortable with me leaving out, I hope what emerges is an accurate portrait of the man they loved and respected. (A special note of thanks as well to Lamar's first wife, Rose Mary Carr. Her keen memory and generosity of spirit were crucial to telling Lamar's story.)

In writing about Lamar's life, I wanted to see where he spent his time, and I am grateful for the tours of his past homes I received. Norma graciously showed me the home where she and Lamar lived for the last two decades of his life; Teresa Amend allowed me to visit the beautifully refurbished Mount Vernon, where he grew up, and Gene Phillips opened the doors of the Gaywood mansion where Lamar and Norma lived from 1971 to 1987. Thanks to Virginia Yinger, I also received a window into another of Lamar's homes—the Hill School in Pottstown, Pennsylvania, where he spent five years.

Lamar had fascinating friends, and it's been a pleasure spending much of the past two years traveling around the country and talking with several of them. Tom Richey (who shared a bulging box of correspondence with and articles about Lamar), Edward "Buzz" Kemble, Don McIlhenny, Phil Jones, and Phil Woods were all helpful.

For someone who worked as much as he did, it's not surprising that Lamar forged many of his deepest friendships at the office. Jack Steadman and Carl Peterson were crucial in providing insight into his leadership and thought processes, as well as accounts of many of his most important decisions. One of Lamar's most significant relationships was with Hank Stram, and I deeply appreciate the help from Hank's son, Dale Stram, who shared so many memories of his father, as well as Hank's 1969 playbook, and the text from his team talks that season. Among the legendary Chiefs, I'm particularly grateful for the time and candor of Willie Lanier, Len Dawson, Bobby Bell, and Jim Lynch, as well as Buck Buchanan's widow, Georgia. I would love to write a book about that special 1969 Chiefs team one day.

In the meantime, someone *ought* to write a book about the pilgrims who came to Dallas in the late 1960s and early '70s, and spawned one of the hotbeds of American youth soccer. The English expats—including Mike Renshaw, Kenny Cooper, Sr., Dick Hall, and Bobby Moffat, as well as Tornado coach Ron Newman—were integral in spreading the gospel of soccer, and doing so door-to-door when necessary. The sprawling eighteen-field complex in Frisco, Texas, is not merely their gathering place but also, to a certain degree, their legacy.

At the NFL, I'm grateful for the help of commissioner Roger Goodell, former commissioner Paul Tagliabue, Jeff Pash, Greg Aiello, and Joe Browne, as well as Steve Sabol and David Plaut at NFL Films. At Major League Soccer, commissioner Don Garber and president Mark Abbott (who shared Lamar's copious notes on the original MLS single-entity prospectus) were invaluable, as were Lamar's friends and partners, Philip Anschutz and Robert Kraft. I also appreciate the time and insight of Sunil Gulati and Dan Flynn at the U.S. Soccer Federation.

In tennis, I'm grateful for the patient attention of (and extensive loaned materials from) Rod Humphries, who walked me through his vision of the history of pro tennis one afternoon in Houston, and of longtime WCT executive director Mike Davies. Over breakfast one morning in St. Louis, Butch Buchholz—one of the original "Handsome Eight"—sat down with me and lucidly explained how things were, and how they changed when the WCT came along.

Along the way, I received plenty of assistance from many at Hunt Sports and Hunt Midwest, especially from my friend and Chiefs historian Bob Moore (who first suggested me for the project, and then endured numerous drafts of the work in progress), as well as John Wagner, Ryan Petkoff, Alan Tompkins, Kathy McDaniel, Suzanne Cornett, Kristen Deahl, Lee Derrough, and Kim Rutter, as well as Al Hill, Jr.'s assistant, Joy Waller. I also received a great deal of help from Lamar's former executive assistant, Thom Meredith.

At Andrews McMeel, I am indebted to Hugh Andrews for taking on this project; for the trenchant editing eye of Chris Schillig; as well as gifted copyeditor Elizabeth Degenhard; David Shaw; Susie Morris; Cliff Koehler; Amy Worley; Kathy Hilliard; Lynne McAdoo; and Kirsty Melville.

The process of assembling this material was made bearable by the expert transcription work of Shannon McCormack (and her trusty aide, Russ Dummerth), as well as the labor of my underpaid research assistant, Michael Galvin. I also received some valuable ad hoc research assistance from Ed Krzemienski, Ross Lillard, Nancy Gates, and Bob Jacobi, Jr. Once again, Saleem Choudhry, at the Pro Football Hall of Fame, was both helpful and accommodating.

In this book, like all the others, I have been sustained by the friends and relations who put me up—and put up with me—during the book's long gestation period. My girlfriend, Ivy Tominack, provided companionship and countless gourmet dinners in St. Louis. My mother, Lois MacCambridge, delivered endless moral support and gentle reminders when I fell behind schedule, which was—let's face it—pretty much the entire time. My friend Trey Gratwick and his children Tyler and Ashley were my home away from home during my many trips to Kansas City. Chris and Jenny Bosworth provided room, board, and exquisitely good company during the Great Dallas Super Bowl snowstorm week of 2011. I also received accommodations from dear friends Kevin Lyttle in Austin, David Zivan in Indianapolis, and Joe Bienvenu and Holly Tominack in Baltimore. (They weren't the only ones: In addition to the hospitality of Dale and Janet Stram during my Louisiana jaunt, Smokey Stover and his wife Johnette fed me a wonderful dinner during a late-night trip through Louisiana.)

For their abiding support and friendship through this project and over the years, I am indebted to Reggie Givens, Greg Emas, Laura Pfeifauf, Angie and Tom Szentgyorgyi, Andy Lovins, Brian Hay, Rebecca Tominack and Glenn Hachey, Dr. Gerald Early, Pat Porter, Bill James, Russell Smith, Loren Watt, Stan Webb, Larry Johnson, Hal Cox, Susan Reckers, Jane Girson, Robert Draper, Chris Brown, Tony Owens, Michael Hurd, Michael Sutter, Joanne Stouwie, Riza Raffi, John and Lois Stob, Nicole and James Stubbe, Kristin Elizondo, Rosie Roegner, Jeff Groene, Neal Richardson, Marilyn Breitling, Scott Granneman, Denise Lieberman, and David Hale, I also want to thank my friends in the business, most especially Grant Wahl, Joe Posnanski, Dan Jenkins, John Walsh, Bob Costas, Bob McGinn, Vahe Gregorian, and Alex Wolff. As for coaches Brian Billick and Larry Kindbom, I am thankful not only for their friendship but also for the continuing education in football they've provided. As ever, the more I learn, the more I appreciate how little I know.

I am deeply grateful for my dear friend and confidante Robert Minter (who in addition to everything else, did some crucial last-minute research in Dallas for me, on the 1939 Cotton Bowl); my fellow road warrior Rich Moffitt, who talked me through it all; and the many friends at my regular Friday lunch, who've given me love, support, and plenty of hard-earned wisdom over the years.

In addition to Bob Moore, Zivan, Kindbom, and Minter all read parts of the early manuscript. Together, they saved me from a lot of mistakes, but the ones that made it through are all my own. (If you find others, please send me a note at maccambridge@mac.com, so I may correct them for future editions of the book.)

As always, I owe a special note of thanks to my patient and irrefutably wise agent, Sloan Harris of ICM, as well as Rick Pappas. They have been with me throughout this great adventure, and it would not have been conceivable for me to get here without them.

Finally, I owe my deepest gratitude to my children, Miles and Ella. They have grown up with my books, gamely tagged along for many work-related road trips, grown accustomed to the view from inside several football and soccer stadiums (and, I must admit, a few sports bars as well), and have endured the constant interruptions, phone calls, and e-mails with patience and good humor. Through it all, they have been loving, supportive, and understanding; they continue to be my greatest source of inspiration and joy.

MJM, St. Louis, May 2012

SOURCE NOTES

EPIGRAPH AND PROLOGUE

Epigraph: *Homo Ludens*, Johan Huizinga; "My Passport Was at Shortstop," Wilfrid Sheed, *Sports Illustrated*, November 11, 1968; author interview with Lamar Hunt, 2001.

Prologue: Details from the visit to the Cotton Bowl were gleaned from two author interviews with Lamar Hunt, 2000–2001, as well as interviews with Caroline and Herbert. Lamar Hunt noted that he vividly remembered the 1939 Texas Tech–St. Mary's Cotton Bowl as his first, beginning a personal streak of attending the Cotton Bowl for more than fifty years in a row, though his sister Margaret once said that Lamar likely had gone to the first and second one as well, because "we always took you everywhere." In this case, Lamar's specific memory—from the eyes of a six-year-old who was already captivated by sport—seems more reliable than his older sister's general notion that he always came along, especially since contemporaneous accounts, and Lamar and Herbert's own recollection, indicate that wasn't the case. Also: *I'll Tell You One Thing*, the *Dallas Morning News*, January 1–3, 1939; *Football Texas Style*, Kern Tips; *The Great State Fair of Texas*, Nancy Wiley; *The ESPN College Football Encyclopedia*, Michael MacCambridge; Sam Blair's "The Roots and Fruits of the Cotton Bowl Classic," from *The Dallas Morning News*, December 16, 1978; "Lamar Hunt, a Force in Football, Dies at 74," *New York Times*, December 15, 2006; "Chiefs Owner Lamar Hunt Dead," *USA Today*, December 14, 2006; "Lamar Hunt, Chiefs Owner and Sports Legend, Dies at 74," ESPN.com, December 14, 2006, and broadcast transcript from *SportsCenter*, December 14, 2006. *The Franchise: A History of Sports Illustrated*, Michael MacCambridge; *America's Game: The Epic Story of How Pro Football Captured A Nation*, Michael MacCambridge; "Biggest Cheapskate in Big D," by Jack Olsen, *Sports Illustrated*, June 19, 1972; "Tale of the Hunts," *Ultra Magazine*, July 1988; "Lamar Hunt: The Backyard Player Who Made Big-Time Tennis," by Kim Chapin, *Sport*, September, 1972; "It's Chiefly Business with Lamar Hunt," *Kansas City Star Sunday Magazine*, October 11, 1970; "He's A Modest Super Chief," *Southwest Scene, the Dallas Morning News Sunday Magazine*, May 3, 1970; "A Texas Tycoon's Million-Dollar Team Is Making Tennis A Booming Business," John

J. Green, *The Detroit News Sunday News* Magazine, June 6, 1971; "It's Lamar Hunt's Game Even if Packers Roll, 42–14," Sandy Grady, *Philadelphia Bulletin,* January 15, 1967; "Lamar Hunt—Facts and Fiction," Wells Twombly column; *The Sporting News,* December 5, 1970; "Hunt Looks Back at 40 Years of Chiefs Football," Bob Gretz, *Chiefs Report,* Red Friday issue, NFL Week #2, 1999; "A Hunt for Economy," Charles Thobae, *Texas Sportsworld,* March 1985; Don Garber interview; David Dixon interview; Lamar Hunt interview; Clive Toye interview; Sharron Hunt Munson interview; Norma Hunt interview; Roger Goodell interview; Marty Schottenheimer interview; Dick Vermeil interview; Jack Steadman interview; Thom Meredith interview; Len Dawson interview; John Newcombe interview; Pat Williams interview; Dan Jenkins interview.

CHAPTER ONE | LATE ARRIVAL

Many of the scenes in this chapter were taken from Margaret Hunt Hill's excellent *H. L. and Lyda* (written with Burt and Jane Boyar). Several of Lamar's personal recollections, as well as details on the family history as related by Herbert and Bunker, came from the unpublished interviews that the Boyars did with each of the family members while preparing to collaborate with Margaret Hunt Hill for her book. Some of the additional details of Lamar's early years, in both Tyler and Dallas, come from notes and documents he stored in four boxes, which were later recovered from the attic of Mount Vernon, as well as the signed letter from the nine-year-old Lamar that Caroline Hunt saved from her personal papers. Also: Lamar Hunt interview; Lamar Hunt birth certificate, El Dorado County, Arkansas; Herbert Hunt interview; *H. L. and Lyda; The Big Rich: The Rise and Fall of the Greatest Texas Oil Fortunes,* Bryan Burrough; *Texas Rich: The Hunt Dynasty from the Early Oil Days Through the Silver Crash,* Harry Hurt III; *Hunt Heritage,* H. L. Hunt; Margaret Hunt Hill interview with Boyars; author visit to Charnwood in Tyler, Texas; author visit to East Texas Oil Museum; Caroline Hunt interview; Lamar Hunt letter to Caroline Hunt, undated, circa 1941; Lamar Hunt unpublished interview with Boyars; *200 Years of Sports in America,* Wells Twombley; *The Pro Football Chronicle,* Dan Daly and Bob O'Donnell; Dan Jenkins interview; Herbert Hunt interview; Bunker Hunt interview; Al Hill, Jr., interview.

CHAPTER TWO | MANSION ON THE HILL

Much of the detail from this chapter came from an interview the author did with Lamar Hunt April 20, 2000, when Hunt drove by Mount Vernon and parts of the Lakewood area, and spoke of his childhood. The author also visited Mount

Vernon in 2010, receiving a tour from Teresa Amend, who along with her husband John, purchased the estate in 2000, after the death of Ruth Ray Hunt. On April 16, 2002, Lamar returned to Mount Vernon for a speech for the Dallas Historical Society ("Lamar Hunt Notes for Remarks at Dallas Historical Society Meeting," Lamar Hunt, delivered April 16, 2002), in which he recalled growing up in the home. "It was the best speech he ever gave," said Norma, and much of its detail is included in the chapter. Also: Buddy Rupe interview (originally done for *America's Game*); Lamar Hunt unpublished interview with the Boyars; Lamar Hunt letter to Caroline Hunt, January 15, 1940; Herbert Hunt interview, *H. L. and Lyda*; "Developer Buys Lakewood Center," Steve Brown, *Dallas Morning News*, June 22, 2011; Sam Blair interview; Bob Chilton interview; "Just Plain H. L. Hunt," Tom Buckley, *Esquire*, January, 1967.

CHAPTER THREE | "HERBIE"
Much of the background for this chapter came during the author's visit to The Hill in September 2010. Additional background information from Virginia Yinger, the Hill School. Also: Graham Humes interview; Lamar Hunt interview; Herbert Hunt interview; Tom Richey interview; Johnny Fisher interview; Phil Woods interview; Jim Yonge interview; Dick O'Shaughnessy interview; Lamar Hunt unpublished interview with Boyars; Bunker Hunt unpublished interview with Boyars; Herbert Hunt unpublished interview with Boyars; *Whatsoever Things Are True*, Willis Pierre, Hill School Publications, 20TK; *The History of The Hill School, 1851–1976*, Paul Chancellor; *The Dial, 1947; The Dial, 1948; The Dial, 1949; The Dial, 1950; The Dial, 1951; H. L. and Lyda*, Hill; *Doak Walker: More Than a Hero*, Whit Caning; "Ultimate Hero: Doak Walker, *the* All-American, Built a Legend," Sam Blair, *Dallas Morning News*, September 26, 1986; "Southwest Has A New Crop of Super Rich: Is This the Richest Man in the U.S.?", unsigned, *Life*, April 5, 1948; *Lamar Hunt and the Founding of the American Football League*, Tom Richey; "Doak Walker of Southern Methodist," *Life* (cover), September 27, 1948; "Southwest," Amos Melton, *Street & Smith's Football Yearbook*, 1948; "The Southwest," George W. White, *Illustrated Football Annual*, 1948; "The Southwest," Curtis Bishop and Wilbur Evans, *Street & Smith's Football Yearbook*, 1949; "Walker Ends Brilliant Career Against Notre Dame," Bill Rives, *Dallas Morning News*, December 3, 1949; "Southwest," Flem Hall, *Street & Smith's Football Yearbook*, 1950; "Great Rivalries, No. 2: Army vs. Navy," Jack Zanger, *Sport*, October 1969; "Sport's Hall of Fame: Doak Walker," Arnold Hano, *Sport*, October, 1969; telegram, from Mr. and Mrs. D. Gordon Rupe, Jr., and Buddy, to Lamar Hunt, June 3, 1951.

CHAPTER FOUR | "POOR BOY"

The best recollection of Lamar's life during college comes his first wife, Rose Mary Carr, and his friends and teammates on the football team, and friends and fraternity brothers in the Kappa Sigma Fraternity. The author received a tour from Ed Bernet of some of Lamar's favorite haunts on and near the SMU campus. Also: Rose Mary Carr interview; Lamar Hunt interview; Lamar Hunt unpublished interview with Boyars; Herbert Hunt interview; *The Dial, 1950* (Lamar Hunt's copy); LeVon Massengale interview; *The Great State Fair of Texas,* Wiley; *SMU Ponies, 1951,* Lamar Hunt scrapbook; Phil Jones interview; Roger Blackmar interview; Ed Bernet interview; Don McIlhenny interview; Al Hill, Jr., interview; Norma Hunt interview; Bob Chilton interview; Bill Adams interview; Buddy Rupe interview; personal travel journal of Phil Woods, 1952; "Games I Have Seen This Year," journal of Lamar Hunt; *TV Guide,* October 26–November 1, 1951; "Fireworks in the Football Feud," Bill Stern, *Sport,* September 1950; *America's Game,* MacCambridge; Bud Shrake interview; Bunker Hunt unpublished interview with Boyars; Joe James interview; three-ring binder belonging to Lamar Hunt at SMU, date unknown; *You Know Me Al: A Busher's Letters,* Ring Lardner; *Do You Know Your Baseball?,* Bill Brandt; *If I Were in Your GOLF Shoes,* Johnny Farrell; *Youth's Courtship Problems,* Alfred L. Murray; Raymond Berry interview; Forrest Gregg interview; *1954 SMU Team Prospectus*; John Marshall interview; "Mister, He Kissed Her," music by Hoagy Carmichael, lyrics by Frank Kautzmann.

CHAPTER FIVE | A MAN ALONE

The beginning of Lamar Hunt's professional career also witnessed the beginning of his remarkably detailed and thorough recordkeeping. Among his personal papers were hundreds of subject and idea files, much of his correspondence (especially from 1980 onward) and a majority of the paperwork that he accumulated while planning and forming the American Football League. Also: Lamar Hunt interview; *H. L. and Lyda,* Hill; Daniel Hunt interview; Rose Marry Carr interview; Bob Wilkes interview; Buzz Kemble interview; letters from Tom Richey to Lamar Hunt, undated, circa 1951–56; John Marshall interview; "Test Your Horse Sense," column by Dr. George W. Crane, *Dallas Morning News,* September 1, 1943; Bill Adams interview; LeVon Massengale interview; Carl Shannon interview; Sam Hunt interview; Don McIlhenny interview; Letter from Al Hill to Lamar Hunt, February 23, 1956; postcard from Lamar Hunt to Rose Mary Hunt, April 20, 1956; Tom Richey interview; "The World's Richest Men," Robert E. Bedingfield, *New York Times Magazine,* October 20, 1957; Jake Cobb interview; Bob Chilton interview; Buzz Kemble interview; Dan Jenkins interview; Mack Rankin interview; *Grand Expectations: The United States, 1945–1974,* James T. Patterson; *America's Game,* MacCambridge; Lamar Hunt deposition in *AFL v. NFL,* US 12599; Stormy Bidwill interview; Bill Mercer interview; Bud Adams interview; Bunker Hunt unpublished interview with Boyars; "Original 6; First Year's Operations," notes by Lamar Hunt on a new football league, February 1959.

CHAPTER SIX | SURVEYING THE FIELD

Letter from Lamar Hunt to James Ralph Wood (and 200 other Dallas "business opinion leaders") to survey Dallas businessmen on attitudes toward pro football in Dallas, March 13, 1959; Walter Robertson interview; Tom Richey interview; *America's Game,* MacCambridge; Bud Adams interview; Barron Hilton interview; Stormy Bidwill interview; Don Weiss interview; Bert Bell, Jr., letter from Ole Haugsrud to LaMar Hunt [sic], August 24, 1959; Lamar Hunt memo to Davey O'Brien, July 1959; Bert Bell Testimony in "Senate Subcommittee on Antitrust and Monopoly," *Organized Professional Team Sports Hearings,* 86th Congress, 1st Session, July 1959, S. Res 57 on S. 616 and S. 886; Mickey Herskowitz interview; Lamar Hunt unpublished interview with Boyars; Jack Steadman interview; Letter from W. E. Rhodes to Bert Bell, February 24, 1958; Ralph Wilson interview; Rose Mary Carr interview; Mack Rankin interview; *A Proud American: The Autobiography of Joe Foss,* Joe Foss; Davey O'Brien letter to Lamar Hunt, July 21, 1959; "The Hunt Won't Start on NFL's Property," Bud Shrake, *Dallas Times Herald,* July 31, 1959; "Dallas' First Pro? Meredith Wants In," Louis Cox, *Dallas Times Herald,* August 1, 1959; "Hunt Off and Running on Organizing Tour," *Dallas Times Herald,* August 2, 1959; "The Hunts: Family Next Door," unsigned, *Dallas Morning News,* August 9, 1959; "Press Release," Richard White, Conrad Hilton Hotel, August 14, 1959; letter to First National Bank, from Barron Hilton, Lamar Hunt, Bud Adams, Harry Wismer, D. E. O'Shaughnessy, Nash J. Dowdle, Max Winter. E. W. Boyar, H. P. Skoglund, Robert L. Howsam; "Estimated Operation of Dallas Club for 1st Year," Lamar Hunt worksheet, circa 1959; "Possible Cities," Lamar Hunt worksheet, circa 1959; "American Football League: A Projection," prospectus prepared by Barron Hilton and Los Angeles Chargers, September, 1959; telegram from Lamar Hunt to Fritz Crisler, September 15, 1959; letter from Lamar Hunt to Fritz Crisler, October 19, 1959; "Hunt Looks Back at 40 Years of Chiefs Football," Bob Gretz, *Chiefs Report,* Red Friday Issue, 1999; letter from Gregory R. Dillon to American Football League owners, November 16, 1959; letter from Lamar Hunt to William H. Sullivan, November 18, 1959; Tom Richey interview; letter from Lamar Hunt to American Football league owners, December 3, 1959.

CHAPTER SEVEN | "GO TEXAN!—GO AMERICAN!"

Postcard from Bunker Hunt to Lamar Hunt, October 2, 1959; Lamar Hunt interview; Bob Wilkes interview; telegram from Bud Wilkinson to Lamar Hunt, October 1959; Hank Stram interview; *They're Playing My Game*, Hank Stram, with Lou Sahadi; "H.W. McNutt Jr., 81: His Company Sold Fruitcake to World," by Claire Noland, *Los Angeles Times*, September 16, 2006; "Competition in Texas," unsigned, *Sports Illustrated*, September 14, 1959; Jay Michaels letter to Joe Foss, March 17, 1960; Gary Cartwright interview; Bob Halford interview; Bill Mercer interview; Dan Jenkins interview; Dale Stram interview; Lamar Hunt letter to Martana TK, October 19, 1999; Chris Burford interview; *Winning It All*, "Hunt's Light Shining after 25 Years," Bob Gretz, *Kansas City Times*, September 1, 1984; "Forerunners Feel Bonded to Early Roots," Kent Pulliam, *Kansas City Times*, September 1, 1984; Joe McGuff; Smokey Stover interview; letter from Ruth Ray Hunt to Lamar Hunt, September 7, 1960; Mack Rankin interview; Jack Steadman interview; Roger Blackmar interview; Rose Mary Carr interview; Ed Bernet interview; Caroline Hunt interview; letter from Lamar Hunt to Joe Foss, November 17, 1961; Al Michaels interview; American Football League minutes, annual meeting, January 10, 1962; Personal and confidential memorandum, Jack Steadman to Lamar Hunt, October 17, 1962; Personal and confidential memorandum, Jack Steadman to Lamar Hunt, October 18, 1962; Len Dawson interview; Stu Stram interview; David Dixon interview; *TV Guide*, December 22–28, 1962; Lamar Hunt, Jr., interview; Tom Richey interview; Herbert Hunt interview; Abner Haynes interview; "Texans Now Rule AFL Kingdom," Sam Blair, *Dallas Morning News*, December 24, 1962; "Battle Nerves Buffet Texans," Bud Shrake column, *Dallas Morning News*, December 24, 1962; "Delirium Grips Victorious Texans," unsigned, *Dallas Morning News*, December 24, 1962; "Triple in 11th Inning Wins It: Texans Grab AFL Title," Gary Cartwright, *Dallas Times Herald*, December 24, 1962; "The Happy Return of the Champions," Blackie Sherrod column, *Dallas Times Herald*, December 24, 1962.

CHAPTER EIGHT | THE HEART OF AMERICA

Details on the negotiated move from interviews with Lamar Hunt, Jack Steadman, David Dixon, Mary Dixon, as well as an account in *Winning It All*, Joe McGuff. Additional newspaper accounts: "Texans to Head for Kansas City—If," Gary Cartwright, *Dallas Morning News*, February 9, 1963; "Hunt Okays Kansas City Bid for Texans," UPI wire story, *Chicago Tribune*, February 9, 1963; "Promises Must Be Met, Hunt Says," unsigned, *Dallas Morning News*, February 10, 1963; "Move Underlines AFL Shakiness," Arthur Daley, New York Times New Service, February 11, 1963;

"The Hunt for Peace," Gary Cartwright column, *Dallas Morning News,* February 10, 1963; "AFL Is Better Off in Kansas City," Steve Weller column, *Buffalo Evening News,* February 11, 1963; "Texans Will Move Here," Chris Burford interview; Jerry Mays letter to Lamar Hunt, undated (circa spring 1963); Len Dawson interview; Norma Hunt interview; Abner Haynes interview; Rose Mary Carr interview; Lamar Hunt letter to TK, March 1963; "Kansas City: Cosmopolis of the Heartland," Frederic A. Birmingham, *Saturday Evening Post,* September 1975; Bobby Bell interview; Ernest Mehl, *Kansas City Star,* May 22, 1963; "Texans Say Official Adios," unsigned, *Dallas Morning News,* May 23, 1963; "Hunt Announces Kansas City Deal," unsigned, *Dallas Times Herald,* May 22, 1963; "Bartle in Cloak-and-Dagger," James J. Fisher, *Kansas City Star,* May 23, 1963; "KC Gets Texans," UPI wire story, *Orlando Sentinel,* May 23, 1963; "Chiefs Really Going," Frank Boggs, *Dallas Times Herald,* June 21, 1963; "Baseball Fans Helped KC Land Football Team," Bob Gretz, *Kansas City Star,* September 26, 1982; "Homecoming Game: Lamar Hunt's Chiefs Return to City He Surrendered," Gerry Fraley, *Dallas Morning News,* November 22, 1995; Lamar Hunt, Jr., interview; Dale Stram interview; Curtis McClinton interview; "Neck, Spinal Cord Injuries Cause of Johnson's Death," unsigned, *Wichita Eagle-Beacon,* September 10, 1963; letter from Eddie Robinson to Lamar Hunt, October 28, 1963; Jake Cobb interview; Bill Adams interview; "The Disciples of St. Darrell on a Wild Weekend," Dan Jenkins, *Sports Illustrated,* November 11, 1963; Bill Mercer interview; Bob Halford interview; *Warren Commission Report,* Testimony of Connie Trammel Penny, File No. DL-44-1639; *They're Playing My Game,* Stram; Dan Jenkins interview; Lamar Hunt letter to Dick Ebersol, February 27, 2006; Ralph Wilson interview; *America's Game,* MacCambridge; Bud Adams interview; Tom Werblin interview; Jake Cobb interview; Lloyd Wells interview; "Was This Their Freedom Ride?" Ron Mix, *Sports Illustrated,* January 18, 1965; Don Klosterman Interview Transcript from Interviews done for HBO documentary *Rebels With a Cause*; Lamar Hunt, Jr., interview; Sharron Hunt Munson interview; "Portrait of a Super-Patriot," Robert G. Sherrill, *The Nation,* February 24, 1964; "Hunt Strikes Ink," unsigned, *Newsweek,* January 18, 1965.

CHAPTER NINE | "I BELIEVE WE SHOULD 'COIN A PHRASE'..."
Lamar Hunt letter to Chester "Chet" Simmons, March 13, 1964; "Without Them, We're Wichita," Michael MacCambridge, *The Sporting News,* August 11, 1997; "Wolves Wail as Chiefs Prevail," *Kansas City Times,* November 30, 1965; *Winning It All,* McGuff; Norma Hunt interview; Len Dawson interview; *America's Game,* MacCambridge, John Martin interview; Lamar Hunt interview; "On With the

Golden Game," Tex Maule, *Sports Illustrated,* September 13, 1966; "Here's How It Happened," Tex Maule, *Sports Illustrated,* June 20, 1966; Tex Schramm interview; "After Foss, A Hotter Pro War," Edwin Shrake, *Sports Illustrated,* April 18, 1966; *Slick,* Mark Ribowsky; "War Declared on AFL's Rival," William Wallace, *New York Times,* April 29, 1966; "Act of Provocation," Arthur Daley column, *New York Times,* May 19, 1966; Mickey Herskowitz interview; *Player of the Year: Roman Gabriel's Football Journal,* Roman Gabriel; Buddy Rupe interview; Lou Spadia interview; "Joint Statement, National and American Football Leagues," NFL press release, June 8, 1966; Al Davis interview; *Rebels With a Cause,* HBO documentary film, 2009; "NFL vs. AFL in Title Game This Season," unsigned, *St. Louis Post-Dispatch,* June 9, 1966; "Early Road to Merger Paved With Irony," Gary Cartwright, *Dallas Morning News,* June 12, 1966; "Who Put the Super in Bowl," Sam Blair, *Dallas Morning News,* January 20, 1979; "Sharron Won't Be at HER game," Pat Truly, *Fort Worth Star-Telegram,* January 6, 1977; letter from Lamar Hunt to Pete Rozelle, July 25, 1966; Don Weiss interview; Bill Adams interview, Buzz Kemble interview; *AFL Pictorial,* game program, Kansas City Chiefs vs. Buffalo Bills, October 2, 1966; Jake Cobb interview; Phyllis Stram interview; Jack Steadman interview; "Sporting Comment," Joe McGuff column, *Kansas City Star,* December 30, 1966; Corky Flynn interview; "12,000 Greet the Chiefs," unsigned, *Kansas City Times,* January 2, 1967; "Chiefs Roll to Super Bowl, 31–7," Bill Richardson, *Kansas City Times,* January 2, 1967; Herbert Hunt interview; *When Pride Still Mattered,* David Maraniss; *Kansas City Chiefs,* Dick Connor; *The Super Bowl: Celebrating a Quarter-Century of America's Greatest Game,* Ray Didinger; *The Other League,* Jack Horrigan and Mike Rathet; "Gate Crashers and Frog Legs," Will McDonough, in *A Game of Passion: The NFL Literary Companion,* edited by John Wiebusch and Brian Silverman.

CHAPTER TEN | NEW FRONTIERS

The venerable soccer writer Paul Gardner's work on the rise and eventual demise of the NASL is the standard against which all other accounts are measured. Gardner was kind enough to provide four pages of notes from an interview he did with Lamar Hunt at the Roosevelt Hotel, January 7, 1971. Much of the correspondence surrounding the world tour of the Dallas Tornado came from a personal file in Lamar's papers, which included a day-by-day recap of events by his administrator Paul Waters, and from Mike Renshaw's eminently readable (though as yet unpublished) memoir, *Just a Life.* Also: *1966 Uncovered: The Unseen Story of the World Cup in England,* Peter Robinson and Doug Cheeseman, text by Harry Pearson; Lamar Hunt letter to Paul French, December 5, 2005; "What It Was on TV Screen Was Soccer," unsigned, *Dallas Morning News,* July 31, 1966; "When the Reality of a Lead Doesn't Quite Live Up to its Legend," Dave Kindred, National Sports Journalism Center, October 1, 2010; *Constitution: North American Soccer League,* August 23, 1966; "Agreement Between United States Soccer Football Association, Incorporated and North American Soccer League," December 28, 1966; letter from Lamar Hunt to Michael Lewis, September 30, 2002; *Introducing Dundee United Football Club,* self-published booklet, Dundee United Football Club, undated, circa 1967; "Tornado in Stormy Deadlock, 2–2, Bob St. John, *Dallas Morning News,* June 15, 1967; "Tornado Gets 'Whipped', 2–0," Roy Edwards, *Dallas Morning News,* July 2, 1967; "Tornado on the Skyline," Bob St. John, *Dallas Morning News,* June 27, 1967; "Soccer is Simple?," unsigned, *Newsweek,* April 24, 1967; "To Start A League," Roy Edwards column, *Dallas Morning* News, March 11, 1968; Herbert Hunt interview; Norma Hunt interview; Jerry Colangelo interview; *Nice Guys Finish Last: Sport and American Life,* Paul Gardner; Kyle Rote, Jr., interview; Bob McNutt interview; Bill McNutt interview; Lamar Hunt interview; David Dixon letter of agreement to Lamar Hunt and Al Hill, Jr., September 15, 1967; "Chiefs Smash N.F.L. Bears, 66–24," Bill Richardson, *Kansas City Times,* August 24, 1967; *Winning It All,* McGuff; Mary Dixon interview; Mike Davies interview; "World Championship Tennis: Net Result," Lamar Hunt, *Saturday Evening Post,* April, 1976; Butch Buchholz interview; Donald Dell interview; "A Chronological History of World Championship Tennis," unsigned, WCT publicity department, circa 1990; "Lamar Hunt and the Opening of Tennis: A Synopsis," unpublished paper by Bob Moore; Richard Evans Interview; "A Texas Tycoon's Million-Dollar Team Is Making Tennis a Booming Business," Green; Al Hill, Jr., interview; *Open Tennis,* Richard Evans; Mike Davies interview; Wayne Henry interview; "Leaning on Fruitcake," from Scorecard, *Sports Illustrated,* August 26, 1968; Alan Rothenberg interview; Bobby Moffat interview; *A Kick in the Grass,* Clive Toye; "Development Coordinating Committee Report to the Board of Directors of the North American Soccer League," Clive Toye, chairman, September 30, 1968; Clive Toye interview; "Soccer: Ambition Unlimited and a Major Program Now Under Way," United States Soccer Football Association press release, September 11, 1969; Buzz Kemble interview; "The Big Daddy of Sport," Edwin Shrake, *Sports Illustrated,* September 7, 1970; Bill Adams interview; "If Not Alcatraz, How About Candlestick?," Melvin Durslag column, *Los Angeles Herald-Examiner,* July 30, 1969; proposal for Alcatraz commissioned by Lamar Hunt; Sharron Hunt interview; Lamar Hunt unpublished interview with Boyars; Bill Adams interview; "2nd-Class Citizen," Charles Maher column, *Los Angeles Times,* November 25, 1969.

CHAPTER ELEVEN | ON TOP OF THE WORLD

Among Lamar Hunt's papers was a detailed scrapbook of the Chiefs' 1969 season (assembled by a season-ticket holder, who sent it to Lamar some years later), with almost every story written during the season by *Kansas City Star* sports editor Joe McGuff, beat writer Bill Richardson, and staff writer Gary D. Warner. The two books published the fall after the Chiefs' title—Len Dawson's autobiography, *Len Dawson: Pressure Quarterback* (with Lou Sahadi) and McGuff's *Winning It All: The Kansas City Chiefs and the AFL*—provide the best accounts of that championship season. Also: Lamar Hunt interview; Willie Lanier interview; Lloyd Wells interview; Curtis McClinton interview; "The Black Athlete—A Shameful Story," Jack Olsen, *Sports Illustrated,* July 1, 1968; Abner Haynes interview; Hank Stram interview; Dale Stram interview; memo from Jack Steadman to Lamar Hunt, undated, circa 1961; *Full Color Football: The History of the American Football League,* NFL Films, 2009; Stu Stram interview; Bobby Bell interview; Hank Stram letter to Kansas City Chiefs players, undated, circa summer 1969; *America's Game,* Michael MacCambridge; "The Unflappable Lamar Hunt," Ed Fite, *Cleveland Press SporTime,* October 9, 1969; "Chiefs Stop Oakland," Bill Richardson, *Kansas City Star,* August 3, 1969; "K.C.–Raider Rivalry Heats Up Again," Bill Richardson, *Pro Football Weekly,* date unknown, circa August 14, 1969; "Chiefs Show Nixon Their Best," Bill Richardson, *Kansas City Star,* August 24, 1969; "Chiefs Turn Ram Defense to Shambles," Mal Florence, *Pro Football Weekly,* September 4, 1969; "AFL Will Prevail in Super Bowl Again," William N. Wallace, *Pro Football Weekly,* September 18, 1969; Lamar Hunt memo to Jack Steadman, TK, 1968; Lamar Hunt letter to Tony DiPardo, October 30, 1969; Lamar Hunt memo to Jack Steadman, November 10, 1969; "KC Had the Hot Hand," Robert F. Jones, *Sports Illustrated,* November 24, 1969; Bill Grigsby interview; *Len Dawson: Pressure Quarterback,* Len Dawson, with Lou Sahadi; Len Dawson interview; Ed Budde interview; "Chiefs Fight from Agony to Triumph," Gary D. Warner, *Kansas City Star,* January 5, 1970; "Sporting Comment," column by Joe McGuff, *Kansas City Star,* January 5, 1970; "Lamonica's Moveable Feast: He Was the Main Dish," Robert F. Jones, *Sports Illustrated,* January 12, 1970; "The Survival of Len Dawson," *The Sporting News,* January 11, 1970; Lamar Hunt unpublished interview with Boyars; "Vikings All the Way—Say, a 31–7 Romp!," William N. Wallace, *Pro Football Weekly,* January 15, 1970; *Winning It All,* McGuff; "Sporting Comment," column by Joe McGuff, *Kansas City Star,* January 12, 1970; "Vikings Are Made 13-Point Favorite," unsigned, *New York Times,* January 7, 1970; *The Super Bowl,* Didinger; "Namath, Dawson Reported Among Those to be Called in Gambling Inquiry," Charles Friedman, *New York Times,* January 7, 1970; *Super Bowl Chronicles,* Jerry Green; Tom Bettis interview; Will Hamilton interview; Buzz Kemble interview; Tom Richey interview; Norma Hunt interview; "Miracle Sunday," Tom Leathers, *Town Squire*, January 8, 1970; "Call by Nixon Cheers Lenny," Dick Young, *Kansas City Times*, January 12, 1970; "Len's Nightmare, Len's Dream," Shelby Strother, *Super Bowl XXXIV Program*, January 31, 2000; "Hail to the Chiefs: Kansas City Carved Out a Lasting Legacy in the First Super Bowl in New Orleans," Jim Gigliotti; *Super Bowl XXXI Program*, January 26, 1997; "Wham, Bam, Stram!," Tex Maule, *Sports Illustrated*, January 19, 1970; *Going Long: The Wild 10-Year Saga of the Renegade American Football League in the Words of Those Who Lived It*, Jeff Miller; "Parting Shot," John Garrity, *Sports Illustrated Presents NFL '95*; "Some Suggested General Subjects for 'Repartee' with Hall of Fame Players at Silver Celebration Dinner," memo from Lamar Hunt to Bill Grigsby, September 5, 1984; Steve Sabol interview; telegram from H. L. Hunt to Lamar Hunt, January 11, 1970.

CHAPTER TWELVE | GLOBETROTTER

Mike Davies interview; Al Hill, Jr., interview, Rod Humphries interview; "A Chronological History of World Championship Tennis," internal document of World Championship Tennis,1990; "Lamar Hunt and the Opening of Tennis: A Synopsis," unpublished paper by Bob Moore; "Winner Takes $50,000, Loser, $1 Million," Joe Jares, *Sports Illustrated*, December 6, 1971; Dick Hall interview; Bobby Moffat interview; Mike Renshaw interview; Neil Cohen interview; Kenny Cooper interview; *Just a Life*, Mike Renshaw (unpublished memoir); "Soccer's Greatest Games: The Longest Game in NASL History," Temple Pouncey, *Soccer Digest*, September, 1979; "The Game I'll Never Forget," Ron Newman, as told to Barry Janoff, *Soccer Digest*, July 1982; Kyle Rote, Jr., interview; Bob McNutt interview; Bill McNutt III interview; Ron Newman interview; Clive Toye interview; Paul Tagliabue interview; Ruth Woosnam interview; Norma Hunt interview; Verne Lundquist interview; Temple Pouncey interview; Hank Stram interview; Stu Stram interview; Phyllis Stram interview; Jack Steadman interview; Len Dawson interview; Jack Steadman letter to Lamar Hunt, April 22, 1970, with Hunt's handwritten reply; Lamar Hunt letter to Tony DiPardo, May 14, 1970; Lamar Hunt letter to Jack Steadman, October 20, 1971; "The late great Morgan Maxfield," James Kindall, *Star Magazine, Kansas City Star*, July 18, 1982; Otis Taylor interview; Clark Hunt interview; Lamar Hunt, Jr., interview; Norma Hunt interview; "The Football, Tennis, Soccer and Spending King of American Sports," Melvin Durslag, *TV Guide*, November 20, 1971; "Tuning Up for a New Hunt Ball," Curry Kirkpatrick, *Sports Illustrated*, May 22, 1972; Bud Collins interview; Butch Buchholz interview; Richard Evans interview; *Open Tennis*, Evans; "Lamar

Hunt Buys Jim Ling's House," Jim Stephenson, *Dallas Morning News,* November 4, 1970; "Lives in a Mansion," Frederick "Shad" Rowe, *Grant's,* September 16, 1988; Donald Dell interview; Billy Sullivan Enshrinement speech for Lamar Hunt, July 29, 1972; Lamar Hunt Enshrinement speech, July 29, 1972; Bobby Bell interview; Len Dawson interview; "The Best Stadium in the World," Gaylon White, *KC Fan,* September, 1972; Lee Derrough interview; Dale Stram interview; Charles Getty interview; Lamar Hunt letter to Jack Steadman, October 24, 1978; Lamar Hunt notes on meeting, November 25, 1974; Lamar Hunt letter to Hank Stram, December 20, 1974; Lamar Hunt notes on coaching interviews, undated (circa January 1975); Lamar Hunt interview notes with Paul Wiggin, January 15, 1975; Ann Roach interview; Willie Lanier interview; Jan Stenerud interview.

CHAPTER THIRTEEN | "YOU WANT TO ACCOMPLISH THINGS"
One of the most lucid glimpses of H. L. Hunt later in life comes from Chapter 9 in the Edwin "Bud" Shrake novel *Strange Peaches,* during which the story's protagonist, John Lee, is summoned to visit Big Earl at his mansion. Shrake once confided, "That was the closest I could come to straight reporting, and still call it fiction." Also: Lamar Hunt interview; Norma Hunt interview; Rose Mary Carr interview; Sharron Hunt Munson interview; Lamar Hunt, Jr., interview; *H. L. and Lyda,* Hill; "H. L. Hunt and the Vatican," unsigned, *American Century,* April 2, 1969; "Executives: Rich and Strange," unsigned, *Newsweek,* December 9, 1974; "The Hunt Heirs Play for High Stakes," *Business Week,* February 17, 1975; "Daddy's Money," Harry Hurt III, *Texas Monthly,* April 1978; Donald Dell interview; "Number One Sportsfan," Gay Yellen, *Tennis Illustrated,* February 1975; "World Championship Tennis—a Reflection," by Lamar Hunt, *WCT Finals Program, 1991;* Jack Steadman interview; Richard Evans interview; Norma Hunt interview; Barry Frank interview; Ivan Irwin interview; Al Hill, Jr., interview; Cliff Drysdale interview; Bill Adams interview; Clark Hunt interview; Lamar Hunt, Jr., interview; Sharron Hunt interview; Kyle Rote, Jr., interview; Bobby Moffat interview; Letter from the Publisher, *Sports Illustrated,* September 3, 1973; "Big D Reduced to Atoms," Bud Shrake, *Sports Illustrated,* September 3, 1973; *The Ball Is Round: A Global History of Soccer,* David Goldblatt; *Soccer in a Football World: The Story of America's Forgotten Game,* David Wangerin; Kenny Cooper interview; Temple Pouncey interview; Blackie Sherrod column, July 8, 1974; "Curtain Call for a Legend," Jerry Kirshenbaum, *Sports Illustrated,* June 23, 1975; Paul Tagliabue interview; "From Kids to Pros . . . Soccer Is Making It Big in U.S.," unsigned, *U.S. News & World Report;* "Soccer, American Style," Paul Gardner, *New York Times Magazine,* May 4, 1975; "Suddenly, Soccer is No. 1," Carl Reich,

San Francisco Examiner, April 26, 1975; Wayne Henry interview; Bill Adams interview; *America's Game,* MacCambridge; Jim Lynch interview; Lamar Hunt memo to Jack Steadman, October Tk, 1977; "Coach, You're Fired," Ron Reed, *Sports Illustrated,* March 13, 1978; Ann Roach interview; "Hunt Replies to Criticism," Lamar Hunt letter to *Kansas City Star* columnist Dick Mackey, *Kansas City Star,* November 12, 1977; Bruce Rice letter to H. Don Krouse, November 4, 1977; Lamar Hunt letter to Bruce Rice, November 9, 1977; Jim Seigfried interview; Tom Bettis interview; *Where Else Would You Rather Be?,* Marv Levy; Marv Levy interview; Jack Steadman interview; Jim Schaaf interview; "The Life and Lists of Lamar Hunt," Bryan Burnes, *Star: The Sunday Magazine of the Kansas City Star Magazine,* May 28, 1978; *Nineteenth- and Twentieth-Century American Paintings, Drawings, Watercolors, and Sculptures,* Sotheby's Auction Catalog, October 25, 1979; "Would You Pay $2.5 Million for That Painting?" Michael Ennis, *Texas Monthly,* April, 1980.

CHAPTER FOURTEEN | THE CRISIS

"An American Fortune: The Hunts of Dallas," L. J. Davis, *Harper's,* April 1981; "The Billion-Dollar Gambler," *Newsweek,* April 7, 1980; "A Scandal for the Hunt Clan," James R. Gaines with Peter S. Greenberg and Anthony Marro, *Newsweek,* March 24, 1975; "Hunts in Hock: Big Silver Debts Force Brothers to Mortgage Most of Their Empire," George Getschow and Roger Thurlow, *Wall Street Journal,* May 27, 1980; "The Hunt Brothers: Battling a Billion-Dollar Debt," John A. Jenkins, *The New York Times Magazine,* September 27, 1987; Ivan Irwin interview; Bunker Hunt unpublished interview with Boyars; Herbert Hunt interview; Jim Seigfried interview; Jack Steadman interview; "Hunts Bare Financial Souls in Statements," Allen Pusey, *Dallas Times Herald,* May 28, 1980; Press Statement, from N. B. Hunt, W. H. Hunt, and Lamar Hunt, May 31, 1980; Norma Hunt interview; Marv Levy memo to Lamar Hunt, date TK; Ann Roach interview; Jim Schaaf interview; Gary Heise interview; Lamar Hunt memo to Jack Steadman, December 19, 1982; Lamar Hunt letter to Bob Gretz, September 16, 1982; John Mackovic interview; Les Miller interview; Wayne Henry interview; Rod Humphries interview; Thom Meredith interview; *North America Soccer League: A Strategic Plan 1978–1987,* Committee Report, 1978; A *Kick in the Grass,* Toye; Clive Toye interview; Kent Kramer interview; Bob McNutt interview; *Hail to the Chiefs,* Bob Gretz; Deron Cherry interview; Lamar Hunt memo to Jack Steadman, November 27, 1986; Nick Lowery interview; Tom Richey interview; "Dallas: A True Story," Stephen Fay, *(London) Sunday Times,* June 22, 1980; "Bunker's Gamble Goes Sour," Stephen Fay, *(London) Sunday Times,* June 29, 1980; "On the Record: Lamar Hunt," Don Pfannenstiel, *Kansas*

City, December 1981; "Rozelle Optimistic Despite NFL Storm," Bob Gretz, *Kansas City Times,* September 5, 1983; "The Lamar Hunt Story," Ron Boyd, *Dallas Times Herald,* April 19, 1984; "Don't Write Off the NASL Yet," Jim Ruben, *Soccer Digest,* October 1981; "Why 1982 Is a Key Year for the NASL," *Soccer Digest,* May, 1982; "A Trimmed-Down NASL Pins New Hope on Team America," Michael Lewis, *Soccer Digest,* April/May, 1983; "The NASL: It's Alive But on Death Row," Clive Gammon, *Sports Illustrated,* May 7, 1984; Jack Steadman letter to Lamar Hunt, January 20, 1983; "Hunt Says Football Just a Business," Vickie Long, *Kansas City Times,* December 14, 1984; "Bunker Hunt to Sell His Stock of Racehorses," unsigned, *Dallas Times Herald,* September 24, 1987; "Hunts Take a Gamble in Silver Case," Walter M. Rogers, *Dallas Morning News,* February 23, 1988; "Hunts Still Fighting Losses From Silver Crisis," Steve Coll, *Washington Post,* March 20, 1988; Clark Hunt interview; Daniel Hunt interview; Jack Steadman letter to Lamar Hunt, December 24, 1987; Dick Vermeil interview; Lamar Hunt interview; "Chiefs Owner Responds to Gansz Stories," Lamar Hunt letter to the editor, *Kansas City Star,* January 24, 1988; Jack Steadman letter to Lamar Hunt, November 4, 1988; Carl Peterson interview; Lamar Hunt's Weight Log Entry, January 1, 1989; "Hunt Saga: Lost Riches, Cloudy Future," Michael Sawicki, *Dallas Times Herald,* August 9, 1988; "Hunts Conspired to Corner Silver Market, Jury Says," Phil Shook, *Dallas Times Herald,* August 21, 1988; "Peru Firm Is Awarded Over $130 Million In Case Involving Hunts' Silver Scheme," Ann Hagedorn and Leonard M. Apcar, *Wall Street Journal,* August 22, 1988; "Lamar Hunt Sets Settlement of Suits by Silver Investors," Ann Hagedorn, *Wall Street Journal,* April 3, 1989; "Hunts Put Trusts in Chapter 11," Walter M. Rogers, *Dallas Morning News,* December 2, 1987; "The Hunts: They're Rich, But You Can Find 'em in the Phone Book," Ann Crittenden, *Kansas City Star,* January 6, 1990; "Big Shake-up for Chiefs," Rick Gosselin, *Kansas City Times,* December 9, 1988.

CHAPTER FIFTEEN | RENAISSANCE

There's no more authoritative writer on the Chiefs' rise to perennial contenders than Bob Gretz, whose book *Hail to the Chiefs* nicely captures the turnaround from the late '80s gloom to '90s revival. Additionally: Carl Peterson interview; Jim Seigfried interview; Bob Moore interview; "WCT, You Didn't Leave Us The Way You Found Us," by Tom Koch, *Buick WCT Finals Program,* 1988; Marty Schottenheimer interview; Lamar Hunt interview; Tim Connolly interview; Derrick Thomas interview; "Without Them, We're Wichita," Michael MacCambridge, *The Sporting News,* August 11, 1997; "Chief Chief: A Squire Interview with Lamar Hunt, Owner of the Chiefs," unsigned, *The Squire,* October 15, 1992;

Tony Dungy interview; Daniel Hunt interview; Lamar Hunt letter to Dave Smith, October 5, 1992; Kevin Ross interview; Georgia Buchanan interview; Clark Hunt interview; Sharron Hunt interview; Alan Rothenberg interview; Dr. Robert Contiguglia interview; Lamar letter to Buzz Kemble, undated, circa spring 1990; Bob McNutt interview; Mike Davies interview; Al Hill, Jr., interview; Rod Humphries interview; Butch Buchholz interview; Arthur Ashe letter to Lamar Hunt, undated, circa September 1990; Frew McMillan letter to Lamar Hunt, October 1, 1990; Bill Adams interview; Wayne Henry interview; "Sports People: TENNIS; Hunt and Barrett Elected to Hall of Fame," *New York Times,* March 3, 1993; Jake Cobb interview; Roger Goodell interview; Jeff Pash interview; Joel Bussert interview; Steve Schanwald interview; "A Whole New Ball Game," Kathleen Tibbetts, *SMU Magazine,* Spring, 1994; Jim Graham interview; "World Cup Soccer," Laurie Shulman, *SportsPulse,* June 1994; Bob McNutt interview; Robert Kraft interview; Clive Toye interview; Mark Abbott interview; *Viva Brazil!, Sports Illustrated* (cover), July 25, 1994; Joel Bussert interview.

CHAPTER SIXTEEN | "HAVEN'T WE DONE THIS BEFORE?"

The most complete historical account of Lamar Hunt's love of soccer was "The First Father," an interview by Michael Lewis that appeared in the January 2003 issue of *Soccer Digest*. An unedited version of Hunt's answers also appeared in his papers (Lamar Hunt letter to Michael Lewis, September 30, 2002). Also: "Major League Soccer, L.P. Business Plan and Confidential Memorandum," November 10, 1993; Lamar Hunt letter to Alan Rothenberg, November 29, 1993; "Hunt Has Prostate Cancer," Randy Covitz, *Kansas City Star,* January 20, 1999; Mark Abbott interview; Clark Hunt interview; Tim Latta memo to Lamar Hunt, July 29, 1996; Susie Stephens interview; Lamar Hunt, Jr., Marty Schottenheimer interview; "Without Them, We're Wichita," Michael MacCambridge, *The Sporting News,* August 11, 1997; Doug Newman interview; memo from Doug Newman to Lamar Hunt re: Arrowhead events mailing, April 22, 1998; Tom Richey interview; Carl Peterson interview; Jack Steadman interview; "Crew Ready to Open New Stadium," unsigned, May 12, 1999; "Crowning Moment for Columbus," unsigned, May 12, 1999, CNNSI.com; SportingNews.com; "Major-League Gamble," Todd Jones, *Columbus Dispatch,* May 14, 1999; "Few Problems, Many Accolades for Opener," Ridge Mahoney, *Soccer America,* May 31, 1999; "Crew Kicks Its Way into History with Win at First MLS Stadium," Tales Azzoni, *Ohio State Lantern,* May 17, 1999; "In Soccer, Bigger Isn't Always Better," Bob Hunter column, *Columbus Dispatch,* May 14, 1999; "For Openers, This Was an Event," Bob Hunter column, *Columbus Dispatch,* May 16, 1999; "Crew Feels Right at Home," Craig

Merz, *Columbus Dispatch,* May 16, 1999; Jim Seigfried interview; Bill Adams interview; Wayne Henry interview; Norma Hunt interview; Philip Anschutz interview; Doug Logan interview; Doug Newman interview; Ron Newman interview; John Wagner interview; Jamey Rootes interview; "Lamar Hunt Notes for Remarks at Dallas Historical Society Meeting," Hunt; Sharron Hunt interview; Buzz Kemble interview; Mark McCullers interview; Robert Kraft interview; Don Garber interview; Paul Gardner interview; "The Re-Tooling of MLS: It's About Time," Ashley Jude Collie, *Soccer Digest,* March 2000.

CHAPTER SEVENTEEN | FINAL SEASONS

Norma Hunt interview; "Cup City!: Meola's Wizardy Lifts KC to First Title," David Boyce, *Kansas City Star,* October 16, 2000; "Goodness, Gracious: Hunt on Hand for Every Nerve-Racking Moment," Hearne Christopher, Jr., *Kansas City Star,* October 16, 2000; "Wizards Reward Lamar Hunt," Paul Gardner, *Soccer America,* October 30, 2000; "Once Again, the Wizards Found a Way," Ridge Mahoney, *Soccer America,* October 30, 2000; Lamar Hunt letter to Bob Gretz, June 9, 1999; "Sports Day Forum: Should the NFL Rotate the Thanksgiving Day Games Instead of Playing Them in Dallas and Detroit Every Year? Yes" Lamar Hunt, *Dallas Morning News,* December 9, 1999; *Long-Range Goals,* Beau Dure; Mark Abbott interview; Tim Leiweke interview; Alan Rothenberg interview; Sunil Gulati interview; Lamar Hunt memo to Jim Smith and Mark McCullers, December 19, 2000; Memo, Lamar Hunt to Bob Moore, November 1, 1999 (circulated later between Moore and Carl Peterson), Hunt Papers; Lamar Hunt letter to Paul Tagliabue, February 12, 2001; Don Garbert interview; Philip Anschutz interview; Clark Hunt interview; Daniel Hunt interview; Mark Abbott interview; Robert Kraft interview; Norma Hunt interview; Sharron Hunt interview; Kathy McDaniel interview; Susie Stephens interview; Jeff Pash interview; Jim Holland interview; Bill McNutt III interview; Dan Flynn interview; Brad Hunt interview; Robert Contiguglia interview; Dick Vermeil interview; "A Hunt Family Affair," Alan Peppard column, *Dallas Morning News,* April 28, 2002; Lamar Hunt interview; Lamar Hunt, Jr., and Sharron Hunt interview; John Wagner interview; "His Love for Game is Still Growing," Steve Davis, *Dallas Morning News,* August 6, 2005; "F.C. Dallas Investor-Operator Lamar Hunt to be given U.S. Soccer Federation Lifetime Achievement Award," unsigned MLS press release, September 15, 2005; Don Garber remarks prior to Lamar Hunt receiving U.S. Soccer Federation Lifetime Achievement Award, September 15, 2005; Jim Irsay interview; Ralph Wilson interview; Dan Rooney interview; Paul Tagliabue interview; Lamar Hunt letter to Phil Anschutz, July 13, 2006; Lamar Hunt letter to Michael Lewis,

September 30, 2002; "The First Father," Michael Lewis, *Soccer Digest,* January, 2003; Len Dawson interview; John Marshall interview; Ryan Petkoff interview; Bob Moore interview; Bobby Bell interview; Bill Adams interview.

EPILOGUE

Kyle Rote, Jr., interview; Willie Lanier interview; Pat Schottenheimer interview; *The Prize: The Epic Quest for Oil, Money, and Power,* Daniel Yergin; Paul Tagliabue interview; Jim Irsay interview; Teresa Amend interview; "For Mrs. Hunt, It's a Game of No Misses," Brad Townsend, *Dallas Morning News,* January 23, 2011; "Oil in the Family," Alan Peppard, *Vanity Fair,* June 2008; Don Garber interview; Lamar Hunt letter to Michael Lewis, undated, circa 2002; Don Garber interview; *Fair Ball: A Fan's Case for Baseball,* Bob Costas; Clark Hunt interview.

AUTHOR INTERVIEWS

Mark Abbott, Bill Adams, Bud Adams, Teresa Amend, Philip Anschutz, John Beake, Bobby Beathard, Bert Bell, Jr., Bobby Bell, Ed Bernet, Raymond Berry, Stormy Bidwill, Roger Blackmar, Sam Blair, Anne Marie Bratton, Mike Brown, Joe Browne, Georgia Buchanan, Butch Buchholz, Ed Budde, Neil Buethe, Chris Burford, Joel Bussert, Hamilton Carothers, Rose Mary Carr, Gary Cartwright, Ron Chapman, Deron Cherry, Bob Chilton, Jake Cobb, Neil Cohen, Jerry Colangelo, Bud Collins, Tim Connolly, Dr. Robert Contiguglia, Ken Cooper, Sr., Gunther Cunningham, Steve Danzansky, Mike Davies, Len Dawson, Scott Debolt, Donald Dell, Lee Derrough, David Dixon, Mary Dixon, Cliff Drysdale, Tony Dungy, Richard Evans, Caroline Hunt, Bud Collins, Mike Davies, Len Dawson, Frank Deford, Johnny Fisher, Corky Flynn, Dan Flynn, Barry Frank, Don Garber, Paul Gardner, Charles Getty; Roger Goodell, Jim Graham, Forrest Gregg, Bill Grigsby, Sunil Gulati, Bob Halford, Dick Hall, Will Hamilton, Abner Haynes, Robb Heineman, Gary Heise, Wayne Henry, Mickey Herskowitz, Al Hill, Jr., Barron Hilton, Jim Holland, Ted Howard, Jack Huckle, Graham Humes, Rod Humphries, Brad Hunt, Bunker Hunt, Clark Hunt, Daniel Hunt, Herbert Hunt, Houston Hunt, Lamar Hunt, Lamar Hunt, Jr., Norma Hunt, Ray Hunt, Sam Hunt, Jim Irsay, Ivan Irwin, Joe James, Dan Jenkins, Phil Jones, Robert Kelleher, Robert Kraft, Kent Kramer, Jack Landry, Jr., Willie Lanier, Rod Laver, Tim Leiweke, Scott Le Tellier, Marv Levy, Janie Lewis, Ross Lillard, Doug Logan, Nick Lowery, Verne Lundquist, Jim Lynch, John Mackovic, John Madden, Wellington Mara, John Marshall, John Martin, LeVon Massengale, Curtis McClinton, Mark McCullers, Howard McHenry, Don McIlhenny, Bill McNutt

III, Bob McNutt, Kathy McDaniel, Bill McDermott, Bill Mercer, Thom Meredith, Al Miller, Les Miller, Carol Modean, Bobby Moffat, Bob Moore, David Munson, Sharron Hunt Munson, Doug Newman, Ron Newman, John Newcombe, Dick O'Shaughnessy, Jeff Pash, Carl Peterson, Ryan Petkoff, Gene Phillips, Frank Pitts, Temple Pouncey, Tom Pratt, Mack Rankin, Mike Renshaw, Tom Richey, Ann Roach, John Roach, Walter Robertson, Dan Rooney, Jamey Rootes, Bert Rose, Ken Rosewall, Kevin Ross, Alan Rothenberg, Kyle Rote, Jr., Pete Rozelle, Buddy Rupe, Steve Schanwald, Tex Schramm, Jim Seigfried, Marty Schottenheimer, Pat Schottenheimer, Carl Shannon, Bud Shrake, Neil Smith, Lou Spadia, Jack Steadman, Judy Steadman, Hank Steinbrecher, Jan Stenerud, Susie Stephens (Ritchie), Smokey Stover, Dale Stram, Hank Stram, Phyllis Stram, Stu Stram, Paul Tagliabue, Otis Taylor, Derrick Thomas, Denny Thum, Clive Toye, Jim Trecker, Dick Vermeil, Grant Wahl, John Wagner, Joy Waller, Don Weiss, Tom Werblin, Lloyd Wells, Bob Wilkes, Pat Williams, Gene Wilson, Ralph Wilson, Phil Woods, Ruth Woosnam, Jim Yonge.

Note: Bert Bell, Jr., Stormy Bidwill, Hamilton Carothers, Gunther Cunningham, David Dixon, Tony Dungy, Forrest Gregg, Mickey Herskowitz, Lamar Hunt, John Madden, Wellington Mara, Bert Rose, Buddy Rupe, Tex Schramm, Bud Shrake, Lou Spadia, Hank Stram, Otis Taylor, Don Weiss, and Lloyd Wells were originally interviewed for the 2004 book *America's Game*; Pete Rozelle was originally interviewed for the 1997 book *The Franchise*; Derrick Thomas was originally interviewed for a 1997 article in *The Sporting News*.

BIBLIOGRAPHY

Anderson, A. A. *Experiences and Impressions: The Autobiography of Colonel A. A. Anderson*. Freeport, NY: Books for Libraries Press, 1970.

Barone, Michael, and Grant Ujifusa. *The Almanac of American Politics 2000*. New York: Three Rivers Press, 1999.

Brandt, Bill. *Do You Know Your Baseball?* New York: A. S. Barnes and Company, 1947.

Brown, Stanley H. *H. L. Hunt*. Chicago: Playboy Press, 1976.

Burrough, Bryan. *The Big Rich: The Rise and Fall of the Greatest Texas Oil Fortunes*. New York: Penguin, 2009.

Caning, Whit. *Doak Walker: More Than a Hero*. Edited by Dan Jenkins. Indianapolis: Masters Press, 1997.

Chancellor, Paul. *The History of the Hill School*. Pottstown: The Hill School, 1976.

Connor, Dick. *Kansas City Chiefs*. New York: Macmillan, 1974.

Copeland, Lara. *Historic Photos of Kansas City*. Nashville, TN: Turner, 2006.

Costas, Bob. *Fair Ball: A Fan's Case for Baseball*. New York: Broadway, 2000.

Daly, Dan, and Bob O'Donnell. *The Pro Football Chronicle*. New York: Macmillan, 1990.

Davies, Richard O. *America's Obsession: Sports and Society since 1945*. Fort Worth, TX: Harcourt Brace College Publishers, 1994.

Dawson, Len, with Lou Sahadi. *Len Dawson: Pressure Quarterback*. New York: Cowles Book Company, Inc., 1970.

Didinger, Ray. *The Super Bowl: Celebrating a Quarter-Century of America's Greatest Game*. New York: Simon & Schuster, 1990.

Dodd, Monroe. *Journeys Through Time: A Young Traveler's Guide to Kansas City History*. Kansas City, MO: Kansas City Star Books, 2000.

Dure, Beau. *Long-Range Goals: The Success Story of Major League Soccer*. Washington, DC: Potomac Books, 2010.

Eisenberg, John. *Cotton Bowl Days: Growing up with Dallas and the Cowboys in the 1960s*. New York: Simon & Schuster, 1997.

Evans, Richard. *Open Tennis: The First Twenty Years*. London: Bloomsbury, 1988.

Farrell, Johnny. *If I Were in Your GOLF Shoes*. New York: Holt, 1951.

Felser, Larry. *The Birth of the New NFL: How the 1966 AFL/NFL Merger Transformed Pro Football*. Guilford, CT: The Lyons Press, 2008.

Fitzgerald, Ken. *Dallas, Then and Now*. San Diego, CA: Thunder Bay Press, 2001.

Foss, Joe, with Donna Wild Foss. *A Proud American: The Autobiography of Joe Foss*. New York: Pocket Books, 1992.

Gardner, Paul. *Nice Guys Finish Last: Sport and American Life*. London: A. Lane, 1974.

Goldblatt, David. *The Ball Is Round: A Global History of Soccer*. New York: Riverhead Books, 2008.

Green, Jerry. *Super Bowl Chronicles: A Sportswriter Reflects on the First 30 Years of America's Game*. Indianapolis, IN: Masters Press, 1995.

Gretz, Bob. *Hail to the Chiefs*. Urbana, IL: Sagamore Publishing, 1994.

Gruver, Ed. *The American Football League: A Year-by-Year History, 1960–1969*. Jefferson, NC: McFarland, 1997.

Haskell, Harry. *Boss-Busters and Sin Hounds: Kansas City and Its Star*. Columbia, MO: University of Missouri Press, 2007.

Hazel, Michael V. *Historic Photos of Dallas*. Nashville, TN: Turner, 2005.

Hill, Margaret Hunt. *H. L. and Lyda*. Little Rock, AR: August House Publishers, 1994.

Hill, Patricia Evridge. *Dallas: The Making of a Modern City*. Austin, TX: University of Texas Press, 1996.

Horrigan, Jack, and Mike Rathet. *The Other League: The Fabulous Story of the American Football League*. Chicago: Follett, 1970.

Hoskins, Alan. *Warpaths: The Illustrated History of the Kansas City Chiefs*. Dallas: Taylor Publishing, 1999.

Huizinga, Johan. *Homo Ludens: A Study of the Play-Element in Culture*. Translated by R. F. C. Hull. London: Routledge, 1949.

Humphries, Rod. *A Guide to World Championship Tennis and Media Information—1980*. Dallas: World Championship Tennis, 1980.

Hunt, H. L. *Hunt Heritage: The Republic and Our Families*. Dallas: Parade Press, 1973.

Isaacson, Darlene. *Kansas City, Then and Now*. San Diego, CA: Thunder Bay Press, 2007.

Jackson, David W. *Kansas City Chronicles: An Up-to-Date History*. Charleston, SC: The History Press, 2010.

Jenkins, Dan. *Saturday's America*. Boston: Little, Brown, 1970.

———. *I'll Tell You One Thing*. Emery, CA: Woodford Press, 1999.

Jose, Colin. *North American Soccer League Encyclopedia*. Haworth, NJ: St. Johann Press, 2003.

Kaplan, Fred. *1959: The Year That Changed Everything*. Hoboken, NJ: John Wiley and Sons, Inc. , 2009.

Kowet, Don. *The Rich Who Own Sports*. New York: Random House, 1977.

Lardner, Ring. *You Know Me Al: A Busher's Letters*. New York: C. Scribner's Sons, 1925.

Lyons, Robert S. *On Any Given Sunday: A Life of Bert Bell*. Philadelphia: Temple University Press, 2010.

MacCambridge, Michael. *The Franchise: A History of Sports Illustrated Magazine*. New York: Hyperion, 1997.

———. *America's Game: The Epic Story of How Pro Football Conquered a Nation*. New York: Random House, 2004.

———, ed. *The ESPN College Football Encyclopedia: The Complete History of the Game*. : ESPN Books, 2005.

———, ed. *ESPN Sports Century*. New York: Hyperion, 1999.

Maule, Hamilton "Tex." *The Pro Season*. Garden City, NY: Doubleday, 1970.

McGinn, Bob. *The Ultimate Super Bowl Book*. Minneapolis, MN: MVP Books, 2009.

McGuff, Joe. *Winning It All: The Chiefs of the AFL*. Garden City, NY: Doubleday, 1970.

McKenzie, Michael. *Arrowhead: Home of the Chiefs*. Lenexa, KS: Addax, 1997.

Michener, James A. *Sports in America*. New York: Fawcett Crest, 1976.

Miller, Jeff. *Going Long: The Wild 10-Year Saga of the Renegade American Football League in the Words of Those Who Lived It*. New York: McGraw-Hill, 2003.

Montgomery, Rick, and Shirl Kasper. *Kansas City: An American Story*. Kansas City, MO: Kansas City Star Books, 1999.

Olsen, Jack. "Biggest Cheapskate in Big D." *Sports Illustrated*, June 19, 1972.

Patterson, James T. *Grand Expectations: The United States, 1945–1974*. New York: Oxford University Press, 1996.

Pierre, Willis. *Whatsoever Things Are True: Volumes I and II*. Bloomington, IN: Xlibris, 2009.

Posnanski, Joe. *The Good Stuff: Columns About the Magic of Sports*. Kansas City, MO: Kansas City Star Books, 2001.

Richey, Tom. *Lamar Hunt and the Founding of the American Football League*. Rochester, NY: Mercury Print Productions, 2009.

Robinson, Peter, and Doug Cheeseman. *1966 Uncovered: The Unseen Story of the World Cup in England*. London: Mitchell Beazley, 2006.

Rodriguez, Sally. *White Rock Lake: Images of America*. San Francisco: Arcadia, 2010.

Rosenthal, Harold, ed. *American Football League: Official History, 1960–69*: The Sporting News, 1970.

Schirmer, Sherry Lamb, and Richard D. McKinzie. *At the River's Bend: An Illustrated History of Kansas City*. Woodland Hills, CA: Windsor Publications, 1982.

Shapiro, Michael. *Bottom of the Ninth: Branch Rickey, Casey Stengel, and the Daring Scheme to Save Baseball from Itself*. New York: Times Book, 2009.

Shrake, Edwin. *Strange Peaches*. New York: Harper's Magazine Press, 1972.

Simonson, John. *Paris of the Plains: Kansas City from Doughboys to Expressways*. Charleston, SC: The History Press, 2010.

Stallard, Mark. *Kansas City Chiefs Encyclopedia, Second Edition*. Champaign, IL: Sports Publications LLC, 2004.

Steidel, Dave. *Remember the AFL: The Ultimate Fan's Guide to the American Football League*. Cincinnati: Clerisy Press, 2008.

St. John, Bob. *Tex! The Man Who Built the Dallas Cowboys*. Englewood Cliffs, NJ: Prentice Hall, 1988.

Stram, Hank, with Lou Sahadi. *They're Playing My Game*. New York: William Morrow, 1986.

Taylor, Otis, with Mark Stallard. *Otis Taylor: The Need to Win*. Champaign, IL: Sports Publishing LLC, 2003.

The Dial, 1947. Pottstown, PA: The Hill School, 1947.

The Dial, 1948. Pottstown, PA: The Hill School, 1948.

The Dial, 1949. Pottstown, PA: The Hill School, 1949.

The Dial, 1950. Pottstown, PA: The Hill School, 1950.

The Dial, 1951. Pottstown, PA: The Hill School, 1951.

Tinling, Ted, with Rod Humphries. *Love and Faults: Personalities Who Have Changed the History of Tennis in My Lifetime*. New York: Crown Publishing, 1979.

Tips, Kern. *Football Texas Style: An Illustrated History of the Southwest Conference*. New York: Doubleday, 1964.

Toma, George, with Alan Goforth. *Nitty Gritty Dirt Man*. Champaign, IL: Sports Publishing LLC, 2004.

Toye, Clive. *A Kick in the Grass*. Haworth, NJ: St. Johann Press, 2006.

Trecker, Jim. *1979 Official North American Soccer League Guide.* North American Soccer League, 1979.

Twombly, Wells. *200 Years of Sport in America: A Pageant of a Nation at Play.* New York: McGraw-Hill, 1976.

Wahl, Grant. *The Beckham Experiment: How the World's Most Famous Athlete Tried to Conquer America.* New York: Three Rivers Press, 2010.

Wangerin, David. *Soccer in a Football World: The Story of America's Forgotten Game.* London: WSC Books, 2006.

Weiss, Don, with Chuck Day. *The Making of the Super Bowl: The Inside Story of the World's Greatest Sporting Event.* Chicago: Contemporary Books, 2003.

Wiley, Nancy. *The Great State Fair of Texas.* Dallas: Taylor, 1995.

Williams, Rusty. *Historic Photos of Dallas in the '50s, '60s and '70s.* Nashville, TN: Turner, 2010.

Winters, Willis Cecil. *Fair Park.* Mount Pleasant, SC: Arcadia, 2010.

INDEX